Where the Pools
Are Bright and Deep

Books by Dana S. Lamb

On Trout Streams and Salmon Rivers (1963)
Bright Salmon and Brown Trout (1964)
Woodsmoke and Watercress (1965)
Not Far from the River (1967)
Some Silent Places Still (1969)
Green Highlanders and Pink Ladies (1971)
Where the Pools Are Bright and Deep (1973)
Commentaries for *Sporting Etchings* by A. Lassell Ripley
  (1970)

Where the Pools
Are Bright and Deep

Dana S. Lamb

with illustrations by Eldridge Hardie

WINCHESTER PRESS

Many of the articles in this collection have appeared in other publications. Grateful acknowledgment is made to the editors of *The Anglers' Club Bulletin* (New York), *The Atlantic Salmon Journal* (Montreal), *Flyfisher's Journal* (London) and the books *Fishing Moments of Truth* and *Hunting Moments of Truth* (Winchester Press, 1973) for permission to include these articles.

In "Perchance to Dream," the lines from W. B. Yeats' "The Song of Wandering Aengus" (copyright 1906 by Macmillan Publishing Co., Inc.; renewed 1934 by William Butler Yeats) are reprinted by permission of Macmillan Publishing Co., M. B. Yeats, Macmillan of London and Basingstoke and the Macmillan Co. of Canada. In "Toward Canada," the lines from Robert Frost's "Stopping by Woods on a Snowy Evening" (from *The Poetry of Robert Frost* edited by Edward Connery Lathem, copyright 1923, © 1969 by Holt, Rinehart and Winston, Inc., copyright 1951 by Robert Frost) are reprinted by permission of Holt, Rinehart and Winston, Inc. and Jonathan Cape Ltd. The title *Where the Pools Are Bright and Deep* is the first line of the poem "A Boy's Song" by James Hogg (1770-1835).

Library of Congress Catalog Card Number: 73-78826
ISBN 0-87691-110-6 (regular edition)
ISBN 0-87691-124-6 (limited edition)

Published by Winchester Press
460 Park Avenue, New York 10022

Printed in the United States of America

In affectionate tribute
to the Reverend Robert A. Bryan and to Faith,
all royalties are for
the Quebec Labrador Mission Foundation.

IN MEMORY OF A NINETEEN-YEAR-OLD SERGEANT
FROM VERMONT
MY GREAT-UNCLE, LEWIS LAMB.
Accounted by his comrades in his native state's
8th Regiment of Veteran Volunteers
as "noble, generous and brave,"
he fell while fighting well at Cedar Creek
at harvest time in 1864.

Contents

New Brunswick Morning · *1*

Going Out to Get the Mail · *4*

Pride Goeth Before a Waterfall · 7

Perhaps (An Adirondack Episode) · *13*

Should Auld Acquaintance Be Forgot · *16*

Halcyon Days — and Nights · *19*

On the North Shore · *21*

Season's End · *24*

The Gift Is to the Giver · *27*

March Brown · *31*

A Foolish Consistency Is the Hobgoblin of Little
    Minds · *33*

Further Details on Request · *37*

Late Thunderstorm · *39*

I Should Have Gone · *42*

A Sort of Accident · *44*

Not Always What They Seem · *47*

Grouse Gunner's Prayer · *50*

I Still Fish—Badly, but I Fish · *53*

Perchance to Dream · *57*

The Blind Man and His Dog · *60*

Oh Wind, If Winter Comes · *63*

Toward Canada · *66*

I Am a Purist · *69*

Closing Camp · *72*

The Pig Pen Pool · *74*

Regardless of the Fog · *78*

What Then Unless Somebody Cares? · *80*

The Crossing of the Caribou · *84*

Hopefully It's—You Know—Like I Said · *92*

How Far Off Is Next July · *95*

Hey, Look at That! · *99*

God Tempers the Wind · *104*

The Nymph Fisherman · *107*

Old Roger's Funeral · *114*

Neither Could Ponce de Leon · *120*

Where the Action Was · *124*

Noises in the Night · *127*

Well Anyway—Almost · *130*

All Good Lies Are Not on Putting Greens · *134*

The Possum Hound · *139*

An Old New Englander Looks Back · *145*

Where the Pools
Are Bright and Deep

New Brunswick Morning

We hear the chore-boy's footsteps on the porch, the crackle of the flames that gnaw his offering of white birch logs, the rumbling in the belly of the stove. Through the open door, as he departs, we glimpse the moving water, smooth and gray beneath the mist.

Here, where the passing salmon pause to rest beside the underwater rocks, calm and quietness prevail. But upriver, where around a bend unyielding cliffs stand guard to herd rebellious currents through a narrow gorge, the river rages like a panther in a trap, its roaring carried by the wind across long miles of wilderness.

Well bundled up against the early morning chill, we take the trail that leads to steaming coffee, ham and eggs and buckwheat cakes before the open fire where the mounted moose heads hang; the mist is lifting as the sun surmounts the eastern hills.

Below the windows of the lodge, the surface of the great Home Pool is sparkling as the sunlight gains in strength. Above the voices of the guides now gathered on the gravel beach the tread of heavy horses on the covered bridge sounds hollow as the week's supplies are brought in from the railhead settlement.

An ancient truck with cargo of canoes and fishermen and guides is driven off to distant salmon swims above the gorge, and one by one the boats still on the beach put out from shore to take their "sports" downriver.

We take our time because we've drawn the pools adjacent to the camp. That means a cocktail and a home-cooked meal at noon; a short siesta undisturbed by flies, a chance to cover all the water thoroughly. We both are happy and relaxed.

Ed takes the pool above the bridge; I start to fish in front of camp. We still need sweaters, though the hint of frost will soon be dissipated by the sun. I tie on a Rusty Rat; Ed holds up a Silver Gray. He says he won't fish dry until the air is warmer than the water and he spots a fish.

My guide begins a yarn about a bear cub that the cook kept in a lumber camp some seasons back, and in the middle of his story stops to light his pipe. He puts some fly dope on the inside of his hat and looks upstream; he lights his pipe again and turns to look a second time.

"Any action up above?" I ask.

He spits and kills a blackfly on his wrist and waits

awhile before he says: "Looks like they're going to the bank; looks like they have a salmon on."

"Let's watch them land the fish before we drop; I'll just make one more cast," I say.

Suddenly the water bulges and I feel a salmon's heavy pull; this is no grilse. Swallow-swift the line swoops out and down the pool, and, far below, a big fish jumps, then wallows like a crocodile. The salmon is well hooked; the battle's joined. Remembering a famous old-time angler's paraphrasing of the poet's lines, I shout: "The snail is doing tailspins on the thorn."

I feel that, for that day at least, all's right with Robert Browning's world, as well as Ed's and mine.

Going Out
to Get
the Mail

I'm going out to get the mail," the old man said. "I'll be back soon."

He went off down the lane and paused to watch a partridge drag a wing and try to lure him from the chipmunk-colored chicks that blended with last autumn's leaves beside the old stone ivy-covered wall. A hundred yards ahead the weathered platform for the milk cans stood, beside the post box, just across the covered bridge. An oriole was singing somewhere in the upper branches of the elms, and behind him, where contented cats crouched purring in the corncrib's shade, a barnyard rooster crowed.

It wasn't far from buttery to river bank, but Zephaniah Brown moved slowly on this long-familiar walk. How many times, in something over sixty years, he'd made the same short journey down the hill; how many different things he'd hoped to find inside the box where wrens had often tried to build a home in competition with the rural free delivery and parcel post.

Way back, the "funnies" in the Sunday papers, early in the week, brought Zephaniah *Buster Brown, The Katzenjammer Kids, That Son-in-Law of Pa's* and *Uncle Munn* to read in raptured whispers to himself. In boyhood days a package might contain a clutch of setting eggs from Lester Tompkins' prize Rhode Island Reds or a headlight for an Iver Johnson bike. Sometimes a long-saved-up-for catcher's mitt, a muskrat trap or pair of hockey skates was what he looked for at the junction of the rough and rutted lane and river road.

Now, as with the family setter dog at heel he made this long-familiar trip he thought of endless disappointing visits to the place as well; times in hopes, forever vain, of finding scented letters from a girl who never wrote or something from an editor besides rejection slips. Today there was no letter from his son; just appeals for contributions to what the writer, in each instance, called "a worthy cause," a statement from the Grange, an Orvis catalogue.

Before he went back up the hill he sat down on a fallen tree to watch the stream. This was the place and time of day he missed his old companions most; the place and time he felt most poignantly the absence of his son. He wondered how the fishing was in Indochina now and whether any stretch out there was half as good as this below the bridge.

Idly thumbing through the catalogue, he came across a lovely bamboo rod, its worth unquestioned, but its cost beyond his grasp. So beautiful, this work of art, he couldn't put its picture down. And then — why is it that we sometimes know — he looked and saw the big and legendary trout commence to feed on mayflies underneath the bridge.

"I ought to go and get my good old Sears and Roebuck pole," he thought. "But, no; I'll post the place and let the dogs run free and save that fish for Jonas when he comes back from Vietnam. And darned if I don't buy him that there fancy rod."

The old man started for the house. The hill seemed steeper than before. He didn't get back as soon as he had said he would; they found him when they went to look. Zephaniah Brown was luckier than many men. He never learned that Jonas wasn't coming home; the lovely rod was never bought. But just perhaps, somewhere, somehow old Zephaniah smiles again as Jonas, with a priceless rod of Tonkin cane, brings to the net his father holds a gold and crimson four-pound trout — and lets it go.

Pride Goeth
Before
a Waterfall

I thought that I was pretty good; a man who owns the proper gear *should* learn to cast in fifty years of fishing streams almost too numerous to count. True, I'd never mastered entomology, but that defect would not show up where I was bound. As the plane droned eastward down Duplessis County's rocky coast a score of angling triumphs came to mind, inspired by a photograph that fell out of my pocketbook. It showed three salmon weighing just a shade below one hundred pounds taken on the Molson water of the Bonaventure. These fish, for several days, had lain where they could easily be seen from where the guides directed us to cast; only when I'd overruled these men who generally know best, crossed the river, and changed the angle and the fly as well would these great silver monsters take. The cast had been a long, long cast, and I was proud, although the biggest one, through no known fault of mine, had "got away."

I thought about the plaudits of a company of anglers on the railroad tracks as I stood casting up a long straight line below the millrace of the Kennebago power dam; about the time when Wendle Collins, the man whom Edward Hewitt called the greatest fisherman of all, approved the way I cast my Hendrickson onto the oil-smooth glides below Cooks Falls.

It was satisfying to recall the admiration Deeside's Donald had displayed when I put out a floating line to probe for far-off salmon just above his warden's shack; the reluctant laudatory grunts coming from the dour Scot who guided me one afternoon at Harmony. It seemed but just a little time since Richard Platt and I had fished a Catskill stretch they called "the lake"; I'd taken half a dozen wild brown trout from underneath the distant bank when Dick quit fishing and sat down. "I want to watch the master work," he'd said.

There'd been trout days on Adirondack streams and salmon days on the Matane when friends who fished with me had said: "Nice work."

Oh I was good all right, I guessed, and here I was about to waste two thousand dollars and a precious week in chuck-and-chance-it fishing in an inlet of the Gulf for salmon scarcely bigger than an old-time Rangeley trout.

Below the plane a lighthouse and a lugger came in view. The water from a river high up in the hills cascaded down into the sea. A few miles farther on the craft turned inland and splashed down beside the rustic buildings of a sportsmen's camp.

The water where the pilot beached the plane looked much less like a river than a lake. The head guide and the man assigned to me were there to take my gear ashore and show me where I was to sleep. They said that dinner would be served at eight; the others had gone out to fish. In answer to their inquiry as to when my guide should come for me I said he needn't come at all; I'd just unpack and rest that afternoon. They seemed surprised.

We met for cocktails in the lodge a little after eight. I learned that eight o'clock for dinner meant more nearly nine. Tom Burns who'd organized the trip did not appear; he had some business down at Rocky Point where he and Pete, his guide, would spend the night and get an early start next day at Lord Buckminster's pool. However, Mrs. Burns was there to tally up the anglers' scores.

"Tom says it will be difficult to do as well as our group did last year," she said, "but maybe we can beat the men who had the camp last week."

She turned to me and asked: "What did you do? Not even any trout?"

I didn't say I hadn't fished. "Nothing to report," I said.

When morning came I turned my back on all — or nearly all — the good things that a fat man shouldn't break-fast on and went down toward the Gulf until I reached the pool that I had drawn across the river, not far from where Tom Burns was floating stone flies from his anchored boat.

I waved to Tom and waded out from where I'd left my dory and my guide and made a short cast with a small Black Dose. Almost immediately I hooked a grilse, gave it the butt and called for Philip and the net.

I took the long-nosed pliers from the pocket of my wading coat and quickly twisted out the hook. Then, as I held the fish upright and let it go, I heard a howl of protest from the farther bank.

"Don't worry, Tom, I won't keep more than four," I called. "I always count a fish released as one against the number I'm allowed."

"But the record, man, the record!" he roared, letting his fly hang in the current.

"We can put him in the record, Tom; he weighed three pounds and three-eighths — male fish, of course."

Tom's guide turned to him and said: "He must have used a pocket scale and weighed the net."

Tom looked suspicious.

"Have you a pocket scale?" he asked.

Just then a six-pound salmon seized his trailing fly and Tom forgot about my grilse. I set about the task of catching up; I realized I was low rod for the camp. It wouldn't do to be the one to cause our team to fall behind the one which had the camp the week before.

For a little while it seemed I might succeed in reestablishing what was now a somewhat tarnished reputation. Five minutes after Pete dispatched Tom's fish I tried a variation of a Royal Wulff. Cast carefully, it seemed as though a fish had bulged beneath the fly, and on the third cast after that a salmon took. I say a salmon by design since the pull was powerful, the back fin like the fins of salmon rising on the Restigouche. With the butt piece in and drag just right I tapped the rod to cause a jump; a sulking fish too long conserves its strength. The tactic worked; the salmon jumped — all twenty pounds of it I'd say. With the leap I let the rod down momentarily, then tightened up and waited for the fish to make a run. And then the fly came back to me —

"You gave him slack," Tom shouted in disgust.

I heard Pete say: "He shouldn't hold a fish that hard."

Pete had a better motor than my guide; he beat us back to camp by half a mile. When we arrived he held the little salmon up beside two grilse for me to see. Bob Jones was weighing his two grilse, and Arthur Brown had three. "Those guys know how to fish," Tom said.

For the rest of that humiliating week I tried to show that I knew how to fish as well. I tried to raise another salmon; tried each day to kill at least a brace of grilse. But small success and smaller popularity were mine. My explanations weren't listened to; my opinions were ignored; my favorite jokes at cocktail time elicited no laughter and few smiles.

The last day came and once again I fished across the pool from Tom. A northeast wind was blowing in my face, and though I sought to overcome this handicap I couldn't get my variant upstream or send my Rusty Rat to where I wanted it. At lunch, Tom lectured me on how the rod itself should do the work, the stiff elbow, the horizontal line behind, and all the things that—forty years before—John Alden Knight, my fishing partner and my friend, had advocated or condemned. As low man on the totem pole there wasn't much that I could say.

That afternoon, the last of all, I fished a pool not fifty yards from camp while Mrs. Burns sat on the front porch of the lodge and watched. Three times that afternoon I hooked a grilse; three times I played it carefully, and then three times the fish got off. As dusk came on I raised a salmon but it wouldn't take. When the other fishermen came back I called it quits and joined them by the open fire for a drink.

Mrs. Burns had come inside and sat there totting

up the catches all of us had made. "These men know *really* how to fish," she said.

She turned the pages of the record book and came to mine and then — "I have some good advice for you," she said. "There's a company called Orvis near our summer place in Manchester, Vermont. Why not come up and stay with us and take some courses at their fishing school? I'll bet if you do that you'll catch two times as many fish and *really* have some fun next year."

The camp cook's dog came through the kitchen door and licked my hand, regarding me with soft and sympathetic gaze. I bowed my head.

Perhaps
(An Adirondack
Episode)

L ast night the white-pine seeds the squirrels hadn't har-
vested were scattered by a wasteful wind. Cruelly striking from the north, the cold intruder robbed the hard-
woods of their gaudy autumn dress and carpeted the forest
floor with flaming red and apple-yellow leaves.

As though excited by the frost, the chalk-white
birch trees seem to shine against the darkening background of the spruce. Although it's snowing on the mountain tops whose peaks, all season long, are capped with

white, the friendly river sparkles in the sun; not yet imprisoned by the winter's wall of ice, it sings a song of welcome to the creatures on its banks.

No one preoccupied with management of rod and reel, no one intent on hooking trout while being jostled and harassed, can pay court to a river like the man who walks alone. He who worships at the waterside without a thought of fame or food may reap a rich reward some months before the violet and the *Iron fraudator* come up, song birds come north to build their nests and baby animals are born. It is the quiet contemplative ones, I think, who learn to know a river well: its channels, currents, rocks and depths; its sand bars, springs and gravel beds.

Almost every trout stream has a so-called Schoolhouse Pool, and all of those I know are beautiful. As I walk, this morning, through the pines to where I took a three-pound trout one rainy Sunday forty years ago a ruffed grouse up behind me on the ridge begins to drum. I pause; then go on down to where I see the two big rocks. The larger one is undercut. With a stick I probe the dark, deep hollow out of which I took my still-remembered big brown trout; no fish comes out. I scan the gravel beds upstream for spawners; it is the season and the place, but nothing stirs the shallows where the redds should be.

Why, where the current slides along the bigger boulder's side, is no fish lying in the sheltered depths? Has an otter found the spot? Why are no breeders on the gravel bar? Could the raccoons answer that?

Above the sound of water running over rocks I hear the drumming of a grouse again. Why should these furtive woodland birds send signals down the forest aisles so many snows before their mates will nest beneath some blowdown or beside an old stone wall? Are they indicating that the area is theirs?

Up on the road beside the ruin of the little back-woods school I call my dog and start the car. The season's over and the days are short; we must head south. Perhaps if I had time to go down to the pool below the run . . .

Should Auld
Acquaintance
Be Forgot

I never knew until last month Jock Menzies, whom we salmon anglers all will miss, had gone to join that hearty host of Scots who used to take their brown trout from the burns and lochs and from the swaying kelp beds of the Hebrides; their salmon from the Tay and Spey and from the Aberdeenshire Dee. And when some symptom of my sadness at our loss was manifest, the one van Dyke would call "My Lady Gray Gown" brought me comfort as she always does. From some safe place she brought a long-forgotten letter dated 1929. Its author was a Scottish lady (I use that word advisedly) who, in my early youth, had been our cook. The letter, written to my mother, had accompanied a wedding cake—a promised gift to me when I should find a wife.

Too sincere and sensitive this letter is to hold up for the gaze of those who aren't familiar with the background of the case. But some things in it I can tell—and no harm done; they cheered me up.

"When you," our dear old Fraser said, "were last in Glasgow you were only twelve miles from the little village I came from; it is not far from Loch Lomond. There is a beautiful glen close by and the castle on the hill across from it is where I started out—nearly 100 bedrooms."

This put me in mind of the claim made in a backwoods Carolina church that David Cohn had built himself a palace with a hundred rooms in Paris, France, where every room contained a pleasure lady and a barrel of drinking whiskey, a sensational canard well calculated to embarrass a supposed millionaire before a needy and expectant congregation; and sweet revenge for having done Roark Bradford bad by capturing Old Mose, a king-sized dreamed-of catfish that Roark himself had longed to catch.

The letter—getting back to that—goes on to say that since the First World War the ladies to whom the castle on the hill belonged have lost their money and now keep a tea room in the glen.

But then she tells more happily about a Massachusetts wedding breakfast she has recently prepared: "chicken salad, lobster salad, cold crabs, cold gelatins, two cold hams, little chickens boned and stuffed, cold roast beef, chicken pies, steak and kidney pie and *a beautiful big salmon sent from Canada.* I boiled it whole, then let it drain, hired a platter for it as it was 24 pounds (we did not have one big enough) then skinned it and masked it over with mayonnaise and decorated it with truffles and pimentos and had chopped aspic around it; it did look a picture. The hot dishes were Irish stew and pork and beans, Boston brown bread and biscuits."

Pages past the snacks described above the letter ends with wishes for our health and happiness. Bless you, Annie Fraser from the glen — twelve miles from where they build the ships, and not far from the Bridge of Wier whence my old friend, Bob Campbell, came by freighter years ago to fish the Beaverkill with me — well up, on posted water where the woods were silent and the trout were wild. "Now you come back and fish with me," he'd said. "It won't cost much for food because it's only whisky we'll be drinking when we're not at home. Don't say you can't afford to come."

As I write I hold Bob's brother Ian's inscribed copy of the records of the West of Scotland Angling Club. Since its founding — 1834 — "Remarks" beside the early members' names all state starkly "Dead" except for one who's "dropped" and one "killed falling from his horse."

It's too late now; I wish I'd gone.

Halcyon Days — and Nights

The men who never knew the Willowemoc and the Beaverkill when Johnnie Woodruff fished the downstream pools at night, the boys from Binghamton were making whoopee at the Antrim bar, goateed Les Petrie and his hard-of-hearing pal, Fred Nagle, floated fanwings near the old DeBruce Club Inn, and Hewitt and La Branche were household words; the men who never fished with Richard Hunt, Pop Robbins or Joe Knapp — those men, I say, are welcome to their youth.

In days of traveling salesmen, shaving mugs and railroad trains; in days when livery-stable owners saw — or should have seen — the writing on the woodshed wall, imported brown trout settled in beside the boulders in the Beaverkill and in beneath the Willowemoc's overhanging banks to challenge masters of the anglers' newfound art, the men who now disdained the use of "chuck-and-chance-it" underwater flies presented downstream to a witless native trout.

But lest you whippersnappers think I only speak of bigger fish; of fewer anglers on the streams; of wilder, unspoiled countryside and fewer posters on the trees, let me explain. There were some lovely people in the valley at that time. Frank Keener; there is one I can't forget. Frank owned and ran the Antrim Lodge where Morgan partners, artists, railroad engineers, sportsmen, bums, ambassadors, industrialists and politicians of renown wolfed luscious, tender sirloin steaks, drank deep, told lies about their trophies of the angle or the chase and, in the evening, came alive.

Like many others, I loved Frank; why wouldn't I? When I was ill he doctored me; when I was broke he cut my bill in half. Yes, indeed, I really loved, admired, thought the world of Frank.

And Frank, God bless him, thought the world of me; admired me; at least I thought he did.

And then one autumn day when all our group, no longer after trout, were hunting partridge on the hills we came into the bar at Bloody Mary time and put three ruffed grouse down in front of us. Frank tended to our wants and smiled and asked: "Who shot those birds?"

My son, ten times as proud as though he'd killed the partridges himself, replied: "Dad got them all."

"The hell you say!" said Frank.

On the North Shore

A half mile seaward of the smother of the surf the yacht drops anchor in the Gulf. In the purple afterglow a dory puts out from the river mouth. And now, as seals and seagulls vanish in the dusk, an angler leaves the larger vessel's polished decks and takes his place amidships in the smaller boat. An outboard motor coughs and roars; bells ring aboard the yacht; the skipper waves and turns the bowsprit toward the distant coast of Newfoundland.

Light-years above the ghostly northern lights, the constellations — vast, serene and diamond-bright — illuminate the sky beyond the glacier-rounded outcrop of the tundra's hills. Back down the faint and frothy furrow that the outboard motor plows, the darkness from the shadowed shorelines meets and closes in.

And now at last the river widens and the lodge's lights come into view; the cabins stand in silhouette against a slowly rising moon; the camp dog barks, and voices sound across the water as the motor throttles down.

The small waves slap and slurp against the underpinnings of the dock. A half a dozen guides appear to greet the angler and to carry in his gear. The other gentlemen — they say — will fly on down the coast from Seven Islands in the morning. They tell him that the fishing has been poor but that the men who've just flown home have left some good-sized sea trout with the cook, in case he'd like one for his dinner.

Inside the lodge a mouse is rustling in the unburned papers in the fireplace; the evening meal is cheerless and the lights are dim. Someone has left a book called *Pools and Ripples* on the table by the door. "The man with a rod or gun," the author says, "sees more and feels more in the woods than if he were to go empty-handed."

The angler wonders whether that is true as he recalls Thoreau's philosophy. The solemn sage of Walden Pond suggests, as every reader doubtless knows, that one should "leave the gun and fish pole behind so that he may better distinguish the proper objects of his life."

The lonely fisherman gets up and builds a drink. "Right now the proper objects of my life are fish," he tells the empty room. He takes Bliss Perry's book and walks back to his cabin waiting underneath the moon. The bed is soft; the light is dim; outside he hears the lapping of the water on the rocks; the rumble of a waterfall; that night he reads no more.

The rain that came at dawn has stopped, but tall grass hanging down across the paths between the cabins and the lodge is sopping wet. The sky is like damp dirty wool; the hills invisible behind the clouds; the river sullen underneath the fog; no plane will fly to camp that day. Until the afternoon the angler stays indoors, testing leaders, setting up his rods, arranging flies. But in the gray and gloomy afternoon he asks his guide to show him all the pools his group — when they arrive — will fish. He isn't favorably impressed. He likes to cast his flies where he can see the salmon he is casting to, not just to blindly float or work a fly at random over water which may well be blank. Before he calls it quits he brings to net two undersized unwanted grilse. Dejectedly he tells his guide to head for home.

A second lonely night has passed; the morning sunshine sifting through the trees is glistening on each drop of dew. The fisherman, although his hair is white, quite suddenly is young again. He sets out joyously while squirrels chatter in the branches overhead and out behind the quarters of the guides the robins sing. In the Home Pool where the salmon rest before they fight their way up through the falls he hooks a big one on a Badger Variant. The salmon leaps and shakes the hook. The fish — well over fifteen pounds — is gone, but now the angler hears the seaplane's motors in the west. *His friends are coming, and the fish are in.*

Season's End

The first fall day has come and gone; less than a week
before the season's close remains. The water in the
Beaverkill is low and clear; no trout are showing in the
pools. Diehard determined fishermen who rise at dawn go
home at dark with empty creels. Because the tiniest of flies
cast deftly where the water quickens in the runs are known
to yield such meager dividends, few anglers line the Antrim bar on midweek nights; or line the banks next day
between the Junction and the Delaware.

Beneath an oak beside Ferdun's a solitary station wagon stands. Its driver, sobered by advancing years, prefers to sit and watch one pool and not to wander, as was once his wont, along this river that he loves so well. This is not his first time on the scene but, after one nostalgic trip from wooded top to bottom of the valley of the Beaverkill, this peaceful place has been his choice for quiet contemplation and to wait for trout to rise.

For perhaps an hour every day he works a streamer in the upstream run, floats a variant down Ferdun's current lanes or, with a Leadwing Coachman, probes the broken water at the long pool's tail. But for the most he occupies the front seat of his car, his rod aslant against the hood, his waders, jacket and his net all close at hand.

The leafy surface of the rich brown earth is dappled as the sunlight filters through the still-green leaves; the glade is resonant with joyous songs of birds. The robins, warblers, swallows and the summer yellowbirds are flocking up before they start their long flight south. The solitary angler's gaze pursues their fitful progress from the maples to the sycamores or out across the placid pool.

He reaches for a book he's brought along; part of its title, *Fishless Days*, seems apropos. He reads and as he does he seems to travel to a land where it is always afternoon. Forgetting where he is he laughs so loudly that the chipmunks scramble for the rocks; a shadow falls across his face, a lump comes in his throat, he sheds a tear. He rolls his thoughts back forty years to days when Catskill trout *were* trout and they were —

Crack! An acorn from the topmost branches hits the radiator hood. The startled reader lifts his head; out where the water flows along the farther shore a trout is feeding avidly.

The fish presents no problem to a fair to middlin'

dry-fly man. That Friday afternoon the happy angler holds it in his net; its size and shape and coloring delight the captor as he carefully works out the hook. "Almost like old times," he thinks. Behind him where his Pontiac is parked a car door slams; he hears the crunch of gravel as a Ford and then a Chevrolet come down the hill. The weekend fishing has begun; the owner of the station wagon turns and slowly wades ashore. He takes his waders off, takes down his rod.

A man who stands beside him rigging up regards him with surprise. "I saw you with a darned good trout; don't tell me that you're through and going home? We still have two more days to fish."

The lucky angler smiles and nods his head. "I hope you fellows hit it right," he says. "I've had my fun; I'm going to quit while I'm ahead."

The Gift Is
to the Giver

Past islands where the Flatlands Indians are cutting
fiddleheads, the tasty not yet fully opened ferns, the
salmon hasten toward upriver pools. Old-timers on the
lower Restigouche remember when the big fish used to
pause above Tidehead and hold there long enough to take
the fly instead of running up beyond "the meeting place of
waters."

Deterred, some years ago, by budget-wrecking fishing fees, my wife and I set out to try some bargain-base-

ment angling on the Restigouche—way down among the islands at its mouth.

"A traveling fish won't take," our friends all said. "The trip will be a waste of time."

Despite this sound advice, we went ahead. A friend beloved by both of us, old Reggie Shives of Campbellton, found us a friendly small motel, got us some so-called salmon water for a "song," put us in touch with Austin Adams, retired railroad engineer who knew the river up and down, its salmon and the people on its banks. Austin, in his younger days, had held a lease on many well-known salmon pools. He supplied us with the necessary boats and guides, including Ken, his son, as fine a man as ever dipped a paddle, poled a sport upstream or made an angler's time pass pleasantly—regardless of the catch.

No wide selection of exotic dishes graced our table at the first day's evening meal; no steward brought the wine around. But at a piano in a corner of the little dining room our host played music we had loved since college days while pine logs in the open fireplace fought off the chill that came up from the river when the sun had set.

Each day we went forth hopefully; *some* traveling fish would surely take, we thought. Each night we went home happily—though empty-handed—grateful for the priceless things the quiet river had bestowed: glimpses of the birds and animals, good companionship and hearty appetites.

True, we might have left our rods at home. I took but one small fish; my better half took none. But then, the final afternoon of all, from beyond a wooded island point, there came a roaring down the evening breeze. My partner's guide to whom the cries were audible pulled anchor and took off upstream while his passenger looked forward with a wild surmise.

And now, around the point, they came on Austin Adams in a boat alone. His rod was bent and it was obvious that he was fast to something bigger than a grilse.

"Here, take me rod," he shouted. "You've not had any luck. I want for you to play and land this fish. He's not wore out; I haven't held him hard."

Although "the missus" didn't want to rob her would-be benefactor of perhaps his season's only fish, she knew that she must grant his wish. And she was well rewarded when she did by Austin Adams' happy smile.

The men who guided us among the islands long ago have gone to fish around the bend where taking thirty-pounders run throughout the year and sand flies never bite. But Austin Adams, now too old to fish alone — with prudence — still spends the summer on the river in his boat with just his dog for company.

Upriver where I fished this year, while my partner, cooped up in her hotel room, fought back a more than common cold, the fishing has been tolerable. I came in yesterday — the last day of our trip — and found my vastly better half was out.

"Madame, she goes for fish," the room clerk said.

I worried as I drank my Scotch and waited for her safe return. She came at last, all radiant and free from her late bronchial distress.

"I got two lovely fresh-run fish," she said, "the sea-lice still aboard on both. The smaller one is packed in snow and ready to take home."

"Where is the larger one?" I asked.

"Oh, you would have been so thrilled," she said. "I took it down to Austin Adams' camp. He'd just come in, without a fish of course, alone. He seemed so tired and discouraged. I guess that we would be downhearted too, at eighty-four. I said: 'I've come to pay you back your fish.'

"He looked surprised. He said: 'But the salmon that you talk about was not as big as this.'

" 'But you forget,' I said to him, 'I owe you twelve years' interest in the silver of the Restigouche.'

"You should have seen his smile!"

"I guess I should," I said, *but I see yours.*"

March Brown

The opaque, off-white sky hung moist and low above the bleak and somber countryside. Fallen branches and dry autumn leaves had carpeted the forest floor while walnut shells and winter-wizened fruit lay rotting on the dead grass of the lawn. The furrows where the plow had left its mark were cocoa-brown. A tawny bird of prey swung out across the fallow fields where ancient arrowheads are buried deep, to land high on a leafless limb to pluck the feathers from a murdered quail.

Beneath the arbor where the gray-brown grape vines twined around the old fence rails the quiet white-throats searched for hidden seeds, while perching in the yews nearby the sober-plumaged turtledoves made mournful music all that sunless afternoon. The brook, made turgid by snow water from the hills, was filled with flotsam and with mud. The muskrats, as the dusk came on, swam out from underneath their reedy igloo in the drab and winter-stricken swamp. And now, like shadows 'round a fire in the night, the solemn unseen owls mourned as sadly as the doves.

I wished, now that these gloomy dark-brown days in March were at an end; I wished I might have had some "glimpses that would make me less forlorn." But there was little hope; I went to bed and lay there on the edge of dreams of pitching horseshoes back of Byron Blanchard's Adirondack Mountain House, and bells that ring on Sundays in the valleys where I used to fish.

Just this side of sleep I felt the freshening wild east wind and heard the dreadful demons of the forest howl as lightning zigzagged up and down the darkened hills and thunder raged and rolled and roared. And now, despite the terrors of the stormy night, I fell back to forgetfulness and slept the winter slumber of the bear; no thoughts, no worries and no dreams.

When I came awake again much later on, the stars were steady and the night was still. A planet like a great green lantern in the springtime sky hung where I could see it from my bed. The fiery traces of a meteor blazed a passage through the midnight's silver air. I heard the clear eternal language of the stars. I knew the winter, like a snake, had shed at last its worn-out skin; the countryside would soon be joyous, glad and green. The spring was being born again; I'd need some March Browns in my fly box pretty soon.

A Foolish Consistency
Is the Hobgoblin
of Little Minds

Near the big bow window of the Porpoise Inn, Don
Parker looked across the sparkling waters of the bay
to where the deep-sea fishing boats were coming out of
hibernation at the inlet's weathered docks. He saw the season's first white sails stand out against the azure sky beyond a distant sandy point of land and watched, nearby,
three mallard drakes converging, in a friendly way, on the
small gray lady of their choice.

Between the dry martini and the well-iced clams,

Don Parker sighed contentedly; Suffolk County in the spring was hard to beat. He ordered sautéed soft-shell crabs — the little ones shipped up from Maryland — an artichoke with Hollandaise, a plate of watercress, a demitasse and Brie.

"Tonight I'll go to Friede's Riverside," he thought, "for Löwenbrau, smoked eel and shad roe from the Nissequogue."

"How fortunate I am," he muttered to himself, "to be here where the sweet warm spring is in the air, the crocuses are up, the songbirds coming back, the pheasants crowing everywhere, the quail about to nest — and there are restaurants like this."

Just then a member of the Big Bend Club came in and stopped to speak with Don.

"How lucky that you're here and not upstate," he said. "Bert Cable told my brother when Ed called him up last night, they've had a week of snow and freezing rain; the Beaverkill's discolored and it's up above its banks. No one is taking any trout."

"Luck, that you found it out in time," Don said. "You would have frozen half to death and never caught a thing except perhaps pneumonia."

"But damn it all, I didn't find it out in time," said Arthur Burns. "I've burned my bridges at the office, and I've told Lucille to take the children out to Illinois to see her folks. I have to either waste my time alone at home or go."

Don Parker shook his head and frowned and said, "It's hard to tell you what to do; those Catskill counties are a mighty dreary place in weather such as that that you describe. Why not drop by my house tomorrow and we'll shoot clay birds and worry down a drink?"

"OK, I'll call you up to check," Burns said and took a table by the bar.

In the creek behind Don's house that afternoon the sunlit waters gleamed like polished platinum; a thousand broadbill idled there, a hundred geese stood on the banks and thought of eggs to cover and of nests. Between the weeping willows and the tall marsh grass the Wilson snipe were feeding by the springs; red-winged blackbirds rode the swaying cattails in the swamp; the maples showed a touch of reddish brown.

Don filled his lungs with salt sea air and went indoors. Who could leave so beautiful a place this lovely time of year? He headed for his well-loved books, but on the way he turned aside; he turned aside to have a quick look at his rods and reels before he took up *Leaves of Grass, The Horse's Mouth,* or *War and Peace.*

The rods had just come back from Orvis in Vermont; the varnishing was perfect and the nickel fittings shone. The ferrules fit; the guides were neatly bound. Don set up every renovated rod: the best that Orvis made themselves, two Paynes, a Leonard, Gillum, Edwards, and a rod that Garrison had built, rare treasures these of Tonkin cane, rods for big Norwegian salmon and for small New England trout.

Don saw that every reel seat fit its reel; that lines that floated, lines that sank were of the proper size and weight to let an angler fling a fly just right. He tested every nylon leader and a dozen points of gut — he thought he needed gut sometimes to put a number eighteen floater where he wanted it.

He saw the flies he hadn't looked at since last season's close; the nymphs, the nets, the waders and the brogues. And suddenly he saw that it was getting dark. He put his duffle in a bag and changed his clothes. "Regardless of the icy rain, high water and the mud," he thought, "despite no sun, no hatches and no fish, I've got to go. There *might* be something doing in a feeder brook or underneath the bank; perhaps a bucktail or a salmon fly will take a trout. I'll find some place to get a hot dog on the way."

When Arthur Burns called up that night to find out when to bring his gun and shells next day somebody said, "I'm sorry, Mr. Parker isn't home; he left here just a while ago to go upstate. I think that you can reach him at a place they call the Antrim Lodge; he said you'd know."

Further Details
on Request

A rushing rivulet descends from mountain ledge to mountain ledge to where a deep and long blue lake, well nourished by its icy springs, lies sleeping in the summer sun. Off toward the east an opening in the trees presents a view of where the silver current of the outlet surges through uncharted forest channels toward the sea.

An hour since — it seemed a long, long time — back down the hills, a dozen miles among the pine trees and the crags, we'd left salt water and the last bleak farm. And now, a deer, two partridge broods, a fox and bull moose later on we were — we hoped — approaching camp.

We'd waited all that morning for the guides who never came. And when it seemed we might be doomed to stay forever in the shabby little coastal town, we took a chance and since we knew there was a God who watches out — I don't know why — for sinners from "the States," we headed up a rough and seldom traveled road into the foothills of the Gaspé mountain range.

Now here beside this lovely, lonely lake, headwaters of a sister salmon stream, we listened to the croak of ravens, watched the sailing shadows of the clouds, waited for a snowshoe hare to cross the rutted wagon track we hoped was our right road and drove our cautious way across the gullies and the rocks that lay ahead.

High on a ridge where one could look down from the crumbling edges of a cliff — which I could not — the sunshine glittered in the distant depths below on water downstream from the camp we sought. I screwed my courage to the sticking point and put the car in second gear and in due course we pulled up on the flats where smoke was fragrant and the river sang.

Unloaded, happy and relaxed, we set our rods up while we drank our Scotch, dined on lobster brought in by our tardy but unworried guides and watched a black bear from the window as we went to bed. That night we dreamed good Gaspé dreams; all dreams in camps like this are good, and in the morning on the river all our dreams came true, as I can tell you in detail if you should really want to know.

Late Thunderstorm

On golden, after-season days when wind-stirred, painted maple leaves come fluttering down to float awhile on quiet shallows near the bank, I like to loaf beside the river in the shade and watch the swirling current claim its red and yellow cargo for the long voyage to the sea.

Below the boulders in midstream where deepening water quickens over undersurface stones, the secrets of the river bed are guarded by a camouflage of weaving shadows, shifting foam and silver spray. I am content. I do not lie in wait to spy upon what happens later on the redds as, in the spring, I do not spy upon the oriole's homemaking in the upper branches of the elms. I cannot understand why window shades to private rooms, in modern times, are seldom drawn. I sympathize with all my heart with nature's right to privacy.

Here, where a hundred homespun years ago the mighty salmon used to spawn before the snowflakes gathered strength, we now perforce accept with thankfulness the presence of a beautiful, though less august successor from abroad. In this river, on the banks of which I take my ease, this brown- and crimson-spotted alien was introduced by sportsmen when my father was a boy. We know it came from Britain, but from just where no one knows. Perhaps its forebears rose to mayflies on a placid midland stream, grew fat on heavy feeding in a loch or occupied some brawling bourn that plunged down from the heights — where sheep were only small white dots up toward the sky — to join the waters of the Irish Sea.

The songbirds and the swallows now have gone. I know the salmon won't come back. The brown trout have a holiday from fishermen before they spawn. As for myself, I'm glad that I need only dream: too late to put my waders on and cast a fly; too soon to struggle uphill with my gun, and there seems nothing I must do to fortify my self-respect. I plan to stay there all day long, to dream about the season past; the trout that broke my leader in the Junction Pool; the one that didn't get away, and weighed a little over two pounds and a half; the partridge chicks, the pups, the woodcock's nest.

I plan to read Walt Whitman's *Leaves of Grass;* to watch the clouds. And then the summer — long dead though I thought it was — shows in those same clouds its savage anger at my indolence. It stirs up trouble on the mountain tops. The sudden tumult on the heights sweeps down to rage along the water course with thunder, lightning and high wind combined with blinding sheets of rain.

Fortunately there is an empty camp nearby; I have a key. I cower there and watch the battle in the sky until the storm and day are spent. The rain has stopped, but water from the roof drops sulkily. The stars come out and still the way toward home is dark. I stoop below the branches spreading from the birches' snow-white trunks; the cobwebs hang like snares across the trail and water lies in unseen pools along the path. I'm glad, at last, to see the village lights.

I Should Have Gone

I should have gone for partridges today. Foul weather never kept a real grouse gunner in the house. This freezing rain would drive the biddies to the evergreens and deaden sounds of footsteps in the fallen leaves. I knew just where the birds would be; I should have gone.

Of course it's not much fun to hunt alone without a dog, and hard to get a shot without at least one partner working with you in the woods. Two hundred miles of icy roads beneath a downpour from a leaden sky is not a pleasant thing to contemplate. To dine without companions in a roadside restaurant and spend — now that the tavern where I used to stay is gone — a lonely evening in a motel room are prospects which do not allure. But still, the season ends two days from now; I should have gone.

Perhaps by now the rain upstate has stopped; the skies have cleared. Perhaps Walt Baker's wife would mind the store so he could hunt with me this afternoon. That hemlock grove between the orchard and the lake has not been posted since the owner died last year. Then there's the heavy cover out behind Bill Allen's hen house on the hill and that hot spot where thorn apples grow along the brook, below the graveyard's old stone wall. If I could muster up the energy to work these covers carefully between now and tomorrow noon I ought to get a bird or two, even if I hunted them alone.

Outside, despite the freezing rain, a while ago, I heard a pheasant cackle in alarm, and from my window I can see a covey of Long Island quail busy at the feeder underneath the old white pine. There is game enough right here to occupy a gunner with the will to brave the elements, but who would shoot his guests, his neighbors and his friends? Just let me bag one final brace of wild ruffed grouse; no double mind you, I'm not good enough for that. Just let me have the energy and aim to bring two tufted fantailed woodland birds back to the kitchen of my favorite chef, and I will never load my twenty-gauge again. But one must face the fact that partridges fly faster every year; the hills get harder every year to climb. I should have gone.

A Sort of
Accident

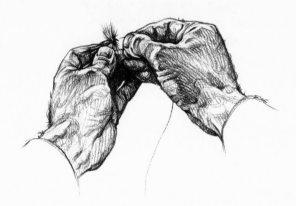

On this summer afternoon the sunlight lingered on Vermont's green hills while down beside the little spring-fed brook, the shadowed valley—bathed already in the mist—was waiting for the stars to guide the gentle Jerseys from their milking sheds back through the hoof-high pasture grass to where the clover clustered in the bottom lands.

Jim Easton parked his car and climbed the old stone wall, rod butt forward-tucked beneath his arm. He made his way downhill along a cattle path to where the tiny tributary stream made junction with the river. Here, where in the heat of noon the dairy herd would stand and drink, there was, at dusk no sound or sign of life except the *beep* of nighthawks hunting insects in the sky, the barking of a collie far away, and, now and then, a ghostly glimpse of bats that skimmed the placid surface of the junction pool.

As night closed in the rainbows rose along the bank where cold clear water from the brook had cut a channel through the sand to where the larger stream was wide and deep and cooled by its own underwater springs. This was neither time nor place for niceties and, in the fading daylight, Jim tied on a white hair fly which, in early afternoon, he knew that any river trout would shun, but "in the dark all cats are gray." His offerings were avidly accepted now and all went well until a brown trout bigger than its brothers with the crimson sides broke the leader as it lunged in terror to avoid the lowered net.

Halfway between regret and admiration of the fight the fish had made, the solitary angler went ashore and sat down on a rock where he could safely use his pocket flashlight tying on another fly. Just as the yellow beam swept out across the level pastureland he heard a bellow from the center of the field. Against the skyline where the moon was coming up Jim saw a hulking monster trotting toward the rock. As frightened as the big brown trout had been five minutes earlier, Jim left the light on to attract the bull and crossed the river to the shadowed farther shore, crouching there against a gravel bank in fervent hope of being undiscovered by the beast.

The more enraged by what he could not understand, the giant Jersey pawed the ground, displaced and doused the light and set out savagely to find his enemy. And when some little stones from where his quarry quivered in the dark slid down the bank the bull began his stalk.

45

The only thing that Jim could do was run, no easy job in waders and at night. He might have prayed; he needed to. Ten feet downstream the water deepened to above his waist. He thought the bull would get him now for sure — and then he saw the boat tied to a stump.

Jim cut himself and broke his nails in wrenching out his fishing knife to slash the rope. He seized a broken oar and thrust the leaky rowboat out into the deep, swift water at midstream.

Saved? Above the bellows of the thwarted bull he heard below the frightening thunder of the falls; he feared he'd have to go ashore before the murderous animal was left behind. But now a second miracle preserved his life: a fence loomed up; the animal was stopped; the falls avoided and the shore was safe.

Soaked with river water, blood and perspiration, Jim Easton walked back to his car on trembling legs. He drove back to his little wayside inn and went into the room that served as bar.

"Know who owns that land about a half a mile above the falls?" he asked.

"Yup," the barkeep said. "Bill Tucker owns that place; he comes in here most every afternoon."

"When you see him next, give him this dollar bill. I had a sort of accident and had to take his boat downstream a hundred yards or so and cut the rope. He'll need a new one when he brings it back to where it was."

"OK," the barkeep said. "I will, but I should think a man should ought to have more sense than go out on the river in the night alone."

"I guess you're right," Jim Easton said. "There seem to be some hazards now and then."

He shook himself and lit a cigarette; his fingers trembled as he struck the match.

"Give me a double shot of rum," he said.

Not Always
What They Seem

Solemnly and slowly the moonlit water flowed between the river's darkly shadowed banks. It might have seemed to one well versed in fantasy as though he and the figures from a favorite fairy tale were sailing down a magic, silver stream that flowed from dark and fragrant forests far up in the New Brunswick hills down toward a sleeping sunless sea.

Old Archie Lufkin dipped the tin cups in the pail of water from the brook and handed 'round the bottle we had brought. Above the rumble of the fire in the little stove we heard the sound of voices as the guides beached their canoes: laughter, animated talk, and, now and then, a gay French snatch of song.

We asked Old Archie what was being said; he didn't know. "I never learned to understand them Frenchmen."

I looked out through the open window at the heavens high above the pines and realized that I'd never learned to understand the stars. A great horned owl calling, like the baying of a distant hound, sent chills and tremors coursing up and down our spines. "What's that?" my cousin Harry asked and edged up closer to the stove.

"Fine fishermen we are," I said. "We ought to speak the language of the habitants; to know the names of insects that the fish are feeding on; which star up there at night is which; what plants and flowers grow along the banks; the songs and calls of all the birds."

"I wish my wife was here," said Archie, as he poured himself another drink. "She knows most all the sounds we hears here in the woods; the birds, the animals and sometimes even just the bugs. But sometimes she don't recognize the things she sees."

"How come?" I asked.

"When I come out last spring to guard the pool," he said, "my wife, she come along to give the shack a homey touch. She brung them rugs you see there on the floor and put them nice white curtains in the windows back of where we're settin'. About that time there was a bear hung out around the place and when Christine got everything fixed up and we was eatin' dinner here by lantern light, that bear he stuck his head in through the window right beside her chair. And when he did them curtains covered up his ears and hung down all around his face. 'My

Lord,' says Christine, 'who'd a thought a nun would come a peekin' in at night way out here in the woods.'

"Christine, she ain't been out here since that time and neither has the bear."

We smoked in silence since we knew the sound of chuckling outside in the night was no more than the river running down across the bar.

Grouse Gunner's Prayer

Give me a woodlot and an orchard by a long-abandoned barn; a cattle pasture where thorn apples grow; an old rail fence along the bank above a bog that feeds a sparkling little alder-bordered stream wherein the brook trout soon will spawn and, when the flight from farther north is on, the woodcock chalks abound. Give me the long gray grass that crowns a gentle knoll that slopes down to the sun-baked hardhack and a stand of small white birch. Give me the remnants of a briar-guarded wall, a carpet of the forest's fallen leaves beyond its mossy heaps of stones; faint traces of a one-time wagon track between the trunks of ancient oaks; a grove of evergreens, the rhododendron thick along its edge.

Give me a frosty morning on the gold and crimson hills; time-tested friends with whom I long have shared the secrets of the woods: the places where the partridge feed; which way the birds are apt to fly. Give me a snow-white setter, steady, sound and slow, who never ranges, like a quail dog, far ahead and always marks a grounded grouse; an easy-handling twenty-gauge that fits my shoulder and my arm; the strength to climb the ridges and to work the swamps and swales.

Never let me fail to gauge the distance and the speed of flying birds, to shoot straight at the target and with skill — or else to cleanly miss and not to maim. Don't let me fail to give the man who hunts beside me his full share of shots, and credit for a grouse he claims that I at first had thought had fallen to my gun. No matter how far off I am from home or whether I am coming back, don't let me fail to thank the farmer who has let me hunt behind his house.

Give me kind thoughts about the country boy who may, with rabbit hound and twenty-two, have spoiled my cover for that lovely autumn day; about a gunning partner's over-eager Brittany who puts 'em up a hundred yards ahead — I know the owner of the ill-trained dog regrets the ruin of the hunt far more than I.

Give me the eyes to see and ears to hear; to see the work of glaciers many thousand years ago in spreading boulders bigger than a woodshed or a poultry pen beneath the pines where, in this eon's later age, the bears and bobcats den; to watch, high overhead against the blue, the miracle of bird migrations toward the south; to see, while sitting silent on a drumming log, the deer go down the hill in single file; to briefly glimpse a hunting fox; to hear the music of a distant waterfall, the chorus of a flight of crows, the chatter of a squirrel not yet gone to ground, the echoes of a shot — far off.

This is my prayer — or some of it. But who has need to pray in words? Awareness of man's dreams and knowledge of his needs exists. Today kind Providence has granted every wish a man could have. My dog lies at my feet as I await my friends. I take my brace of biddies from the pocket of my shooting coat and kneel to drink the water of an ice-cold spring.

I kneel and stay there on my knees awhile to thank my God — whatever God may be — and *yours*.

I Still Fish — Badly,
But I Fish

The jay in the woods never studied the gamut,
Yet trills pretty well to me.

Walt Whitman

The man who fishes in Quebec and can't speak French is missing something that he shouldn't miss; likewise the angler on a brown trout stream who never studied entomology. As long as salmon freely take and trout rise avidly, the fisherman won't keenly feel his weakness and his lack. But let the salmon stay at sea or sulk or let the dwindling trout schools feed selectively, disdaining imitations which are inexact, and Piscator, if unprepared, will soon feel wholly incomplete.

A willingness to murder grammar, energetic pantomime and mutual goodwill may oftentimes surmount the language barrier which tends to separate the passenger amidships from the guides who man the Gaspé boats. But woe to him who wades alone where trout are feeding on a hatch he can't identify.

With the passage of the years, I've grown increasingly aware of this. To take one's share of wild brown trout on hard-fished Eastern streams, a fisherman should study Preston Jennings, Ernest Schwiebert, Arthur Flick and half a score of other entomologists, and just to study will not do; one has to learn, discern, identify and memorize the mayflies of a dozen states. Some years ago I found I was too old a dog to learn these tricks. It followed that I wasn't catching trout and felt I never could again; my confidence was lower than the belly of a snake. I thought of giving up the sport last spring and almost did; an accidental meeting tipped the scales toward one more try.

Dining by myself one evening at the Club, I recognized Tad Hillman's voice and turned and saw him sitting at a table just behind my own, alone. Close friends at college and on Adirondack camping trips, we hadn't met in fifteen years; we wasted little time in joining forces for a talk about old times.

The most cherished memories that we shared were of our early after-college years when we were blessed with luck for which we ever since have thanked our stars; the luck of having found the fishing that we did on New York's then unspoiled Ausable. Our recollections drifted back and centered on those halcyon days when almost no one joined our little group of dry-fly fishermen except for, now and then, a friendly countryman more prone to fish that lovely river with a brace of *wet* flies than with worms.

Tad Hillman, who had driven down from Montreal, could not withstand the urge, he said, to pay a visit to the river that we both had loved.

"I didn't fish at all," he said. "There were too many guys with spinning rods, and cars parked everywhere along the stream. But I got all choked up when I left Wilmington and drove up through the Notch and thought about Guy Jenkins' twenty-inchers taken there, above the fox farm where Ray Bergman and Bill Randebrock had once disdained as nuisances all trout below a full fat fifteen inches long."

"What did they take them on those days?"

"Oh I don't know; perhaps a Fanwing or a Hendrickson. Lee Wulff had not dreamed up his famous flies as yet."

"Yes, I remember how Lee tied them in his teeth the year I came, and how Stan Berry took a three-pound trout on one below the concrete bridge."

"There was a crowd of minnow-dunkers on that bridge when I drove past," Tad said. "I didn't stop. I drove on up to Dead Dog Bend where Johnnie Easton caught that fish that hung in Byron Blanchard's dining room. The place looked just the same except for people up and down the bank with spinning rods. In the glide beside the road where Freddy Nagle took the record fish one year, a trout was rising and a guy was working on it with a variant. Inconsistent though it may have been I breathed a prayer for both the fisherman and fish before I put the car in gear and drove to the lagoon."

Ah, the lagoon! I looked across the room and seemed to see again the gravel-bottomed run where George La Branche, one late spring afternoon, on deftly placed Pink Lady, took — and released — five handsome trout that averaged just below two pounds. I thought about the deep black water underneath the bank where monsters lurked that only minnow-men could hope to tangle with; the boulders at the downstream bend that sent the current swinging in below dark branches of the ancient hemlock trees where "Chiseljaws" had seized my Hendrickson and made me famous for a year or two—and proud for ten.

"That's where you took your four-pound trout, I think," I heard Tad Hillman say. "I guess you took him on a Brown Bivisible; you fished with Fred and John so much, and Fred, at least, used almost nothing else."

"No, it was a Hendrickson. But Don Bell got one just about as big that day, up by the ski jump, on a Badger Spider. It didn't seem to matter much what fly you used."

"It didn't seem to matter much what fly you used." The words stuck in my mind long after we had said goodnight. When Tad went out to get his car, I went in to the bar to nurse a nightcap and to think. Who had that fellow been from Philadelphia who fished in shorts and carried nothing but a box of Spent-Wing Coachmen hanging from his Sam Brown belt? He'd caught as many trout as any two of us. How had I done so well those carefree happy naive days with just a Fanwing where no hatch was on and little else to cast to rising trout than half a dozen stiffly hackled patterns, either gray or buff or brown?

The tide within my highball glass was getting low; time perhaps to order one more for the road. I idly turned the pages of a magazine and saw a picture of an ear of corn. An ear of corn; it rang a bell. Standing on the bridge at Upper Jay some twenty years before I'd dropped some yellow kernels pilfered from the Blanchard's hens and watched the big trout lying in the cool, clear current from the tributary brook swirl up to suck them in.

The man behind the bar said: "Closing time; you'd like another drink?"

"No thanks," I said. "I'm leaving early for a drive upstate; I want to be bright-eyed and bushy-tailed. I aim to bring my family back a mess of trout."

Perchance to Dream

I went out to the hazel wood,
Because a fire was in my head,
And cut and peeled a hazel wand,
And hooked a berry to a thread;
And when white moths were on the wing,
And moth-like stars were flickering out,
I dropped the berry in a stream
And caught a little silver trout.

William Butler Yeats

The moonlight came in through the window by my bed. The snow outside was two feet deep but, lying endlessly awake, I seemed to hear the noises of midsummer night as though the mournful music of the locusts and the katydids was being played back somewhere in my room on tape. Of course I didn't hear the whippoorwill; I hadn't heard a whippoorwill since World War One. But otherwise the sounds were all the same. This grew monotonous; I pulled the shade down all the way and lay there thinking in the dark.

A lot of things I thought about weren't pleasant things; like the time my favorite hunting dog was killed, or when I'd climbed a big white column on our porch and slid back down onto the awning hook and pushed back up from where I was impaled and raised my arm and looked and seen the just-missed purple artery. But when a car went by the house, or there was pounding in the ancient pipes, I usually could change my thoughts.

The thing I always tried to think about was fishing in the River X; that was definitely the best. I call it River X because I have to keep the place I go when I can't sleep a secret so it won't be all fished out. From late in May until the fall it has good salmon runs of heavy fish; no grilse, though now and then a five-pound sea trout takes the fly. The tributaries harbor big brown trout, sly as foxes and as wild as hawks.

When I fish this River X on sleepless nights it isn't any trick at all to think of water up above its banks. This makes the racing current give my heavy bucktail life and often fools some mammoth, hook-jawed cannibal a feeder stream is better off to be without. Sometimes I exercise my nighttime wizardry to bring a dilatory run of salmon up the river from the bay where it has overlong been preying on the capelin schools. But usually I just let nature take its course, content to choose a month to suit my mood and try my luck.

Sometimes I start my fishing at the Forks. I almost always take a limit there: long skinny West Branch salmon and the chunky kind that go up to the lake that feeds the wider, smoother branch. There is a gravel bar where you can beach your fish and use your pliers to get out the hook or cut the leader if the barb is pulled in deep.

If there are no salmon showing at the Forks, it isn't more than fifty yards to where Big Crystal Creek comes in.

Big Crystal is a first-rate brown-trout stream: pocket water, glassy slides and long still pools where twelve-foot leaders are a "must," cold shaded springs, no competition for the fly life or spawning beds. There are no trash fish, and somehow the salmon seem to pass this little river up, although the ice has hollowed out deep places underneath the rocks; places where a brown trout often lies that's bigger than a grilse.

Usually I think about these places where I fish the most. I think about the salmon and the butter-yellow browns. But last night, when the winter moon was full, I tried to think of something else to while away the dark and plodding, leaden-footed hours. I tried to think — and did at last — of deer trails through the woods to where a violet-bordered brook was born. I heard a partridge drum — or thought I did — and now, far down the little watercourse, a flicker sounded its alarm. Agile as a wildcat and as keen — for I was young again last night — I worked my way on down the brook through blowdowns and across the boulders on the banks until a ten-foot waterfall that marked the junction with another brook was musical and rainbow-bright.

Here at the secret meeting place of sparkling waters in the woods my mentor was goat-footed Pan, not Skues, Hewitt or La Branche, as with a little willow wand and baited hook I took a half a dozen crimson-spotted trout, the lovely, silver *Salvelinus fontinalis*. So exquisite they were there on a bed of ferns I raised the shade to let the moonlight in, but now the moon was down behind the hill; there was a fainter different light. The colors of the brook trout faded in the dawn; the waterfall at last was still; I slept.

The Blind Man
and His Dog

I turned reluctantly away one afternoon from looking at
the camp supplies displayed in Abercrombie's window.
With hosts of others homeward bound from work I waited
for the traffic light to change. My thoughts were joyous
thoughts of snow still on the Catskill mountain tops and
rivers running brim full past the budding alders on the
flooded banks; of woodcock flighting northward to the
nesting grounds and partridge drumming in the spring-
awakened woods. I might have thought I heard the peepers

in the swamp at home and smelled the fresh fine smell of mint along the margins of our brook. But then my thoughts abruptly changed; I saw the blind man's dog.

Hers were the saddest eyes I've ever seen; unhappy, opaque eyes that focused only on unfeeling crowds and on the passing traffic in the city's streets her master could not see; eyes no longer even dimly lit by fading memories of a carefree puppyhood or sparked by hopes of nursing puppies of her own.

The shuffling beggar's pace was tortoiselike; the sounds of his guitar less musical than the infrequent clink of minor coins into his little dented metal cup. Only a master's overwhelming love could compensate for endless days like this, but nothing in the dog's brown eyes would indicate that she was loved or thought of by the man who owed so much to her as other than a necessary tool.

My heart turned over as I passed her by. In a few short hours Trigger and his mate, Suzanne, would guide me past emerging crocuses and daffodils to where the banded quail were feeding on the hill. At that same time this sidewalk dog would guide the blind man past the rat-infested buildings of the slums to where perhaps a weary woman waited with a meal of odds and ends. Sometimes no doubt the gleanings of the neighbors' garbage pails would serve to keep this necessary animal alive, and it was fortunate no healthy exercise would serve to interest her in food.

Not so the setters on the Suffolk County hill who with gayly waving tails would gallop through the unmown winter rye, undiscouraged when they paused on point to have the blank shells bring no birds to earth. With smiling eyes the dogs would listen to my praise for work well done and follow eagerly at heel to where their overflowing bowls of beef and meal would be attacked with relish and with glances up of gratitude.

Later, as the night came on, these dogs of mine, caressed and spoken softly to, would stretch out on a favorite rug before the open hearth and watch the fire till the time arrived to go out to their clean and cozy kennels and their dreams of woodcock holding close beside a spring or perhaps of pheasant cornered in the corn.

Meanwhile on the chilly unswept floor of some ramshackle ghetto flat, the city dog would now be lying down to wait for morning, the tragedy of her existence compounded by awareness that, for the man for whom she lived her life, the morning light would never come.

Small wonder that long after I had left the blind man and his dog behind the haunting sadness in their only pair of eyes found some reflection in my own.

Oh Wind,
If Winter
Comes

The shifting curtain of the clouds obscured the brilliance of the upper sky; while brittle leaves whirled crazily across the lawn I heard — far off beyond the dunes — the rolling thunder of the surf. I watched the seagulls struggling inland from the bay, and saw the wild ducks losing headway as they bucked the gale.

The barking of the bird dogs in their barrels on the south side of the barn gave notice that the mailman had arrived, and as the snowflakes started suddenly downwind I went out to the post box by the gate.

Back at the big Dutch door that led into the darkening hall the cold nipped at my heels with icy teeth as though to drive an alien indoors, away from where its master, winter, now was fully in command. Without delay or backward glance, I shot the bolt and sought the comfort of the fire in the shadow-paneled living room. An envelope addressed from Canada now caught my eye.

"Your letter," wrote my friend, Emile, "is here with me this year three month before the crows come back, so I am glad to hear from you by your letter just received. I am happy too, that you are in good health and ready early for the salmons to come back.

"First of all I want to wish you many mile of pleasant driving with your car. Now you have companion for your traveling and hope you will have pleasure with this dog.

"For the fishing season we don't know. Twelve feet of snow and maybe more is on the river on the ice; the ice is very big and, for sure, we have more snow before the spring is very late to come. All these heavy snow and ice will make sometime much water in the river very high; the place you like for fishing best should fish good many days and maybe weeks. I watch close when the ice is going to the bay and write to you so you are coming when the first run is arrive.

"And now, my friend, I have surprise for you; the Government has ask the paper company to put the dam in operation when the ice is no more in the river and use the fishway for the salmons. The Provincial Government in Quebec City say there will be no more the nets close by the rivers on the Gaspé coast this year. What, my friend, you think of that?

"So I hope that what you hope and what I hope will be like that. I hope we have many salmons in the river when the summer come, and big one like ten year ago.

"I give your greeting to Armand Gaston and to Pierre Coté and they both say, 'bonne chance' to you."

I put the letter down and while I thought about my friends up north, the cat jumped on my lap and looked up at my face; she flexed her dainty toes and purred — regardless of the howling wind and driving snow outside — as though the sun were shining and the year were at the spring. Listening to her joyous song, I almost heard the orioles and, in the fire's flames, I saw a little river and a covered bridge and Emile smiling, with my salmon in his net.

Toward Canada

This dour afternoon the ocean seems a vast and Godfor-
saken waste. Born in the distant windswept depths its
mighty rollers boil and thunder 'round the lighthouse
rocks or plunge, as white-topped breakers, on the trembling sand. No ships, no smoke, no fishing boats, no sails
are visible between this lonely coast and Spain. The river,
swollen by late-season rains, pours its waters out to sea and
sends a call of welcome to the salmon of the autumn run
now nosing in across the bars.

In the swamps and on the forest green, tinges of bright red appear. Behind the saltbox houses and the weathered barns, the long grass in the open fields is turning gray. The cattle gather at the pasture gates, the crows are winging toward their roosts, and now and then, oncoming motor cars put on their lights.

As is the case so often I am on my way, but am not headed north-northeast with rod and reel and more flies than I need or can afford. This time I'm driving toward the border where the motels all have vacancies, the roadside restaurants are boarded up and summer folks have left for home. I'm going up along the shore to see where William Fowler writes his sonnets on New Hampshire's coast; to see where, every hour of the day and night, year after year, the famous firm of L. L. Bean sells fishing tackle, guns and camping gear; to see where Ellis Briggs shoots woodcock in the swales between the St. Croix and the big St. John.

I'm going north to look for salmon in the rivers where no salmon anglers fish; to talk with guides who have no sports to guide; to learn the ways of people undisturbed by aliens; to learn about the birds and animals and fish.

As October's sun begins to set behind a bank of drifting clouds, I cut off down a little lane along a creek that leads to Stephen's cabin on the margin of the marsh. No one is there, but I know where the key is hidden on the rafters of the shed. I light the stove and heat a can of pork and beans. The coffee bubbles on the stove; the toast turns brown. The evening turns to dusk and then to dark. The clouds are blown away; the moon shines out.

And now I see, far up above, a scattered multitude of stars. I listen to the noises of the night: the rustle of a raccoon in the reeds, the muted thunder of the surf beyond the shadowed outline of the dunes, the happy gabble of the geese. I inhale the salty, heady, low-tide fragrance of the mud.

A flight of black ducks shoots between me and the moon, headed up the river toward the woods. Ten miles upstream — if they keep on — they'll see the stars reflected in the lake; another mile above the birch trees and the pines will bring them to the pool where Steve and I have planned to build our camp.

The words of Robert Frost come to my mind:

The woods are lovely, dark, and deep,
But I have promises to keep,
And miles to go before I sleep,
And miles to go before I sleep.

I make myself a promise there and then to drive along the rutted woods road through the dark, to see the eyes of animals reflected in the headlights' beams, to see — between the trunks of trees — the moonlight on the placid lake, to hear the owls hunting on the hills, to listen for a wildcat or a fox.

I wash the dishes, leave a note and lock the door. Back in the little crossroads town at Foster's store, I fill the tank with gas, buy food enough to last and say goodnight. I have my flashlight and my sleeping bag.

"Aren't you afraid to go alone?" Ma Foster asks.

"Afraid of what?"

I start the car; I hope the things I've read about the harmlessness of bears are true.

I Am a Purist

Some of the stars were visible that night despite the dusky cover of the clouds, but none of them as clear as that which shone beside the green-gold glitter of the sun against the day-old crescent moon. I put my rod across the old rail fence, unclasped my net and dropped it on the grass, climbed through the bars and picked my tackle up and crossed the pasture to the water's edge.

I had my waders on of course, my rod strung with a sinking line, a heavy leader and a Black Dose salmon fly. I knew the river bottom well; I knew the pool I'd come to fish, the runs and shallows at its head and tail. Carefully I took my stance where I could cast and let the current do the rest. My hopes were high.

In a nearby beaver pond the chorus of the peepers celebrating spring was shrill. I heard the snort of farmer's horses out to pasture for the night, the barking of the watch dogs down at Jay, the bleat of sleepy, streamside sheep. I watched the moon and stars play hide-and-seek up in the clouds. I cast repeatedly and hoped.

Cloud followed cloud across the sky; the minutes and the hours passed. No evidence of big Ausable trout was manifest though I was sure such trout were there. And then, as loneliness, discouragement and chill were added to my weariness, I heard — plainly in the shallows down below the pool — the telltale splashing of a monster brown trout herding frightened minnows up on shore, whence it could seize them as they came back one by one. Now, in my flashlight's shielded beam, I changed the fly. Careful not to raise a wave I stole downstream and cast a bucktail toward the lurking cannibal. My aim, it seemed, was accurate. As I started my retrieve I felt resistance and I struck to set the hook. It held; I took in line for just a foot or two before my would-be victim took it back. I brought the creature back toward me again; once more it powered toward the other bank. This went on until elation turned to doubt.

I waded in regardless now — what could I lose? I shone the light down on the stream and there — caught on a submerged willow branch — I saw my lure; a bucktail is a lure — say what you will.

Listening to a whippoorwill I walked back through the dampness, dew and clouds of fireflies to where I'd left my car beside the road. Despite the beauty of the night I was resolved to fish in future when a man should fish, in sunshine, safety and with friends, and with a stiffly hackled, well-cocked floating fly. Big fish be damned!

Closing Camp

The salmon season's over and the camp is closed. The last canoe is paddled down to where the river meets the Gulf; to where the lamps are being lit in houses bordering the road between the airstrip and the beach. From here the far-off running lights on transatlantic vessels, dimly seen, shine through the dusk; stout freighters, full and down, with final cargoes of the year. With hearty handshakes and good wishes for the winter months the suntanned seignior boards the old twin-engined plane which takes off into moonlit skies toward Seven Islands, Montreal, New York.

Now, as the aircraft burrows westward through the clouds, the passenger may cast his thinking back to where his summer happiness lies sleeping in the shadows of his silent lodge of logs. Perhaps he thinks fair weather will not soon be gone. Perhaps he thinks he might have had another golden month; a month of open fires crackling in the hearth, of sunlight on the tundra in the dawn, of late run salmon showing in the pools, of sunsets fair as sunrise in the spring. Perhaps he thinks of silver nighttime merging into brisk and bracing day when, on the glacial outcrop of the hills, the wolf packs of the barren lands give tongue in music weird as are the Northern Lights to serenade the morning star.

Suddenly he sees a countless galaxy of stars; the chorus of the wolves he hears in dreams is drowned out by the thunder of the waterfall he's left behind that afternoon. A fellow traveler turns to him and says: "There's Seven Islands down below; I guess we'll make the plane for Montreal all right."

The rumble of the motors ends as flight three-thirty-one glides to a stop.

The Pig Pen
Pool

We called the place the Pig Pen Pool; there used to be a pig pen in the orchard at the downstream end. Not far beyond a weatherbeaten paint-starved barn, an empty silo, battered by a century of winter winds, leans toward the ruins of a once substantial house. A half a mile across the fields outbuildings of the dwellings fronting on the county road today house Chevrolets and snowmobiles instead of hens.

The brookies in the Pig Pen Pool have yielded to

the European trout; shy fish, sophisticated, sly and strong, with vast distrust of man's deceits. The local barefoot boys long since have found the brown trout are no easy marks; their elders of the chuck-and-chance-it school have for the most part seen their offerings disdained, have gone to fish elsewhere for perch and bass and left the canny foreigners alone.

Where the river rubs against a steeply slanting wooded hill the rocks and rhododendron offer shaded shelter in the water's dark-green depths. Down there, beside the cooling crystal springs that stir the snow-white pebbles and the sand, the great elusive stream-bred beauties lie; longed-for, unreachable and seldom seen.

Upstream the boisterous waters bubble down between the stones to coast in foam-flecked slicks and gentle glides along the banks, with now and then an underwater thrust that shifts the currents till they join in joyous union with the calmer waters of the Pig Pen Pool. Below the pool itself, the streambed widens out and loses depth before the river gathers strength and races on again in endless searching for the sea.

On these fertile quiet-water flats, well shaded on the angler's side by apple trees and elms, the fly life is so rich uncounted schools of trout, if undisturbed, would gather there to rest and batten on the summer's never-ending feast. If wading were done carefully or not at all in water not above the knee, a man who cast as far as Ellwood Colahan and daintily as Richard Hunt, who matched the hatch as well as Schwiebert, Atherton or Flick and crept up on his prey as cautiously as George La Branche, might have such sport, when duns were up, as few of us have ever dreamed about.

Unfortunately for those who deeply care for solitude there is, from season's opening till its end, a long parade of those equipped with hobnailed boots that starts down at the Junction Pool and crunches ceaselessly on up with spashing disregard through silent secret places in the stream, then thunders off around an upstream bend before the stirred-up water downstream clears.

To take a brace of fifteen-inches from the Pig Pen Pool is difficult; the unresponsive trout of size lie deep within the safety of the rockbound pool and dare not venture forth to risk the shallow water hazards at the tail. The fish that work their way upstream to reap the harvest of the hatching duns are shy, plagued as they are by memories of mayflies harboring a hook.

Success demands a break in the parade, a little time at least alone, a sunken leader long and delicate and curved, a fly that imitates the natural, no drag, much luck. One evening when I nursed a cold at home and fishermen all day were thick as gnats, a man whose company I love went out alone at dusk and, casting science to the winds, ignoring subtlety, put out a fanwing to the center of the pool. The fish whose viscera our cats enjoyed that night was nearly two feet long.

And now, inspired by the recollection of this feat of long ago, I sit beside the Pig Pen on an old stone wall: the violets beside my felt-shod feet are fragrant as the apple blossoms overhead, the sun has left the water and the light wind dies. A hush comes on the valley and the birds are still. The shadows creep across the fields and up the hill. The dancing mayflies suddenly are gone; the daylight fades. The moon comes up; the tiny lanterns of the fireflies appear. Backwater bullfrogs croak as planets take their places in the sky, and toads commence their mournful music in the swamp.

Now trout no longer surface-feed on tiny insects dimly seen. But what of that? Three trout that I have taken on a spent-wing at the spinner fall lie on the clover in the bottom of my creel; they are enough. And now, as Skues might have said, the gates of fairyland are opened on a lovliness beyond all thought of sport. May God forever guard the Pig Pen Pool, and keep it as it is tonight for our grandsons and their grandsons and brothers of the angle every spring until the endless end of time.

Regardless
of the Fog

The stars are shrouded by the mist tonight; the moon has abdicated from her realm. Beneath the fog that hangs between the hills the coal-black river rushes toward the sea. The partridge perches close against the tall dark pine tree's trunk, but in the alder-bordered swales no wakeful woodcock pokes its bill in search of worms; no wild geese gossip as they glean the farmers' fields; no black ducks dabble in the shallows where the brook trout spawn. These migrants will not leave their summer homes until the frost is on the pumpkin and the locust orchestras are stilled.

The travel-weary driver turns his jeep in off the blacktop road and risks the muddy ruts that lead up to the silent camp. With dog at heel he turns the lamp wick up and leaves the porch door open while he gets undressed. Outside the rain commences to come down.

What rotten luck, the old grouse gunner thinks, November in the Catskills with this heat. He wonders if the bobcats, on a night like this, are seeking shelter in their caves beneath the rocks, and if the fox that barks behind the camp on moonlit nights is curled up cozily beneath some blowdown on the ridge. He calls his dog to stroke his head and say good night but Rap already has gone fast asleep. As raindrops patter on the roof he lies down on the blankets of his bunk and seems to see his dog on point beside a brook or bringing back a biddy from across an overgrown stone wall. Deep within the world of dreams he smiles and sighs with sweet content; regardless of the fog, the heat and rain how wondrous, here among the mountains is the peaceful Land of Nod.

What Then
Unless Somebody Cares?

The sun groped feebly through the gray December sky. Alarmed by some slight movement in the tall marsh grass, the black ducks standing on the river ice took wing; a corporal's guard of grumpy hunched-up gulls remained, indifferent to the threatened depredation of a fox. No other creatures were abroad except the crows that gossiped on the branches of a long-dead elm, two snow-white swans that sailed majestically downstream where wind and waves had kept a channel open by the farther shore and, in the shelter of a holly tree, a mockingbird.

This was the shortest day in all the year. Henceforth succeeding days would each be just a fraction longer than the last; each day would be a little closer to that perfect day in June when Andrew Dawley took the net, the cushions and the tackle bag and walked ahead along the path that led to where the Gaspé boat was drawn up on the gravel beach.

Repelled by the winter morning's dank and dismal atmosphere, old Arthur Jones, out walking with his Labradors, went back inside the house and shivered slightly as he hung his shooting jacket on a peg beside the gun-rack in the big front hall. In the living room he struck a match and lit the kindling in the fireplace. He added half a dozen cedar logs and smiled to see the dogs creep up to watch the flames.

He watched the fire like the dogs and when he briefly closed his eyes he saw his well-loved friends of summertime beside their kitchen cooking stove. The little house in which they lived lay now half buried in the northern snow. He seemed to hear the growl of tractors snarling at the drifts that swept in from the river flats across the highway leading to the town.

The big black Labs by now were fast asleep, their muffled barks and twitching paws mute evidence of dreamland, races with the stable cats, forbidden hunts for cottontails and challenges to battle with the dogs from down the road.

Now sleep was overcoming Arthur Jones. He nodded as he dozed and gave vent to a snore or two, but soon the children's voices that he dreamed he heard were real. A roaring pack of boys and girls running hell-for-leather in full cry burst in shouting through the kitchen wing, where they had paused to ascertain what Grandma and her helper, Mrs. Chase, were planning for the noonday feast. Amidst quick hugs, knocked-over chairs, cavorting dogs and noisy mixed-up talk, one question came out finally, at last: "May we go out and feed the pigs?"

Old Arthur Jones stood up and rang a bell to summon Stephen Case, who earlier had fed the poultry and the livestock, laid the fires, gone to get the mail and now was free.

"Steve," he said, "these youngsters here would like to see their friends, the pigs, and any other animals you've got out by the barn. I count on you to see they don't fall in the pen or stick their fingers in the rattrap in the empty chicken yard. Don't let them get in Bessie's stall, she kicks; or leave the corncrib door unlatched. We've had our troubles with the squirrels and the rats."

Steve Case's weatherbeaten face was crinkled in a mile-wide smile. "Come on, all of you," he said, "just let me leave these letters I've brought in."

The herd of small fry thundered toward the door in Stephen's wake with Dad and Mum and Uncle Bob all dragged along. Now, left alone, old Arthur Jones picked up the mail.

"All dividends they seem to be," he said. "I'll let Miss Martin cope with them next week. But this one here is postmarked 'Canada,' Christmas card perhaps from Andrew Dawley and his wife."

It was a Christmas card all right, but inside was a note from Andrew's cousin, Billy Moore: "I thought that you should know," it said "that Andrew and his wife were hurt real bad. They skidded coming down the hill and hit a big truck going fast toward Montreal. Both of them are laid up in the hospital downtown. The doctors say she may get well by spring, but doubt that they can save my cousin's leg.

"You knew, I guess, that Andrew's oldest boy was

drowned last fall, and at the Club his father was laid off—too old.

"I promised Andrew that I'd send this Christmas card; both he and Mary Jane was hurt too bad to write."

For some moments Arthur Jones was stunned. Who would cook and care for all the children in the Dawley house? Could the old man cope at eighty-three? How could Andrew guide next spring—with just one leg? What other gainful work was there for him to do? How many years would pass before the younger Dawley children made their way in life? What prospect of survival could there be for this fine family that he'd learned to love?

Arthur Jones was thoughtful and depressed. But now he heard the family coming back; all of them were gay and joyful and they sang. "'Tis the season to be jolly" came across the frozen lawn where playful Labs retrieved the children's rubber balls or ran in frantic happy figure-eights.

From the kitchen Mrs. Jones appeared to herd the family in to where the roast goose waited for the knife.

"Let's all be quiet now for silent grace," she said. "And yet since Uncle Bobby's here, perhaps he'll ask the blessing of this meal."

While little girls looked down demurely at their plates and little boys glanced sidewise at the food to come, their uncle called on God to make them all aware of what had been so bountifully bestowed.

"And make us conscious of the needs of others" was the final thing he said.

The children wondered why, at these few simple words, old Arthur, not much given generally to prayer, murmured reverently "AMEN."

The Crossing
of the Caribou

You didn't drive or fly to Maine when I was young;
you took the train. As the engine gathered speed you
saw the outer city's lights come on, and when you walked
across the lurching platform to the dining car you caught
the soft warm smell of tar.

Now, more than likely, seated by the window waiting for your order of lamb chops in ruffled paper pants,
Maine sweet potatoes and green corn, a bluff and suntanned
stranger took the seat across the table and began to talk.

Perhaps he'd say, "I heard you say you didn't want

that Kennebec boiled salmon; said you'd catch your own next week. You must be heading for my state."

"Yes sir, I'm headed up to Maine."

"I'm traveling down to Maine myself," he'd say; "that's what I call my stampin' ground. But I'd consider this a mite too late; we mostly quit our salmon fishing in the Bangor Pool the end of June."

Then you might tell him you were going after land-locks near Fort Kent and say that some of them were pretty big—larger than some sea-run fish.

And possibly he'd say he knew that that was true; some Portland friends of his had taken ten-pound land-locks in Sebago Lake. But he, himself, preferred to fish a river than a lake.

"That's why I take my holiday this time of year," I'd say. "I like to fly-fish in the thoroughfares instead of trolling in the lakes. Those landlocked salmon leave deep water in the fall; you find them in the streams between the lakes. I guess they want to have their spawning beds pre-pared a month or two before the winter closes in."

The train now shudders to a stop; the waiter brings the ice cream and the macaroons; I pay the bill. The strang-er smiles and says: "Penobscot's had its finest season yet this year; it might just be the same up by the border. I hope it is; I wish you luck."

Murmuring a word of thanks, I walk on back—the scent of marshes and low tide is strong—to where my lower bunk is ready for my dreams. The train rolls onward in the night, racing with September's orange moon. I see it—always even with the train—slicing silently through banks of clouds; I am happy, healthy and content, and need no opiate to make me sleep. That's about the way it was in 1921.

Next morning in the sleeping car, the porter

helped those people who were bound for Rangeley and its sister lakes to shift their rods and duffle to another train. Augusta took its toll of Belgrade fishermen with reservations at the Liar's Paradise. Bangor was the stopping place where some of us bade goodbye to the businessmen, the folks who came to close their summer homes on Mount Desert or salmon anglers headed for the Miramichi. Here I turned off for Osprey Lake.

My car was hitched up now to ancient shopworn mates behind a locomotive short on paint. But if equipment wasn't all that one could wish, the service was. The trainmen — it was difficult to tell just who was which — were calm and kind. Each waistcoat pocketed a fat, gold watch with massive chain; each wallet in a man's blue jacket held encyclopedic information on New England's railroad trains, and every well-fed fellow had a heart made glad by helping out his fellow man.

"Keep a close watch out this window now; we're coming to a mighty likely place to see a moose," one said.

Another said: "I think you'd be right smart to get a coat or sweater from your bag before we get much further on. If you're headin' in for Marchand's camp, I guess you'll wish you had on something warm the time you get across the lake to Marchand's dock."

Osprey Lake, the only village on the wooded shores of Osprey Lake, was so all-fired starved for entertainment that its residents — except the folks too sick or hurt to walk — turned out to watch the coming of the day's one railroad train. Among them, Philippe Pluard, alerted by employers at the big lake's only sportsman's camp, was quick to greet the single passenger to leave the train.

"I am Philippe Pluard, who will be your guide," he said. "I put your baggage in the boat and then I go and get the mail. When it is ready we will go to camp."

Osprey is a major unit in Aroostook County's Rushing River Chain of Lakes. From its low surrounding hills the forests march down to the water's edge, endless ranks of evergreens without a gap for farmhouse or for summer camp. Some years before the time of which I write, young salmon of a migratory strain were introduced and outlets of the lower lakes were wired off so fish could not escape downstream. Ultimate return from their traditional feeding places in the sea had long been blocked by unenlightened industry. Fortunately, the system's larger lakes served well as little inland oceans, providing smelts and other sustenance as well as absence of extremes in water temperatures. From the safety and the comfort of their depths the fish ran up or down connecting streams; down in spring to feed on spawning smelt; and up in the fall, themselves to reproduce. While each year thousands fished the Beaverkill for trout, and hundreds sought the salmon in the Restigouche and the Miramichi, only a corporal's guard competed for these lovely native fish of Maine.

Eagerly I looked back from the sunset toward the night; toward camp and toward next morning on the thoroughfare.

On the dock our host stood in the dusk. The gentle, well-loved Pierre Marchand with mellow, low-pitched voice called out a greeting and my name. With well-tied knots the boat was soon secured against the weathered float's protected landward side; the men transferred my baggage to a cabin on the rocks. Philippe turned up the lamps, put fresh wood on the fire and brought a pail of water from the spring while Pierre showed me the ropes.

"The path leads up the little hill to where we eat," he said. "You'll hear the bell and see the lanterns in the windows of the lodge. The rods we always keep inside the screen to protect the handles from the porcupines. That running water that you hear is coming from a big lake up above us here, Round Lake. It was beside these camps of ours the caribou would cross the river every year; my father saw them swim across the year he died. That was many years ago; they say they never crossed again, but just this season one dark night when I was here alone in camp I thought I saw the caribou go by. The fog was thick, there was no moon; I can't be sure. I'll leave you for a little while and see you later at the lodge."

Next morning, off the nearby river's mouth, we took a turn or two with Philippe paddling in the stern and Gray Ghost trolled behind, but I only caught a single, small-sized trout. I'd never heard of Theodore Gordon, Halford, Skues, Hewitt or La Branche but, all the same, this seemed a dull and unrewarding form of sport. With a Jock Scott and a Silver Gray we moved up to the Outlet Pool.

The Outlet Pool looked promising enough to make it fun to fish regardless of results. I cast at least a hundred times and let the current swing the flies around. The patient Pluard changed position; changed the flies, to no avail, and at last suggested that we go upstream, eat our luncheon in the clearing by the warden's shack at the outlet of Round Lake and fish up there that afternoon.

"Sounds to me a good idea," I said. "Let's go ashore and get our slickers and our mackinaws in case the weather changes."

When we started out again and went a mile or so upstream, Philippe leaned on his pole and said, "M'sieur Marchand, he say he wish you luck. He say he sorry not to see you at the lodge last night; he had bad dizzy spell and he not feel so good. He say he like to take you out for fish one day and be your guide himself before the season close. He say he have good dream big salmon sleep at mouth of brook outside long gravel bar at outlet of Round Lake. He say sometime you fish close in with big Green Drake; he think you catch."

"Let's hope our good friend Pierre is well again when we get back to camp tonight," I said.

My guide stood thoughtful for a while, then crossed himself and leaned on his pole and pushed up through the fallen, floating. yellow hardwood leaves until we saw, a little way ahead, a wide expanse of ruffled blue, Round Lake. There he ran our craft ashore, unloaded pots and pans, tin plates, canned goods, the tableware and such beside the bench that served the warden as a restful watching post beside the pool. With his hunting knife he shredded kindling from a white-birch log, cut fodder for a fire with his little axe and, in ten minutes, served a first-rate woodsman's lunch at which the moosebirds were our uninvited, rather pushy guests.

The warden who had lunched at Campbell's camp some miles beyond the islands in Round Lake, came by and joined us in a cup of coffee and a chat before he left to spend the night at Osprey Lake. When he was out of sight we lay down on our blankets in the shade and slept. We woke up in the middle of the afternoon and both at once gave thought to Marchand's dream of salmon, big and eager for the Green Drake fly, where Round Lake's ice-cold brook ran in outside the gravel bar.

"Let's go out, Philippe," I said.

We did, and, as we left the inlet, I saw a bull moose with a rack of horns of trophy size feeding in the lily pads. We watched him tearing at the roots and heard the water dripping when he raised his head from nostrils which he turned toward us suspiciously. Cautiously we eased back in behind the bar and drifted through the pool and killed a three-pound fish and took it down to camp to give to Madame Marchand who, we hoped, would cook it

89

for Pierre. Then, happy and relaxed, I went to bed, ignoring dinner bells.

The wind lashed 'round the cabin all night long, the autumn rains came streaming down from raven skies. I awoke well rested and without the urge to get out on the river and to fight the elements. Philippe was standing by the stove. "M'sieur Marchand was taken to the hospital last afternoon," he said. "The warden, he don't like the way he look when he came by. He take him down."

"Philippe," I said, "you ask Madame if you can take her down today to see M'sieur. I know that he will be all right, but think, perhaps, she'd like to go."

"Merci," he said and went away.

For two days the storm kept up. I cowered in my cabin, read a book, fished fitfully the nearby Outlet Pool and slithered up the muddy path for cheerless meals.

After this the sun came back, likewise Philippe Pluard.

"M'sieur is better; he will be all right. He think we go, and Madame say so too, and spend two days, last days, where Round Lake run into top river pools. I have blankets and plenty food in my canoe. We sleep in warden's shack; he say OK. Your friend, Pierre, he think you get big salmon early in the morning at the brook. When you are ready, call; I wait for you."

All day I felt a kinship with Pluard upriver in the quiet woods. When evening came we talked about the caribou Pierre Marchand had thought he'd seen; about the dream Pierre had had about the fish. Before we went to sleep Philippe had said: "You come again next year; you come back anytime and tell me, I will go with you. I will anytime go anywhere with you."

We ate our breakfast in the gray before the dawn and got out to the brook as it was getting light. No bull moose stood among the lily pads, no wind came down the lake to block the progress of my fly; my Green Drake landed where I wanted it to land. Just as the sun came out and warmed the air I saw the boil and felt a pull; a big fish ran along the bar and jumped. I saw a lovely silver fish, the biggest of its kind I'd ever seen. It leapt and diamonds flashed and sparkled in the sun; again, again and yet again. And then, at last it came to net, the miracle Pierre Marchand had seen in dreams.

"Let's go back down to camp; perhaps Pierre is back," I said. I found it difficult to speak.

"Perhaps there is another here."

"Perhaps there is, Philippe, but let us go."

We weighed the salmon on the kitchen scales. "Is Pierre back?" I asked the cook. "We have a salmon just for him."

"Pierre will not be back," somebody said. "Pierre is dead."

Down at the Legion Hall in Osprey Lake you'll see a salmon mounted under glass by Herbie Welch. The brass plate reads: "This salmon weighing sixteen pounds is here in memory of Pierre Marchand who told us where and how to take it on a fly the last day in September, 1921."

Underneath there are two names, Philippe's and mine. Now, after many years together in the woods, Philippe cannot go with me any more. Philippe like his old friend and mine, Pierre, has seen the crossing of the caribou.

Hopefully It's—
You Know—
Like I Said

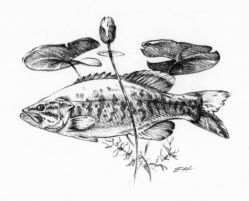

G ee, Uncle George," the youngster said, "I thought
you'd never come to visit us, with all those things—
you know—you have to do in managing that mink ranch
down to Circleville. I thought—you know—you might
forget how many bass you used to catch when—you
know—you and dad were boys. I sure am—you know—
glad that you've come back. Ma's talked—you know—so
many years about how—hopefully—you'd come."

"Well Bill, I've come and I am hopeful; hopeful I

can latch onto a mess of husky smallmouths like the ones we used to take. Let's get on to the boat house and see what kind of guide you are."

Out on the lake his uncle baited with a gob of worms. "I'm always hopeful when I start to fish," he said.

Young Bill impaled a hellgrammite and for an hour both the youngster and his older relative—though changing bait—were hopeful that a smallmouth, nosing through the depths, would seize the lure. Then Bill, whose minnow had dropped off, declared: "It's like I said; they must be biting over there beside the reef. If you are—you know—ready let's go give that place a try."

Old Uncle George chewed on his fifteen-cent cigar. "What are we waiting for?" he asked.

Bill cut the engine as the water shallowed near the reef. He said: "It might be—you know—good around these rocks."

This time, before the boat had drifted to a halt, each one had dropped a lip-hooked frog to swim across the gravel bar and past the water lilies near the bank. Each one expected action but the frogs were undisturbed.

"Maybe we'd better move again," Bill said, "it's getting late."

The motor droned on down the lake to where the sunken channel of a brook came out across a little harbor full of stumps. The sun was sinking like the old man's hopes. "It's like I said; things ain't the way they used to be," the old man said. "It ain't much use, but I'll try one more cast before I quit. Hand me that box of frogs."

Bill fumbled for the biggest frog.

"Hopefully," he said, "you'll—you know—get a big one just before we quit."

His uncle bit his moist cigar. He cast and saw the bullfrog, flying free, swim unmolested to the reeds along the shore. Bill said: "Gosh darn it, Uncle George, it's — you know — Uncle George . . ."

"Young man, I damn well don't know nothing even though you keep on telling me I do, excepting that I know damn well there ain't no fish in this damn lake; let's go back to that damn boat house and trade that sarsaparilla that you brung for something with a little more authority."

How Far Off
Is Next July?

The upper branches of the leafless maples gleam like silver burnished by the sun; the gulls go over flashing white against the pale-blue background of the sky. Beside the creek the weeping willows droop as though aware their ancient hollow trunks will not withstand the first strong blast of winter wind. Disturbed by Teddy and his dog, five hundred black ducks feeding where the ice has not yet formed now spring aloft and thunder off across the marsh. The boy stands watching as the dark flocks swirl and separate and coalesce and separate again in seeking safety high above the distant woods or out — far out to sea — across the dunes. The dog, with scarce an over-shoulder glance, goes on to trail a running pheasant in the reeds.

Teddy now removes the number sixes from his gun, looks down the barrels, drops the shells back into place; pulls off the safety, pushes it back on again. But now he sees his preparations are in vain; too closely followed to the water's edge, a cackling pheasant cock takes flight — well out of range — and in the tall brown grass no sign of life remains except the black Lab's slowly waving tail. Dejectedly the youngster calls the dog to heel.

"Come on, Romaine" — he bends and strokes the old retriever's coat — "let's see what's going on at Grandpa's house."

"OK, boss," his hunting partner seems to say, "but I know where those quail are apt to be right now."

Relationships between a gunner and his dog are close; the youngster rightly reads the message in his canine friend's brown eyes.

"We'll try the quail some other time," he says. "The hunt went through those fields not long ago; the birds must all be in the briars now. Let's you and I go in the back door first; perhaps we'll get a hand-out from Christine."

No one is in the kitchen when they go inside but when they find the pantry cookie jar is full they pause en route to Grandpa's den to practice petty thievery — share and share alike. But now, alerted by the click of Romaine's toenails on the sanded floor, the Conklin pointers, Pilot Plant and Pebble Beach, come trotting from the hall to see what's up. The rumble in each bird dog's throat is silenced by a bribe, and with the contents of the cookie jar appreciably reduced, Teddy and his escorts go on to the den.

Here the senior Conklin is seated in his leather arm

chair by the window looking out across the creek. "Well, Ted," he says, "come in; sit down. Let's see that gun. Romaine, you'd better drop; you too, Plant and Pebble, no more growling, down you go, *now drop*."

Making sure the gun's unloaded and the dogs are properly behaved, the old man lights his pipe and smiles. "I saw you pass that cloud of close-up ducks without a shot," he says. "You could have had your limit with one shell."

"Yes sir," his grandson, Ted, replies, "but Dad has told me not to shoot into a bunch of birds, no matter what."

"Your dad is right. But how about that pheasant that Romaine put up?"

"I think, sir, it was out of range. I might have hit the bird, I guess. I might have hit it hard enough to break a wing and make it easy for a fox to kill or wound it badly so it wouldn't live. I knew there wasn't any chance of killing it right off the way my father says you always used to kill your birds."

Ted's grandpa was well satisfied. He said: "My boy, I think you'll do, I'd offer you a cookie if I didn't know you'd helped yourself—and given all the dogs a case of worms to boot."

Now they hear the telephone; Grandmother answers it and calls downstairs: "Oh Ted—I mean big Ted—the call's for you; I think it's Jean Paul calling from Quebec."

Her husband lurches from his chair and goes across the hall to talk; the conversation lasts a long, long time.

The fire flickers and the three dogs doze; outside the winter twilight closes in on afternoon. Young Ted turns on the lights and while his father's father's voice drones on and on he looks at sporting prints and etchings on the wall and dreams. He dreams that he is casting from a Gaspé bank and, where his fly comes 'round above a rocky ledge, a salmon's dorsal fin and tail come up; he has a rise. He dreams — though wide awake — two Frenchmen hold his boat in place with steel-tipped poles while in the run across and toward the farther bank two twenty-pounders lie beneath his floating fly. He dreams that casting from a rock, he feels a mighty pull and sees his bamboo rod tip bend. He dreams — and then he hears his grandpa's lifted voice: "Hold on, Jean Paul, don't hang up yet," the old man says. "Forget what I have said about July. I have a friend who'll fish with me; he's just come in and told me that he can. You tell Pierre I'll take those two rods for the first ten days; I'll send a check. I want the best guides you can get; this young friend of mine has never fished in Canada before."

With wild surmise the youngster grasps what's being said. In ecstasy he rushes out across the hall. "Oh Grandpa, is it really true? — How long? — How long?" he asks, "before we start? I just can't wait."

The boy's excitement now infects the dogs; the senior Conklin tries to calm them down. "Don't be impatient, Ted," he says, "it took the Incas fifty years to build their palaces; you only have to wait six months. Now go on home; it must be suppertime. We'll talk some more about our trip next time you come."

A jubilant young Ted bursts out the door and races down the path toward home. "How far off is next July?" he asks himself. "Grandpa must be kidding about those fellows in Peru; he must have meant a hundred days, not fifty years."

The moon is just a pearl-white sickle, low above the dark mass of the woods; overhead the sky is bright with light from stars that may have left their sisters in the firmament long centuries ago. Six months, young Ted will find as time goes on, is not so very, very long.

Hey, Look
at That!

The springtime mountain air was sweet; the sun was shy behind the clouds; the swallows had at last come back to pluck emerging mayflies from the surface of the stream; the robins caroled from the lilacs on the village lawns.

I watched the water as I drove along the river road. I'd fished a dozen likely spots without a thing to show; my legs were heavy and my creel was light. I wouldn't leave the car again, I vowed, unless I saw some rising trout.

A host of memories were crowding into consciousness: Fred Nagle's highly colored two-pound trout taken on a bucktail in Ferdun's; the snakes that frightened Johnnie Woodruff on the hill above the Schoolhouse Pool; the big fish Walter Dette brought in from the Hendrickson and laid on Keener's Antrim Bar. I thought about the time Cy Coggins called across to me at Cairn's: "How big do chubs in Catskill rivers grow? If they don't ever reach four pounds, I've lost a damned good rainbow trout." I thought about dark nights when William Mackey, conservationist of striped bass, authority on duck decoys, as expert with a minnow as with Whirling Dun, was caught for longer than he liked in someone's cast-off, sunken bedsprings; this, a hundred yards above the Wagon Tracks where, in the blackness of another moonless night, the one and only Sparse Grey Hackle groped his way above the rapids toward safety on a bank, lit only now and then by lights of passing milk trucks rumbling down the hill.

Despite the lapse of many years I thought, as I approached the Mountain Pool, of two five-pounders taken by an angler shot with luck one day when Bergman and Bill Randebrock were casting just behind the man with horseshoes in his tackle bag. I thought about my son's first fourteen-incher on a floating fly; a fish that leapt two feet above the pocket water by the railroad bank just as its captor took an icy bath; about the comments of Ray Camp and Jimmy Deren the day I raised and lost a big one underneath the bridge; my trout the cat had stolen just below Cook's Falls, the one I'd kept to show Tom Collins I could sometimes get one just as big as his.

Down by the culvert where Ed Meyer used to fish I thought I saw a splash and then a circle where a fish came up. I put the brakes on coming to a stop. I saw that Ernie Maltz and Lil were hip-deep in the water casting tiny flies.

There wasn't really room for three to fish; I thought I'd drive away before they knew that I was there.

My progress was accompanied by a shout: "Hey, park your car by Tillie Smith's and come on down; they're rising here like crazy and some are heavy fish. Come down!"

"God bless you, Ernie Maltz," I thought. "How kind and generous you are! I like you much too well to share your pool and spoil your fun."

Pretending that I hadn't heard, I drove away. Beside a heavy run below the road I stopped. Here was the place where on one evening long ago, Tad and I had put our waders on and tried to win the Anglers' Outing prize.

Tad, that afternoon, went down the river to a place where he could cross. Beside the car I cast out to the center of the run from roadside rocks. I was perhaps a hundred yards above my friend, my friend who never missed a woodcock or a grouse and yet would say to me a dozen times each fall: "Nice shot, you killed it clean. My shot was not within a mile of it; that bird is yours." When I knew well that such was not the case.

I was, I say, a long way up above my friend when, coming up and up and up, I saw the biggest trout I've ever seen. My leader was too light and long to deal with something in the ten-pound range; it would take some time to change. The hatch might not last long; I should have called to Tad.

Instead, with trembling hands and backward glance, I tied another leader on; put on a different, larger variant. My friend was closer, but he hadn't seen what I had seen. I cast again but cast a bit below Leviathan, a practice cast. And, as my luck would have it then, a sixteen-incher took the fly.

In water strong and fast as this it takes a little time

to land a stream-bred fish as big as that, to let it go and fluff and oil the fly. When I was set to cast again the hatch had ended; Tad was opposite across the stream; Leviathan had gone down deep to occupy his cave among the rocks. My hope to bring this trophy fish to net had all but died.

"There was a big one rising where you're casting now," I said.

I prayed the monster wouldn't rise once more and take his fly. And later though I often went back to the place again — alone — I never saw that fish again. If I'd been Ernie Maltz, Jack Rolls, John Easton or Ed Zern, I'd have yelled: "Hey — look at that!"

And, although a wise fast-water fish that large perhaps could not be taken on a trout-size, floating fly, we might have had a story we could share with other fishing friends throughout the years.

I turned my thinking off — it's not too difficult — and drove on down below the junction with the Delaware. I knew one place where trout as big as salmon ought to feed at dusk. No one was on the island which I sought to reach; I was alone. I waded in and found the current treacherous and swift; I thought that I could make it but I wasn't sure; I paused.

"Oh well," I thought, "why not? You might as well risk going on from here to higher things — to 'graduation' as the saying goes. Who wants to live forever on a planet where he never takes a trout that he can brag about?"

I took another step and slipped. I stopped and felt the current strong against my legs. The forest leaves behind me seemed to murmur warnings in the evening breeze: "If you think you were lucky getting into college when you did, just try Valhalla now and see what's really tough; far too many nicer guys than you are on the waiting list."

Carefully I made my way back to the darkening bank and wondered, as I stood among the ferns, how many fishermen would call a friend to come and cast if they should spot a rising ten-pound trout.

God Tempers
the Wind

One June evening back in 'twenty-two I happened into
Henry Metz's General Store. A dozen older men were
gathered at the counter in the rear where Mr. Metz sold
meat. In the center of the crowd was tall and lanky Steven
Smith; his arms were waving and his goatee wiggled like a
thing alive. Folks said that Mr. Smith had brought a trout
to leave in Metz's icebox until he'd shown it off enough to
eat; it must be big, I thought. I elbowed through the
throng to have a look. *I'll say that trout*, as Adirondack

brown trout go, *was big;* it must have weighed at least five pounds.

"Whatja use to take him, Steve?"

"See him rise when you was settin' up there on the road?"

"Mayflies hatchin' or was he chasin' minnas up the bank?"

Steven Smith ignored them all, telling them—although they heeded not—his recent troubles at the farm. He harped on how the hired man had gotten drunk and left that morning when the tractor wouldn't start; on how a coon had found a loose board in the laying house and killed a dozen leghorn hens; on how the power saw was on the blink, the rats were in the corncrib, and the kids were all puffed up and broken out with poison oak.

"All them things that happened at the farm is durned tough luck," somebody said when Steven Smith ran out of breath. "But tell us, Steve, about this whopper you brung in. I ain't seen anything that size since Wilder Lambert built the milldam down below the forks."

The owner of the big trout seemed to ruminate before he scored a bull's eye on the cuspidor beside the icebox door. He looked down at his prize; his furrowed face and eyes of faded blue lit up. He smiled.

"Well sir, when Mary blowed her top because the pigs was rootin' up her garden, 'long with all them other things I give up hope and went to fishin' Dead Dog Bend. I ain't seen a legal trout in Dead Dog Bend in twenty years. But I guess mebby somehow the Lord, He kinda felt I'd had my share of havin' things go bad. Yessir, that's just the way He musta felt. I thought the deal—now that I think of it—was fair enough."

We all gazed silently upon the monster fish the farmers called a "German Brown," the biggest we had ever seen. We knew that Steven Smith was right; the Lord—we should have known this all the time—had not short-changed our friend.

The Nymph
Fisherman

Freddie Skillman was a ladies' man, the object of his fellow anglers' secret admiration. Tall, wasp-waisted, mellow-voiced and strong, he utilized his eyes the color of the summer sky, his courtly manners and his charming smile to great effect. While the rest of us were casting furtive glances at some lovely creature on the Calicoon express Freddie would contrive, in some way known alone to him, to lure the lady to the club car for a tête-à-tête — a tête-à-tête the more enjoyable for Fred because the patent envy of his friends was manifested by their grumbles and their scowls.

Evenings on the porch of Donald Campbell's Willowemoc Lodge while after-dinner talk concerned the day's events, what fly we'd used, what trout we'd caught and where we'd fished, we often heard, above the creaking of the swing behind the screen of honeysuckle vines, the happy laughter of the pretty daughter of the house at some soft-voiced sally of our handsome friend.

Fishing on the Beaverkill we often came upon some lovely listener seated on a mossy rock intent on Freddie's lecture on the art of angling for a trout or understanding birdsongs and the flowers in the spring-enchanted woods.

Most weekends while the rest of us were fishing open water on the Housatonic or the Battenkill our lady-killer mouthed sweet nothings to some tycoon's daughter at the Paradise or Blooming Grove. We weren't exactly pleased on summer Mondays when he showed up at the Anglers Club with tales of conquest and perhaps a trophy trout from the Southside or from Rolling Rock. And yet we mourned this boon companion's loss when business took him off to represent his firm in Baton Rouge.

We grieved because our fishing trips became just ordinary trips in search of trout without the sideshows now like those when Freddie, in a Catskill high school gym, tripped the light fantastic with a blushing beauty queen, or when he'd given us the eye across the lobby of the old DeBruce Club Inn while drinking cocktails with a movie star.

With our flirtatious friend's departure everything began to change. New highways brought a faceless horde of fishermen to streams where once a friendly group of purists cast their flies. These ubiquitous newcomers rose at dawn and stayed out late, preempting every likely stretch and using every method that the law allowed to fill their creels with harvests of the river's dwindling crops. Then, too, infirmities appeared within our ranks: Tad's bad knee made it difficult for him to wade; I found it hard to see my fly; Dave's arthritis made him miserable; Tom tired quickly and was short of breath. Long trips and longer hours on a brawling, crowded, fishless stream were out; the time had clearly come to change our ways.

And yet it took some years to find a place with chef and chambermaids where we could cross the creek without a staff and guides would net our fish and lug our gear; a place where we were waited on and comfortable and didn't have to break our necks to creel sometimes a more than legal trout. The waiting list, of course, was long; a score of older members had to die before the last of us were members of the club; the last, that is, except for Freddie Skillman, whose retirement was imminent and who would doubtless come back North and want to join.

I wrote that we would like to sponsor him, suggesting that he come up to the club the week before his Yale reunion to try the fishing and to look around. "And, by the way, old boy," my letter said, "what reunion is this now?"

He took me up by telegram: "Expect you for lunch the Sphinx June fifth, am bringing necessary gear."

"My goodness, Fred," I said the day we met, "not a gray hair in your head. How do you do it after all these years?"

"I attribute my eternal youth to virtue and a quiet life of piety."

"The same old Fred," I said. "I hope you're going to like our new setup at Calder Creek; the others went up there last week even though the heavy rains made fishing not much fun until a day or two ago. Tad says he likes the food. Tom claims that it's the only place where he can sleep, and Dave declares that looking at our streamlined waitresses makes him forget his aches and pains."

Freddie Skillman gave a start. "You order two martinis — Poodles Gin; I'll be right back. I want to talk to Carl about some things I need that he can send a boy out for so we can start when we have finished lunch; I guess you'd like to get to Calder while it still is light enough to fish."

My friend returned just as the cocktails came; we settled down, relaxed, to talk about old times. The time passed pleasantly and we were quite surprised to see the crowd was thinning out when Carl came to our table with a package in his hand.

"Excuse me, gentlemen," he said, "I thought perhaps that Mr. Skillman might wish to have a look at what we'd bought; because the shop was out of several things we told the boy to ask for, he took the liberty — because the time was short — of accepting several substitutes."

Freddie cleared his throat. "I'm sure those changes will be quite all right."

"For one thing, sir, they had no 'Renaissance for Men' but they were certain that you'd like 'Cellini's After Shave' as well. The 'Ponce de Leon Gray Away' comes only in the larger bottles now with the spray attached. As for — "

"It's all right, Carl," Fred tried to interrupt, "whatever you have got will do."

If looks could kill, Carl would have perished instantly. But he was on his verbal horse and galloping with blinding speed.

"As I was saying, sir," he clattered on, "the most expensive perfume that they had was one they guaranteed your lady friends would like; gift-wrapped as you instructed, sir."

The unintended audience was at an end as, with a minimum of words, we started on our journey from the club to Calder Creek.

Calder Creek was lovely on that springtime afternoon. Except for Ruth and Edith May, young ladies from the nearby hotel school whose jobs were waiting on the tables in the members' dining room, the club was empty and as quiet as the tomb. But several guides were pitching horseshoes out back on the lawn; one took our bags and showed us to our quarters on the lodge's second floor. Conscious of a tugging at my sleeve, I introduced my friend to Ruth and Edith May.

"I'd rather stay with you two girls than catch the biggest trout that ever swam," he said. "I've heard your praises sung by friends, but never thought the things they said could be half true."

"Come on, Fred," I said, "Bill's waiting for us on our beat below the mill; we don't want to miss the hatch of Evening Duns. It doesn't last all night, you know."

Perhaps the words "all night" rang some sort of bell. At any rate he followed me upstairs although he didn't hurry into fishing clothes and, after pawing through his bag, went back down with two small packages, gift-wrapped.

"There goes the perfume that Carl talked about," I thought.

When at last I diverted Freddie from romance to trout and Bill, our waiting guide, had shown him where to fish, the hatch was on. Occupied with casting to some rising trout I concentrated on the task at hand, instructing Bill to wait on Skillman, who was on the beat below. That afternoon I could have filled my creel with fourteen-inchers, if I'd wanted to, but I kept on trying for a record trout; I knew there were some in the stream but none was tempted by my fly.

Finally, the hatch of mayflies tapered off; the rise had ended and I waded wearily ashore. Surprised, I saw that Freddie and our guide were seated on a fallen tree trunk watching me.

"Why did you quit so soon?" I asked. "No luck?"

"Oh yes," Fred said, "my hand has never lost its skill."

"He says that one three-pounder is enough," Bill said. "He says it would be rude for him to show the members up."

We trudged back to the lodge where, as the custom of the Calder Creek Club was, Fred's fish, as largest of the day, was laid out on a platter on the bar. Then, although we would have liked to dine together at the club, we found we must drive over to a private camp to spend the evening with the senior members who would judge if we were right in recommending Freddie Skillman for inclusion in Calder Creek's somewhat exclusive membership.

Back finally at the lodge, I went behind the bar on which the big trout lay surrounded by its fresh and icy watercress. Fred lingered on the porch to listen to the near-by waterfall and watch the moon.

As Ruth and Edith May approached to view the fish the air seemed redolent with scent of Chanel Number 5.

Ruth said: "Your friend is awfully cute."

I saw Freddie coming through the door, although the girls could not because their backs were toward him as he came within earshot.

"He's just a doll; I'm *so* glad he got that fish."

I saw Fred's smile.

"Bill says that *for his age*," said Edith May, "he's really quite a fisherman. And he's *such* a kindly nice, old gentleman!"

I couldn't bear to look at Fred. I poured out two stiff drinks and handed one to him across the bar.

"Let's take these nightcaps up to bed," I said. "I think if we old codgers want to get an early start we'd better hit the hay."

I never asked my friend again just what reunion he would now attend; I was getting ready for my thirty-fifth.

Old Roger's Funeral

Old Roger wasn't really old despite his more than four score years; the adjective stood guard before his name in token of his friends' affection and esteem. Old Rog had taught me everything I knew about the salmon in the Restigouche; my memories of that noble watercourse were doubly rich because of him. Although he now no longer acted as a guide I planned to seek him out as soon as I was settled in at camp, inviting him to lunch with me and share my rod that afternoon.

I left Aroostook County in the quiet time before

the dawn, the mountains darkly outlined like a pride of lions sleeping underneath the stars, and found the morning in the valley where the Tobique meets the big St. John. Alas, no Indians were fishing in the Narrows there as once in summertime they always were before New Brunswick's need for power caused the building of the three great dams. I turned on speed and turned my thinking of the old days off but, after breakfast at an early-opening restaurant, I looked ahead instead of back and thought again about the smell of woodsmoke at the camp, the sound of rapids and, with luck, a friendly drink with Rog.

Now, at intervals along the forest-bordered road were rock- and root-strewn fields of fireweed with — here and there — a patch of daisies lending cheer and contrast to the somber background of the evergreens. The gate at last; the rough and narrow rutted road; the sight of water glinting through the trees; the cabins standing in a row; the lodge. For the season and the time of day the clearing in the woods was strangely still; none of the fishermen were on the porch or paths; a single guide was busy at the water's edge. This man I recognized as Andrew Frost, who had guided me each season since the time Old Roger had retired. He came to greet me and to help me with my bags.

"Hello, Andy, where is all the crowd?" I said.

"There is no crowd, sir."

"No crowd; how come?"

"No salmon, sir."

"No salmon! How can that be, Andy?"

"For one thing, sir, there's been no rain; the water's very low. Another thing, they're taking hardly any in the nets. The gentlemen has mostly all gone home, and Mr. Arnold's gone to town. That leaves you all the river here; I guess it makes no difference where you fish."

"Well, we'll give it a try," I said, "but first, while I unpack my gear, I'd like to have you telephone Old Rog and ask him to come up for lunch and maybe fish with us this afternoon."

"You didn't know, sir?" Andrew seemed surprised. "Old Roger died three days ago."

"*Old Roger's dead?* I didn't even know that he was sick."

"He wasn't sick, sir. Old Roger was too tough for that. It was a motor accident — a logger's truck; his funeral is this afternoon."

At first I was too stunned to speak, but then I said: "What time's the funeral? We must go."

"Four o'clock, sir. If we take our lunch out in the boat we'll have a lot of time to take a look at all the pools before we have to start downriver in the afternoon. It just might be a salmon has moved in somewhere last night."

"All right," I said. "And just in case we locate one I'll bring my waders."

Andrew first poled up to Sailor's Run. Surprisingly there were no salmon milling there below the rapids in the great, deep hole where a fish will almost never take, but where the fellows working for the hatchery can always count on netting gravid fish each fall to strip. This was a most unhappy omen and it was, in consequence, without much hope that we dropped down across the shallows into Ireland's Flats.

Here, with half a dozen pools to go until we reached our lowest pool, Brown's Gulch, we figured that we had two hours left before we must be on our way to Campbellton. Accordingly, we wasted little time on this and the adjacent pools where we could scan the bottom with our Polaroids but pushed on down to fish the Elbow Pool. And then, with half an hour left, I put my waders on and cast a sparsely dressed, low-water fly out toward a long black shadow in the shallow water near the tail. As the Blue Charm drifted past the shadow moved; we'd found our fish.

"We'll take this one for dear Old Rog. We'll leave it at his daughter's house this afternoon," I said.

I checked the leader and the fly. Carefully I cast again as Andrew watched the salmon from the bank.

"He moved again, sir. I think that he will take."

Fifteen minutes passed and now the fish—a good one we could see—ignored the fly. I tried a small Black Dose, a tiny Rusty Rat, a larger Night Hawk and a little Silver Gray. The fish disdained them all.

"What time is it?"

"It's ten to two. Why don't you try a dry fly, sir?"

I waded stealthily ashore and opened up my dry-fly box. Daintiest of all the contents was a Darbee Variant. With a barrel knot I lengthened the leader I'd been fishing with with a finer strand; I oiled the stiff and honey-colored hackles of my fly and floated it across the unresponsive fish's nose.

"He doesn't want it," Andrew said.

"What time is it?" I asked again.

"It's two o'clock, sir, time to go. Why not try just one more fly?"

I tried an oversized white Wulff.

"I'll just put on a stone fly as a last resort," I said.

"He moved, sir! Yes, he moved for that."

I cast again, again, again. Trembling in my haste I tried a tandem hackled fly that Arseneault had tied for me; *the big fish swirled.*

"What time is it?" I shouted as I dried the fly.

"It's two-fifteen, but sir, I think Old Roger wouldn't like it if you left a salmon you could see. It's ten to one he'd rather have you out here working on a fish than sitting down there in the funeral home."

Just then a change in light or angle gave me a clear view of the fish. Even for the Restigouche the fish was big. I said, "I guess you're right," and wondered if I'd told the truth.

Through that long and sunny afternoon I fished the tail of Elbow for that fish. We stayed until the swallows and the cedar waxwings disappeared and evening drew the daylight down beyond the pines. Then, wearily I sat down on a rock while Andrew pulled my waders off. Back at camp I bathed and changed and took the whisky bottle from my locker at the lodge. I saw two places set at table for the evening meal. Alone I built and nursed a drink and thought about Old Roger as I looked out at the moon.

The cook came in to tell me dinner would be ready soon.

"The waitress has gone home," he said. "There's so few folks has stayed to fish. Mr. Arnold should be in by now; he come back up from Roger's funeral just about the time that you and Andy come back in. Him and Henry Hall who's guiding him this year went out to fish a drop or two. They seen a salmon yesterday and figured he might take a fly tonight after the sun was off the water."

I heard a step and voices on the porch and saw a flashlight gleam.

"Come out and look at this here fish," somebody said. "He must go close to thirty pounds."

Mr. Arnold came into the room and shook my hand.

"I hope I haven't held you up," he said. "Harry Hall and I have been at Campbellton this afternoon and just got back in time to cast a fly over this salmon that we spotted yesterday. Funny thing about that pool we took him from; they never seem to take a fly until it's really getting dark."

I offered my congratulations and a drink. "I drink to your 'good luck,' " he said. "I leave for Boston in the morning; you'll have the river to yourself."

I crossed my fingers and expressed regret that I'd not have his company. I knew where I would go as soon as he had left; I wouldn't miss him and I wouldn't wait for dusk. I asked: "Oh, by the way, where did you take that lovely salmon that you just brought in?"

"He was lying in the tail of Elbow Pool," he said.

"Did you say *Elbow Pool?*" I asked him shakily.

I trembled as I once more filled my glass.

Neither Could
Ponce de Leon

I thought I'd find him at the Antlers Bar. Last time I'd looked into the mirror there I'd seen him smiling at some secret thought. Long-limbed and lean, his hair bleached by the sun, I'd heard him talking to the man who served the drinks and listened to the laughter as he lied about the trout he'd caught that day.

The fellow tending bar came close to where I sat. "Where's Frank tonight?" I said.

He looked surprised; put out some beers, flicked off

the suds. He said: "I guess you must mean Frankie Cassidy. He's not been here for twenty years or more than that perhaps."

That was a shock. It sort of stopped me in my tracks. "I'll have a shot of that Old Rosebud rye," I said, "no water; just a piece of ice."

"You must mean this Four Roses," the new bartender said.

"No," I said, "I don't. Give me a beer."

I looked around the room. Nobody looked familiar; there didn't seem to be a lot of fishermen. The man I looked for wasn't there. On the way out I stopped at the jukebox. All the listed songs were new to me. If I'd seen "I Can't Give You Anything but Love" or "Five Foot Two, Eyes of Blue" I might have put a quarter in and asked one of the girls to dance. I went back to my motel room and went to bed.

For a long time I could not relax. I kept trying to get comfortable. I tasted the cucumbers that I'd had for dinner. I thought of the things back home I'd come to Roscoe to forget. It was so late when I finally fell asleep at last, I didn't get up early in the morning as I'd planned to do to look for him out on the river.

The early hours on the Willowkill in May are gentle, bright and beautiful. I knew he never liked to miss this magic time of day. But as I'd missed the best part of the morning, I went over to Kay's restaurant. By all odds he would be there, cheerfully putting away an enormous breakfast no matter how much he had had to drink or how late he had been awake the night before.

No one was sitting at the counter on a stool, no one was sitting in a booth. I ordered soft-boiled eggs, dry toast and tea. I didn't have much appetite and the fact that the waitress disregarded my instructions and brought the toast in burnt and cold and soggy with the melted butter didn't help. When she started chattering about how warm the weather was, I paid my check and got out quickly as I could. The trousers that I'd bought the year before were tight around the waist; I went back to my room and changed.

Then, because I knew his favorite pool was at the forks, I drove up there and parked the car. He wasn't anywhere in sight, but I got out, rigged up, pulled on my waders and began to fish. There was a hatch of Hendricksons and the trout were coming up. I took a pair of fourteen-inchers. This would have thrilled the fellow I was looking for, but he had never fished for salmon, as of recent years I had, and hence I didn't feel that fourteen inches was a trophy fish.

When the sun warmed up the water and the trout no longer showed, I drove on up to Alice Black's. I thought perhaps I'd find him sitting on the terrace there or floating flies along the wall out front, but when I got up to the gate I saw the place was posted by another owner. The new name didn't ring a bell. A warden drove up close beside my car. "What can I do for you?" he asked suspiciously.

"I'm looking for a man I know," I said. "He used to fish here as a guest of Mrs. Black."

"Mrs. Black's been dead a good ten years," the warden said.

I tried again to let him know I was OK. "Perhaps you know my friend Irving Potter."

"Oh yes, I know Irv Potter. He's a fine old gentleman." (I knew Irv Potter wasn't old.) "He used to fish this river with a fly. Nowadays they mostly spin."

So far I wasn't having any luck. I put the car in gear and drove on up the road until I reached the Gardner place. The sun was hot on my bald head as I walked up to the house. I saw May Gardner's mother sitting on the porch. She looked much older than I thought she would. I didn't think that she'd remember me. I asked if I could fish a while.

"Why Peter Brown, you rascal you," she said. "Don't you pretend you don't know Maisie Gardner just because I wouldn't let you kiss me when you came up in your father's Stutz."

Right then and there I felt that I was really old. I said: "Why May, you know that I remember you. I don't really want to fish. I came in just to say hello for old times' sake."

Later at the Antlers Bar I said: "OK, I'll take the Four Roses."

"You find that fellow you was looking for?" the barkeep asked.

"No, Fred," I said — by then I'd learned the fellow's name — "I know now that I'll never find the guy."

"Oh yeah? Perhaps he's dead?"

"Not dead exactly; no, not dead — just different, very different, not the same."

He shrugged and turned to fill an order for a rye and ginger ale.

Where
the Action Was

My uncle was conductor on the Denver – Rio Grande in 1868. He fixed for me to travel free to Abilene where I could buy myself a hook and line, get back aboard and wait until the locomotive stopped to take on water just a few miles outside town. That's where I'd seen that monster trout my heart was set on taking back to Emmy Lou, to show her that that Eastern dude she always talked about wasn't any better fisherman than I. The afternoon was hot as I went into Bowman's General Store to get myself a fishing rig. I planned to organize my tackle and my bait and lay around beneath the trees out where the river ran into the lake and wait for dusk. I hadn't come this far to botch the business up. I'd keep low against the moon; no shadows where they hadn't been before; no dislodged stones; no sudden movements.

I went into the Silver Dog to cool off and to quench my thirst. For a moment I forgot the train and asked the barkeep for a second shot, and then I heard the whistle toot and when I came out on the street I saw the cars were rolling down along the track. It was too hot to make a run for it; I'd have to walk. I cursed the weather and the train, the place, my luck, the trout and things in general. I hadn't noticed that the sheriff, Gentleman Jim Slade, was standing on the station platform talking with a pretty girl just come to town to join the pleasure ladies at the Silver Dog.

"Young man," he says, "this lady here ain't used to language like the kind you've just been using in her presence and I think, young man . . . "

No man was going to "young man" me. I took my Stetson off and bowed and swept the ground. "A thousand pardons, sir," I said.

He bowed and as he straightened up I shot the man between the eyes. He fell; the woman screamed; I took the sheriff's horse and rode off out of town as fast as I could make the big bay gelding go. An hour later in a thicket by a stream I saw the swishing of a horse's tail. I sneaked up close and saw a man far gone in drink, unconscious on the ground. I struck the fellow on the temple with a rock and killed him where he lay. I exchanged hats and took his money and his rough and rugged chestnut horse and left the sheriff's heaving worn-out bay beside the body of the drunk, then rode on east across the state.

For a little while I worried that I might get caught. But Uncle Bill had used his head. From the train he'd heard the shot and seen the smoke, and when some fellow said the killer looked like me he said: "By George you're right he did, but my brother's boy is riding herd up north in Canada this year."

I didn't dare go hunting for that trout again for several years, but when I did, by Jove, there was the fellow by the self-same rock, and looking twice as big. Funny thing though—I could never get that fish to take the bait; *some guys have all the luck!*

Noises
in the Night

Detailed long since to duty with the stable guard, I used to listen to the troopers called "The Picket Line Quartet." They made sweet music underneath the stars; they sang *John Peel* and *Jeffrey Amherst, Hail Cornell* and *Old Nassau.* And just before the bugler sounded taps they sang *Brahm's Lullaby.* For hours then there were no noises in the night except perhaps the snort or pawing of a horse; the Squadron slept. Against all regulations I slept too sometimes, despite my shoes and spurs and starchy dungarees, hidden from the sergeant in the feed tent on a bag of oats.

The men who sang so well in 1929 now sing no more unless to horses stabled in the sky. The Squadron sleeps, but often I do not, despite the absence of the watchful sergeant of the guard; despite soft pillows, sleeping pills; no dreaded brassy early notes of reveille. I say I cannot sleep and yet sometimes I do when lulled by soporific noises of the night; the sounds on which the drowsy camper builds his dreams.

Sometimes I hear, or think I hear, ships' bells, the throbbing of the engines on a freighter out at sea, the throaty foghorn of a lighthouse on an island in the Gulf, wave beats on a ghostly gravel beach, the splash of homing salmon at a river mouth, the rush of running water over rocks, the mystic music of the wolves.

Sometimes, in dreams though wide awake, I listen to untimely midnight merriment of celebrating Gaspé French that dies away as locomotive whistles on a train from Montreal and Mont Joli comes roaring down to cross the pitch-black Restigouche en route to distant Halifax.

Sometimes I hear, while seeking sleep, the honking of the wild geese, passing overhead, the eerie yurr of foxes in the shadows on the lawn, the repetitious whippoorwill, the whurr-r of little owls in the apple trees, the crowing of the roosters on a neighbor's farm, his collie's barking at the moon.

At other times at night I hear, far off, the striking of the valley's white church tower clock, the crackling of the fire on the open hearth beside my streamside camping place, the frantic flight of minnows in the shallows where the big trout hunt.

And there sometimes, as clouds obscure the moon, the tree frogs sing, the mallards gabble in the reeds, the loons call weirdly on the lake, the horned owls hoot up in the woods and on the ridge a bobcat or its furry victim screams, I can't tell which. I am asleep and happy and at peace and have no need to worry or to dream.

Well Anyway —
Almost

G ene Hill, a winsome wingshot with a nimble pen, has made another of his many hits when he infers that records kept by gunners are of little lasting joy.

Likewise an angler, with the passing years, will find his memories more flexible than facts. My recollections, happier by far than what is written in my conscientious day-to-day accounts, put dull statistics in the shade. That's why dust gathers on the leather cover of the *Fishing Log* I've hidden way back underneath the eaves.

Long, long ago, my diaries lay open on the table in

my den. On winter evenings, with my shorthair pointer and my glass of Highland Malt, I'd watch the flaming cedar logs chase shadows up the paneled walls and think about the salmon rivers that I loved.

"Perhaps this year I might start off in May," I'd tell myself. "It would cost me even less than staying home to fish in Nova Scotia; let me see . . ."

I'd put my desk light on and read: "St. Mary's: May 18th; the moon three-quarters full, the weather clear and cold, the water fifty-eight at ten a.m. no fish seen anywhere by anyone, one salmon taken here last week."

I'd turn the pages past the Moser, Ecum Secum, Gold, LaHave and Midway. "Black flies, black flies and more black flies," I'd read. "But fishing hopeless; going home."

About then maybe Johnnie Bench from down the road would hammer on the door. I'd bid him welcome, take his coat and bring him his Old Taylor on the rocks. While I was doing this and getting something extra for my glass, he'd likely finger through my diary and say: "I guess you'll have to find some other place to go this year than that Cap Chat. Says here your seven rods took just one fish in seven days. Could that be right?"

Of course you'd have to say something about the need for taking bad luck with the good, and things like that, and get him interested in what the pointer's ear looked like after his battle with the big raccoon. And afterward you learned to keep your records under lock and key or just to read excerpts from them to prove a point before you put them out of sight again.

So much for diaries or record books, although I could recount their frequent interference with my dreams. But let us turn to witnesses, perhaps the greatest hazards that the storytelling angler must confront.

A loyal wife, though on the scene, will often let an angler's lies slip by without comment, but not so little boys. I was a boy who fished with Father on the Belgrade Lakes in 1906; I know! Accustomed only to the rather homely smallmouth bass, I was entranced when Father caught an out-of-season trout. Our guide was law-abiding and we let it go. This trout was more endowed with beauty than with brains; it took the hook a second time and once again was gently put back in the lake. But when two minutes later it was flopping on the floor boards of the Naphtha launch again the guide considered this a message from on high and socked it with a monkey wrench.

Just then the warden's motorboat came by.

"What luck?" the game protector asked.

"Oh, pretty good," our skipper said. "A funny thing just now, we caught a trout and let it go. And then we caught the trout again and let it go again."

The warden primed his carburetor, spun his wheel.

"And then we caught the trout again," I said.

A half a century beyond that date I took my largest-ever Adirondack brown trout on a floating fly.

"He's two feet long," I shouted to my better half up on the nearby road from which we'd seen the rise.

Just then Bill Rawle *who used to be a friend* came by. The picture that he took hangs on my wall; the trout lies there on Bill's stretched tape. Sure, nineteen inches and a half is good, but — damn it all — because of Bill the fish lost four and five-eighths inches then and there.

The humbling diary I disdain. Witnesses are something else again; you can't throw them behind an attic trunk, and so I cast my flies, these days, alone or with French guides who wouldn't talk in English if they could. In recent years I've tangled with some mighty fish: I've dealt with salmon up to fifty pounds (it's hard to find an

Eastern stream where one can fish alone for trout). And let me tell you what a thrill it is to have a fifty-pounder wolf a Wulff!

Some envious and less successful fishermen with squalid souls express their doubts of my veracity.

"If you take salmon of that size, why don't you bring one in some time?" they ask. "We've never seen a scale in your canoe; how can you *prove* that you had three fish over forty-five last year?"

To guys like that I have an answer: *"How can you prove that I did not?"*

I figure that should shut them up.

All Good Lies
Are Not on
Putting Greens

Age, angina and arthritis, along with several minor ills, had hobbled and depressed Jim Boone. His scatter guns and fishing rods were put away; his bird dog, old, stiff-legged and half blind, lay dozing quietly beside the hearth at Bob White Farms; his favorite books stood untouched on their shelves. Old Jim beguiled the tedium of leaden-footed hours spent alone by gazing out across the fields to where the hills came down to meet the creek, daydreaming of those happy half-remembered days when he was young.

But underneath the weariness, inertia, ennui and pain, a latent spark of joie-de-vivre survived that flared to flame when kindled by the company of those old friends with whom he'd shared ideas and sport in youthful days. And when the tinder was the presence of his grandson, Dave, the flame shot high and bright.

The old man had few visitors. The house was off the beaten path of friends, remote from those of flagging energy and failing strength who gladly would have traveled often to its doors if distance hadn't intervened. His grandson had a family and a job. He loved his father's father well, but had to parcel out his time: the lion's share for spouse, support and special things at home; the residue for Granddad Jim.

One sparkling autumn day when gliding gulls sailed down the dark blue ocean of the sky and robins gathered for their southern trek, Bill Schultz brought in a load of logs to fill the wood box and the bin beneath the stairs.

"Mabel says she feels cold weather coming on."

"You tell your wife those sausage cakes she gave me for my breakfast were just the thing the doctor ordered. If she knows as much about the weather as she does about a frying pan we'd better batten down the hatches and get ready for Jack Frost."

The setter thumped her tail against the floor and raised her head. Suddenly she struggled to her feet with lifted ears and padded down the hall to greet Dave Boone, who let her lick his hand and learn by sniffing at his knees about his shorthair pointer Rap, a present from the elder Boone.

"Hello Granddad! Hello Bill!" Dave shouted as he came into the room. "By Jove, J. B., you look as young and strong as Bill. If you feel half as healthy as you look you should be ready when the flight arrives. What say we get some practice with my twenty-gauge? I've got the hand traps and the clay birds in the car."

"Yes sir, Mr. Boone," Bill said. "I'll bet you wipe the eye of both of us; it's all that I can do to hit a woodcock with a twelve."

Good cheer was now contagious and the old man smiled.

"Not quite so fast, my boys; not quite so fast. I haven't gotten healthy overnight. I'll tell you what I can do — and I will. If Dave can get a week off from the mill, and Mrs. Schultz will let Bill go, I'll treat you to a trip upstate: steaks, bedrooms, beer and gasoline; the works. You drive up Sunday afternoon and shoot till Friday noon. Then come back here and make a full report. We'll talk about the woodcock later on."

When Jim Boone paused, Dave looked at Bill and smiled.

"It's so long since I've shot a grouse," they heard Jim softly whisper to himself.

And so it was that on an evening when the lighted jack-o'-lanterns glowed, Dave Boone and Bill ate dinner at a little Catskill inn, let Rap run free before they put him in his station-wagon box, laid out their guns and shooting clothes and set their clocks for six a.m.

The shooting trip, it should at once be said, was no success. Torrential rains took up two days; the car required half a day's repairs while greasy men in overalls with monkey wrenches smoked and joked and disappeared for intervals while grounded gunners fidgeted and cursed their luck or lack of same. The covers that Dave sought to hunt on Wednesday afternoon were posted every twenty feet. Few birds fed on the acorns on the hills or in the orchard of an old abandoned farm.

From where a friendly farmer's cattle grazed, six birds were started by the overeager Rap beneath thorn-apple trees and one was bagged. Another brace was taken down along a brook. Bill missed a woodcock as the gunners walked back to the car on Friday noon, and that was all. They heard the weekend hunters' fusilade as they ate lunch.

Back at Bob White Farms, Bill fed the dogs and helped his wife to set the table. Dave went in and showed Jim Boone the birds.

"We only brought three biddies home," he said. "We gave the rest to friends of yours; so many people asked for you I thought we might not have enough to go around."

The tired eyes of old Jim Boone lit up; he lit a long-forbidden fine cigar and offered one to Dave.

"So there were lots of birds," he said. "The dog worked well? That's fine; I thought those rumors that the birds were scarce weren't true."

About then, Bill brought in the cocktail glasses and the ice and stood with open mouth as Dave described the covers he and Bill had worked; the swarms of partridge that they'd seen and shot; the great performance of the dog.

"We hit the hot spots that you showed me when you shot with Dad, and took our limit every day," Dave said. "The only woodcock that we got were native birds; we left them with the fellow at the Lodge."

Jim Boone poured out an extra drink for Bill, Old Forester aged sixteen years.

"I'll tell you what I'm going to do," the old man said. "I can't go through those swamps or up those hills, just now at least. But I can knock those ringnecks kicking down at Bob Bean's pheasant farm.

"We'll have another drink and after dinner, Dave, you get Guy Jenkins on the phone and make a date. And let me kid old Guy a little bit about the woodcock that he missed the last time we were out near Utica, I think it was in 1925."

Jim Boone was singing as he started for the dining room: "Oh what a time I had with Minnie, the Mermaid, down at the bottom of the sea."

Dave winked as Bill took out the cocktail tray.

"Whoever claimed that lying wasn't ever justified?" he said.

The Possum Hound

S ince childhood I've disdained details. Most vivid of my
memories concerns an argument with an educator of
that distant day, tersely terminated and decided in her own
favor by my mother's unique rebuttal of her opponent's
scholarly supporting evidence.

"Of what interest are *facts* to me?" she said.

This recollection, ever since, has had a baleful influence on my philosophy, my fishing and my practical
affairs. But lest you seek a show of modesty from me, I
know, as Whitman says in *Leaves of Grass*, "I know I am

august." I know few challenge my acknowledged standing at the top, my standing at the very pinnacle of that fly-fishing art wherein so few will claim equality; the art, that is, of hardly ever catching fish.

Oh, there were times when I was inexperienced and young when I caught fish. I caught sophisticated wild brown Adirondack stream-bred trout, amazing entomologists like Preston Jennings, famous for his *Book of Trout Flies*, built by Gene Connett at Derrydale. But that was in the days before I knew about the things I didn't know about. When I sought the company of masters of that less polluted age, I got a shock.

I heard the great Ed Hewitt talk of stone flies, caddis grubs, terrestrials and Mayfly nymphs, emerging duns, their molt, brush hatch and nuptial flight; the spinner fall. Dick Hunt might recommend the skittered spider or the wet fly fished upstream; the dry fly — as a variation — down.

I went to Tappen Fairchild's home and saw a four-pound Catskill trout my host had taken from a shallow brush-surrounded pool — no mean achievement even for an angler of the very foremost rank.

I borrowed esoteric books that dealt with barometric pressures, air and water temperatures, life cycles and emergence dates of scores of ever-changing creatures of the streams, all called by lengthy Latin names and sporting in their final flights perhaps four wings, six legs and extra tails.

I listened to John Alden Knight expound his theory of the pull of sun and moon, and experts on stream strategy like George La Branche discuss the curve and bump and steeple casts.

I marveled at the things that Henry Ingraham knew about the rivers' underwater life, and watched while

Dr. Burke, Jack Atherton and later Schwiebert and de Feo tied their flies.

This scholarly and scientific atmosphere, alas, was far too rare for any fact-disdaining chuck-and-chance-it fisherman like me who'd won no honors in his alma mater's ivied halls; the encyclopedic knowledge which went in one ear, went out the other and was gone. I went off to the Battenkill with Junebug-imitating brown bivisibles and nothing else. I left my Fanwing Royals at home; Ray Bergman said they represented nothing in real life. I felt that there was something missing, something wrong; all the trout I got that trip were small and soft and freshly stocked.

Tom Collins tipped me off about the great fly-tying pros: Scotch lassie, Betty Grieg and Reuben Cross, Art Flick, the Dettes and Darbees. I bought a half a gross of well-tied, stiffly hackled flies and took them to the rivers that I'd thought I owned: West Canada, the great Chazy, the Salmon, Saranac, Ausable, Delaware and Beaverkill. They floated nicely but I caught few fish.

Guy Jenkins pointed out when I came home mid-season hatches often came in early afternoon and not when I went out to fish at sunrise or at dusk. Later when the weather and the fly life changed, Bill Mackey asked me why I hadn't changed my methods with the temperature, the water levels and the flies.

"Why use Cream Variants and Light Cahills when all the naturals are gray?" he asked. "Why stick to Gordon Quills when *Iron fraudator* has long been gone?"

I couldn't fish the nymphs of duns whose scheduled emergence dates were imminent—a practice recommended by a fellow member of the Windbeam Club—because I didn't recognize the nymph or know when duns were due.

I got so hopelessly confused, I lost all confidence, I couldn't wade the way I should; I couldn't cast the way — till then — I had; and then it was I started catching hardly any trout and knew at last why Preston Jennings and Chip Stauffer were amazed when I'd come in to Byron Blanchard's Adirondack Mountain House when they were there with browns too big to fit my creel.

A friend below the Mason-Dixon Line about that time, in talking of his family dogs, referred to them as possum hounds. "What is a possum hound?" I asked. "A possum hound," he simply said, "is just a coonhound that has failed."

As far as fishing went right then, I knew I was a possum hound.

Of course a possum hound, though worthless, has a happy life, and troutless days by human possum hounds have their rewards. Nobody laughs while dealing with a two-pound trout on 5X gut. But I have laughed when little boys below the hamlet of Cooks Falls have said: "Sir, please don't give our cat that chub you caught, our mother doesn't like to have our cat eat fish."

Whatever skillful wielder of a bamboo rod, concerned about the netting of a rainbow he's been after for a month, has turned and seen a doe and tiny spotted fawn behind him watching from the woods, or glimpsed a baby woodchuck peeping from the safety of its sandy streamside home?

Whoever, waiting for a big brook trout to rise, has let his bird dog have the fun of splashing through the stream in joyous search for water rats?

Whatever expert, working on a rising brown, has watched a mother partridge stealing up the hill with chipmunk-colored chicks in tow or seen the beavers working in the dusk? Whoever bent on taking home a heavy creel has time to read a book of verses underneath a bough? Whoever fired up to be the day's high rod will gather mint beside a brook for juleps when he gets back home?

Oh yes, a possum hound has lots of fun. He loves the winged miracles that fly across the satin surfaces of the stream, the crimson-spotted ivory-bellied trout with backs of silver-gray or chocolate-brown, the light wind stirring in the willows and the scent of new-mown hay, the sunrise and the sunset and the vast blue sky at noon.

If only he could name the flowers and the bird songs and the trees, as well, of course, as all the flies. And if, beyond these daytime things he ought to be familiar with, he knew, when he went home at night across the fields, which star was which, his happiness would be complete. But how unfortunate it is that aging possum hounds can seldom learn new tricks.

An Old New Englander Looks Back

L ast night I raised my tankard of New England rum and
drank deep to the days two hundred years ago when,
on the clear undammed Connecticut, a man too busy with
his cows and crops to salt his own, might buy his year's
supply of salmon — when the run was on — for just one cent
a pound or less; to days when gay aristocrats would gather
on the Merrimack for sport as fine as any offered on the
Moisie or the Restigouche; to days when Cotton Mather's
thunderings against the sin of catching fish for fun were

drowned out by the roar of fish-filled rapids on the Kennebec, Penobscot and the Androscoggin. I drank to days in Massachusetts colony when crops were fertilized by fragments of the salmon catch the sated hired hands refused to eat, and dogs were hobbled lest they dig and rob the corn hills of the colonists.

Are those days gone beyond recall? Perhaps. And yet I thought I heard a whisper in the springtime wind that spoke of growing interest on the part of those whose forebear's moored their ships at Plymouth Rock in bringing back the good old unpolluted days when salmon spawned where mills today discharge their waste and all the brooks were filled with trout.

Can it be done? It will be difficult, but still . . .

"A man's reach should exceed his grasp, or what's a heaven for!"

Commercial Auto

At press time, this edition contains the most complete and accurate information currently available. Owing to the nature of license examinations, however, information may have been added recently to the actual test that does not appear in this edition. Please contact the publisher to verify that you have the most current edition.

This publication is designed to provide accurate and authoritative information in regard to the subject matter covered. It is sold with the understanding that the publisher is not engaged in rendering legal, accounting, or other professional services. If legal advice or other expert assistance is required, the services of a competent professional should be sought.

To submit comments or suggestions, please send an email to errata@dearborn.com.

Published by DF Institute, Inc.

Printed in the United States of America.

ISBN: 0-7931-6435-4

PPN: 5937-0101

05	06	10	9	8	7	6	5	4	3	2	1
J	F	M	A	M	J	J	A	S	O	N	D

····· Table of Contents

ACKNOWLEDGMENTS   vii

INTRODUCTION   ix

UNIT 1
COMMERCIAL AUTO LOSS EXPOSURES   1
The Need for Commercial Auto Coverage   1
Commercial Auto Coverage Forms   6
Monoline or Package Coverage   9
What is a Commercial Auto?   12
Commercial Auto Underwriting   17
Summary   23
Unit 1 Review Questions   24
Answers To Unit 1 Review Questions   26

UNIT 2
BAP SECTION I—COVERED AUTOS   27
Business Auto Coverage Form Overview   27
Covered Auto Symbols   29
BAP "Covered Auto" Case Studies   37
Summary   38
Unit 2 Review Questions   40
Answers to Unit 2 Review Questions   41
Case Study Answers & Rationale   42

UNIT 3
BAP SECTION II—LIABILITY COVERAGE   43
The Need for Auto Liability   44
Who is an Insured?   49
Coverage Extensions and Exclusions   53
Summary   62
Unit 3 Review Questions   63
Answers to Unit 3 Questions   64

UNIT 4

BAP SECTION III—PHYSICAL DAMAGE   **65**

Insuring Agreements   65
Physical Damage Exclusions   70
Other Physical Damage Considerations   73
Summary   76
Unit 4 Review Questions   77
Answers to Unit 4 Review Questions   78

UNIT 5

CONDITIONS, DEFINITIONS AND ENDORSEMENTS   **79**

Section IV—Business Auto Conditions   80
Section V—Definitions   94
Auto Medical Payments Coverage   99
Business Auto Endorsements   101
Summary   113
Unit 5 Review Questions   115
Answers to Unit 5 Review Questions   116

UNIT 6

TERRORISM COVERAGE OPTIONS   **117**

Terrorism Endorsements   118
Terrorism Acceptance Forms   120
Terrorism Coverage Rejection Forms   128
Prior Approval Property and Liability Forms   130
Liability Nuclear Hazard Exclusions   132
Summary   133
Unit 6 Review Questions   135
Answers to Unit 6 Review Questions   136

UNIT 7

THE GARAGE POLICY   **137**

The Need for Garage Policy Coverage   138
Section I—Covered Autos Described by Numeric Symbols   144
Section II—Liability Coverage Covers Garage Operations   148
Garage Coverage Exclusions   153
Garagekeepers Coverage Section III   157
Garage Coverage Sections IV, V and VI   163
Auto Service Risks Market   169
Summary   172
Unit 7 Review Questions   173
Answers to Unit 7 Review Questions   174

UNIT 8

OTHER COMMERCIAL AUTO FORMS   **175**

Truckers Coverage Form   176
Motor Carrier Coverage Form   188
Summary   193
Unit 8 Review Questions   194
Answers to Unit 8 Review Questions   195

UNIT 9
RATING THE BUSINESS AUTO POLICY 197
Determining the Premium 198
Summary 210
Course Summary 211
Answers to Unit 9 Rating Problems 212

REVIEW TEST 215

GLOSSARY 219

APPENDIX 231

▪▪▪▪▪ **Acknowledgments**

The publisher would like to acknowledge the following individuals for their contributions to the development of this text:

- Cheryl L. Koch, CPCU, CIC, ARM, AAI, API, AAM, AIM, AIS, ARP, ACSR. Ms. Koch is owner of Agency Management Resource Group, an insurance training and consulting firm located in Lincoln, California. She is a contributor to industry periodicals, the author of several technical publications, and a frequent speaker at insurance events nationwide

- Phyllis A. Travis, Esq., J.D., CCLA, FCLA, CTS. Ms. Travis is a member of the Massachusetts bar and has over 25 years experience as a claims professional in the property and casualty insurance industry

- Diane M. Lamyotte, CPCU, AU, MA. Ms. Lamyotte is a freelance writer and editor who specializes in insurance and financial services products

This course includes copyrighted and proprietary material of Insurance Services Office, Inc., with its permission. Copyright, Insurance Services Office, Inc., 1990-2004.

ISO does not guarantee the accuracy or timeliness of the ISO information provided. ISO shall not be liable for any loss or damage of any kind and howsoever caused resulting from your use of the ISO information.

▪ ▪ ▪ ▪ ▪

····· **Introduction**

T he purpose of this course is to provide an in-depth review of the Insurance Services Office (ISO) commercial auto forms, October 2001 edition.

This comprehensive course is written for claims, underwriting, and producer professionals. The course focuses primarily on the ISO October 2001 edition of three forms: (1) Business Auto Policy Coverage Form, (2) Garage Coverage Form, and (3) Truckers Coverage Form. To provide a comprehensive overview of the function, utility, and application of commercial auto coverage, two additional forms (the Business Auto Physical Damage Coverage Form and Motor Carrier Coverage Form) are also briefly reviewed.

Throughout this course, we will use a number of real life examples and key points to underscore the important coverages, exclusions, and limitations of commercial auto policies.

Learning Objectives

When you have completed this course, you should be able to:

- explain the main coverages, exclusions, and conditions of the Business Auto, Garage, and Truckers' Coverage Forms;

- explain who is an insured under each of the commercial auto forms;

- describe how the ISO numerical system defines coverage under the Business Auto, Garage, and Truckers' Coverage Forms;

- determine risk eligibility for the commercial auto forms;

- distinguish when commercial auto coverage should be written as a Business Auto Policy or incorporated into a Commercial Package Policy;

- identify 2001 ISO coverage form changes;

- explain the federally mandated terrorism coverage requirements and options for commercial auto policyholders;

- explain the key elements for rating commercial auto policies and identify key rating factors; and

- determine the premium for commercial auto liability and physical damage coverages, and non-owned auto and hired auto coverages.

■ ■ ■ ■ ■

Course Learning Features

Dearborn has structured its P&C courses to teach students how to use policy forms to understand and verify coverages. The course examines the current ISO coverage form for each line of insurance that is being explained. Whether the carriers you represent use this form or a variation, a comprehensive understanding of its coverages and conditions will help you competitively position your products in the marketplace and better analyze client needs.

ISO Review Link

Throughout the course, we have provided excerpts of the Business Income forms relevant to the content. These form excerpts provide an effective way to reinforce the concepts treated in this course by examining the exact language of the ISO form as the course progresses.

Commercial Auto Appendix

The Appendix is an excellent tool to enhance your understanding of this course. It includes reference charts and samples of policy forms explained in this course. Referencing actual ISO forms will help you understand the content of this course.

Glossary

A glossary is provided at the end of this text and includes definitions of key terms. These key terms are identified in bold throughout the text. When a term is bold, refer to the glossary for a definition.

Real Life Applications and Questions

Real Life Application

We use a number of hypothetical scenarios to help you apply concepts to everyday issues. Many of these scenarios include questions that reinforce the course instruction discussed in the scenario. The icon shown on the left identifies a scenario as a Real Life Application. Answers to any questions following the hypothetical appear in footnotes at the bottom of the same page. Question numbers are consecutive within a chapter.

Study Questions

There are questions at the end of each unit. These questions provide a check for understanding of important concepts. Answers to these questions appear on the last page of each unit.

Review Test

The 25-question Review Test supplied at the end of this text helps you prepare for the state CE exam if you are taking this course for CE credit.

State Continuing Education Exam

If you have not already done so, you can obtain a 50-question exam by ordering from Dearborn Customer Service at 1-800-824-8742. Instructions about monitoring and proctoring the exam are available on the outside of the exam package.

Important Information

The information contained herein is provided to assist you in your efforts to learn about ISO's 2001 Commercial Auto policy forms. This program is designed to provide accurate and authoritative information in regard to the subject matter. It is sold with the understanding that the program is not engaged in the rendering of legal, accounting, or professional services. If professional advice is required, the services of a competent professional should be sought. Any names appearing in this publication are fictional and have no relationship to any person living or dead.

Many state insurance regulators amend ISO forms with their own mandated endorsements. You are responsible for determining the difference between the ISO forms and endorsements used in this course and the forms approved for use in the states where you write coverage. In addition, many insurers develop their own policy forms.

Earn A Competitive Advantage

Whether the carriers you represent use standard ISO forms or their own modified forms, a comprehensive understanding of the ISO forms used in your state will allow you to distinguish specific company policy features and compete more effectively.

1

Commercial Auto Loss Exposures

T he term *commercial auto* is used for those auto risks not written under a personal auto policy, including named insureds who are individuals, partnerships, corporations, joint ventures, and governmental entities. The term can also include fleets of private passenger vehicles, trucks, trailers, semitrailers, and other vehicles.

In this unit, we will compare **Personal Auto Policies (PAPs)** to Business Auto Policies (BAPs) as well as reviewing the Insurance Services Office's development of commercial auto coverage. Basic underwriting guidelines and ratings will also be explained.

When you have completed this unit, you should be able to:

Learning Objectives

- differentiate between the Personal Auto Policy (PAP) and the Business Auto Policy (BAP);

- identify the factors that determine the classification of a commercial vehicle;

- explain the commercial auto coverage form options;

- determine what type of risks should be written under commercial auto forms; and

- explain how business auto and alternate coverage forms are used in monoline versus commercial package policies.

■ ■ ■ ■ ■

■ THE NEED FOR COMMERCIAL AUTO COVERAGE

Like personal auto owners, commercial auto owners are subject to both property and liability loss exposures. Commercial auto exposures, however, are generally excluded in Commercial Property and Commercial General Liability Coverage forms. In many cases, commercial auto exposures are also excluded in personal auto coverage forms.

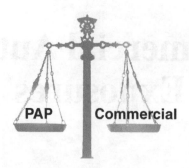

Avoiding duplicate coverage and multiple carrier complications is the reason some loss exposures are excluded in one policy form and covered in other forms better suited to treat the risk.

ISO policy forms are intended to act in concert with one another, not duplications in coverage.

Selecting the Property Coverage Form

Comprehensive insurance programs are used to offset both personal and commercial risk exposures. It is not always easy to differentiate between these risks, or to determine which policy form is really needed.

For instance, corporations lack a personal identity by legal definition and thus have only commercial exposures; while sole proprietors, **partners**, and individual owners of limited liability companies could potentially be exposed to both commercial and personal liability.

Coverages are similar in both the commercial auto policies and the Personal Auto Policy (PAP), but there are some specific differences in policy application, as illustrated below.

Personal Auto Policies Protect Individuals

Individuals who own vehicles often insure them with a Personal Auto Policy (PAP). The PAP (ISO form PP 00 01) combines physical damage insurance on the automobile with liability insurance for claims arising out of the ownership or use of the vehicle.

The PAP is designed to cover a named insured (not a corporation) and a resident spouse and may be written for private passenger vehicles used in business.

However, certain underwriting restrictions and exclusions in the PAP may create the need to insure business vehicles under a commercial auto form. For example, all of the following may warrant commercial auto coverage:

- vehicle ownership;

- vehicle size and **classification** restrictions;

- vehicles used for public conveyance (taxis); and

- garage operations or auto dealerships.

Vehicle Ownership

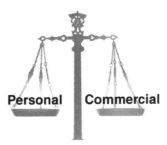

For insurance purposes, vehicles are classified as either:

- private passenger vehicles—motor vehicles such as passenger cars, station wagons, pickups, etc., owned by the named insured and used mainly for non-business activities by individuals residing in the same household; or

- commercial autos—motor vehicles of the truck type, including tractors, trailers, and semi-trailers, used for the transportation or delivery of goods or merchandise or for other business purposes.

Private passenger vehicles can be written on either a PAP or commercial auto policy depending on their ownership and use.

Vehicle Size and Classification Restrictions

Personal auto policies have the following size (gross vehicle weight) and use restrictions:

- Pickup or vans cannot exceed 10,000 pounds GVW.

- Pickup trucks or vans cannot be used in the delivery or transportation of goods and materials, unless used in farming or ranching, or incidental to business of installing, maintaining, or repairing furnishings or equipment.

For example, a person who owns a 10 ton gross vehicle weight dump truck for personal use would be required to insure it using a business auto policy because of the size of the vehicle.

Vehicles Used for Public or Livery Conveyance

The insured's liability arising out of the ownership or operation of a vehicle while it is being used as a public or livery conveyance is not covered by the PAP. A public or livery conveyance is one that is held out to the public or private parties for hire, such as taxis, limousines, commuter vans, and busses.

These types of business exposures must be insured using a commercial auto policy. This PAP exclusion does not apply to a share-the-expenses car pool.

Garage Operations or Auto Dealerships

The PAP excludes liability for use of vehicles while the insured is employed or engaged in the business of selling, repairing, servicing, storing, or parking vehicles. For example, a person employed as a parking valet would not be covered for bodily injury or property damage that occurs while driving a customer's vehicle.

This exclusion includes road testing and delivery (such as that performed by car dealers), but it does not apply to the ownership, maintenance, or use of personal autos. In other words, the valet's PAP would cover liability arising out of the use of his owned vehicle.

Commercial Auto Policies Protect Businesses

When a business is solely owned, the insured may have the option of insuring autos under either a PAP or a Business Auto Policy (BAP).

The Insurance Services Office (ISO) Business Auto Coverage Form (CA 00 01) provides selected liability and physical damage coverages on vehicles used for commercial purposes. The BAP consists of the Business Auto Coverage Form, the Declarations Page, and applicable endorsements.

Personal vs. Business Auto

Coverages are similar in both the PAP (used to insure individuals) and the BAP (used to insure a business).

The following chart summarizes the key characteristics of the Personal Auto Policy (PAP) and the Business Auto Policy (BAP).

Key	Personal Auto Policy	Business Auto Policy
Ownership	Four-wheel vehicles owned by individuals or married couples who reside in the same household.	Land motor vehicles, trailers, and semitrailers designed for travel on public roads owned or operated by individuals, unicorporated associations, joint ventures, governmental entities, partnerships, or corporations.
Use	Vehicles used to go to and from work or school, on a farm, a ranch, or in business.	Vehicles that are used for any business purposes, including transportation of goods, materials or merchandise.
Type of Vehicles	Pickup trucks, panel trucks, and vans not exceeding 10,000 pounds gross vehicle weight and not used to transport goods or materials (unless the use is incidental to the insured's business of installing, maintaining, or repairing furnishings, or equipment or for farming or ranching.	Trucks with a gross vehicle weight exceeding 10,000 pounds. Private passenger vehicles and lighter trucks are also eligible for coverage.
Number of Vehicles	Maximum of four vehicles.	Any number of vehicles with different rates based on the number.

Commercial Auto Policies Protect a Business

As shown above, although individuals and businesses face many of the same automobile exposures, a business cannot purchase a PAP to cover its vehicles because the PAP is designed to cover a named insured and a resident spouse.

To address this problem, ISO developed a Business Auto Program to cover exposures that are unique to business. These exposures include the potential for a business to be held liable for an employee's use of automobiles the employer owns or for use of employee-owned vehicles in the employer's business.

The Business Auto Program is compatible with other business and commercial policies such as the **Commercial General Liability (CGL)** policy and the NCCI Workers' Compensation and Employers Liability insurance policy. Coverage can be written as a stand-alone (BAP) or as part of a **Commercial Package Policy (CPP).**

Non-Owned Autos May Be Covered Under the BAP

A business that does not own autos still may need a Business Auto Policy. Non-owned autos include vehicles used for business purposes that are not owned, leased, hired, or borrowed by the insured. A non-owned loss exposure exists, for example, when employee's own auto is used for making sales calls or deliveries for a commercial insured.

For example, salespeople may cover their personally owned autos with PAPs, but use them in the course of their business. If a loss occurs, the PAP covers bodily injury and property damage. The businessowner may also have some liability exposures because the **employee** was performing work on behalf of the business. Without a BAP of its own, a business cannot be assured of coverage for non-owned auto exposures.

Insurance Coverage Needed for Borrowed Autos

Real Life Application

Delores, the manager of Anderson Office Products, is short one employee on a busy day and calls her neighbor, Hector, to run a business-related errand using his own vehicle. While doing so, he is involved in an accident.

1. How can Anderson Office Products protect itself if it is named in a lawsuit arising out of Hector's accident?

■ COMMERCIAL AUTO COVERAGE FORMS

Automobiles owned or operated by individuals, unincorporated associations, joint ventures, government entities, partnerships, or corporations, or autos that are not eligible for PAPs because of auto type, can be insured under a **commercial auto insurance** form.

As the next unit will discuss, the appropriate commercial auto form can be written as a mono-line policy or it can be added as part of a commercial package policy (CPP). This unit will briefly look at the five available coverage forms.

Business Auto Coverage Form Covers Business Use

The Business Auto Coverage Form is the most widely used commercial auto form. It is used to insure a wide variety of vehicles owned or used by a business.

Private passenger vehicles, vans, pickups, trucks, and panel trucks may all be covered under this form. However, because the definition excludes mobile equipment, certain vehicles such as bulldozers, certain construction equipment, and farm machinery cannot be covered.

The form provides physical damage and liability coverage. **Medical payments**, uninsured motorists, and personal injury protection may be added by endorsement.

Policies May Be Tailored to Cover Specific Risks

The Business Auto Coverage Form has two major coverage parts: **Liability** and **Physical Damage**. These are the exposures common to most businesses.

However, a policy can be tailored to cover specific risks by using **endorsements**. For example, the policy may be endorsed to cover medical payments, uninsured

---

Answer and Rationale

1. A BAP protects an insured for losses arising out of the use of both owned and non-owned autos. Hector's vehicle, being used on behalf of Anderson Office Products, is an example of a non-owned auto.

motorists, or hired cars.

Business Auto Coverage for Personal and Business Vehicles

Business auto coverage is flexible enough to meet the needs of most businesses except for truckers, garages, and auto dealerships. Typically, business auto coverage is included as part of a commercial package policy (CPP) and may be used to insure both personal and business vehicles. This is a common practice because many business owners prefer to insure all of their vehicles under a single policy for convenience.

Premium considerations can also apply because insuring private passenger automobiles under a business policy may be less expensive than purchasing a personal auto policy for the same purpose.

Covering Business Auto Physical Damage Only

The Business Auto Coverage Physical Damage Form (CA 00 10) is used, where permitted by law, to limit coverage on business vehicles to Physical Damage coverage only. No liability coverage is provided.

This choice would apply to situations where the insurer wants to write the commercial auto coverage but is uncomfortable with a particular auto that the insured owns (e.g., a particular vehicle presents extraordinary risk).

For example, assume the insured has a fleet of private passenger autos used for sales calls and one large truck. The truck is used to transport goods to another state for a friend of the insured. Because the truck is transporting property for another, it is considered a shipper and might be better covered by a specialty carrier. For simplication, the insured may purchase physical damage coverage from the carrier issuing the BAP and insure the liability exposure with a trucking specialist.

The coverage can be purchased as a stand-alone policy or as part of any other commercial auto coverage form.

Physical Damage Form Mirrors BAP Coverage

The coverages in the Business Auto Coverage Form (CA 00 10) are identical to the physical damage coverage in the BAP, which is explained in detail later in this course. Therefore, CA 00 10 will not be examined further in this course.

Garage Risks Present Additional Hazards

In many cases, it is possible to classify a risk as either an auto exposure or a general liability exposure. A garage operation, however, has both liability and auto exposures that must be addressed. In addition to the potential liability if a customer is injured on the property, the garage may also provide towing and auto repairs that create vehicle liability exposure.

The **Garage Coverage Form** (CA 00 05) combines a business auto policy with the commercial general liability policies to accommodate businesses who are in the auto sales or dealership business.

The Garage policy functions as a multi-line policy because it has additional premises, operations, and commercial property exposures. The form is discussed in more detail later in this course.

Truckers Coverage Form Used for Transporting Goods

When vehicles are used to transport goods, materials, or commodities for another entity, that operation involves special risks.

The **Truckers Coverage Form** (CA 0012) was developed for trucking operations. The basic coverages are the same as those provided under the Business Auto Policy, with two exceptions:

- coverage is available for trailers owned by others and in the insured's possession; and

- the insured's trailers may be covered when they are in the possession of others.

These trailer interchange agreements are common in the trucking industry. ISO also offers the **Motor Carrier Coverage Form** (CA 00 20) which is limited to vehicles transporting goods across state lines. Both coverage forms are state-regulated and issued by specialty carriers.

Motor Carrier vs. Truckers Coverage Forms

Many states have enacted motor carrier laws that pertain to the intrastate transportation of persons or property for hire. The Motor Carrier Coverage Form (CA 00 20) was created in response to a number of changes in motor vehicle carrier regulations that may not be properly addressed by the Truckers Coverage Form (CA 00 12).

It is important to remember, however, that the differences between these two forms are very slight. There are minor differences in the *Definitions, Coverage Symbols, Who Is An Insured,* and the *Other **Conditions*** sections.

Truckers Form Covers Transportation of Property, Not People

The major distinction between the Motor Carrier Form and Truckers Coverage Form is in their definition of a motor carrier.

- The Motor Carrier Coverage Form includes coverage for an insured engaged in the business of transporting persons or property.

- The Truckers Coverage Form provides coverage for transportation of property only.

■ MONOLINE OR PACKAGE COVERAGE

Commercial auto coverage can be written on a monoline basis or as part of a CPP. A monoline policy contains a single coverage part or line of insurance. CCPs are multi-line policies that contain two or more coverage parts or lines of insurance.

The most common way to provide insurance for a larger business or organization is with a Commercial Package Policy (CPP). This policy may include coverage for liability, automobiles, commercial property, crime and fidelity, and other major lines of insurance. A common Declarations Page is combined with separate insuring agreements for each type of coverage. This approach allows the insured to select the coverage needed and tailor it to the needs of the insured's business.

Creating a Monoline Policy

The Business Auto, Garage, Truckers and Motor Carrier Coverage Forms, when combined with a Declarations Page and any applicable endorsements, create a **monoline policy**.

The monoline policy is used when the insured only needs commercial auto insurance.

Coverage May Be Monoline or Package

The CCP requires at least two coverage parts (e.g., business auto and commercial general liability).

The following coverages are eligible for the CPP:

- Commercial auto

- Commercial property

- Commercial general liability

- Commercial crime

- Commercial inland marine

- Boiler and machinery

- Farm

- Professional liability

- Employment-related practices liability

Packages Provide Simple Format

The package approach allows many of the items that are common to all or most of the coverage parts to be included only once, which provides insureds with a simpler policy format. The required forms in a CPP are listed below:

- Common policy declarations

- Common policy conditions

- Specific coverage form(s)

- Specific coverage form declarations

- Specific coverage general conditions form

- Applicable endorsements

Multiple forms can be added to the CPP to create a total insurance solution with one policy and one premium billing.

CPP Standarizes Coverage Forms

The CPP was designed to:

- simplify placement and updating;

- standardize insurance forms;

- eliminate duplicate coverage and gaps;

- provide premium discounts; and

- provide easy-to-read language.

CPP Benefits the Consumer

The CPP benefits the consumer by providing:

- comprehensive coverage in single package;

- one premium notice and common renewal date;

- aggregate premiums to receive discounts; and

- standardized coverage and ease of use.

Common Policy Conditions Apply to All Coverages

The common policy conditions must be included in either a monoline or package policy.

These conditions include *cancellation, changes, inspection, transfer of interest,* and *right to **examine the insured's books and records**.*

Declarations Indicates Coverage That Applies to Vehicles

The **Declarations Page** (or **Dec Page**) includes detailed information regarding risks, coverages, and vehicles.

Specific items on the Dec Page include the following:

- Name and address of the insurer

- Policy and endorsement numbers

- Name and mailing address of agent/producer

- Name and mailing address of policyholders

- Designation of insureds

- Coverage symbols and selection

- Premium charges and deductibles

- Limits of liability (coverage limits)

- Aggregate limits (policy limits)

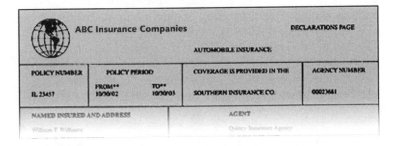

✓ *Helpful Hint:* A sample of a Dec Page is included in the Appendix.

Numerical Symbols Describe Vehicle Coverage

The Dec Page also includes information about covered autos on the policy, as denoted by coverage **symbols**. The symbols are numeric and a description of the covered auto designation symbols is included for each coverage form.

The symbols are not the same for each coverage form but some correspond to those used in other forms.

The description of covered auto designation symbols is reviewed in detail later in this course.

■ WHAT IS A COMMERCIAL AUTO?

ISO does not define the term commercial auto in its Commercial Lines Manual (CLM). However, which autos are to be rated under each subsection of the Rules section of the manual are identified.

The types of vehicles that may be covered as commercial autos include the following:

- Private passenger types

- Vans

- Pickups

- Trucks and panel trucks

- Truck tractors and fifth wheels

- Semitrailers and kingpins

- Full trailers and service or **utility trailers**

Commercial Definition of "Auto" Differs from PAP

The PAP defines *your covered auto* to mean any vehicle shown in the Declarations, a newly acquired auto, a trailer, or a temporary substitute vehicle.

The commercial auto forms define the term *auto* as follows:

> *"Auto" means a land motor vehicle, "trailer" or semitrailer designed for travel on public roads but does not include "mobile equipment."*

This definition is broad and includes most vehicles commonly used in business.

Mobile equipment, which includes bulldozers, farm machinery, forklifts, and other vehicles, is not covered. These vehicles are usually not licensed for use or intended to be driven on public roads.

Inland Marine and CGL Cover Mobile Equipment

To properly insure a given risk, it is critical to understand the distinction between mobile equipment and autos. Generally, mobile equipment includes land vehicles that are not designed for use on normal public roads. **Automobiles** are vehicles licensed and used on public roads.

The property coverage for these items would be covered in an Inland Marine Form, and the liability would be covered in the Commercial General Liability (**CGL**) policy.

What is Mobile Equipment?

The term *mobile equipment* refers to any of the following types of land vehicles, including any attached machinery or equipment:

- Bulldozers, farm machinery, forklifts, and other vehicles designed for use principally off public roads

- Vehicles maintained for use solely on or next to premises the insured owns or rents

- Vehicles that travel on crawler treads

- Vehicles, whether or not self-propelled, maintained primarily to provide mobility to permanently mounted power cranes, shovels, loaders, diggers, or drills or to road construction or resurfacing equipment (such as graders)

- Other vehicles that are not self-propelled and are maintained primarily to provide mobility to permanently attached equipment such as air compressors, pumps, generators, cherry pickers, and similar devices used to raise or lower workers

- Other vehicles maintained primarily for purposes other than the transportation of persons or cargo

Mobile Equipment Liability Covered While Towed or Transported

Mobile equipment is specifically excluded from the definition of *auto* because this coverage is better provided under other policy forms.

The liability exposure is generally picked up by a standard commercial general liability (CGL) policy. The only exception is mobile equipment that is being transported by an auto.

Under Part C of Section I—Covered Autos, the Business Auto Coverage Form picks up liability coverage for mobile equipment, if the mobile equipment is transported or towed by a covered auto with liability coverage. The form also provides liability coverage for trailers with a load capacity of 2,000 lbs or less and temporary substitute autos.

Liability coverage is extended for these vehicles because they do not significantly change the loss exposure. In essence, they simply become an extension of a **covered auto.**

Liability Coverage Provided for Towed Mobile Equipment

Liability coverage is only extended for mobile equipment that is being transported or towed by a covered auto because while it is being transported or towed, the mobile equipment does not drastically change the liability exposure. When the equipment reaches its destination, liability coverage ends.

For example, a driver towing a bulldozer to a construction site is assumed to be in control of both vehicles. Should an accident with resulting injuries occur, it would be difficult to determine whether the vehicle being driven or the bulldozer being towed caused the injuries or property damage.

Self-Propelled Vehicles Are Covered Autos

The following types of vehicles with permanently attached equipment are not considered mobile equipment under the BAP. The BAP's definition of auto includes permanently attached equipment designed primarily for:

- snow removal;

- road maintenance, but not construction or resurfacing; or

- street cleaning.

Coverage exists because the equipment is permanently attached and the vehicles are designed primarily for use on public roads. Again, they present liability exposures that are an extension of the covered auto.

Coverage applies for cherry pickers and similar devices mounted on automobile or truck chassis used to raise or lower workers. In some situations, coverage applies for other similar devices including air compressors, pumps, and generators, and including spraying, welding, building cleaning, geophysical exploration, lighting, or well servicing equipment. These are described below.

■ *ISO FORM*

K. "Mobile equipment" means any of the following types of land vehicles, including any attached machinery or equipment:

1. Bulldozers, farm machinery, forklifts and other vehicles designed for use principally off public roads;

2. Vehicles maintained for use solely on or next to premises you own or rent;

3. Vehicles that travel on crawler treads;

4. Vehicles, whether self-propelled or not, maintained primarily to provide mobility to permanently mounted:

a. Power cranes, shovels, loaders, diggers or drills; or

b. Road construction or resurfacing equipment such as graders, scrapers or rollers.

5. Vehicles not described in Paragraphs **1., 2., 3.,** or **4.** above that are not self-propelled and are maintained primarily to provide mobility to permanently attached equipment of the following types: **a.** Air compressors, pumps and generators, including spraying, welding, building cleaning, geophysical exploration, lighting and well servicing equipment; or

b. Cherry pickers and similar devices used to raise or lower workers.

Some Have Features of Auto and Mobile Equipment

Some vehicles, such as a cherry picker, have features of both mobile equipment and autos. A cherry picker is a maneuverable vertical boom with an open bucket or cage at the end from which a worker can perform aerial work such as pruning trees or repairing electrical lines.

A cherry picker is not considered mobile equipment, although it has some characteristics of mobile equipment. When the cherry picker itself is being used, it is treated as mobile equipment and the CGL would cover liability exposures that arise from its operation. When the vehicle is being driven with the cherry picker collapsed in the bed of the truck, it is covered by the BAP.

This is an example of how ISO has crafted the forms to work together. When special needs arise, the form is flexible enough to allow insurers to create special symbols or policy language to cover the needs of a particular risk.

Add Mobile Equipment Coverage by Endorsement

In some cases, the insured may wish to have certain items that meet the BAP definition of mobile equipment insured as autos. This can avoid a coverage dispute when different carriers provide coverage for CGL and BAP exposures.

The CA 20 15 Mobile Equipment endorsement specifically provides coverage for mobile equipment under the BAP, Motor Carrier, and Truckers Coverage Forms.

✓ *Helpful Hint:* A copy of this endorsement is available in the Appendix.

Only Autos Listed on the Dec Page Are Covered

As explained earlier, the term *auto* refers to any vehicle except mobile equipment, provided it is a **land motor vehicle**, trailer, or semi trailer designed for travel on public roads.

Thus, mopeds and motorcycles, motor homes, cars, trucks, tractors, trailers, three-wheelers, and any tractor-trailer combination qualify as autos under the business auto coverage forms.

The forms cover only autos that are described on the Declarations Page.

Trucks Are Vehicles Used to Haul Items

For commercial auto purposes, a truck is an automotive vehicle suitable for hauling items. When a truck has a cab but no body and is used to pull large trailers or vans, it is called a tractor. When a truck consists of a tractor and trailer together, it is called a trucking rig.

Trucks are classified by gross vehicle weight (GVW), the maximum loaded weight for which a single vehicle is designed (as specified by the manufacturer). Trucks are classified as:

- light trucks (GVW of 10,000 lbs or less);

- medium trucks (GVW of 10,001—20,000 lbs); or

- heavy trucks (GVW of 20,001—45,000 lbs).

Truck Tractors and Fifth Wheels Pull Other Vehicles

The compartment in front of a motor vehicle in which the truck driver sits is called a cab. The cab may be permanently attached to a trailer or it may be a separate unit to which a trailer is attached.

Some cabs are specially constructed to pull heavy vehicles. A truck-tractor is a motorized automobile, equipped with a fifth wheel, used to pull other vehicles. A fifth wheel is a round steel or metal plate that rests on the truck-tractor and is used for attachment to the semitrailer.

ISO divides truck-tractors into two weight classes dependent on their gross combination weight (GCW). The **GCW** is the maximum loaded weight for a truck-tractor and the semi-trailer(s) for which the truck-tractor was designed (as specified by the manufacturer). The two weight classes are

- heavy truck-tractors (GCW of 45,000 lbs or less); or

- extra-heavy truck-tractors (GCW of over 45,000 lbs).

Semitrailers and Kingpins

A **semi-trailer** is trailer that has wheels only in the rear. The front is supported by the towing vehicle or truck-tractor and a semitrailer is connected the truck-tractor by a fifth wheel coupling device. These trailers may be used to haul a variety of items from bulk commodities to heavy excavation and construction materials.

The kingpin is the bolt or steel "pin" under the semitrailer that provides a coupling device for connection with the truck-tractor. It connects with the fifth wheel to join the truck-tractor and semitrailer.

Full Trailers and Service or Utility Trailers

The final type of vehicle that may be covered as commercial autos are full trailers and service or utility trailers.

A full trailer has an axle or axles at the front and rear of the trailer. This construction allows the trailer's weight to rest on its own wheels. The full trailer is connected to another trailer or semitrailer by a draw-bar and hitch. Smaller trailers with a load capacity or 2,000 lbs or less are called service or utility trailers.

■ COMMERCIAL AUTO UNDERWRITING

The application for commercial auto insurance begins with a review of the application. Most applications include information about the:

- producer, carrier, and type of policy requested;

- applicant information;

- premises information;

- nature of the business operations;

- general information;

- prior carrier information; and

- loss history.

The application will also indicate whether the client is requesting a mono-line or package policy.

Insurance Rates Reflect Common Hazards

After the application is reviewed, the rating process begins. The Insurance Services Office (ISO) developed a classification system to group policyholders in classifications of commercial **risk**, so that insurance rates can reflect the **hazards** common to those classifications.

This section will discuss the primary factors that affect the ISO Business Auto Classification system. Commercial auto rates are based on primary and secondary rating factors. The primary classification for trucks, trailers and tractors is based on:

- weight class;

- business use; and

- radius of operation.

A secondary classification for vehicles belonging to special industry classes, such as truckers, farmers, and dump or transit mix trucks and trailers, is also used.

Weight and Type of Vehicle Begins Classification

The underwriter begins to determine classifications by reviewing the size and type of vehicles to be insured. The size class is determined by the gross vehicle weight (**GVW**) or the gross combination weight (**GCW**) of each vehicle.

Once the GVW or GCW is ascertained, the actual class is then determined based on the GVW or load capacity as depicted in the following classification charts:

Vehicle Classification	GVW in Pounds
Light trucks	10,000 or less
Medium trucks	10,001 to 20,000
Heavy trucks	20,001 to 45,000
Extra heavy trucks, includes truck trackers	45,001 or more
Trailer Classification	**Load Capacity in Pounds**
Trailer, if not considered a semi-trailer	2,000 or less
Service or utility trailer, any trailer or semi trailer with < 2,000 lbs. load capacity	2,000 or less
Semi-trailers are equipped with a fifth wheel coupling to be used with a truck-tractor rig	2,001 or more

The Business Use of Vehicles Is Also Considered

In addition to their size and weight, business autos are rated based on their use. This is because the accident potential for a particular vehicle is increased or decreased based in part on the way that vehicle is used.

There are three business use auto rating classifications:

Service Use

This business use auto rating classification applies to vehicles when they are used for the transportation of employees, tools, equipment, or supplies to or from a job site.

Retail Use

Rating category that includes vehicles used for retail pick-up or delivery to households.

Commercial Use

Rating category that includes all uses of commercial vehicles other than those specifically included in the Service or Retail categories.

Long Distance Driving Means Greater Risk

The **radius of operations** is another factor used in rating commercial trucks. ISO has clarified that the radius should be determined based on a straight line from the street address of the principal garaging and is measured as a straight line rather than in road miles.

Trucks travelling more than 50 miles are assumed to face greater risks because of driver fatigue and higher speeds.

Radius of Operations

Factor used in rating commercial trucks based on the distance travelled from the principal garage location. Risks are assumed to be greater for trucks traveling long distances (usually more than 50 miles) because of driver fatigue and higher speeds than for those confined to a small area. It is customary to measure the radius by a straight line rather than by road miles.

Three **radius classes** are available:

Local

A commercial auto rating classification for any vehicle not frequently operated beyond a 50-mile radius of the vehicle's principal garage location.

Intermediate

A commercial auto rating classification for vehicles that customarily operate within a radius of between 51 and 200 miles of the vehicle's principal garage location.

Long Haul

A commercial auto rating classification for any vehicle that is customarily driven at a distance of over 200 miles from its garage location. When long haul is the proper class to use, zone rates apply to any vehicle that is not classified as Light in the size class.

Fleet Classification Reduces Premium

After the size, type, business use, and radius of operation are determined for each vehicle, the underwriter must ascertain whether the vehicle is part of a **fleet** (a group of automobiles owned and managed by the same person). The economies for an insurer of covering a significant number of vehicles under a single policy allows them to offer a discounted premium on automobile fleet policies.

The number of vehicles determine whether a fleet exists:

- Fleet—Five or more self-propelled vehicles under the same ownership, not including any mobile equipment.

- **Non-fleet**—Less than five self-propelled vehicles.

Trailers do not play any role in the composition of a fleet. They will however, belong to the same class as the vehicles on the policy.

Vehicles added or deleted after the policy inception will not change the classification until renewal.

Secondary Classification Needed for Special Industry Class

Special rates apply for vehicles in one of eight major industry classes that include:

- truckers;

- food delivery;

- specialized delivery (such as armored cars, mail delivery, etc.);

- waste disposal;

- farmers;

- dump and transit mix trucks and trailers;

- contractors; and

- not otherwise specified (such as logging and limbering).

The secondary classification, like the primary classification, is based on the vehicle's use. There may be different primary classifications for different vehicles on the same policy.

Vehicles Must be Properly Maintained

During the application review process, the underwriter must evaluate the general condition of the vehicles that are to be insured on the policy. Loss and safety specialists, underwriters, and fleet account managers should pay particular attention to the maintenance history on each vehicle.

All of the following are important factors when assessing the risks related to a particular business:

- Age

- Condition

- Person responsible for upkeep

- Dates and times of service

- Major repairs

- Log detailing the rotation schedule

Loss Control Reports Provide Risk Information

Insurance underwriters will request an inspection report from the insurer's loss control area. The loss control report confirms and supplements the information found on the application and will include information about the size of the business, the number of vehicles and their use, the area of operations, as well as other vital information.

Safety

When the insured has a fleet, the underwriter will expect to see a written safety program. The underwriter will review the program to determine how drivers are selected and trained, how equipment is maintained, how accidents are reported, and whether management supports the program.

The underwriter also considers antitheft protection in the garage where the vehicles are stored and security issues of the premises when rating a policy.

Information about All Drivers Must Be Included

Of critical importance is the list of all drivers, including family members and employees who will be using the company vehicles. The drivers list should include:

- name;

- date of birth;

- driver's license or Social Security number;

- vehicles operated;

- frequency of operation;

- Motor Vehicle Record (MVR); and

- loss history of each driver.

At a minimum, underwriters usually require this information before rating a commercial auto policy.

Loss History Should Be Complete and Accurate

Loss history is of critical importance to the underwriting and evaluation of a business auto account. Loss history should include:

- date of loss;

- time of day;

- driver's full name and information;

- vehicle identification number;

- type or description of the accident or loss;

- amount of the loss; and

- whether the loss is open, closed, in reserve, or in suit.

Depending on the frequency, type, and radius of the auto exposure, an underwriter may need other information (such as the training of each driver). Loss prevention programs should also be evaluated.

The Company Should Monitor Driver Records

The following factors are driver-specific **underwriting guidelines**:

- Does the insured obtain periodic motor vehicle records for all company drivers?

- Does the insured have standards of acceptability with respect to driving records and training?

- How are drivers that do not meet those standards handled?

- Does the insured offer a bonus or other incentive for good records and for loss-free or accident-free drivers?

- What type of formal safety program does the insured have in place?

- Are any drivers required to have special licenses?

- How are special licenses handled?

In the event of an auto accident, the claims adjuster will need all of this information to properly investigate the claim.

Complete Information Speeds Application Review

Providing complete information to the insurance company promotes quick underwriting. In addition, accuracy of information may secure a more favorable rating.

The opportunity to receive favorable rates and **scheduled credits** often depends on the agent communicating successfully with the insurance company.

■ SUMMARY

An insured's need to purchase a business auto insurance policy will depend on the types of vehicles owned and how they are used. Insurance professionals should also ask insureds about who will be driving them and whether employees are likely to be driving their own cars in the insured's business. Many underwriting details are needed to complete the commercial auto application.

The next unit will begin the exploration of the Business Auto Coverage Form with an explanation of Section I—Covered Autos.

▪ UNIT 1 REVIEW QUESTIONS

1. Which of the following statements regarding BAPs and PAPs is(are) TRUE?

    I. The BAP is designed to cover vehicles used for business ventures.

    II. The PAP allows coverage for certain business use vehicles.

    III. Vehicles owned by a business are generally not eligible for coverage under the PAP.

    A. I and II only

    B. I and III only

    C. II and III only

    D. I, II and III

2. All of the following are examples of a commercial auto form EXCEPT

    A. Garage Coverage

    B. Truckers Coverage

    C. Business Auto Coverage

    D. Personal Auto Coverage

3. Which of the following is not found on the Business Auto Declarations page?

    A. Coverage territory

    B. List of autos to be covered

    C. Policy period

    D. Named insured and address

4. A vehicle that has an attached cherry picker is always considered to be mobile equipment.

    A. True

    B. False

5. Which of the following is not included in the definition of *mobile equipment*?

    A. Forklift

    B. Grader

    C. Street Sweeper

    D. Power Crane

6. If a given risk uses 15 personal autos for local delivery, the autos should be classified as fleet and service.

    A. True

    B. False

7. Which of the following best lists all of the factors that are important in the decision to underwrite a commercial auto policy?

    A. Loss history and personal history

    B. Loss history and driver history

    C. Loss history, driver history, and safety devices

    D. None of the above

8. How does the underwriting history assist the claims adjuster?

    A. In no way; claims and underwriting have nothing in common.

    B. In no way; the company has to pay regardless.

    C. It will assist to know that a risk was rated with a class radius of 25 miles and was not charged for an out-of-state fleet business, where the accident occurred.

    D. It will assist claims to know where the named insured on a commercial auto policy personally lives.

■ **ANSWERS TO UNIT 1 REVIEW QUESTIONS**

1. **D.** The BAP is designed to cover business ventures, but the PAP allows coverage for certain business use vehicles. Additionally, vehicles owned by a business are generally not eligible for coverage under the PAP. Therefore, the insurance professional must determine when the BAP is appropriate and when the PAP is applicable to business auto protection.

2. **D.** The commercial auto forms consist of the Business Auto Coverage Form, the Garage Coverage Form, and the Truckers Coverage Form.

3. **A.** The coverage territory for an unendorsed BAP is found in the body of the policy itself, not on the Declarations Page.

4. **B.** False. The cherry picker is not always considered mobile equipment, although it has some of those characteristics. When the cherry picker itself is being used, it is treated as mobile equipment and the CGL would cover events that arise from its operation. When the vehicle is being driven with the cherry picker collapsed in the bed of the truck, it is covered by the BAP.

5. **C.** The street sweeper is not considered mobile equipment. The auto definition clearly describes the sweeper as an auto because it is a self-propelled vehicle with permanently installed equipment used for street cleaning.

6. **B.** False. The risk should be classified as fleet and commercial. Service use is reserved for transportation to and from the job site by cars that will only be on the road to and from one location. A car used for delivery will make many trips per day.

7. **C.** All of these records and factors are critical, because the underwriter needs to be able to anticipate the exposures and know how to rate the account (i.e., whether or not the account will be classified as fleet or non-fleet). When there are multiple vehicles, as with a limo company, the driver history and loss history is also critical. Security information, such as antitheft devices on the cars and security protection on the premises, is also important.

8. **C.** All of the history on the rating of the risk is important because it explains the intent of the company when underwriting the policy.

2

BAP Section I—Covered Autos

 ommercial auto policies use ISO's classification of covered autos and coverage symbols to denote coverage. The various coverage forms list the symbols and a description of the covered auto designation symbols.

In this unit, we will discuss eligibility factors and auto symbols, as applied to Section I—Covered Autos of the Business Auto Coverage Form.

When you have completed this unit, you should be able to

Learning Objectives

- discuss the application and use of ISO's Business Auto Coverage Form (CA 00 01);

- define covered auto;

- recognize ISO coverage symbols; and

- explain how these symbols are used in the commercial auto policy to denote coverage.

■ ■ ■ ■ ■

■ BUSINESS AUTO COVERAGE FORM OVERVIEW

The Business Auto Coverage Form (CA 00 01) may be used to insure the automobile exposures of almost any type of organization, with the following two major exceptions:

- Businesses such as auto dealers (which must use the Garage Coverage Form), service stations, auto dealers, repair shops and parking lots, most of which use ISO's auto service risks market segment program.

- Motor carriers for hire that use automobiles to transport property of others, most of which insure their exposures under the Truckers Coverage Form or Motor Carrier Coverage Form.

Truckers Form Covers Transportation of Property, Not People

The major distinction between the Motor Carrier and Truckers Coverage Forms is in the definition of a motor carrier.

- The **Motor Carrier Coverage Form** includes coverage for an insured engaged in the business of transporting persons or property.

- The **Truckers Coverage Form** provides coverage for transportation of property only.

Coverage Form Is the Basis for the Business Auto Policy (BAP)

The Business Auto Coverage Form (CA 00 01) has two major coverage parts, **physical damage** and **liability coverage**, because these are the exposures common to most businesses.

The CA 00 01 form is combined with a Declarations Page and applicable endorsements to create the Business Auto Policy (BAP). The policy can be tailored to cover specific risks by the addition of endorsements. For example, the policy may be endorsed to cover medical payments, uninsured motorists, or hired cars.

The Form Contains Five Sections

The BAP is divided into five major sections:

- Section I—Covered Autos

- Section II—Liability Coverage

- Section III—Physical Damage Coverage

- Section IV—Business Auto Conditions

- Section V—Definitions

Sections II, III, IV, and V will be reviewed later in the course. This unit will be limited to the provisions of Section I—Covered Autos. As you saw in Unit 1, the BAP's definition of *auto* is fairly broad.

BAP Definition of "Auto" Is Broad

As explained previously, the definition of auto in Section V—Definitions of the BAP states:

"Autos" means a land vehicle, "trailer" or semi-trailer designed for travel on public roads but does not include "mobile equipment."

The definition applies to most vehicles commonly used in business.

■ **COVERED AUTO SYMBOLS**

The Business Auto Coverage forms use numeric Symbols 1 through 9 to denote coverage for autos described in Section I—Covered Autos.

Each symbol below represent vehicle categories based on specific ownership and usage.

- Symbol 1—Any "Auto"

- Symbol 2—Owned "Autos" Only

- Symbol 3—Owned Private Passenger "Autos" Only

- Symbol 4—Owned "Autos" Other Than Private Passenger "Autos" Only

- Symbol 5—Owned "Autos" Subject To No-Fault

- Symbol 6—Owned "Autos" Subject To Compulsory Uninsured Motorists Laws

- Symbol 7—Specifically Described "Autos"

- Symbol 8—Hired "Autos" Only

- Symbol 9—Nonowned "Autos" Only

■ *ISO FORM*

SECTION I – COVERED AUTOS
Item Two of the Declarations shows the "autos" that are covered "autos" for each of your coverages. The following numerical symbols describe the "autos" that may be covered "autos". The symbols entered next to a coverage on the Declarations designate the only "autos" that are covered "autos".

A. Description Of Covered Auto Designation Symbols

Correct Coverage Symbols Must Appear on Dec Page

The Business Auto Declarations (CA 00 03) includes a section titled Item Two—Schedule of Coverages and Covered Autos.

The policy states that coverage applies only to those coverages indicated on the Dec Page and only when a charge for those coverages is shown in the premium column. In order to be a "covered auto" for a particular coverage, one or more numeric symbols as described in the "Description of Coverage Auto Designation Symbols" on the Business Auto Coverage Form must be included in Item Two.

Insureds can design the coverage they want by selecting different Symbols for different vehicle types or uses.

A sample of the section titled Item Two — Schedule of Coverages and Covered Autos appears on the opposite page.

BAP Application Limits Coverage Choices

An insurance company may use its own forms and applications. It may also choose the **ACORD®** applications. Whichever the choices, the business auto section of the application limits the coverage options that may be selected. Certain symbols can only be used for certain types of coverage.

For example, Symbol 1 may be selected only for liability. Symbol 2, however, may be selected for liability, medical payments, uninsured motorists, underinsured motorists, and physical damage coverage (excluding towing and labor).

Proper Symbol Selection Is Important

Selecting the proper symbol is vital because it governs the types of vehicles and coverage that will be provided under the policy.

The next sections will explain what autos are designated for coverage by each of the nine ISO symbols. Each of the symbols identifies how:

- the covered auto is owned or used;

- coverage is provided for autos owned at the policy's inception; and

- coverage is provided for autos acquired after the inception of the policy.

Symbol 1 Covers all Vehicle Liability

Symbol 1 offers the broadest scope of coverage under the policy. It applies liability coverage to any vehicle, whether owned, hired, borrowed, or rented by the insured, and for whatever purpose, business or personal use. It makes **any auto** a covered auto for liability purposes.

When Symbol 1 is used, the policyholder is not required to report new vehicles. Newly acquired vehicles during the policy period are automatically covered during the policy period.

Symbol 1 is infrequently used because it is so broad. Underwriters are reluctant to take on the broad exposure and policyholders are reluctant to assume the higher premium associated with such extensive coverage.

POLICY NUMBER: _____

ITEM TWO

SCHEDULE OF COVERAGES AND COVERED AUTOS

This policy provides only those coverages where a charge is shown in the premium column below. Each of these coverages will apply only to those "autos" shown as covered "autos". "Autos" are shown as covered "autos" for a particular coverage by the entry of one or more of the symbols from the Covered Autos Section of the Business Auto Coverage Form next to the name of the coverage.

COVERAGES	COVERED AUTOS (Entry of one or more of the symbols from the Covered Autos Section of the Business Auto Coverage Form shows which autos are covered autos.)	LIMIT THE MOST WE WILL PAY FOR ANY ONE ACCIDENT OR LOSS	PREMIUM
LIABILITY		$	$
PERSONAL INJURY PROTECTION (or equivalent No-fault Coverage)		SEPARATELY STATED IN EACH P.I.P. ENDORSEMENT MINUS $ DED.	$
ADDED PERSONAL INJURY PROTECTION (or equivalent added No-fault Coverage)		SEPARATELY STATED IN EACH ADDED P.I.P. ENDORSEMENT.	$
PROPERTY PROTECTION INSURANCE (Michigan only)		SEPARATELY STATED IN THE P.P.I. ENDORSEMENT MINUS $ DED. FOR EACH ACCIDENT.	$
AUTO MEDICAL PAYMENTS		$	$
MEDICAL EXPENSE AND INCOME LOSS BENEFITS (Virginia only)		SEPARATELY STATED IN EACH MEDICAL EXPENSE AND INCOME LOSS BENEFITS ENDORSEMENT.	$
UNINSURED MOTORISTS		$	$
UNDERINSURED MOTORISTS (When not included in Uninsured Motorists Coverage)		$	$
PHYSICAL DAMAGE COMPREHENSIVE COVERAGE		ACTUAL CASH VALUE OR COST OF REPAIR, WHICHEVER IS LESS, MINUS $ DED. FOR EACH COVERED AUTO, BUT NO DEDUCTIBLE APPLIES TO LOSS CAUSED BY FIRE OR LIGHTNING. See ITEM FOUR For Hired Or Borrowed "Autos".	$
PHYSICAL DAMAGE SPECIFIED CAUSES OF LOSS COVERAGE		ACTUAL CASH VALUE OR COST OF REPAIR, WHICHEVER IS LESS, MINUS $ DED. FOR EACH COVERED AUTO FOR LOSS CAUSED BY MISCHIEF OR VANDALISM. See ITEM FOUR For Hired Or Borrowed "Autos".	$
PHYSICAL DAMAGE COLLISION COVERAGE		ACTUAL CASH VALUE OR COST OF REPAIR, WHICHEVER IS LESS, MINUS $ DED. FOR EACH COVERED AUTO. See ITEM FOUR For Hired Or Borrowed "Autos".	$
PHYSICAL DAMAGE TOWING AND LABOR		$ For Each Disablement Of A Private Passenger "Auto".	$
			$
		PREMIUM FOR ENDORSEMENTS	$
		*ESTIMATED TOTAL PREMIUM	$

*This policy may be subject to final audit.

 CA DS 03 02 04 ☐

Symbols Further Subdivide Categories

By using Symbols 2—9, autos may be further subdivided into autos owned by the insured and all other autos. Under the BAP, owned autos are either private passenger types or other than private passenger types. All other autos include hired autos or nonowned autos.

Hired autos are those not owned by the insured but leased under a contract on behalf or, or loaned to, the named insured. **Nonowned** autos are those vehicles an insured does not own, lease, hire, or borrow, such as an employee's personal auto used in the insured's business.

Symbol 1 "Any Auto" Includes Employee Cars

Pizza companies that provide delivery services but do not have company cars may use Symbol 1—Any Auto coverage on the company BAP. When employees use personal autos to deliver pizza, the use of Symbol 1 provides liability protection for the company.

The primary coverage for an employee's personal car would be the employee's personal auto policy. However, in the event of an accident during a pizza delivery, Symbol 1 affords coverage for any **vicarious liability** which may attach to the employer, the pizza company.

Symbol 2 Covers Owned Autos

Coverage Symbol 2 provides automatic coverage for the insured's **owned autos** of any type owned at the policy's inception or acquired during the policy term. Symbol 2 designates coverage for private passenger vehicles and non-private passenger vehicles owned by the insured.

It also provides liability coverage for non-owned trailers or semitrailers that are attached to the insured's owned power units, such as truck-tractors.

There is no coverage under Symbol 2 for rented, borrowed, or non-owned vehicles.

Symbol 2 may be applied to any coverage which is offered under the Business Auto Coverage Form, except towing and labor which is limited to private passenger vehicles. In other words, Symbol 2 may be used to provide liability, medical payments, uninsured motorists, and/or physical damage coverage.

Commonly, Symbol 2 is used for providing automatic physical damage insurance on a fleet of owned autos. When Symbol 2 is used for physical damage coverage, additional or new autos are generally discovered during the audit after the policy expires. Because coverage has been afforded during the policy term, the discovery of new vehicles can result in additional premiums for the insured.

Symbol 2 Is Used to Limit Coverage to Owned Vehicles

Assume a small corporation needs a fleet of both private passenger and non-private passenger vehicles for its sales staff. All vehicles are directly owned, not leased. Because of the number of miles driven each year, vehicles are frequently replaced.

To avoid any mistakes in providing coverage, the insured wants to insure the fleet automatically for liability and physical damage coverage. He also wants to be sure the coverage is limited to owned autos, not vehicles that are used by employees for other purposes.

Coverage Symbol 2 would be entered in the Liability and Physical Damage Selection boxes in Item Two of the Business Auto Declarations (CA 00 03).

LIABILITY	2	$	$
PERSONAL INJURY PROTECTION (or equivalent No-fault Coverage)		SEPARATELY STATED IN EACH P.I.P. ENDORSEMENT MINUS $ DED.	$
ADDED PERSONAL INJURY PROTECTION (or equivalent added No-fault Coverage)		SEPARATELY STATED IN EACH ADDED P.I.P. ENDORSEMENT.	$
PROPERTY PROTECTION INSURANCE (Michigan only)		SEPARATELY STATED IN THE P.P.I. ENDORSEMENT MINUS $ DED. FOR EACH ACCIDENT.	$
AUTO MEDICAL PAYMENTS		$	$
MEDICAL EXPENSE AND INCOME LOSS BENEFITS (Virginia only)		EXPENSE AND INCOME LOSS BENEFITS ENDORSEMENT.	$
UNINSURED MOTORISTS		$	$
UNDERINSURED MOTORISTS (When not included in Uninsured Motorists Coverage)		$	$
PHYSICAL DAMAGE COMPREHENSIVE COVERAGE	2	ACTUAL CASH VALUE OR COST OF REPAIR, WHICHEVER IS LESS, MINUS $ DED. FOR EACH COVERED AUTO, BUT NO DEDUCTIBLE APPLIES TO LOSS CAUSED BY FIRE OR LIGHTNING. See ITEM FOUR For Hired Or Borrowed "Autos".	$

PHYSICAL DAMAGE SPECIFIED CAUSES OF LOSS COVERAGE		ACTUAL CASH VALUE OR COST OF REPAIR, WHICHEVER IS LESS, MINUS $ DED. FOR EACH COVERED AUTO FOR LOSS CAUSED BY MISCHIEF OR VANDALISM. See ITEM FOUR For Hired Or Borrowed "Autos".	$
PHYSICAL DAMAGE COLLISION COVERAGE	2	ACTUAL CASH VALUE OR COST OF REPAIR, WHICHEVER IS LESS, MINUS $ DED. FOR EACH COVERED AUTO. See ITEM FOUR For Hired Or Borrowed "Autos".	$

✓ **Helpful Hint:** A sample of the BAP Declarations Page is included in the Appendix.

Symbol 3 Covers Owned Private Passenger Autos

Symbol 2 is used for owned private passenger and non-private passenger vehicles owned by the insured. Symbols 3 and 4 further subdivide those vehicles into owned private passenger vehicles only and other than private passenger vehicles only.

Symbol 3 is used for owned private passenger autos only. Automatic coverage for private passenger autos acquired during the policy period is provided.

This symbol does not include trucks, buses, or any kind of automobile not owned by the insured. It also excludes nonowned trailers, which could be covered under Symbol 2.

Towing and labor may be added because this category is for private passenger vehicles only.

Symbol 4 Covers Autos Other Than Private Passenger Autos

Symbol 4 applies to owned autos other than private passenger vehicles only and includes acquired vehicles of the same classification during the policy period.

Symbol 4 provides coverage for owned autos other than private passenger autos. These autos include pickup trucks, vans, and truck-tractors. Symbol 4 also extends coverage for non-private passenger vehicles acquired during the policy period.

Liability coverage may be extended to trailers or semitrailers while they are attached to owned power units. Symbol 4 may also be used to cover trucks, truck tractors, busses, taxies, motorcycles, trailers, and emergency vehicles.

Symbol 3 May Cover Vans and Delivery Trucks

Sometimes the choice between Symbols 2, 3, and 4 may not seem clear-cut.

Assume a bakery business owns and uses only delivery vans for its business. Symbol 4 would be used.

But, if instead of the vans, the insured has a few private passenger autos which are primarily used by company employees for both business and personal use, Symbol 3 should be used.

If the insured has both private passenger autos and vans, Symbol 2 should be used.

Coverage Options May Be Selected

Symbol 4, like Symbol 3, designates specific coverages for vehicles. For example, an insured may want to cover private passenger autos for **Comprehensive** (Symbol 3) and Specified Causes of Loss on other than private passenger autos (Symbol 4). This strategy would enable the insured to save on premiums.

Although it can be used for any coverage offered under the BAP, Symbol 4 is seldom used because most insureds need one of the broader coverage choices available.

Symbol 5—Owned Autos Subject to No-Fault

Symbol 5 provides coverage for No-Fault on those vehicles owned or acquired during the policy period. Symbol 5 is normally used only for **personal injury protection (PIP) coverage** in the state in which the vehicles are principally garaged or in which they are licensed. Coverage is only provided for those autos required to have it by state law.

The benefits provided are consistent with the requirements of the state where the auto is principally garaged or licensed.

Symbol 6—Owned Autos Subject to a Compulsory Uninsured Motorist Law

Symbol 6 provides coverage on those vehicles owned or acquired during the policy period for **Compulsory Uninsured Motorist Laws**. Symbol 6 is normally used only for uninsured motorist coverage and provided only for autos required to have this coverage by state law.

The insured cannot reject this coverage as stipulated by the state where the auto is licensed or principally garaged.

Symbols 5 and 6 Provide Specific Coverage

Assume an insurance company owns vehicles that are assigned to adjusters who investigate claims within a given territory or region. Presume that one of the states within the region, State A, has a compulsory uninsured motorists and no-fault law, and State B is a compulsory uninsured motorist jurisdiction only.

Coverage Symbols 5 and 6 would be used to insure owned vehicles in State A for compulsory coverages; only Symbol 6 would be used for owned vehicles in State B to denote uninsured motorists coverage.

Symbols 5 and 6 Address State Regulations

Symbols 5 and 6 are used respectively only for owned autos that are required to have either no-fault coverage (Symbol 5) or uninsured/underinsured motorist (UM) coverage (Symbol 6) in states that mandate such coverage.

An endorsement must be attached to the policy when either symbol is used. The symbol cannot be used with any other coverage under a business auto form, and typically applies in situations where the vehicle is used in a state that requires the coverage.

Owned Autos Acquired after Policy Begins

If Symbols 1, 2, 3, 4, 5, or 6 are entered into Item 2 of the Declarations Page, any auto that the insured acquires during the policy period is automatically covered during the policy period. The insured does not need to report the change to the insurance company. At the end of the policy period, the insurer will conduct an audit to determine the actual auto exposures that existed during the policy term.

The BAP charges an estimated premium based on the auto exposures shown on the Declarations Page at the policy's inception. The final premium due the insured (or the return due the insured) is determined at the time of the audit.

Symbol 7 Is Used to Schedule Specifically Described Autos

Coverage Symbol 7 provides coverage for only those autos specifically described to the insurance company at the beginning of the policy period, and for which a premium is shown in the policy. It also provides liability-only coverage for any trailer owned by the insured while it is attached to a covered auto.

Coverage is extended to include any auto of the same class (i.e., owned or non-owned) which the insured acquires in the policy period, but the insured must also report the newly acquired vehicle to the company (unlike other symbols) and request the coverage within 30 days of the acquisition.

This requirement is in sharp contrast to Symbols 1—6 used for owned autos that do not require the insured to report new vehicles during the policy period. The use of Symbol 7 places a burden on the insured to report any changes to the insurance company. Carriers use this underwriting tool to ensure they are receiving an adequate premium for specific autos.

Symbol 8 Covers Hired Autos

Symbol 8 applies to hired autos only, or only those autos which the insured leases, hires, rents, or borrows. If Symbol 1 is used, the insured does not need to list Symbol 8 for liability.

The coverage does not include vehicles which are owned by employees, their partners, or members of their household. Thus, a vehicle borrowed from an employee by the named insured is not covered under this symbol (but coverage may be provided under Symbol 9).

Symbol 8 may be used alone or in conjunction with Symbols 2, 3, 4, 7, or 9 for liability or physical damage coverage. Typically, Symbols 8 and 9 are written together to assure that both hired and nonowned autos are covered.

Symbol 9 Extends Coverage to Nonowned Autos

The last coverage symbol listed on the BAP is Symbol 9, coverage for nonowned autos. This coverage is excess only and is only used for liability coverage. In other words, the vehicle owner's insurance provides primary coverage.

The main purpose of this symbol is to cover the insured's vicarious liability when employees use their own autos on behalf of the named insured. If Symbol 1 is used, Symbol 9 is unnecessary.

Typically, this is the coverage purchased to protect against liability arising from the use of employee-owned vehicles.

■ BAP "COVERED AUTO" CASE STUDIES

There are seven different risk scenarios in this lesson. Choose the coverage Symbol (or Symbols) that would offer the best coverage option for the scenario given. The coverage option to which the Symbol will apply is Liability. The answers to the seven case studies are found on page 42.

Symbol 1—Any Auto will not be given as an answer choice because, even though it does offer the broadest coverage available, insureds may be unwilling to pay the additional premiums associated with this broad coverage. Further, some insurance companies are not willing to offer this coverage.

Please select from the Symbol(s) below as your recommendation for the following cases:

Symbol 2, 3, 4, 5, 6, 7, 8, and/or 9

Case 1: Hired Commercial Trucks

An insured has two private passenger type vehicles and frequently borrows and hires commercial trucks.

Case 2: Compulsory Insurance Law

An insured lives in a state that has a compulsory insurance law but the insurer refuses to offer Symbol 2.

Case 3: Frequent Trailer Use

The insured frequently borrows and uses trailers owned by others. They only want to insure autos they own.

Case 4: Adding Broader Coverage

The insured has Symbol 2 coverage and wants to make sure the BAP provides the broadest protection possible.

Case 5: Limited Coverage

Which symbol(s) would provide coverage for the narrowest class of vehicles?

Case 6: Owned Cargo Van

The insured only wants to cover owned private passenger autos and is thinking about buying a cargo van.

Case 7: Owned and Used Vehicles

The insured has Symbol 7 for physical damage and wants to know which symbols cover the liability loss exposure for both owned and acquired vehicles.

■ SUMMARY

The BAP provides coverage for the broadest range of organizations and vehicle types, although vehicles collectively described as mobile equipment in the definitions section of the BAP are specifically excluded. Coverage for this equipment is achieved through a combination of CGL and inland marine forms.

Coverage Symbols 1—9 are defined in the BAP under **Section I—Covered Autos**. Coverage is selected by placing the appropriate symbol next to the desired coverage on the Business Auto Declarations Page.

BAP coverage is indicated by applying the proper symbol to the desired coverage. The symbols were developed to account for the most commonly encountered circumstances and to provide a method of differentiating coverage within the same form.

This universal language enables insureds, insurers and interested third parties to understand the depth of coverage at a glance. It is critical to apply the proper sequence of symbols to prevent coverage gaps.

The next unit will look at the liability insurance provided by the Business Auto Coverage Form.

■ **UNIT 2 REVIEW QUESTIONS**

1. Coverage Symbol 1 offers the broadest coverage under the business auto form because

    A. any auto is a covered auto
    B. coverage applies to owned, non-owned, borrowed, or hired vehicles
    C. none of the above
    D. A and B

2. Coverage Symbol 2 does not provide coverage for

    A. non-owned autos
    B. owned trucks
    C. private passenger vehicles
    D. trailers

3. The BAP is designed to write any type of auto, provided the auto is not a private passenger type.

    A. True
    B. False

4. Coverage Symbol 3 is used for

    A. any auto
    B. private passenger vehicles only
    C. owned autos only
    D. owned private passenger autos only

5. Coverage Symbols 5 and 6 are used for

    A. non-compulsory coverage in any state
    B. mandatory No-Fault and Uninsured Motorist Coverage
    C. optional No-Fault and Uninsured Motorist Coverage
    D. owned autos only

6. As a general rule, the definition of *auto* in the BAP does not include

    A. mobile equipment
    B. semi-trailer
    C. trailer
    D. motorcycle

■ ANSWERS TO UNIT 2 REVIEW QUESTIONS

1. **D.** Symbol 1 applies liability coverage to any auto and applies to any class of vehicle whether owned, non-owned, borrowed, or hired.

2. **A.** Symbol 2 applies to owned autos only. Non-owned, hired, rented or borrowed vehicles are not covered with this symbol. Remember, the policy definition of *auto* includes land motor vehicles, trailers, or semi-trailers designed for use on public roads, but does not include mobile equipment. Trucks and private passenger vehicles are included in this definition.

3. **B.** False. The BAP is designed to write autos used in a business. These autos include private passenger vehicles and larger commercial vehicles. A major restriction on BAP eligibility applies to vehicles used to haul property for hire. Vehicles included in this category can be insured on the Trucker's Coverage Form.

4. **D.** Coverage Symbol 3 is for owned private passenger autos only. Coverage Symbol 3 is used when an insured wants to use different coverage on private passenger owned autos used in business than he does with the commercial fleet vehicles. Additionally, it permits the limitation of coverage on the larger vehicles.

5. **B.** Coverage Symbol 5 is used for mandatory No-Fault Coverage, and Symbol 6 is used for mandatory Uninsured or Underinsured Motorist Coverage. This symbol is not appropriate where coverage is optional, and non-compulsory means not required (i.e., optional). This is a coverage that does not apply to owned autos only—it only applies to owned autos which have to carry a state-mandated PIP No-Fault or UM statutory coverage.

6. **A.** Mobile equipment is specifically excluded from the definition of *auto* in the business auto policy, because other policies provide coverage: i.e., liability under the commercial general liability policy (CGL), unless it is being transported by an auto. Mobile equipment that is being transported or towed by a covered auto is included under the BAP for liability coverage. Mobile equipment physical damage is typically covered under a heavy equipment floater on a commercial property or inland marine policy.

■ CASE STUDY ANSWERS & RATIONALE

1. Symbols 2, 8, and 9

Symbol 2 applies to owned autos only and Symbol 8 applies to hired autos only that are not leased, hired, rented, or borrowed from an employee, partner, or member of the insured's household. Symbol 9 applies to nonowned autos used in the insured's business, including autos owned by employees, partners, or members of the insured's household.

2. Symbol 6

Symbol 6 applies to owned autos garaged or licensed in a state subject to a compulsory uninsured motorist law.

3. Symbol 2

Symbol 2 applies to owned autos, including any auto acquired after the policy begins. It also covers trailers for liability, whether owned or not.

4. Symbol 2

Symbol 2 coverage is the broadest protection possible unless the insured is willing to pay the additional premiums associated with the broad coverage of Symbol 1.

5. Symbols 3 and 4

Symbols 3 and 4 restrict the type of auto to private passenger only and other than private passenger, respectively.

6. Symbol 7

Symbol 7 provides coverage only for the autos specifically described to the insurance company at the beginning of the policy period. Newly acquired vehicles of the same class must request the coverage within 30 days of the acquisition.

7. Symbol 2

Symbol 2 applies to owned autos, including any auto acquired after the policy begins.

3

BAP Section II—
Liability Coverage

L **iability coverage** is provided to protect the insured against a number of claims or losses that could be financially devastating.

Although the sources of liability for commercial autos is similar to that of personally owned autos, the potential loss severity is often greater for commercial autos. The size and weight of commercial autos and the public's tendency to look for large loss settlements when a loss involves a company or corporation tend to result in larger lawsuits.

We continue with the Business Auto Policy in this unit, and focus on the provisions of Section II—Liability Coverage.

When you have completed this unit, you should be able to:

Learning Objectives

- recognize the legal elements necessary to establish liability under Section II—Liability Coverage insuring agreements;

- identify who is an insured under Section II—Liability Coverage;

- describe the liability coverage extensions and supplementary payments;

- describe and apply liability coverage and exclusions; and

- explain how the limits of liability affect claim settlements.

■ ■ ■ ■ ■

■ THE NEED FOR AUTO LIABILITY

As stated previously, the BAP is divided into five major sections:

- Section I—Covered Autos

- Section II—Liability Coverage

- Section III—Physical Damage Coverage

- Section IV—Business Auto conditions

- Section V—Definitions

Sections III, IV, and V will be reviewed later in the course. This unit will be limited to the provisions of Section II—Liability Coverage.

BAP Provides Liability and Physical Damage Only

Key Point

Unlike the Personal Auto Policy (PAP), the Business Auto Policy (BAP) includes only liability and physical damage coverage sections.

Medical payments and uninsured motorists coverages must be added to the policy by endorsement. These coverages are optional because some business clients do not wish to provide or pay for these coverages on vehicles used in business and operated only by employees.

Definitions of Liability and Exposure

Liability is a specific legal finding of fault against one who has breached a duty or obligation owed to another by imposition of law. Liability is not the same as exposure, although the two terms are often confused.

Exposure means that the insured has a potential risk of liability arising from certain operations or conduct (e.g., failure to safely maintain the tires on fleet vehicles).

When the insured has reason to know that a potential risk of injury or damage exists and does not address the safety issue, there is exposure for potential legal liability flowing from the actions of the insured.

Four Elements Needed to Establish Liability

The insurance company is required to pay all sums the insured is legally required to pay as damages as a result of **bodily injury** or property damage to which the insurance applies.

To establish liability under Section II, the investigation of the claim must first reveal:

- the insured owed a legal duty of reasonable care to a third party;

- the insured breached, or failed to meet, that legal obligation;

- those actions or inactions directly or indirectly caused an accident, as defined in the policy; and

- the accident resulted in bodily injury or property damage to which the policy applies.

Based on all the facts and circumstances, all four elements have to be established for liability to result against an insured.

Does the Insured Have Legal Liability?

Real Life Application

The insured owns a fleet of vehicles that are used as pool cars for adjusters. The fleet is insured under a BAP. An adjuster for the company signs out a company car to attend a mediation, a specific business purpose.

On the way to the mediation, the right front wheel falls off, strikes a pedestrian, and causes an injury.

An investigation reveals that the insurance company is the owner of the vehicle and has a legal duty to the public to safely maintain the company cars. The mechanic, an employee of the insurance company, forgot to put on the lug nuts when he rotated the tires before lunch.

1. Based on these facts, is it probable that legal liability has been established?

Coverage Section Spells Out Insurer's Duties

Part A. Coverage of Section II—Liability Coverage of the Business Auto Coverage Form acts as the insuring agreement. This section of the insurance contract contains the obligation of the insurer to pay covered claims, subject to specified conditions and exclusions.

Answer & Rationale

1. **Yes.** Based on the facts provided, legal liability has been established.

    1. The insurance company has a legal duty to the public to safely maintain the company cars. (Duty owed)

    2. The mechanic breached his duty by failing to replace the lug nuts. (Duty breached)

    3. The mechanic failure to replace the lug nut caused the accident. (Causation)

    4. The pedestrian was injured as a direct result of the collision. (Damages for bodily injury)

All four elements necessary to establish legal liability are present on these facts. The facts also reveal that the policy will apply to the damages, and that an accident within the meaning of the policy occurred.

Section II provides liability coverage for:

- bodily injury (**BI**) or property damage (**PD**) resulting from the ownership, maintenance, or use of a covered auto; and

- expenses to defend, investigate, and settle claims.

> ■ *ISO FORM*
>
> **A. Coverage**
>
> We will pay all sums an "insured" legally must pay as damages because of "bodily injury" or "property damage" to which this insurance applies, caused by an "accident" and resulting from the ownership, maintenance or use of a covered "auto".

Auto Liability Covers Injury to a Third Party

The BAP is a legal contract between two parties: the insurer and the insured. Under the terms of the insuring agreement, the insured (the first party listed or **first named insured**) pays a premium to the insurer (the second party). In return, the insurer agrees to pay for covered losses to the insured's property. Generally, the insurer pays the insured directly for property losses.

It is important to remember that the BAP also covers the insured for liability losses involving a third party. When a third party suffers a bodily injury or property damage loss and the insured is found legally liable, the insurer pays the third party directly for these damages.

The bodily injury or property damage to a third party must be a result of the ownership, maintenance, or use of a covered auto under the policy.

The insurer only pays if:

- the insured has a legal obligation to pay damages because of bodily injury or property damage to which the policy applies;

- the property damage or bodily injury is caused by an **accident** as defined in the policy; and

- a covered auto is involved.

>
> We will also pay all sums an "insured" legally must pay as a "covered pollution cost or expense" to which this insurance applies, caused by an "accident" and resulting from the ownership, maintenance or use of covered "autos". However, we will only pay for the "covered pollution cost or expense" if there is either "bodily injury" or "property damage" to which this insurance applies that is caused by the same "accident".

The BAP Is Not Subject to an Aggregate Limit

The most the insurer will pay for damage in any one accident is each limit of insurance shown in the policy declarations. The BAP is not subject to an aggregate limit.

Policies may carry a combined single limit of liability (CSL) for both bodily injury and property damage or may be issued with split limits, i.e., a single limit for property damage and a single limit for bodily injury.

An example of a CSL is $500,000 per accident for bodily injury and property damage. An example of a split limit is $100,000 per person for bodily injury, $300,000 per accident for bodily injury, and $50,000 for property damage.

Financial Responsibility Laws Dictate Coverage Amount

Some states have financial responsibility laws that require motorists to prove they are able to pay for injuries or damage to others as a result of the ownership or operation of autos. Commercial auto owners are generally subject to the same laws that apply to personal autos.

When a state has **financial responsibility** laws, the BAP must provide the minimum amount of coverage required by the laws of the state in which the autos are principally garaged.

States without financial responsibility laws usually have **compulsory auto insurance statutes**. These laws require a vehicle owner or operator to have minimum automobile liability coverage before the vehicle can be registered or licensed.

Some Pollution Costs Are Covered

The BAP Exclusions section excludes virtually all liability for pollution damage. However, in the insuring agreement, the insurer agrees to pay all sums the insured becomes **legally obligated** to pay as a result of a covered pollution cost or expense. There must be bodily injury or property damage to which the insurance applies that is covered by the same accident. For example, the cost to clean up fuel that leaked from a car after an accident would be covered.

The BAP defines "covered pollution cost or expense" as any cost or expense arising out of:

- any request, demand, or order; or

- any claim or suit by or on behalf of a governmental authority demanding that the insured or others test for, monitor, clean up, remove, contain, treat, detoxify, or neutralize, or in any way respond to or assess the effects of pollutants.

Pollution Payments Are Limited

The insurer is obligated to pay when an accident results from the ownership, maintenance, or use of covered autos and the insured is legally required to pay for either bodily injury or property damage to which the insurance applies.

There is no separate limit for pollution cost or expense. The cost incurred reduces the per accident limits available to pay for other covered losses.

Pollution coverage is limited by a broad pollution exclusion (discussed later in this unit).

The Insurer Has a Duty to Defend the Insured

The insurer has the right and duty to defend any insured against a suit seeking damages for bodily injury, property damage, or covered pollution costs under the policy, and reserves the right to investigate, settle, or defend any suit or claim as it deems appropriate.

However, there is no duty to defend any insured against a suit seeking damages for bodily injury or property damage or a covered pollution expense to which the policy doe not apply.

The insurer's duty to defend or settle ends when the liability coverage limit of insurance has been exhausted by payment of judgments or settlements.

Does the Insurer Have a Duty to Defend?

Real Life Application

Baker's Bread Company has a BAP with a combined single limit (CSL) of $300,000. The company receives a lawsuit for a claim valued in excess of the limits. The investigation reveals that Baker's Bread is legally responsible for the loss.

The adjuster settles the claim for the limits of $300,000, with the appropriate release which discharges the named insured from any further liability, in exchange for the policy limit payment.

A dismissal is filed with the applicable court.

2. Does the insured have any further duty to defend the insured?

▪ WHO IS AN INSURED?

Under an insurance contract, the **named insured** is an individual, business, or organization that is specified in the Declarations by name as the insured(s) under a policy.

Other insureds may be covered without being named, but may be included for coverage as insureds or additional insureds by other provisions (e.g., the policy **definitions**). The named insured is responsible for premium payments, receipt of notices, and adjustment of losses.

BAP Broadens the Definition of an Insured

Insureds under a business auto policy include the insured designated on the **Declarations** Page, employees, and household members; individuals who work for an auto servicing, repairing, parking, or storing business; partners and their household members; and other drivers using an insured vehicle with the permission of the named insured.

To restate this simply, insureds include:

- named insured for any covered auto;

- anyone else while using, with the insured's permission, a covered auto the insured owns, hires, or borrows; and

- anyone else who otherwise is not excluded and who is liable for the conduct of an insured, but only to the extent of that liability.

> ### ▪ ISO FORM
>
> **1. Who Is An Insured**
> The following are "insureds":
> **a.** You for any covered "auto".
> **b.** Anyone else while using with your permission a covered "auto" you own, hire or borrow except:

Answer & Rationale

2. The insurer has no additional duty to defend the insured because the BAP liability coverage limit has been exhausted in full and final settlement.

The Definition of Insured Has Five Exceptions

Although the policy states that an insured includes anyone "using with your permission a covered 'auto' you own, hire or borrow," there are five exceptions to this definition.

1. Under exception 1.b. (1) of "**Who is An Insured**," the owner or person from whom the named insured borrows or hires an auto is not an insured under the BAP. Because it is assumed that the auto owner has auto coverage, the borrowed or hired auto would be considered a covered auto under the owner's BAP.

For example, assume Bob is the named insured under a BAP and borrows a car from Jim. If an accident occurs and both Bob and Jim are sued, Jim has no coverage as an insured under Bob's policy but would have coverage under his own.

The exclusion does not apply to a trailer connected to a covered auto. The trailer becomes an extension of the covered auto for liability coverage only.

> ■ *ISO FORM*
>
> **(1)** The owner or anyone else from whom you hire or borrow a covered "auto". This exception does not apply if the covered "auto" is a "trailer" connected to a covered "auto" you own.

Employees Who Lend Autos Are Not Insureds

2. Under exception 1.b. (2) of "Who is An Insured," an employee or an employee's family member from whom the named insured borrows or hires an auto is not an insured under the BAP.

Just as in the first exclusion, it is assumed that the employee or family member who owns the auto has their own auto insurance. Therefore, the borrowed or hired auto would be considered a covered auto under the named insured's own BAP, but the owner of the vehicle would not be considered an insured.

> ■ *ISO FORM*
>
> **(2)** Your "employee" if the covered "auto" is owned by that "employee" or a member of his or her household.

Auto-Related Businesses Have Exclusions

3. Under exception 1.b. (3) of "Who is An Insured," coverage does not apply to anyone using a covered auto while engaged in an automobile-related business other than the named insured's own business.

The purpose of this exclusion is to eliminate coverage under the named insured's BAP for liability that is better covered elsewhere. For example, when someone is working in an auto repair shop and has care, custody, or control of the named insured's vehicle, coverage is better provided by **garagekeepers** coverage or ISO's Auto Service Risks Program.

> ■ *ISO FORM*
>
> **(3)** Someone using a covered "auto" while he or she is working in a business of selling, servicing, repairing, parking or storing "autos" unless that business is yours.

Non-Employee Property Movers Are Not Insureds

4. Under exception 1.b. (4) of "Who is An Insured," people who move property to or from a covered auto are not insureds, unless they are employees, partners, or someone who has leased or borrowed a covered auto.

For example, assume the named insured and two employees are moving furniture from one location to another. When they reach their destination, they realize additional people will be needed to unload the truck. However, these additional people do not become insureds under the BAP. Only the named insured and the two employees are considered to be insureds.

If injured, the additional helpers would seek coverage under their employer's workers compensation policy.

> ■ *ISO FORM*
>
> **(4)** Anyone other than your "employees", partners (if you are a partnership), members (if you are a limited liability company), or a lessee or borrower or any of their "employees", while moving property to or from a covered "auto".

Covered Autos Owned by Partners or Members Are Not Insured

5. Under exception 1.b. (5) of "Who is An Insured," partners or **members** of a limited liability company are not considered insureds under the named insured's BAP if using a covered auto owned by themselves or their households.

As with the other exclusions, this exclusion is intended to eliminate coverage for an auto that is better covered elsewhere. The partner or member should have a separate auto policy.

> ■ *ISO FORM*
>
> **(5)** A partner (if you are a partnership), or a member (if you are a limited liability company) for a covered "auto" owned by him or her or a member of his or her household.

Real Life Application

An insured has several office supply stores scattered throughout the city. Through an agreement with another business, when supplies of ink printer cartridges run low, the insured purchases the needed supplies from that business. He sends a truck covered by a BAP to pick-up the supplies. The employees of the two businesses know one another and often help each other load the truck.

3. If any employee from the other business is injured while carrying the supplies to the truck, does the insured's BAP cover the injury?

Limited Vicarious Liability Coverage Is Provided

Key Point

The definition of "Who is An Insured" includes subpart 1.c that describes another group of people who are insureds under the policy. Basically, coverage applies for those who are liable for the conduct of others. Vicarious liability is a term used to describe a situation where one person is legally responsible for the acts of another based solely on a relationship between the two. This is sometimes referred to as indirect or imputed legal responsibility.

The dictionary defines *vicarious* as "taking the place of another." The legal concept of vicarious liability imposes legal responsibility on a person or entity for causing an injury to someone or something. In reality, that person or entity had nothing whatsoever to do with actually causing the injury. The following relationships may result in an insured's legal liability.

Answer & Rationale

3. Yes, if the named insured is held liable for the injury. If the other business or its employees are sued for injury to a third party, they are not covered under the named insured's BAP policy.

- Parents are vicariously liable for the acts of their minor children.

- Employers are vicariously liable for the acts of their employees while acting on behalf of the employer.

- Organizations are vicariously liable for the acts of volunteers who are acting on its behalf.

The doctrine is commonly applied in the employee/employer relationship. When an employee is negligent on the job, the employer is legally responsible for any damage or injury the employee causes. The concept is helpful to injury victims when the negligent employee is financially unable to pay the judgment, but the employer is capable of doing so.

■ COVERAGE EXTENSIONS AND EXCLUSIONS

Supplementary Payments Paid In Addition to Liability Limits

Insurance contracts typically include **supplementary payments** that are benefit payments under a liability policy in addition to the basic coverages provided by the policy.

In addition to the limit of insurance, the BAP provides the following supplementary payments:

- All expenses the insurer incurs

- Up to $2,000 for bail bonds

- Cost of bonds to release attachments in any suit the insurer defends

- The insured's reasonable expenses, including up to $250 per day for lost wages

- Costs taxed against the insured in any suit the insurer defends

- All interest that accrues after entry of the judgment in any suit the insurer defends

Out-of-State Coverage Extensions Address State Regulations

When the covered auto is used in a state other than the one in which it is principally garaged, some **out-of-state** coverage **extensions** that apply include:

- increased limits of coverage to meet the limits specified by a compulsory or financial responsibility law of the state where the auto is being used; and

- minimum amounts and types of other coverages, such as no fault, required by the state where the auto is being used.

The BAP Policy Lists 13 Exclusions

The BAP excludes liability coverage for

- expected or intended injury;

- contractual liability;

- workers compensation;

- employee indemnification and employer liability;

- fellow employees;

- care, custody, or control;

- handling of property before the property is moved from the place where it was accepted or after it is moved from where it was placed;

- movement of property by mechanical device;

- operations;

- completed operations;

- pollution;

- war; and

- racing.

A more detailed discussion of these **exclusions** follows.

Expected or Intended Injury Is Not Covered

The *Expected Or Intended Injury exclusion* is sometimes referred to as the *intentional acts exclusion*, but the intent is really to make clear the insuring agreement of the coverage that the policy only contemplates the ordinary definition of an *accident*, which is an unexpected and unintended event.

Assume that an insured ran over someone's foot with a covered auto. It may seem from the viewpoint of the injured party that the insured intended the injury and set out to run over his foot, but this is not what triggers the exclusion.

The exclusion only applies if the injury or damage in question is **expected or intended** from the standpoint of the insured (not any other party).

> ■ *ISO FORM*
>
> **1. Expected Or Intended Injury**
>
> "Bodily injury" or "property damage" expected or intended from the standpoint of the "insured".

Liability Assumed Under a Contract Is Usually Excluded

Some insureds assume liability, express or implied, under a written contract. For example, under most construction agreements with a municipality, the contractor agrees to hold the municipality harmless for any accidents arising out of the job.

The BAP excludes liability assumed under any contract or agreement with two exceptions:

- Damages assumed in an insured contract, provided that the bodily injury or property damage occurs subsequent to the execution of the contact or agreement

- Liability that the insured would have in the absence of the contract or agreement

> ■ *ISO FORM*
>
> **2. Contractual**
>
> Liability assumed under any contract or agreement.
>
> But this exclusion does not apply to liability for damages:
>
> **a.** Assumed in a contract or agreement that is an "insured contract" provided the "bodily injury" or "property damage" occurs subsequent to the execution of the contract or agreement; or
>
> **b.** That the "insured" would have in the absence of the contract or agreement.

The Cost of Doing Business is Excluded

In essence, the *Contractual exclusion* is intended to preclude coverage for the cost of doing business, such as a contract to landscape a lawn by a landscaping company or a contract to deliver packages by a messenger service.

Some contracts are incidental to the primary function of the business and qualify for coverage as **insured contracts** as defined in the policy. These are agreements in which the named insured agrees to assume the liability of another to pay for property damage or injuries to third parties, covered under the policy.

What Is an Insured Contract?

Real Life Application

Olympic Insurance Company leases several cars from Full-Service Auto. Under a hold harmless agreement, Olympic agrees to pay any costs or claims that may result from the agreement. It also agrees to hold Full-Service harmless for any liability resulting from injury or damage that results from the use of its autos during the lease.

Sarah, an adjuster for Olympic, uses one of the pool cars maintained under this agreement. On her way to an **arbitration**, she strikes and injures a pedestrian. The pedestrian sues Sarah, the Olympic Insurance Company, and Full-Service Auto.

4. Based on this information, is the agreement with Full-Service an insured contract?

Employment Exposures Are Better Covered Elsewhere

The BAP excludes **workers compensation, employee indemnification** and **employer's liability**. The BAP is not designed to address these two employment exposures.

These exposures are adequately covered under the stand-alone policies designed for each liability, i.e., the workers compensation policy for work-related employee or fellow employee injuries, and the employer's liability endorsement or policy to cover claims arising out of employment-related practices of the insured, such as the wrongful termination of an ex-employee.

Answer & Rationale

4. **Yes.** This is an example of an insured contract entered into by Olympic Insurance, incidental to its business operations, and under which terms it has agreed to **assume the tort liability** of Full-Service to pay for injury or damage to a third party.

■ *ISO FORM*

3. Workers' Compensation

Any obligation for which the "insured" or the "insured's" insurer may be held liable under any workers' compensation, disability benefits or unemployment compensation law or any similar law.

Fellow Employee Exclusion Bars Coverage for Employee Lawsuits

The *Employee Indemnification And Employer's Liability* exclusion potentially allows colleagues to sue insured employees when they cannot sue the named insured. That door for a potential lawsuit is closed by the Fellow Employee exclusion in the business auto, garage, and truckers policies.

The *Fellow Employee* exclusion eliminates liability coverage for an injury to an employee negligently caused by a fellow employee.

■ *ISO FORM*

But this exclusion does not apply to "bodily injury" to domestic "employees" not entitled to workers' compensation benefits or to liability assumed by the "insured" under an "insured contract". For the purposes of the Coverage Form, a domestic "employee" is a person engaged in household or domestic work performed principally in connection with a residence premises.

Owned Property Is Excluded

The *Care, Custody, and Control exclusion* applies to damage to property that is owned by, or in the possession, care, or control of the insured, under the terms of a legal obligation.

The BAP excludes any such damage, as this risk is specifically picked up under other policies. The Garage Coverage Form has garagekeepers legal liability as one of its primary coverage parts, and treats all cars in the **care, custody, and control** of the insured as covered autos for physical damage.

> ▪ *ISO FORM*
>
> ### 6. Care, Custody Or Control
>
> "Property damage" to or "covered pollution cost or expense" involving property owned or transported by the "insured" or in the "insured's" care, custody or control. But this exclusion does not apply to liability assumed under a sidetrack agreement.

Restricted Coverage for Damage Due to Handling of Property

Traditionally, the *Handling of Property exclusion* has been known as the loading and unloading exclusion, because liability coverage is excluded for any property damage or bodily injury which occurs in the process of loading or unloading property if the damage or injury occurs before leaving point A (the point of origination) or after arriving at point B (the intended destination). That damage would be covered under another policy, e.g., a CGL. However, damage that occurs in transit between origin and destination is covered under the BAP.

The CGL, which does not exclude damage to property while in the process of being loaded or offloaded but does exclude damage to property in transit between those two points, works with the BAP to dovetail on coverage gaps.

> ▪ *ISO FORM*
>
> ### 7. Handling Of Property
>
> "Bodily injury" or "property damage" resulting from the handling of property:
>
> **a.** Before it is moved from the place where it is accepted by the "insured" for movement into or onto the covered "auto"; or
>
> **b.** After it is moved from the covered "auto" to the place where it is finally delivered by the "insured".

Mobile Equipment Is Excluded

Two exclusions—*Movement of Property By Mechanical Device* and *Operations*—preclude coverage for property damage or bodily injury arising out of movement of property by mobile or mechanical equipment.

Again, damage to property while being transported from point A to the covered auto, and after it has been offloaded from the auto to destination point B by mechanical device, is not covered under the BAP because it is covered under the CGL.

The same is true of damage to property or bodily injury caused by the operation of mobile equipment, unless the mobile equipment is attached to a covered auto.

Mobile equipment is excluded from the BAP because it is included under the CGL.

> ■ *ISO FORM*
>
> ### 8. Movement Of Property By Mechanical Device
> "Bodily injury" or "property damage" resulting from the movement of property by a mechanical device (other than a hand truck) unless the device is attached to the covered "auto".

Completed Operations Is a Work-Product Exclusion

The BAP is not designed to financially compensate the insured for the risks inherent in doing business. However, it should protect the insured from having to bear the financial burden of property damage or bodily injury to third parties arising out of those **completed** operations.

The *Completed Operations exclusion* applies to liability for property damage or bodily injury arising out of any real or alleged defect in the insured's work, including any materials, parts, or equipment furnished in connection with that work or operations, or work or operations performed on behalf of the insured by someone else such as a subcontractor.

For example, assume a freight company uses plastic packing materials that melt in extreme heat. If books being transported are damaged by the melted packing materials, the damage to the books is covered, but the property damage to the packing material is not because this is a material furnished in connection with the insured's business.

> ■ *ISO FORM*
>
> **10.Completed Operations**
> "Bodily injury" or "property damage" arising out of your work after that work has been completed or abandoned.
>
> In this exclusion, your work means:
>
> **a.** Work or operations performed by you or on your behalf; and
>
> **b.** Materials, parts or equipment furnished in connection with such work or operations.

Leaking Oil, Fuel, or Other Substances May Be Covered

The *Pollution exclusion* precludes coverage for toxic and environmental hazards.

However, the Policy does afford coverage under Section II—Liability for remedial clean-up costs and property damage and bodily injury from an accident in a covered auto which results in an environmental spill. An example of this coverage is the escape of fuel caused by the overturn of a fuel truck.

If the collision is caused by the insured in a covered auto, the costs for the environmental clean-up would be considered as a covered pollution expense under Section II—Liability Coverage.

> ■ *ISO FORM*
>
> **11.Pollution**
> "Bodily injury" or "property damage" arising out of the actual, alleged or threatened discharge, dispersal, seepage, migration, release or escape of "pollutants":
>
> **a.** That are, or that are contained in any property that is:
>
> **(1)** Being transported or towed by, handled, or handled for movement into, onto or from, the covered "auto";
>
> **(2)** Otherwise in the course of transit by or on behalf of the "insured"; or
>
> **(3)** Being stored, disposed of, treated or processed in or upon the covered "auto";

The BAP Complements CGL Coverage

Some of the BAP's exclusions, such as handling of property and movement by a mechanical device, are intended to complement the coverage provided under the commercial general liability (CGL) policy.

In other words, the movement of property before loading onto a vehicle and movement by devices such as conveyor belts represent exposures covered under the CGL, not the BAP.

When properly coordinated, the BAP and CGL work to provide coverage needed by a typical insured without duplicating coverage or creating gaps.

Bodily Injury or Property Damage Due to War Is Excluded

Most insurance policies exclude war or acts of war because they are a catastrophic exposure and are, therefore, not insurable. The BAP is no exception.

The BAP excludes coverage for death or injury caused by acts of war. In this policy, the definition of war includes civil war, insurrection, rebellion, or revolution.

The exclusion applies only to liability assumed under a contract or agreement.

> ■ *ISO FORM*
>
> **12. War**
>
> "Bodily injury" or "property damage" due to war, whether or not declared, or any act or condition incident to war. War includes civil war, insurrection, rebellion or revolution. This exclusion applies only to liability assumed under a contract or agreement.

Racing Is Not Covered

The BAP excludes any covered automobile while it is being used in any professional or organized racing or demolition contest or stunt activity or while practicing for such an activity.

Insurance does not apply while the covered auto is being prepared for a racing, demolition, or stunt activity.

■ *ISO FORM*

13.Racing

Covered "autos" while used in any professional or organized racing or demolition contest or stunting activity, or while practicing for such contest or activity. This insurance also does not apply while that covered "auto" is being prepared for such a contest or activity.

■ SUMMARY

Only liability and physical damage coverage is included in the Business Auto Policy, and primary exclusions are similar to those found in the Commercial General Liability policy. However, with some exclusions, such as the Handling Property exclusion, the CGL dovetails with the BAP to fill in coverage gaps.

Next, we will review Section III—Physical Damage Coverage. The BAP's physical damage section includes comprehensive coverage, specified causes of loss coverage, and collision coverage.

■ UNIT 3 REVIEW QUESTIONS

1. Section II of the BAP provides which of the following coverages?

   A. Physical damage

   B. Workers compensation

   C. Liability

   D. None of the above

2. Which of the following is an insured under the Business Auto Policy?

   A. Permissive user of a covered auto

   B. The named insured on the policy while operating a covered auto

   C. Anyone who has permission to drive a covered auto and is not otherwise excluded as an insured

   D. All of the above

3. The expected or intended exclusion applies to liability for

   A. property damage only

   B. property damage or bodily injury, but only if it is expected or intended from the standpoint of the insured

   C. bodily injury only

   D. property damage or bodily injury, but only if it was expected or intended according to the one who is claiming injury or damage

   D. all of the above

4. The insured moves a table from an apartment and knocks over a lamp in the process, causing the bulb to shatter. The property damage to the lamp is probably

   A. covered under the BAP, if the table was already on the covered auto

   B. covered under the BAP, if the table was not yet on the covered auto

   C. not covered under the BAP

   D. covered under the homeowners policy

5. Under The Insuring Agreements for Section II—Liability, the insurance company has a duty to

   A. pay all damages and all pollution claims

   B. pay all claims and defend all suits

   C. pay all sums the insured becomes legally obligated to pay as damages for property damage or bodily injury, or a covered pollution cost or expense to which the policy applies, caused by an accident involving a covered auto

   D. All of the above

■ ANSWERS TO UNIT 3 QUESTIONS

1. **C.** Section II of the BAP provides liability coverage for property damage and bodily injury. Physical damage is covered under Section III—and workers compensation coverage is not contemplated by a commercial auto policy.

2. **D.** All categories meet the definition of an insured in the "Who Is An Insured" section of the Business Auto Policy, Liability Coverage—Section II.

3. **B.** Liability is excluded for property damage or bodily injury expected or intended from the standpoint of the insured, not the claimant. The intent of the policy is to cover accidents, or unexpected and unintended events. This is sometimes known as the intentional acts exclusion. This is not exactly correct, because even if the insured intends to act in a way certain to cause harm, courts have traditionally held that it is the specific injury or damage that must be intended, based on all of the facts and the circumstances of the case, before liability coverage will be precluded.

4. **A.** This tests the application of the Handling of Property, or loading and unloading exclusion. If the table was already on the covered auto, which is presumably a moving vehicle, then the lamp was probably also on the vehicle, which means the property damage occurred after the property was picked up for transit, but before it arrived at its final destination.

5. **C.** Choice C correctly encompasses the Insuring Agreements under Section II—Liability Coverage. There is no duty to pay all damages and no duty to pay pollution claims and there is no duty to pay all claims or defend all suits.

4

BAP Section III—Physical Damage

U nlike liability coverage that provides coverage for bodily injury and property damage to others arising out of the insured's operation of a vehicle, physical damage insurance provides coverage for physical damage to the insured's vehicle.

This unit will look at the Section III—Physical Damage Coverage of the Business Auto Policy.

When you have completed this unit, you should be able to:

Learning Objectives

- describe the physical damage coverages of the BAP;

- determine whether comprehensive, collision, or specified causes of loss applies to given loss situations;

- identify when coverage for towing and glass breakage apply;

- explain the coverage extensions applicable to Physical Damage Coverage;

- identify the exclusions that apply to this section; and

- recommend limits of insurance and deductibles.

■ ■ ■ ■ ■

■ INSURING AGREEMENTS

Unlike liability insurance that covers the insured's legal obligations for bodily injury or property damage to a third party, the primary purpose of auto physical damage coverage is to cover loss or damage to autos owned by the insured.

Under the BAP's Section III—Physical Damage Coverage, vehicles can be insured for comprehensive, specified causes of loss damage, or collision.

Physical damage coverage can also be written as a stand-alone policy using the Business Auto Physical Damage Coverage Form (CA 00 10). Coverage can also be purchased for autos that are hired, rented, or borrowed by the named insured.

Insureds May Select Coverage Options

Section III—Physical Damage Coverage has its own insuring agreements in the Coverage subsection. In Part A. Coverage, the insurer agrees to pay for loss to a covered auto or its equipment under the type of coverage selected by the insured.

Insureds may choose from four physical damage coverages:

- Comprehensive Coverage;

- Specified Causes of Loss Coverage;

- Collision Coverage; and

- Towing.

A numerical coverage symbol must be shown on the Business Auto Coverage Form Declarations (CA 00 02) to indicate the type of coverage selected for each covered auto. Coverage applies only if a coverage Symbol and premium appear on the Declarations.

Comprehensive Coverage Protects Against Most Losses

Comprehensive coverage is physical damage coverage that can be part of an automobile, garage, or truckers' policy.

It covers damage to the insured's vehicle from causes other than collision or overturn (which are insured separately under collision coverage). Comprehensive losses also include theft, vandalism or fire.

> ■ *ISO FORM*
>
> **A. Coverage**
> **1.** We will pay for "loss" to a covered "auto" or its equipment under:
> **a.** Comprehensive Coverage
> From any cause except:
> **(1)** The covered "auto's" collision with another object; or
> **(2)** The covered "auto's" overturn.

Collision Coverage Protects Against Overturn or Impact

Businesses may elect to insure covered autos against collision damage. This covers physical damage to the insured's vehicle caused by collision or overturn of the vehicle.

Collision coverage provides protection for physical damage to a covered auto caused by striking another object (not just another auto) or by a covered auto's overturn. A stationary vehicle is also covered if it is struck by another object.

The term *collision* is not defined in the policy, but courts have held the coverage is triggered by any impact with another object, regardless of speed, or the vehicle's overturn. In fact, collision coverage would apply for a covered auto that is parked when it is struck and damaged by some object.

Specified Causes of Loss Provides Narrower Coverage

The Specified Causes of Loss (CA 99 14) endorsement may be added to a business auto, garage or truckers' policy to provide physical damage coverage for the specific perils.

This coverage is narrower than comprehensive coverage and is therefore less expensive. The endorsement specifies the perils insured against and gives the insured the ability to reduce premiums by narrowing coverage for covered autos.

If elected, specified causes of loss coverage insures against loss caused by the following **perils**:

- Fire, lightning, or explosion

- Theft

- Windstorm, hail, or earthquake

- Flood

- Mischief or vandalism

- The sinking, burning, collision, or derailment of any conveyance transporting the covered auto (e.g., a ferry that sinks while transporting a covered auto)

Note that collision coverage is not included.

> ■ *ISO FORM*
>
> **b. Specified Causes Of Loss Coverage**
> Caused by:
> **(1)** Fire, lightning or explosion;
> **(2)** Theft;
> **(3)** Windstorm, hail or earthquake;
> **(4)** Flood;
> **(5)** Mischief or vandalism; or
> **(6)** The sinking, burning, collision or derailment of any conveyance transporting the "trailer".

Glass Breakage Is Subject to a Deductible

Glass breakage, hitting a bird or an animal, falling objects, and missiles are all covered under Comprehensive Coverage, if the policy provides that coverage. These perils are mentioned specifically to make it clear that insurance is provided under comprehensive rather than collision coverage because confusion often exists on that point.

If both the comprehensive and collision options are selected and a collision causes glass breakage, the insured may elect to have the glass covered under the collision option to avoid payment of two deductibles (one for comprehensive; one for collision).

> ■ *ISO FORM*
>
> If you carry Comprehensive Coverage for the damaged covered "auto", we will pay for the following under Comprehensive Coverage:
> **a.** Glass breakage;
> **b.** "Loss" caused by hitting a bird or animal; and
> **c.** "Loss" caused by falling objects or missiles.
> However, you have the option of having glass breakage caused by a covered "auto's" collision or overturn considered a "loss" under Collision Coverage.

Special Treatment Applies to Glass Breakage

Real Life Application

The following examples illustrate how glass breakage can be handled differently under the comprehensive and collision coverages.

An insured has comprehensive coverage with a $100 deductible and collision coverage with a $200 deductible. Assume the glass claim cost is $300.

Example 1

Glass is broken in an accident that causes no other damage to a covered auto. The insurer should cover the glass breakage claim under the comprehensive coverage because it has a lower deductible than collision coverage. The insured would pay $100.

Example 2

Glass is broken in an accident that also causes $800 in collision damage. The insurer can elect to cover the glass claim under the collision coverage. The insured pays $200 (the collision deductible) instead of $300, the amount for both deductibles.

Towing Coverage Applies Only to Private Passenger Autos

An optional automobile coverage can be added to the physical damage coverage that provides reimbursement up to a specified limit for towing or on-site labor costs.

If the insured purchases towing coverage, a limit appears on the declarations. Towing coverage only applies to private passenger autos.

Towing and labor charges are covered up to the selected limit for this coverage. All labor has to be performed at the place of disablement for labor charges to be paid.

> ■ *ISO FORM*
>
> **2. Towing**
> We will pay up to the limit shown in the Declarations for towing and labor costs incurred each time a covered "auto" of the private passenger type is disabled. However, the labor must be performed at the place of disablement.

Coverage Extension Granted for Transportation Expense

In the event of a stolen auto, transportation expenses are covered if the insured carries Comprehensive or Specified Causes of Loss Coverage.

The transportation expenses must be incurred because of the total theft of a covered private passenger auto. Coverage is limited to $20 per day for temporary substitute transportation, up to a maximum of $600.

Payments are made available 48 hours after the theft and end when the covered auto is returned to use or the insurer pays for the auto theft claim.

> ■ *ISO FORM*
>
> **a. Transportation Expenses**
> We will pay up to $20 per day to a maximum of $600 for temporary transportation expense incurred by you because of the total theft of a covered "auto" of the private passenger type. We will pay only for those covered "autos" for which you carry either Comprehensive or Specified Causes of Loss Coverage. We will pay for temporary transportation expenses incurred during the period beginning 48 hours after the theft and ending, regardless of the policy's expiration, when the covered "auto" is returned to use or we pay for its "loss".

■ PHYSICAL DAMAGE EXCLUSIONS

Most insurance policies include exclusions that eliminate coverage for specific hazards, perils, property, or locations. Exclusions name what the insurer does not intend to cover under the contract.

Generally, insurers include policy exclusions to:

- eliminate coverage for uninsurable loss exposures;

- assist in the management of moral and morale hazards;

- reduce the likelihood of coverage duplications;

- eliminate coverage not needed by the purchaser;

- eliminate coverage requiring special treatment;

- assist in maintaining premiums at a reasonable level.

Exclusions Describe What the Insurer Does Not Cover

The BAP **Exclusions** section begins with the insurer's statement that it will not pay for loss caused by or resulting from a number of events. No physical damage coverage is allowed for damage to covered autos arising from:

- nuclear explosion, radiation, or hazard;

- war or military action;

- racing or demolition contests or stunting, including prep work for competition; or

- wear and tear, freezing, mechanical or electrical breakdown, or blowouts, punctures, or other road damage to tires.

In addition, the BAP does not cover loss to:

- tape decks or other sound-reproducing equipment unless permanently installed in a covered auto; or

- tapes, records, or other sound-reproducing devices designed for use with sound-reproducing equipment.

Damage Caused by Normal Use Is Not Covered

The policy will not cover losses arising from wear and tear, freezing, mechanical or electrical breakdown, or blowouts, punctures, and other road damage to tires.

The above losses are generally a result of normal wear and tear or owner neglect. They are excluded unless they result from other covered loses.

For example, if a covered auto is stolen and then abandoned in cold weather, freezing damage could occur. In this situation, loss due to freezing would be covered because the damage resulted from theft, which is a covered loss.

Loss to Sound Equipment Is Excluded

The following exclusions apply to sound equipment:

- No coverage for tapes, records, discs, or similar audio, visual, or data electronic devices designed for use with audio, visual, or data electronic equipment (can be added by endorsement)

- No coverage for any device designed or used to detect speed-measuring equipment such as radar and laser detectors

- No coverage for electronic equipment, whether or not permanently installed, that transmits or receives audio, visual, or data signals and that is not designed solely for the reproduction of sound (can be added by endorsement)

■ *ISO FORM*

4. We will not pay for "loss" to any of the following:

a. Tapes, records, discs or other similar audio, visual or data electronic devices designed for use with audio, visual or data electronic equipment.

b. Any device designed or used to detect speed measuring equipment such as radar or laser detectors and any jamming apparatus intended to elude or disrupt speed measurement equipment.

c. Any electronic equipment, without regard to whether this equipment is permanently installed, that receives or transmits audio, visual or data signals and that is not designed solely for the reproduction of sound.

d. Any accessories used with the electronic equipment described in Paragraph c. above.

Permanently Installed Sound Equipment Is Covered

The Sound Equipment, Similar Devices and Related Equipment Exclusion does not apply to equipment that is permanently installed upon the auto, designed for use only with the auto's electrical system, and designed solely for the reproduction of sound.

The BAP covers any other electronic equipment necessary for the normal operation of the vehicle.

■ *ISO FORM*

Exclusions 4.c. and 4.d. do not apply to:

a. Equipment designed solely for the reproduction of sound and accessories used with such equipment, provided such equipment is permanently installed in the covered "auto" at the time of the "loss" or such equipment is removable from a housing unit which is permanently installed in the covered "auto" at the time of the "loss", and such equipment is designed to be solely operated by use of the power from the "auto's" electrical system, in or upon the covered "auto"; or

Dimunition in Value Is Not Covered

The BAP defines diminution in value as the actual or perceived loss in market value or resale value that results from a direct and accidental loss.

For example, assume a covered vehicle is stolen, damaged, and recovered. After the damage is repaired, the insured no longer feels safe driving the car and wishes to sell it. The insured feels the theft and resulting damage has decreased the car's resale value by $5,000.

The insurer will not pay for this loss in market or resale value.

■ OTHER PHYSICAL DAMAGE CONSIDERATIONS

When a covered physical damage loss occurs, the insurer will pay the lesser of:

- the **actual cash value (ACV)** of the damaged or stolen property; or

- the cost of repairing or replacing it with equipment of like kind and quality.

The company will make an adjustment for depreciation and physical condition in determining ACV in the event of a total loss.

If a repair or replacement results in better than like kind or quality, the policy will not allow for the betterment.

> ■ *ISO FORM*
>
> **2.** An adjustment for depreciation and physical condition will be made in determining actual cash value in the event of a total "loss".
>
> **3.** If a repair or replacement results in better than like kind or quality, we will not pay for the amount of the betterment.

Separate Deductibles Apply for Each Covered Auto

A separate deductible applies for each covered auto. Any loss settlement is reduced by the amount of the deductible shown in the Declarations Page.

However, if a covered comprehensive loss is caused by fire or lightning, the deductible shown in the Declarations does not apply.

> ■ *ISO FORM*
>
> **D. Deductible**
> For each covered "auto", our obligation to pay for, repair, return or replace damaged or stolen property will be reduced by the applicable deductible shown in the Declarations. Any Comprehensive Coverage deductible shown in the Declarations does not apply to "loss" caused by fire or lightning.

Form Covers Physical Damage Only

The Business Auto Physical Damage Coverage Form (CA 00 10) is a limited use form. It is a stand-alone policy for physical damage only and does not provide liability coverage.

This form is used in situations where the insured only wants to insure vehicles for physical damage and does not want to pick up the liability exposure.

The language describing physical damage in the Physical Damage Form is the same as in the Section IV—Physical Damage Coverage in the BAP.

BAP and Physical Damage Coverage Form Have Common Provisions

There are common provisions in both the BAP and Business Auto Physical Damage Coverage forms. Both business auto forms use coverage symbols matched to covered autos as in all commercial auto forms, but the numerical sequence is different because liability coverage is not provided.

The Business Auto Physical Damage Coverage Form only has five covered auto designation symbols:

- Symbol 1—Owned autos only

- Symbol 2—Owned private passenger autos only

- Symbol 3—Owned autos other than private passenger autos only

- Symbol 4—Specifically described autos

- Symbol 5—Hired autos only

Coverage is selected on the basis of the appropriate auto designation and that symbol is then placed on the Business Auto Declarations. Physical Damage Exclusions are the same and Definitions are tailored to the limited coverage.

To preview the Business Auto Physical Damage Coverage stand-alone form, turn to page 253 in the Appendix.

Coverage Extension for Loss of Use Expenses

When an insured elects to use the Business Auto Physical Damage Coverage Form, the insured may choose one of three loss of use expenses: Other Than Collision, Specified Causes of Loss, or Collision.

The insurer will pay expenses for loss of use of the hired, rented, or borrowed vehicle without a driver, provided the insured becomes legally liable for these costs under a written contract or agreement.

These expenses will be paid if the loss is caused by:

- Other Than Collision and the Dec Page shows comprehensive coverage for any auto (Symbol 1);

- Specified Causes of Loss and the Dec Page indicates such coverage for any auto (Symbol 1); or

- Collision and the Dec Page indicates collision coverage for any auto (Symbol 1).

The most the company will pay for the loss of use of a hired or borrowed vehicle is $20 per day, to a maximum of $600.

■ **ISO FORM**

b. Loss Of Use Expenses

For Hired Auto Physical Damage, we will pay expenses for which an "insured" becomes legally responsible to pay for loss of use of a vehicle rented or hired without a driver, under a written rental contract or agreement. We will pay for loss of use expenses if caused by:

(1) Other than collision only if the Declarations indicate that Comprehensive Coverage is provided for any covered "auto";

(2) Specified Causes Of Loss only if the Declarations indicate that Specified Causes Of Loss Coverage is provided for any covered "auto"; or

(3) Collision only if the Declarations indicate that Collision Coverage is provided for any covered "auto".

However, the most we will pay for any expenses for loss of use is $20 per day, to a maximum of $600.

■ SUMMARY

The BAP Section III—Physical Damage Coverage section describes coverage for comprehensive, collision, specified causes of loss, towing, glass breakage, and coverage extensions for transportation expenses and loss of use expenses.

Physical Damage Coverage insulates the insured from the undue financial hardship arising from the cost to repair covered autos. With a program of insurance tailored for the specific needs of the insured, such financial burdens can be avoided.

The next unit will look at Section IV—Business Auto Conditions.

■ UNIT 4 REVIEW QUESTIONS

1. Speed is a requirement of collision coverage.

   A. True
   B. False

2. Specified Causes of Loss coverage means

   A. only collision coverage is covered
   B. only physical damage from specified perils is covered
   C. only physical damage from non-specified risks is covered
   D. none of the above

3. Specified causes of loss will cover the insured for overturn if the policy does not specify collision.

   A. True
   B. False

4. The insured has a BAP that covers comprehensive and collision, and has a windshield damage loss. The damage takes place 30 miles from the insured's place of business and the insured rents a vehicle to get back to the office. The rental expense is not covered.

   A. True
   B. False

■ **ANSWERS TO UNIT 4 REVIEW QUESTIONS**

1. **B.** False. Provided there is a collision with another object resulting in damage to the covered auto, the collision coverage is triggered regardless of speed.

2. **B.** Physical Damage coverage is afforded for only those Specified Causes of Loss, or specifically named "perils."

3. **B.** False. Upset or overturn of the vehicles is specifically covered by collision and excluded from specified causes of loss.

4. **B.** False. The rental expense for a substitute vehicle is provided under the Extensions of Coverage as a substitute transportation expense.

5

Conditions, Definitions and Endorsements

T his lesson will continue the review of the BAP with a discussion of the remaining policy sections and some common endorsements. Section IV—Conditions, the requirements imposed on the insured and/or insurer in order for a claim to be paid or the insurance to remain in effect, will be covered first.

Also, some of the most important definitions found in Section V—Definitions will be reviewed and, finally, some of the common endorsements to the Business Auto Policy will be examined.

When you have completed this unit, you should be able to:

Learning Objectives

- describe the conditions that apply to the BAP;

- recognize when a condition is applicable;

- discuss the general conditions;

- distinguish between the loss conditions and the general policy conditions;

- identify and discuss primary definitions; and

- recognize and explain common BAP endorsements.

■ ■ ■ ■ ■

■ SECTION IV—BUSINESS AUTO CONDITIONS

Insurance **contracts** are conditional contracts. The contract remains in effect and the insurer must fulfill its promises to pay for losses only if the insured fulfills the obligations specified in the contract. Among other obligations, the insured must remit a timely premium to the insurer, report losses in a timely manner, and cooperate with claims settlement.

The policy **conditions** explain the duties and responsibilities that apply to the parties to the contract: the insured and the insurer. Some conditions apply to the entire policy; others only apply to specific coverages.

Some Conditions Apply to Entire Policy

The Common Policy Conditions (IL 00 17 11 98) Form must be attached as part of the Commercial Package Policy (CPP). It contains the conditions that apply to all coverage parts that make up the entire policy.

The Common Policy Conditions address policy cancellation, changes, insurer's inspections, premium payment, and **transfer of rights and duties**.

BAP Adds Two Types of Conditions in Section IV

In addition to the Common Policy Conditions, Section IV—Business Auto Conditions of the Business Auto Coverage Form adds two additional condition sections:

- loss conditions; and

- general policy conditions.

These sections indicate the general rules or procedures that the insurer and insured agree to follow under the contract.

Loss Conditions Apply to the Insurer and/or Insured

The five Loss Conditions in the BAP pertain only to situations that might arise when a loss occurs. The Loss Conditions section outlines:

- Appraisal;

- Duties in the Event of Accident, Claim, Suit or Loss;

- Legal Action Against Us;

- Loss Payment—Physical Damage Coverages; and

- Transfer of Rights of Recover Against Others to Us.

A brief discussion of each of these loss conditions follows.

An Appraisal Settles the Amount of the Loss

Under the *Appraisal For Physical Damage Loss* condition, the BAP gives the insured and the insurer the right to call for an **appraisal** if the amount of a covered loss cannot be agreed upon.

The following occurs if either party demands an appraisal for physical damage loss.

- The insured and the insurer each select an appraiser.

- The appraisers or a local court select an umpire.

- An agreement on the amount of loss by two of the above is binding on all parties.

- The insured and the insurer pay the cost of their own appraiser and share equally in the remaining costs of the appraisal, including the umpire's charges.

A decision by any two of the three prescribes a settlement. The arbitration clause binds both parties to this procedure, as well as to the final decision.

An appraisal only involves disagreements between an insured and insurer over loss valuation. For example, the insurer believes a stolen auto is valued at $4,500 and the insured is seeking a payment of $8,000. The appraisal condition applies only to valuation disagreements, not coverage questions.

■ *ISO FORM*

1. Appraisal For Physical Damage Loss

If you and we disagree on the amount of "loss", either may demand an appraisal of the "loss". In this event, each party will select a competent appraiser. The two appraisers will select a competent and impartial umpire. The appraisers will state separately the actual cash value and amount of "loss". If they fail to agree, they will submit their differences to the umpire. A decision agreed to by any two will be binding. Each party will:

a. Pay its chosen appraiser; and

b. Bear the other expenses of the appraisal and umpire equally.

If we submit to an appraisal, we will still retain our right to deny the claim.

An Insured Must Provide Prompt Notification of Loss

One of the insured's most important obligations under the insurance contract relates to the *Duties in The Event of Accident, Claim, Suit or Loss* condition. An insured must give the insurer or its representative prompt notification of loss. The policy does not explain what is meant by *prompt notification*, but it is generally construed to mean "as soon as possible after the loss."

The notice, which may be verbal or in writing, must include details of the loss including:

- how and when it occurred;

- the names and addresses of the insured; and

- injured parties and witnesses (if possible).

■ *ISO FORM*

a. In the event of "accident", claim, "suit" or "loss", you must give us or our authorized representative prompt notice of the "accident" or "loss". Include:

(1) How, when and where the "accident" or "loss" occurred;

(2) The "insured's" name and address; and

(3) To the extent possible, the names and addresses of any injured persons and witnesses.

Insured Has a Duty to Cooperate With Authorities

Any insured must immediately send the insurer any demand, summons, or legal notice received concerning the suit or claim. In addition, the insured must cooperate with the insurer in settling or defending the suit or claim.

An insured must also allow the insurer to obtain medical reports and other information pertaining to the claim and submit to examination by a physician of the insurer's choice (at the insurer's expense), if requested by the insurer.

The *Loss* conditions section indicates that an insured may not assume any obligation or responsibility for loss or make any payments or incur any expenses without the insurer's consent. An insured must allow the insurer to determine if responsibility for loss exists. An insured's attempt to pay or accept responsibility for loss may hinder the insurer's ability to properly defend the insured. An insured may forfeit coverage if these conditions are breached.

> ■ **ISO FORM**
>
> **b.** Additionally, you and any other involved "insured" must:
>
> **(1)** Assume no obligation, make no payment or incur no expense without our consent, except at the "insured's" own cost.
>
> **(2)** Immediately send us copies of any request, demand, order, notice, summons or legal paper received concerning the claim or "suit".
>
> **(3)** Cooperate with us in the investigation or settlement of the claim or defense against the "suit".
>
> **(4)** Authorize us to obtain medical records or other pertinent information.

Additional Loss Conditions Apply to Physical Damage Losses

Additional Loss Conditions apply if a physical damage loss occurs. An insured must:

- inform the police if a theft occurs;

- take steps to protect the auto from further damage;

- permit the insurer to inspect the vehicle before repairs are made; and

- submit to examination under oath and submit a signed statement attesting to the answers of that examination.

> ■ **ISO FORM**
>
> **c.** If there is "loss" to a covered "auto" or its equipment you must also do the following:
>
> **(1)** Promptly notify the police if the covered "auto" or any of its equipment is stolen.
>
> **(2)** Take all reasonable steps to protect the covered "auto" from further damage. Also keep a record

> of your expenses for consideration in the settlement of the claim.
>
> **(3)** Permit us to inspect the covered "auto" and records proving the "loss" before its repair or disposition.
>
> **(4)** Agree to examinations under oath at our request and give us a signed statement of your answers.

Insureds May Force the Insurer to Comply With Its Obligations

Insureds may bring court action to force compliance if the insurer does not comply with its obligations under the BAP. However, the BAP's *Legal Action Against Us* condition indicates that legal action may not take place until:

- all the terms of the BAP have been fulfilled; and

- there has been a final court judgment or a settlement agreed to by the insurer, if a liability loss is involved.

The BAP defends and pays on behalf of an insured, but the insurance company is not a direct party to any legal action. The conditions state that no one can name the insurer in any legal action involving a loss under the BAP. Because juries might consider an insurer to be a source of almost unlimited funds, naming the insurer in a lawsuit could encourage juries to increase the amount of judgments levied against insureds.

■ *ISO FORM*

> No one may bring a legal action against us under this Coverage Form until:
>
> **a.** There has been full compliance with all the terms of this Coverage Form; and
>
> **b.** Under Liability Coverage, we agree in writing that the "insured" has an obligation to pay or until the amount of that obligation has finally been determined by judgment after trial. No one has the right under this policy to bring us into an action to determine the "insured's" liability.

Insurer Has Physical Damage Loss Payment Options

Under the *Loss Payment—Physical Damage Coverages* condition, the insurer has three loss payment options with regard to physical damage losses. The insurer may either:

- pay for, repair, or replace any damaged or stolen property;

- pay for the return of stolen property and be responsible for its repair upon its return; or

- take all or part of damaged or stolen property at an agreed or appraised value.

The insured does not generally have the right to select one of these options. For example, the insured cannot choose a cash settlement over repairing the vehicle.

■ *ISO FORM*

At our option we may:

a. Pay for, repair or replace damaged or stolen property;

b. Return the stolen property, at our expense. We will pay for any damage that results to the "auto" from the theft; or

c. Take all or any part of the damaged or stolen property at an agreed or appraised value.

If we pay for the "loss", our payment will include the applicable sales tax for the damaged or stolen property.

Right to Recovery Is Transferred to the Insurer

The final Loss Condition, *Transfer Of Rights Of Recovery Against Others To Us*, explains the insurer's rights when it makes payment for a loss that was caused by someone other than an insured. This condition is referred to as the **subrogation clause** in many insurance policies.

Subrogation is an insurer's substitution in place of the insured in regard to a claim against a third party for **indemnification** of a loss paid by the insurer. The insurer assumes the legal claim of another and, because it has paid a liability or obligation of the insured, has the right to be indemnified by the third party.

■ *ISO FORM*

5. Transfer Of Rights Of Recovery Against Others To Us

If any person or organization to or for whom we make payment under this Coverage Form has rights to recover damages from another, those rights are transferred to us. That person or organization must do everything necessary to secure our rights and must do nothing after "accident" or "loss" to impair them.

Insurer Assumes the Insured's Right to Recover

Real Life Application

Jim is driving Ace's truck when another truck fails to stop at a stop sign and collides with him. Ace's truck suffers $4,000 in damage. The owner of the other truck denies responsibility and refuses to pay to repair Ace's vehicle.

1. Does Ace have coverage under its BAP for this loss?

Loss Conditions Are the Policy's List of Rules

Loss conditions list the rules by which an insured and the insurer must abide. The major requirements of an insured are to report the loss in a timely manner, protect the property from further damage, and cooperate with the insurer in loss settlement activities.

The exact nature of the required cooperation depends on the type of loss that has occurred.

General Conditions Apply to All Policy Sections

In addition to the Loss conditions in Section IV, there are eight General Conditions in the BAP:

- Bankruptcy

- Concealment, Misrepresentation, or Fraud

- Liberalization

Answer & Rationale

1. Yes. Because Ace has physical damage coverage, Ace's insurance pays for the repairs. Ace's insurer assumes Ace's right to collect the $4,000 from the other truck's owner.

- No Benefit to Bailee—Physical Damage Coverages

- Other Insurance

- Premium Audit

- Policy Period, Coverage Territory

- Two or More Coverage Forms or Policies Issued by Us

Bankruptcy Does Not Relieve the Insurer of Its Responsibilities

Bankruptcy is a legal proceeding in federal court in which a person or company can be released or discharged from all or most of their debts.

The BAP's *Bankruptcy* condition stipulates that the bankruptcy or insolvency of an insured (or an insured's estate) will not affect the insurance company's responsibility under the BAP. The insurer must continue to investigate, defend, and otherwise provide coverage without regard to an insured's financial capabilities.

■ *ISO FORM*

1. Bankruptcy

Bankruptcy or insolvency of the "insured" or the "insured's" estate will not relieve us of any obligations under this Coverage Form.

Insured's Dishonesty May Void the Contract

The *Concealment, Misrepresentation, Or Fraud* condition protects the insurer against an insured's dishonesty.

The BAP is void if an insured attempts to defraud the insurer (e.g., submitting fraudulent claims or inflating the value of items involved in a claim). Coverage is also void if an insured intentionally conceals (e.g., fails to tell the insurer of past losses) or misrepresents (e.g., does not tell the truth about driving records of employees) material facts pertaining to the policy, the covered autos, or the insured's interest in the autos.

The insurer may void (or cancel) coverage if an insured is not entirely truthful about important facts related to the BAP.

> ■ *ISO FORM*
>
> ### 2. Concealment, Misrepresentation Or Fraud
>
> This Coverage Form is void in any case of fraud by you at any time as it relates to this Coverage Form. It is also void if you or any other "insured", at any time, intentionally conceal or misrepresent a material fact concerning:
>
> **a.** This Coverage Form;
>
> **b.** The covered "auto";
>
> **c.** Your interest in the covered "auto"; or
>
> **d.** A claim under this Coverage Form.

The Insurer May Revise the Coverage Form

Insurance companies periodically alter their insurance contracts. Under the terms of the *Liberalization* condition, the change is considered to be a part of all outstanding policies with the same form number, if the change does not require any additional premium.

If the insurer expands coverage and charges an additional premium, the insured must give permission or the insurer cannot change the policy before renewal. If a policy is changed to restrict coverage, that restriction does not apply to the insured until renewal.

> ■ *ISO FORM*
>
> ### 3. Liberalization
>
> If we revise this Coverage Form to provide more coverage without additional premium charge, your policy will automatically provide the additional coverage as of the day the revision is effective in your state.

Bailees Are Legally Responsible for Property in Their Care

An insured may have property in the possession of others for repair, storage, or other reason. A **bailee** is a party in temporary possession of an insured's property for such activities and is responsible for keeping the insured's property safe.

Under the *No Benefit To Bailee—Physical Damage Coverage* condition, the BAP will not provide coverage for any person or organization that holds, stores, or transports property for an insured for a fee. For example, the insured takes a covered auto in for repair. While the auto is in the repair shop, the owner of the shop carelessly sets fire to the building, causing damage to the covered auto. Coverage under the insured's BAP would not protect the **bailee** (the shop owner) who is legally responsible for the loss.

Bailees should have their own commercial property policy to respond to situations where an insured's property is damaged. Bailees cannot expect the insured's BAP to protect them.

■ *ISO FORM*

4. No Benefit To Bailee – Physical Damage Coverages

We will not recognize any assignment or grant any coverage for the benefit of any person or organization holding, storing or transporting property for a fee regardless of any other provision of this Coverage Form.

More Than One Policy May Be Involved

More than one insurance policy may respond to a loss involving an insured's vehicles. The BAP's *Other Insurance* condition describes how the BAP responds when this occurs.

- BAP coverage is primary (pays first) for any auto owned by and covered under the policy for the insured.

- BAP coverage is excess when applied to nonowned autos.

For example, a business owner lends his company car to a neighbor who also has a BAP. The neighbor's policy includes coverage for nonowned autos. Should a loss occur, the auto owner's BAP would be primary and the neighbor's policy would be excess.

■ *ISO FORM*

5. Other Insurance

a. For any covered "auto" you own, this Coverage Form provides primary insurance. For any covered "auto" you don't own, the insurance provided by this Coverage Form is excess over any other collectible insurance. However, while a covered "auto" which is a "trailer" is connected to another vehicle, the Liability Coverage this Coverage Form provides for the "trailer" is:

> **(1)** Excess while it is connected to a motor vehicle you do not own.
>
> **(2)** Primary while it is connected to a covered "auto" you own.

Other Insurance Condition Covers Trailers on Primary or Excess Basis

If an insured tows a trailer, it is covered on a primary basis when connected to a vehicle insured on the insured's BAP. If the trailer is connected to a nonowned vehicle, it is covered on an excess basis.

If the insured loans the trailer to another, the insurance on the borrower's vehicle is primary. Not all types or sizes of trailers are automatically covered by the BAP. General utility trailers are covered; others may have to be added by endorsement.

Hired Auto Physical Damage Coverage for Covered Autos

Hired Auto Physical Damage coverage provides coverage for damage to automobiles that are leased, rented, hired, or borrowed by the insured or its employees for business purposes. This coverage is usually purchased by an organization whose employees rent cars frequently, making it unnecessary to purchase collision damage waiver coverage from the rental car company. The autos must be rented in the organization's name and these vehicles are covered autos under the BAP.

Autos leased, hired, rented, or borrowed with a driver are not intended to be covered under Hired Auto Physical Damage coverage. The owner of such vehicles is responsible for insuring it for physical damage. However, as stated above, a vehicle that is leased, hired, rented, or borrowed without a driver is deemed a covered auto.

Other Insurance Condition Protects Insured and Insurer

An insured may enter into a contract with another to assume responsibility for the other party's actions. The insured's contractual assumption of obligations associated with the use of a business automobile can be covered by the BAP. The BAP's coverage is primary for any liability assumed under an insured contract (as defined in the policy).

Finally, the Other Insurance condition addresses situations in which more than one coverage form or policy applies to the same loss. Whether the BAP is primary or excess, the BAP pays only its own share on a *pro rata* basis.

> ### ▪ *ISO FORM*
>
> **d.** When this Coverage Form and any other Coverage Form or policy covers on the same basis, either excess or primary, we will pay only our share. Our share is the proportion that the Limit of Insurance of our Coverage Form bears to the total of the limits of all the Coverage Forms and policies covering on the same basis.

Multiple Policies Pay Proportionate Share of Loss

Policy A has a limit of $100,000 and Policy B a limit of $300,000 for a total amount of $400,000. A $40,000 loss occurs.

Company A pays 1/4 of the loss (A's limit/total limit available = $100,000/$400,000) or $10,000 and B pays 3/4 (B's limit/total limit available = $300,000/$400,000) or $30,000.

Other insurance provisions of the BAP are important and should be discussed with the insured.

Failure to do so may cause misconceptions on the insured's part, particularly regarding nonowned auto coverage.

Insured's Premiums May Be Adjusted to Reflect Exposure

Although the BAP is issued with an estimated premium based on the information provided at the time of application, the insurance company has the right to adjust the insured's premiums to reflect the actual exposure. The **Premium Audit** condition allows the insurer to collect information about:

- additional vehicles;

- proper rating of existing vehicles; and

- other information pertinent to premium determination.

Premiums may be adjusted either up or down.

> ■ *ISO FORM*
>
> ### 6. Premium Audit
>
> **a.** The estimated premium for this Coverage Form is based on the exposures you told us you would have when this policy began. We will compute the final premium due when we determine your actual exposures. The estimated total premium will be credited against the final premium due and the first Named Insured will be billed for the balance, if any. The due date for the final premium or retrospective premium is the date shown as the due date on the bill.

BAP Coverage Territory Is Limited

The BAP policy period is stated in the Declarations. The **Policy Period, Coverage Territory** condition states that accidents and losses that apply under the BAP are provided during the policy period in the coverage territory. According to this condition, the BAP policy territory is:

- the United States, its territories, and possessions;

- Puerto Rico;

- Canada; and

- anywhere in the world if:

  - a private passenger auto is leased, hired, or rented without a driver for 30 days or less and

  - the insured becomes responsible for a suit brought in the US, its territories and possessions, Canada, and Puerto Rico.

Accidents involving a covered auto while being transported between locations in the coverage territory are also covered. Losses occurring outside the policy territory are not covered by the BAP.

■ ISO FORM

The coverage territory is:

a. The United States of America;

b. The territories and possessions of the United States of America;

c. Puerto Rico;

d. Canada; and

e. Anywhere in the world if:

(1) A covered "auto" of the private passenger type is leased, hired, rented or borrowed without a driver for a period of 30 days or less; and

(2) The "insured's" responsibility to pay damages is determined in a "suit" on the merits, in the United States of America, the territories and possessions of the United States of America, Puerto Rico, or Canada or in a settlement we agree to.

Stacking of Coverage Limits Is Prohibited

It is possible for an insured to be covered by more than one policy issued by the same insurer for the same loss. Under the *Two Or More Coverage Forms Or Policies Issued By Us* condition, the maximum liability of the insurer will be the highest limit available under any single policy.

This provision attempts to prohibit the stacking of coverage limits when more than one policy issued by the same insurer applies to a single loss.

■ ISO FORM

8. Two Or More Coverage Forms Or Policies Issued By Us

If this Coverage Form and any other Coverage Form or policy issued to you by us or any company affiliated with us apply to the same "accident", the aggregate maximum Limit of Insurance under all the Coverage Forms or policies shall not exceed the highest applicable Limit of Insurance under any one Coverage

> Form or policy. This condition does not apply to any Coverage Form or policy issued by us or an affiliated company specifically to apply as excess insurance over this Coverage Form.

■ SECTION V—DEFINITIONS

In response to complaints from insureds and the courts that the terms used in insurance policies were not clearly defined, the insurance industry includes a policy section called **Definitions** in almost every insurance policy.

Although the section does not define every term used in the policy, it defines the most important, frequently used terms. When a defined term is used in an ISO form, it appears in quotation marks each time it appears.

The following pages discuss the more important definitions. It is important, however, to read and understand each definition in this section.

Definition of "Insured" Varies by Policy Section

The BAP's **Section V—Definitions** contains 17 definitions. First, we'll look at the definition of who is an insured under the BAP. According to the Definitions section:

"Insured" means any person or organization qualifying as an insured in the Who Is An Insured provision of the applicable coverage.

In other words, the definition of the term insured may change depending on the coverage section. It is important to carefully read each coverage section to understand its provisions.

The definition goes on to explain that the coverage afforded under the policy applies separately to each insured who is seeking coverage or against whom a claim or suit is brought. However, the most the policy will pay is the Limit of Liability shown on the Declarations Page.

■ *ISO FORM*

G. "Insured" means any person or organization qualifying as an insured in the Who Is An Insured provision of the applicable coverage. Except with respect to the Limit of Insurance, the coverage afforded applies separately to each insured who is seeking coverage or against whom a claim or "suit" is brought.

How Much Will the Policy Cover?

Real Life Application

An employee of the named insured, driving a covered delivery truck, runs a stop sign and is struck by another delivery truck. Both vehicles explode, injuring both drivers and several pedestrians. In addition, several parked cars and the city-owned park suffer damage. In the weeks that follow, several lawsuits are filed against the named insured and its employees. The named insured is covered by a BAP with limits of $500,000. In total, 10 people and the city file lawsuits.

2. Assuming that the named insured is found legally liable and the court awards $200,000 for each of the injured parties, what will the insurer pay?

Some Pollution Cost or Expense Is Covered

As previously discussed, pollution is one the BAP's Section II—Liability exclusions. Pollutants include any solid, liquid, gas, or thermal contaminant, including smoke, vapor, soot, fumes, acids, alkalis, chemicals, or waste.

The BAP provides some limited liability coverage for covered pollution cost or expense if there is other bodily injury or property damage by the same accident to which the insurance applies. For example, when gasoline is discharged from a vehicle after an accident, the cost of removing the fuel and cleaning the area is covered.

> ■ *ISO FORM*
>
> **L.** "Pollutants" means any solid, liquid, gaseous or thermal irritant or contaminant, including smoke, vapor, soot, fumes, acids, alkalis, chemicals and waste. Waste includes materials to be recycled, reconditioned or reclaimed.

"Accident" Includes Continuous or Repeated Exposures

Many insurance policies define an accident as "a sudden, unplanned, and unexpected event, not under the control of the insured, resulting in injury or damage." However, under the BAP, definition is broader.

Answer & Rationale

2. In this case the court will award a total of $2,200,000. Although the coverage afforded under the policy applied separately to each insured who is seeking coverage or against whom a claim or suit is brought, it is limited to $500,000, the policy's Limit of Liability.

Therefore, the named insured is responsible for paying the remaining $1,700,000 out-of-pocket expenses.

> *"Accident" includes continuous or repeated exposure to the same conditions resulting in "bodily injury" or "property damage."*

For example, a covered truck making repeated deliveries to a single location damages a parking lot due to its heavy deliveries. Because the damage was caused by an accident as defined in the BAP, the policy would provide coverage for repairs.

Government Required Clean-Up Is Covered

Covered pollution cost or expense provides coverage for the expense an insured incurs because of a government entity's requirement to clean up pollution. Coverage includes any request, demand, or order, or a claim or suit by a government authority demanding that the insured monitor, clean up, remove, contain, treat, detoxify, neutralize, or in any way respond to the effects of pollution.

Coverage applies in addition to any coverage for bodily injury or property damage provided because of the exception to the pollution exclusion.

> ■ *ISO FORM*
>
> **D.** "Covered pollution cost or expense" means any cost or expense arising out of:
> 1. Any request, demand, order or statutory or regulatory requirement; or
> 2. Any claim or "suit" by or on behalf of a governmental authority demanding that the "insured" or others test for, monitor, clean up, remove, contain, treat, detoxify or neutralize, or in any way respond to, or assess the effects of "pollutants".

Definition Follows Liability Section Exclusions

The pollution exclusion provides no coverage for the cost or transport, handling, storage, treatment, or disposal of pollutants.

Exceptions apply to fuels, lubricants, fluids and gases that escape from the autos normal operating systems.

> ■ *ISO FORM*
>
> "Covered pollution cost or expense" does not include any cost or expense arising out of the actual, alleged or threatened discharge, dispersal, seepage, migration, release or escape of "pollutants":

> **a.** That are, or that are contained in any property that is:
>
> **(1)** Being transported or towed by, handled, or handled for movement into, onto or from the covered "auto";
>
> **(2)** Otherwise in the course of transit by or on behalf of the "insured";
>
> **(3)** Being stored, disposed of, treated or processed in or upon the covered "auto";

Assumption of Tort Liability Is Covered

The definition of an **insured contract** includes a premises lease, sidetrack agreement, or an easement or **license agreement**. It also includes an obligation to indemnify a municipality or the assumption of tort liability.

The definition of insured contract makes it clear that the type of liability being insured is an assumption by one person of a **tort** liability of another. Coverage is provided for bodily injury or property damage to a third party. However, under the Liability section, the BAP does not cover physical damage to vehicles being used by the insured, even if the insured has assumed responsibility for damage.

Coverage for physical damage coverage to borrowed or hired autos may be added to the physical damage section of the policy.

> ■ *ISO FORM*
>
> **5.** That part of any other contract or agreement pertaining to your business (including an indemnification of a municipality in connection with work performed for a municipality) under which you assume the tort liability of another to pay for "bodily injury" or "property damage" to a third party or organization. Tort liability means a liability that would be imposed by law in the absence of any contract or agreement;

Some Contracts Are Excluded

The policy contains exclusions to the definition of insured contract.

- Many railroad companies require contractors who are working near railroad property to provide indemnity to the railroad in circumstances even when the contractor would not otherwise have been liable to the claimant. Such liability will not be covered under the definition of insured contract unless the contractor would have otherwise been liable.

- Coverage does not pertain to auto loan, lease, or rental if done so with a driver.

- Coverage does not include a contract that holds harmless a person or organization that transports property for hire for the insured's use of a covered auto over a route approved for that person by a public authority. For example, an independent trucker contracts to haul goods for another carrier over a route approved for that carrier by the Interstate Commerce Commission. The trucker's BAP will not cover a hold harmless agreement in the contract between the trucker and the carrier.

■ **ISO FORM**

An "insured contract" does not include that part of any contract or agreement:

a. That indemnifies a railroad for "bodily injury" or "property damage" arising out of construction or demolition operations, within 50 feet of any railroad property and affecting any railroad bridge or trestle, tracks, roadbeds, tunnel, underpass or crossing; or

b. That pertains to the loan, lease or rental of an "auto" to you or any of your "employees", if the "auto" is loaned, leased or rented with a driver; or

c. That holds a person or organization engaged in the business of transporting property by "auto" for hire harmless for your use of a covered "auto" over a route or territory that person or organization is authorized to serve by public authority.

New Definition Added

The ISO October 2001 Business Auto Coverage Form adds a statement to its Limit of Insurance section in Section III—Physical Damage Coverage which states that the insurer will not pay for diminution in value.

In essence, the insurer will not pay for the loss in market value or resale value of a covered vehicle. Assume the insured feels he might have received $5,000 more if the truck he sold did not have a large dent and scrapes due to an accident. The insurance company has no obligation to pay the insured the additional $5,000 he "might" have made.

Important Note

As an insurance professional, you should read and understand the definitions section of each coverage form. It is important to remember that definitions may vary by company so each form should be carefully reviewed.

It is vital that you explain any unusual terms to your insureds to prevent later misunderstandings about coverage.

■ AUTO MEDICAL PAYMENTS COVERAGE

The BAP provides liability and physical damage coverage. All other coverage must be added by endorsement. Near the top of each endorsement is a list the coverage forms to which the endorsement may be added to modify coverage. Some endorsements may be used to modify the Business Auto, Garage, Motor Carrier, or Truckers Coverage Forms.

Appropriate covered auto symbols must be indicated on the Declarations Page for every coverage option selected.

This lesson includes a discussion of Medical Payments coverage. Other commonly used endorsements are explained in the following lesson.

✓ *Helpful Hint:* Copies of the Commercial Auto forms and endorsements may be found in the Appendix.

Medical Payments Coverage Is Not Automatically Included

The Business Auto Coverage Form (CA 00 01) does not automatically cover medical payments. When this coverage is needed or desired, a symbol is shown for Auto Medical Payments in Item Two of the policy Declarations Page. The Auto Medical Payments Coverage (CA 99 03) endorsement must also be attached to the policy.

Auto Medical Payments Coverage (CA 99 03) is an optional coverage that may be added to pay for the reasonable and necessary medical and funeral expenses of persons who are injured in accidents while entering into, riding, or exiting a covered auto.

You'll recall that it is important to read the definition of "Who Is An Insured" in both the BAP and any endorsement. The Auto Medical Payments Coverage endorsement applies to the named insured, family members, and other occupants of covered autos.

The endorsement defines a *family member* as:

> *a person related to you by blood, marriage, or adoption who is a resident of your household, including a ward or foster child.*

▪ *ISO FORM*

F. Additional Definitions

As used in this endorsement:

1. "Family member" means a person related to you by blood, marriage or adoption who is a resident of your household, including a ward or foster child.

2. "Occupying" means in, upon, getting in, on, out or off.

Coverage Protects Insured Against Costly Claims

Coverage is indicated by placing the appropriate symbol next to the medical payments option on the Declarations Page.

If included, and in the event of loss, coverage applies without regard to fault. Medical payments limits are usually $1,000, $2,000, $3,000, $5,000, or $10,000 per person.

Medical expenses must be incurred within three years of the date of the accident and benefits for any one person, per any one accident, cannot exceed the limits on the Declarations Page.

Some States Mandate Medical Payments Coverage

Some no-fault states make the inclusion of medical payments up to a certain limit mandatory. The insured may purchase more than the required amount in order to provide better protection.

It is important to note that many insurance companies will not issue medical payments with Symbol 1—Any "Auto" because of the broad application of the symbol.

Employee Coverage Is Better Provided Elsewhere

Coverage for employees is excluded because they should be covered by Workers Compensation coverage.

War, nuclear radiation, and radioactive contamination are also excluded because they are considered to be uninsurable risks.

Real Life Application

Hypothetical Scenario for Medical Payments

Octavio, a driver for a flower shop, takes a customer on a delivery in one of the company's vans. Octavio causes an accident in which both he and the customer are injured.

3. Will the shop's BAP, which includes Medical Payments insurance, cover Octavio's and the customer's injuries?

▪ BUSINESS AUTO ENDORSEMENTS

It is estimated that, in some areas, as many as one in four vehicles do not carry required automobile insurance, even when required by law. To protect against injuries caused by uninsured drivers, businesses can purchase an Uninsured Motorist Coverage (CA 21 17) endorsement. The Limit of Liability for this coverage is shown on the endorsement.

Uninsured Motorist (UM) varies from state to state. In some states it applies only to bodily injury; in others it pays for bodily injury and property damage. The coverage is intended to pays for amounts an uninsured driver is legally obligated, but unable, to pay.

The ISO endorsement applies to both special damages and general damages, such as pain and suffering.

Underinsured Motorists Damage May Also be Covered

In most states, Uninsured Motorists coverage also includes coverage for Underinsured Motorists (UIM).

As part of its definition of an uninsured motor vehicle, the CA 21 17 includes vehicles or trailers that carry only the state's minimum liability limits for the state in which the vehicle is garaged.

If an insured is involved in an accident with a driver that carries only the state minimum liability limits and those limits are less than the Limit of Liability shown on the endorsement, the insured may recover the difference between the other party's liability limits and its Uninsured Motorists Coverage Limit of Liability.

Most States Have Compulsory Uninsured/Underinsured Motorist Laws

UM and UIM coverage is selected by placing the appropriate symbol on the BAP's Declarations Page in the Schedule of Coverage and Covered Auto Section. Most states have compulsory uninsured/underinsured motorist laws and Symbol 6 is used to activate coverage.

The laws vary widely from state to state. If the law is not compulsory, coverage can be provided with Symbol 2, 3, or 7. Compulsory insurance states may allow coverage to be rejected if the insured signs a release stating that coverage is not wanted.

Answer & Rationale

3. The company carries medical payments coverage on the van, therefore the injuries to the customer would be covered. Octavio's injuries, however, would not be covered, and would have to be paid by a workers' compensation policy.

Employee Injuries Are Excluded under BAP

Uninsured/underinsured motorists coverage will pay amounts the insured is legally entitled to collect from other motorists up to the limits of coverage. Underwriters often require UM and UIM limits to be written for identical amounts and limits are often the same as the BAP's liability limit.

Because employees might be the only people operating an organization's commercial vehicles, UM and UIM are often provided only on private passenger type vehicles and pickups or vans. If state law permits, the insured may not wish to provide UM and UIM on commercial vehicles because injuries to employees are excluded under the BAP.

This is an important discussion point when conducting insurance risk analysis evaluations.

Real Life Application

Sue's Hardware has a BAP that also insures Sue's personally owned vehicles. A $1,000,000 limit is provided for uninsured/underinsured motorist coverage. Herman, Sue's friend, is injured one day while operating Sue's automobile. An uninsured driver who caused the accident was determined at fault, but has no personal assets. Herman, who does not own a vehicle, is covered under Sue's policy because he is using the vehicle with permission. His injuries result in $300,000 in special damages.

4. Does Herman have coverage under Sue's policy for his injuries?

Real Life Application

Fast Freight Company is a package delivery service. Employees are the only persons who use the delivery vans. Jeff, a driver for Fast Freight, is injured in a traffic accident. His exclusive remedy is workers' compensation; therefore, neither Medical Payments nor Uninsured Motorists Coverage provides him with any benefits.

Because this situation can easily arise with the use of a commercial auto such as a delivery van, Fast Freight can save a substantial amount of money by not carrying these coverages on its vehicles.

Under the laws of many states, however, uninsured motorists coverage must be included on all policies that provide liability insurance.

Answer & Rationale

4. Yes. The uninsured/underinsured motorist coverage would pay Herman the $300,000 to which he is legally entitled, but unable to collect, from the other driver.

Personal Injury Protection (PIP) in No-Fault States

Personal Injury Protection (**PIP**) coverage varies widely from state to state but generally provides first party benefits for the following costs when they result from a covered accident:

- Loss of income

- Medical payments

- Funeral expenses

In some instances, the law also limits the right of injured motorists to bring suit for certain injuries.

Where required by state law, PIP is specifically endorsed by the ISO state-specific form. The form number varies by state.

Drive Other Car (DOC) Broadens Definition of Who Is an Insured

Many organizations provide company cars to their employees for use in the course of business and as a personal vehicle during off hours. Family members generally may also use these cars to conduct personal affairs.

If these employees do not have their own personal auto coverage, they may not have any coverage if they use or borrow other vehicles. The PAP covers insureds no matter what car they are driving, and this valuable protection is absent if a person does not have a PAP. For example, a BAP does not provide coverage when an auto is used for personal activities, such as a vacation.

The Drive Other Car (CA 99 10) endorsement enables a BAP to provide liability insurance to employees, their spouses, and members of their household while using company cars for non-business exposures. This coverage would also apply to the owners of a corporation who are, by definition, employees of the firm.

Coverage under this endorsement may include liability, medical payments, uninsured motorists, underinsured motorists, and physical damage coverages.

Protection for Personally Registered Vehicles

The commonly used Individual Named Insured (CA 99 17) endorsement provides coverage for a sole proprietor who does not have a PAP, but has personally registered vehicles that are insured under a BAP. When a BAP includes individually registered vehicles, ISO rules require a carrier to attach this endorsement.

When it is attached to a policy, this endorsement approximates the PAP's coverage for the insured, a spouse, and family members who reside in the household. Coverage applies to the use of owned and non-owned autos, but only those of the private passenger type.

This endorsement is important whenever the BAP also insures the business owner's personally registered private passenger vehicles.

Employees May be Included as Insureds

As stated previously in this course, employees are not automatically included as insureds under the BAP for use of other automobiles. If coverage is desired for autos that the named insured does not own, hire, or borrow, it may be added using this Employees As Insureds (CA 99 33) endorsement.

This endorsement extends liability coverage to employees while using covered, non-owned autos for business or personal affairs of the employee. Use of the endorsement indicates that the insured has Symbol 9 (Non-Owned Autos Only) for liability coverage.

Rental Reimbursement May Be Added for Specific Losses

If a covered auto suffers a physical damage loss from a covered cause of loss and is out of service for a reason other than theft, the BAP does not provide coverage for the cost to rent a substitute auto. However, an endorsement may be added to provide coverage.

The Rental Reimbursement Coverage (CA 99 23) endorsement covers expenses incurred to rent another auto because of a loss to a covered auto shown in the policy. Coverage begins 24 hours (the deductible) after a physical damage loss and continues until the vehicle is repaired using due diligence.

The insured must choose the type of coverage desired (comprehensive, collision, or specified causes of loss). Coverage does not apply under the endorsement if the insured has spare or reserve autos that are available for use.

Rental reimbursement is provided for autos that meet the above requirements subject to the maximum limit shown for any one day, the number of days indicated, and the total amount shown for any one period.

Vehicle Lessor Coverage May Be Added

Vehicle leasing is becoming more commonplace, especially for businesses and other organizations. The Lessor—Additional Insured And Loss Payee (CA 20 01) endorsement adds the vehicle lessor (the entity who owns and leases the vehicle) as an additional insured to the BAP.

When leased vehicles are listed on this endorsement, they are deemed to be owned vehicles for coverage purposes and if the lessor is indicated, it is considered as an insured for the designated vehicles. Should a loss occur, payment will be made to the lessor.

If desired, the coverages, limits of insurance, and deductibles may be amended for those autos as described. An additional premium charge may be made for the lessor.

Endorsement Protects the Lender

The Loss Payable Clause (CA 99 44) endorsement allows the bank or finance company that has loaned money for the vehicle's purchase to be paid in the event of a physical damage loss.

The lender usually requires a Loss Payable Clause endorsement for its protection. Normally, no charge is associated with this endorsement.

Protection for Tapes, Records, Discs, and Similar Devices

The Tapes, Records, and Discs Coverage (CA 99 30) endorsement provides coverage for loss to tapes, records, discs, and similar devices that are used with an automobile's audio, visual, or data electronic equipment.

The maximum amount of coverage is $200 and there is no deductible. An additional premium is charged for the coverage.

Important Information Regarding Additional Endorsements

The remainder of this unit provides a list of additional endorsements commonly used with the BAP. When indicated on the form, these endorsements may be used to modify other commercial auto coverage forms.

This information is not included in the state CE exam.

Available Endorsements and Their Uses

The following listing identifies, by number and title, additional endorsements available to modify the ISO's Business Auto Policy. A brief explanation of the use of each is also provided.

Note, however, this section does not address state specific endorsements, changes, or amendments. Copies of these endorsements are not provided in the Appendix. Insurance professionals must determine if these endorsements apply in the states(s) they represent.

Special Type Endorsements:

Additional Insured—Lessor—CA 20 01   This endorsement provides that the policy covers the lessor of property as an insured. This coverage applies only to the use of the property by the named insured.

Sound Receiving Equipment Coverage—Fire, Police, and Emergency Vehicles—CA 20 02   Use of this endorsement applies coverage to any audio, visual, and data electronic equipment that is installed in a covered auto belonging to a police or fire department, and other agencies such as emergency vehicles owned by a political body, volunteer fire department or rescue squad, or volunteer ambulance corps. Without this endorsement the sound receiving equipment would be excluded.

Drive-Away Contractors—CA 20 05   This endorsement provides coverage for the auto not owned while driven with the plates described in the endorsement by an insured responsible for the movement of a motor vehicle or trailer over any public highway for the purpose of delivery from one place to another.

Driving Schools—CA 20 06   The definitions of covered auto and insured change when this endorsement is used. A non-owned auto used for driver training is included as a covered auto, and the definition of the insured is expanded to include any driving instructor and any student while being instructed by the insured or the insured's driving instructor.

Farm Tractors and Farm Tractor Equipment—CA 20 08   This endorsement limits physical damage coverage for farm equipment or a farm tractor. The insurance excludes loss to stationary equipment that can be powered by the covered auto, and loss to any equipment transported by the covered auto. The exception is equipment furnished by the manufacturer as part of the covered auto's delivered price or described in the policy as a covered auto.

Leasing or Rental Concerns—Contingent Coverage—CA 20 09   This endorsement is one of a series of endorsement addressing specific concerns for the lessor of autos. The definition of "leased auto" is included to be an auto leased or rented to a lessee or rentee which requires that the lessee or rentee provide primary insurance to the lessor The endorsement specifies that the insured must be listed as an additional insured on the lessee's or rentee's policy, but at the time of the accident that insurance in not collectible. In this circumstance the endorsement provides coverage.

Leasing or Rental Concerns—Conversion, Embezzlement, or Secretion Coverage—CA 20 10   Another in the series addressing specific concerns for the lessor of autos, this endorsement adds an exclusion to the policy excluding physical damage loss due to theft, conversion, embezzlement, or secretion by any person possessing a covered auto under a lease, sale, purchase agreement, mortgage, or as a rentee or lessee. The insured can buy back this coverage by listing the specific autos or all autos to be covered. There is loss settlement restriction and duties required of the insured in the event of a loss.

Lease or Rental Concerns—Exclusion of Certain Leased Autos—CA 20 11 Liability coverage is excluded in this endorsement for a covered auto which is a leased auto, as defined in the endorsement. If the lessee's or rentee's policy is cancelled, coverage is afforded to the insured for 30 days after the date of cancellation.

Leasing or Rental Concerns—Rent-It-Here/Leave-It-There Autos—CA 20 12 This endorsement addresses the lessor's concern with rent-it-there/leave-it-here autos. The "rent-it-there/leave-it-here auto" is defined in this endorsement as an auto a rentee rents from someone else and leaves with the insured. The liability coverage in the policy is changed to exclude coverage for the owner or rentee of that rent-it-there/leave-it-here auto not owned by the insured.

Leasing Or Rental Concerns—Schedule of Limits For Owned Autos—CA 20 13   The insured may desire different liability limits for the different types of autos insured on the policy. This endorsement allows the insured to choose a specific liability limit for the three categories of autos:

- autos leased or rented under a lease or rental agreement that requires the lessee or rentee to provide direct primary insurance;
- autos leased or rented under a lease or rental agreement that does not require the lessee or rentee to provide direct primary insurance; and
- autos owned by the insured and not subject or a leasing or rental agreement.

Leasing Or Rental Concerns—Second Level Coverage—CA 20 14 The lessor of autos leased or rented under a lease or rental agreement requiring a lessee or rentee to provide primary insurance for the lessor may desire additional liability protection. The second level coverage replaces the liability limits shown elsewhere in the policy or in any lease or rental agreement. The difference between the policy or lease/rental limits is limited to only the insured on the policy, and does not cover the lessee, rentee, any employee of the lessee or rentee, and any person operating the auto with the permission of the lessee, rentee, or their respective employees.

Mobile Equipment—CA 20 15 Mobile equipment is not included in the definition of "auto" in the policy. This endorsement allows the insured to list mobile equipment and provide any policy coverage with specified limits. The listed mobile equipment is then considered an "auto" under the policy. There is a noted exclusion for bodily injury or property damage arising from the operation of machinery that is on, attached to or part of the specified mobile equipment.

Mobile Homes Contents Coverage—CA 20 16 This endorsement provides specifically listed coverages for "covered property", defined as TV antennas, awnings and equipment designed to add additional living space, and other personal property or household furniture belonging to or for which the insured is liable.

Mobile Homes Contents Not Covered—CA 20 17 This endorsement specifically excludes physical damage coverage to mobile home contents, such as the contents except those contents usual to a truck or auto, TV antennas, awnings, cabanas, and equipment designed to create additional living space.

Professional Services Not Covered—CA 20 18 When this endorsement is attached to the Business Auto Policy (BAP), it clarifies that liability for rendering or failing to render professional services is excluded. This endorsement does not apply in New York. No premium credit is normally associated with this endorsement.

Repossessed Autos—CA 20 19 Coverage for the liability or physical damage to repossessed autos may be added by use of this endorsement. The address, limits, rates, and premiums for the coverages selected at each location must be shown to trigger coverage. The formula or components for the computation of the increase in premium are found in the ISO Business Auto Rating Program and the premium basis is the number of autos repossessed. This endorsement may be on a non-reporting or a reporting basis. If **reporting** basis is selected, the reporting options are monthly or quarterly.

Snowmobiles—CA 20 20 For those vehicles described on this endorsement, Liability Coverage is extended. This endorsement only applies in Maryland, New Hampshire, and West Virginia. The formula or components for the computation of the increase in premium are found in the ISO Business Auto Rating Program.

Snowmobiles—CA 20 21   For those vehicles described on this endorsement, either physical damage or liability coverage may be selected and coverage is triggered by insertion of a premium in the appropriate coverage column. Limits and deductibles must also be selected. Additional exclusions apply to snowmobile coverage, some of which may be bought back for additional premium within the endorsement itself. This endorsement does not apply in Maryland, New Hampshire, or West Virginia. The formula or components for the computation of the increase in premium are found in the ISO Business Auto Rating Program, including the charges to be made for the buyback provisions.

Registration Plates Not Issued For A Specific Auto—CA 20 27   Liability coverage is provided for autos while they are using the plates described in the endorsement and for the coverage selected. The insertion of a premium triggers which Liability Coverages are provided. This endorsement does not apply in Connecticut, which has its own version (CA 20 22). The formula or components for the computation of the increase in premium are found in the ISO Business Auto Rating Program. The premium basis is per plate.

Emergency Vehicles—Volunteer Firefighters and Workers Injuries—CA 20 28   Use of this endorsement clarifies that bodily injury liability to volunteer firefighters and volunteer workers while operating a vehicle is excluded if the insured provides, or is required to provide workers' compensation, disability benefits, or other similar coverages. Fellow employee or volunteer worker coverage is also excluded. This endorsement only applies in Florida and New York. No premium reduction is associated with this endorsement.

Emergency Vehicles—Volunteer Firefighters And Workers Injuries Excluded—CA 20 30   When this endorsement is added to the policy, it clarifies that bodily injury liability to volunteer firefighters and volunteer workers is excluded. Fellow employee or volunteer worker coverage is also excluded. This endorsement does not apply in Florida or New York. No premium reduction is associated with this endorsement.

Autos Leased, Hired, Rented, or Borrowed With Drivers—Physical Damage Coverage—CA 20 33   This endorsement provides physical damage for non-owned vehicles designated in the endorsement, for the coverages selected. A physical damage limit and deductible, as well as an estimated cost of hire, rate and premium must be shown for each coverage. The formula or components for the computation of the increase in premium are found in the ISO Business Auto Rating Program. The premium basis is estimated annual cost of hire.

Additional Insured—Lessor Of Leased Equipment—CA 20   Additional insured liability coverage for non-auto, existence hazard only, is given to the lessor of leased equipment for the liability relating to that equipment, when this endorsement is attached to a Garage Policy only. It cannot be used with any other business auto coverage form. An additional premium charge may be made for the lessor.

Designated Insured—CA 20 48   Additional insured liability coverage may be added with this endorsement for the specified person as it relates to their vicarious liability. This endorsement may be used with any of the four coverage forms that provide liability protection. An additional premium charge may be made for the additional insured.

Uninsured Motorists Endorsements:

Split Uninsured Motorists Coverage Limits—CA 21 07   This endorsement gives the insured the ability to split the limits for the uninsured motorists coverage with different amounts for bodily injury each person, bodily injury each accident, and property damage each accident. The premium charged for the uninsured motorist coverage is dependent upon the limit selected.

Split Underinsured Motorists Coverage Limits—CA 21 46   This endorsement gives the insured the ability to split the limits for the underinsured motorists coverage with different amounts for bodily injury each person, bodily injury each accident and property damage each accident. The premium charged for the underinsured motorists coverage is dependent upon the limit selected.

Punitive Damages Exclusion—CA 21 71   When this endorsement is attached to the policy, payments for punitive and exemplary damages are excluded as they pertain to uninsured motorists and underinsured motorists coverages. This endorsement is not available in many states.

No-Fault Endorsement:

Named Individuals-Broadened Personal Injury Protection Coverage—CA 22 01   Coverage is extended to those individuals named or scheduled in this endorsement and they are considered named insureds for Personal Injury Protection only. The formula or components for the computation of the increase in premium are found in the ISO Business Auto Rating Program.

State Cancellation and Suspension Endorsements:

Reinstatement of Insurance—CA 02 38   This endorsement reinstates any coverages that were previously suspended, as of the date of the endorsement. Any premium charges for the coverages that are being reinstated are due and payable.

Suspension of Insurance—CA 02 40   This endorsement suspends the insurance protection of the coverages specified and for the vehicles specified in this endorsement. The unearned premium for the specified coverages and vehicles are returned to the insured if the suspension is 30 days or longer. This endorsement is not applicable in Michigan.

Deductible Endorsements:

✓ *Helpful Hint:* Deductible endorsements can offer some premium reduction

Deductible Liability Coverage—CA 03 01   This endorsement provides for the application of liability deductible that may apply per accident to the liability coverages, per person or per accident to the bodily injury coverage, or per accident to the property damage coverage. This endorsement and endorsement CA 03 02 are similar but with differences as a result of state requirements, so applicability depends upon the state involved. A credit is given towards the premium charged for the coverage the deductible is applied to. This credit is part of the ISO rating program.

Deductible Liability Coverage—CA 03   This endorsement provides for the application of liability deductible that may apply per accident to the liability coverages, per person or per accident to the bodily injury coverage, or per accident to the property damage coverage. This endorsement and endorsement CA 03 01 are similar but with differences as a result of state requirements, so applicability depends upon the state involved. A credit is given towards the premium charged for the coverage the deductible is applied to. This credit is part of the ISO rating program.

100 Dollar Deductible For Completed Operations Does Not Apply—CA 03 03
Use of this endorsement waives the $100 property damage deductible for completed operations work performed by the insured garage operations. This endorsement applies to the Garage Coverage Form only.

Commercial Auto Endorsements:

✓ *Helpful Hint:* Commercial auto endorsements modify coverage.

Explosives—CA 23 01   Use this endorsement to exclude liability caused by the explosion of explosives made, sold, or transported by the insured. This endorsement is not available in Kansas; the endorsement for Kansas is CA 23 21. No change in premium is normally associated with this endorsement.

Multi-Purpose Equipment—CA 23 03   This endorsement amends the liability coverage to clarify that the items listed in the schedule are to be considered mobile equipment and not autos. No change in premium is normally associated with this endorsement.

Trailer Interchange Fire and Fire and Theft Coverage—CA 23 13   This endorsement provides physical damage for trailers and their equipment for the coverages in which a premium charge is shown. Fire or fire and theft may be selected. The formula or components for the computation of the increase in premium are found in the ISO Business Auto Rating Program.

Agricultural Produce Trailers—Seasonal—CA 23 24   This endorsement has been developed to provide coverage for trailers specifically used to haul seasonal agricultural produce. It does not apply to trailers used to transport livestock. The trailer must have a minimum gross vehicle weight of 2,000 pounds or more. The covered trailer(s), the produce to be hauled, and the specific time period the coverage is in effect must be scheduled. An additional premium is charged for each trailer shown.

Coverage For Injury To Leased Workers—CA 23 25   The exclusion for employee indemnification and employer's liability can be amended to provide coverage for injury to leased workers by revising the definition of employee with this endorsement. Any change in premium as a result of this endorsement is at the discretion of the insurer.

Public Transportation Endorsements:

Farm Labor Contractors—CA 24 01   When this endorsement is purchased, liability coverage is provided for the insured while transporting migrant agricultural workers and registers the insured in accordance with the Migrant and Seasonal

Agricultural Worker Protection Act, 29 U.S.C.A. Section 1801. The formula or components for the computation of the increase in premium are found in the ISO Business Auto Rating Program.

Public Transportation Autos—CA 24 02   When the covered vehicle is licensed or used for public transport, the care, custody, or control exclusion does not apply to property of passengers carried in a covered auto. Any change in premium as a result of this endorsement is at the discretion of the insurer.

Single Interest Endorsements:

Single Interest Automobile Physical Damage Insurance Policy (Individual Policy Form)—CA 26 01   This policy provides physical damage coverage to the seller of a vehicle caused by the retail purchaser of that specified auto. This is a self-contained policy and applies specifically to one purchase. The formula or components for the computation of the increase in premium are found in the ISO Business Auto Rating Program.

Single Interest Automobile Physical Damage Insurance Policy (Finance Master Policy Form)—CA 26 02   This policy provides physical damage coverage to the seller of vehicles caused by the retail purchaser of those autos. This is a self-contained policy and applies on a blanket basis for dealers. This endorsement is not available in District of Columbia. The formula or components for the computation of the increase in premium are found in the ISO Business Auto Rating Program.

Common Coverages and Rating Procedures Endorsements

Auto Medical Payments Coverage—CA 99 03   When this endorsement is added to a policy, coverage is provided for auto medical payments for reasonable expenses for medical and funeral services as a result of an accident. The formula or components for the computation of the increase in premium are found in the ISO Business Auto Rating Program.

Drive Other Car Coverage—Broadened Coverage for Named Individuals—CA 99 10   The provisions of the applicable Business Auto Coverage Form are broadened by this endorsement to include the individual and that individual's spouse as an insured, who is specifically designated or scheduled in this endorsement (however, no other family members are automatically included). Each coverage that applies to the scheduled individuals must be selected and the premium charged. The individual may chose to be covered for liability, auto, medical payments, uninsured motorists, underinsured motorist, physical damage-comprehensive, physical damage-collision, or all of those coverages. An entry showing the premium charged for that coverage is the trigger to indicate that the coverage applies. The formula or components for the computation of the increase in premium are found in the ISO Business Auto Rating Program.

Fiduciary Liability of Banks—CA 99 13   This endorsement clarifies that the liability coverage provided does not apply to any damages that occurred before the insured had fiduciary responsibilities for which the insured is liable. No change in premium is normally associated with this endorsement.

Fire; Fire and Theft; Fire, Theft, and Windstorm; and Limited Specified Causes of Loss Coverage—CA 99 14   Use of this endorsement provides limited physical damage coverage for the autos that are scheduled. The coverages that apply are triggered by an insertion of premium by the appropriate coverage. The formula or components for the computation of the increase in premium are found in the ISO Business Auto Rating Program.

Governmental Bodies Amendatory Endorsement—CA 99 15   Any land motor vehicle or trailer owned or leased by the insured that is designed for travel on public roads is considered an auto and not mobile equipment if the only reason it may be considered mobile equipment is that it is used on roads owned by the insured. No change in premium is normally associated with this endorsement.

Hired Autos Specified as Covered Autos You Own—CA 99 16   This endorsement makes the nonowned auto that is specified or scheduled in the endorsement to be treated as a covered auto. This applies to either liability or physical damage coverages.

Individual Named Insured—CA 99 17   Nonowned Coverage is provided for the named insured and family members; however, this endorsement should not be used as a replacement for a personal auto policy. This endorsement offers only a partial remedy and a thorough review of each individual and their circumstances is necessary. Normally, no charge is associated with this endorsement.

Split Liability Limits—CA 99 27   By using this endorsement, the limit of insurance for the liability coverages is changed from a single limit to a split limit for bodily injury liability each person, bodily injury each accident, and property damage each accident. The formula or components for the computation of the increase in premium are found in the ISO Business Auto Rating Program.

Stated Amount Insurance—CA 99 28   For those vehicles that are scheduled in the endorsement, the limit for the physical damage coverages is changed to the least of the actual cash value, the cost to repair or replace, or the limit that is specified in the endorsement schedule. The formula or components for the computation of the increase in premium are found in the ISO Business Auto Rating Program.

Social Service Agencies—Volunteers as Insureds—CA 99 34   This endorsement is designed for social services agencies to cover volunteers. Anyone who is volunteering services to the insured is covered while using covered nonowned vehicles to transport clients or other people to activities necessary to the business of the insured. Coverage is also extended to the owners of the non-owned autos. Any additional charge for the use of this endorsement is at the discretion of the insurer.

Exclusion or Excess Coverage (Hazards Otherwise Insured)—CA 99 40
When a covered auto is insured with another policy or coverage for liability, this endorsement can be used to exclude the Liability Coverage completely for the scheduled vehicle, activate coverage on the specified vehicle when the other insurance expires, or make this insurance excess over the other policy for the specified vehicle only. Any reduction in premium for the use of this endorsement is at the discretion of the insurer.

Employee as Lessor—CA 99 47   Any auto described in the schedule that is leased to the insured by an employee is considered a covered owned auto for liability purposes, and that employee is considered an insured. The formula or components for the computation of the increase in premium are found in the ISO Business Auto Rating Program.

Pollution Liability—Broadened Coverage for Covered Autos-Business Auto and Truckers Coverage Forms—CA 99   Using this endorsement changes the pollution exclusion for liability in the coverage form by excluding only the liability assumed under a contract or agreement. Any additional charge for the use of this endorsement is at the discretion of the insurer.

Covered Auto Designation Symbol—CA 99 54   This endorsement may be used to add a covered auto symbol to any of the Business Auto Coverage Forms and then manuscript a definition for that symbol to describe what is to be considered a covered vehicle.

Audio, Visual, and Data Electronic Equipment Coverage—CA 99 60   This is a buyback endorsement for physical damage coverage to audio, visual, and data electronic equipment that is excluded in the coverage form. This buyback applies only to the equipment that is permanently installed or is removable from the housing units that are permanently installed. Those autos that are covered by this endorsement must be scheduled and a deductible applies. The formula or components for the computation of the increase in premium are found in the ISO Business Auto Rating Program.

Loss Payable Clause—Audio, Visual, and Data Electronic Equipment—CA 99 61   Use of this endorsement adds the provisions that apply to the payment of loss when a loss payable is shown on this endorsement for audio, visual, and data electronic equipment. This endorsement cannot be used in Washington. Normally, no charge is associated with this clause.

Endorsements Customize an Insured's Coverage

The BAP provides coverage for a broad class of risks and can be tailored to meet the unique features of almost any business in any state. For example, coverage parts (such as Medical Payments and Personal Injury Protection (PIP)) are required in some states and not in others. (e.g., New York has a mandatory PIP regulation while Connecticut does not).

Endorsements are available to customize the BAP to meet the needs of most policyholders. Each insurance professional must determine which endorsements are approved for use in their states and by the carriers they represent.

■ SUMMARY

Insurance professionals should review the entire BAP with their insureds, paying special attention to the Conditions and Definitions sections. It is vital that the insured understand the duties and responsibilities imposed under the BAP contract.

The carrier's prompt and equitable disposition of claims under a policy turns on the cooperation of the insured in reporting all losses on time and cooperating with the carrier throughout the investigation, settlement and/or defense of claims. Prompt notice of loss and cooperation are two of the most important conditions of the policy.

This ends the discussion of the BAP. Before we look at another important commercial auto coverage, the Garage Coverage Form, we'll look at the available Terrorism Coverage Options for commercial autos.

■ **UNIT 5 REVIEW QUESTIONS**

1. In the event of an accident, the insured has only to report the loss to the police department. They will automatically alert the insurance company.

   A. True
   B. False

2. Two of the most important duties in the policy are to report claims on time and to cooperate with the insurance company.

   A. True
   B. False

3. Which of the following are conditions under the Business Auto Policy?

   A. Prompt Notice
   B. Duty to Cooperate
   C. Selection of Coverage Symbols
   D. Only A and B

4. As defined in the policy, *insured* means anyone who qualifies as an insured in the Who Is An Insured category of each coverage.

   A. True
   B. False

5. Octavio Flowers transports a customer to a local flower show. While en route, the covered auto is involved in an accident. The Business Auto Policy provides Medical Payments coverage in a maximum limit of $1,000 per person. This coverage is automatically a part of the BAP.

   A. True
   B. False

6. Drive Other Car (DOC) coverage duplicates the coverage in the Personal Auto Policy.

   A. True
   B. False

■ ANSWERS TO UNIT 5 REVIEW QUESTIONS

1. **B.** False. The insured is responsible for reporting the loss to the insurance company or an authorized representative. This duty cannot be transferred to another individual and the police department does not provide this level of service.

2. **A.** True. These are the two primary conditions that trigger the insuring agreements under the policy. Delays in reporting and failure to cooperate often affect settlement or defense costs.

3. **D.** Duty to Cooperate and the Prompt Notice of Claims are two of the primary conditions under the Business Auto Policy and directly affect the carrier's duty to promptly investigate claims.

4. **A.** True. Each coverage part identifies the *insured* in the Who Is An Insured section.

5. **B.** False. Medical Payments is an optional coverage and must be added by endorsement to the Business Auto Policy.

6. **A.** True. Drive Other Car coverage duplicates the coverage under the Personal Auto Policy and applies to listed drivers who have no PAP.

6

Terrorism Coverage Options

T he impact of 9/11/01 on the insurance industry was profound. According to estimates from the Insurance Information Institute, the ultimate insured loss will exceed $40 billion. While this cost is dwarfed by the human toll of this horrific event, the insured loss estimates are more than twice as large as any previous insured catastrophic event.

Pre-9/11

Post-9/11

Insurance companies responded by paying claims with unprecedented speed; however, future loss containment steps were taken with the introduction of the 01/01/02 War or Terrorism exclusions for property and liability policies that made obtaining continued insurance coverage for terrorism difficult if not impossible for many businesses.

■ ■ ■ ■ ■

Terrorism = Economic Concerns

Without terrorism insurance, the economic impact of another terrorist attack would most likely result in bankruptcies, layoffs, and loan defaults. While the government continues to take measures to stop future attacks, it is also clear that a federally sponsored terrorism program is needed to mitigate widespread damage to our economy should another event occur.

TRIA Becomes Law

As a result of the Terrorism Risk Insurance Act (TRIA) signed into law on 11/26/02, all commercial property and casualty insurance polices must offer terrorism coverage.

While all the provisions and features of the TRIA are not summarized in this course, it is important that insurance professionals review the purpose of the act to properly advise policyholders regarding terrorism coverage options.

Following is a direct quote from the TRIA regarding its purpose.

(b) PURPOSE.—The purpose of this title is to establish a temporary Federal program that provides for a transparent system of shared public and private compensation for insured loses resulting from acts of terrorism, in order to—

(1) protect consumers by addressing market disruptions and ensure the continued widespread availability and affordability of property and casualty insurance for terroism risk; and

(2) allow for a transitional period for the private markets to stabilize, resume pricing of such insurance, and build capacity to absorb any future losses, while preserving State insurance regulation and consumer protections.

■ TERRORISM ENDORSEMENTS

The process to elect one of the **Fast Track** liability coverage options varies according to whether the insured has a:

- midterm policy with preexisting terrorism exclusions; or

- midterm policy without preexisting terrorism exclusions; or

- new or renewal policy.

Liability Endorsement Options

This unit discusses the Commercial Auto endorsement options that were part of the Fast Track filings mandated by the Terrorism Risk Insurance Act of 2002. The Fast Track endorsements are approved in all states. Below is a list of the endorsements explained in this unit.

Fast Track Filings Dated 11/02

11/02 Endorsement Option Form Name	CA Number
CA Acceptance Forms	
Exception to Terrorism Exclusion for Certified Acts of Terrorism; Cap on Losses from Certified Acts of Terrorism	CA 23 63
Removal of Terrorism Exclusion; Cap on Losses from Certified Acts of Terrorism	CA 23 64
Cap on Losses from Certified Acts of Terrorism	CA 23 56
CA Rejection Form	
Exclusion of Certified Acts of Terrorism	CA 23 57

The remainder of this unit reviews each of the Fast Track liability endorsement forms by discussing:

- who the form applies to: midterm, new, or renewal policyholders;

- explanation of form coverages, exclusions, or exclusion amendments;

- application of coverage parts; and

- common form provisions.

Fast Track Coverage Options

We will first examine coverage options for midterm, new, and renewal policyholders that accept terrorism coverage.

Midterm policyholders with preexisting terrorism exclusions have the option to:

- *amend* their existing exclusions to cover certified acts of terrorism only (option 1 below); or

- *remove* any preexisting exclusions and cover all acts of terrorism (option 2 below).

New and renewal policyholders without preexisting exclusions will use the *Cap on Losses from Certified Acts of Terrorism* form to cover all acts of terrorism.

Midterm policies with Terrorism Exclusions	New or Renewal Policies and Midterm Policies without Terrorism Exclusions
(1) Coverage for Certified Acts of Terrorism Only	
Exception to Terrorism Exclusion for Certified Acts of Terrorism; Cap on Losses from Certified Acts of Terrorism	N/A
CA 23 63	N/A
(2) Coverage for all Acts of Terrorism	
• Removal of Terrorism Exclusion; Cap on Losses from Certified Acts of Terrorism	CA 23 57
CA 23 64	CA 23 56
• Both the option 1 and 2 forms must be offered to midterm policyholders with preexisting exclusions. The midterm category expires on 11/26/03	

■ TERRORISM ACCEPTANCE FORMS

All CA Fast Track terrorism endorsements are for use with the following forms:

- Business Auto Coverage Form
- Business Auto Physical Damage Coverage Form
- Garage Coverage Form
- Motor Carrier Coverage Form
- Truckers Coverage Form
- Single Interest Automobile Damage Insurance Policy (Texas only)

Liability and Property Endorsement Provisions

All of the CA terrorism endorsements contain two or more of the following Provision Descriptions.

Note the endorsement language that explains the provisions included in this form option.

Definition of Certified Act of Terrorism	"Certified act of terrorism" means an act that is certified by the Secretary of the Treasury, in concurrence with the Secretary of State and the Attorney General of the United States, to be an act of terrorism pursuant to the federal Terrorism Risk Insurance Act of 2002. The federal Terrorism Risk Insurance Act of 2002 sets forth the following criteria for a "certified act of terrorism": 1. The act resulted in aggregate losses in excess of $5 million; and 2. The act is a violent act or an act that is dangerous to human life, property or infrastructure and is committed by an individual or individuals acting on behalf of any foreign person or foreign interest, as part of an effort to coerce the civilian population of the United States or to influence the policy or affect the conduct of the United States Government by coercion.
Amendment to preexisting terrorism exclusion to now cover certified acts of terrorism	With respect to any exclusion of terrorism in this Coverage Form or attached to this Coverage Form by endorsement, such exclusion does not apply to a "certified act of terrorism". That exclusion also does not apply to an act which meets the criteria set forth in Paragraph 2. of the definition of "certified act of terrorism", when such act resulted in aggregate losses of $5 million or less.
Removal of preexisting terrorism exclusions to now cover all acts of terrorism	Any exclusion of terrorism in this Coverage Part, or attached to this Coverage Part by endorsement, is hereby removed
Cap on certified act of terrorism coverage	With respect to any one or more "certified acts of terrorism", we will not pay any amounts for which we are not responsible under the terms of the federal Terrorism Risk Insurance Act of 2002 (including subsequent acts of Congress pursuant to the Act) due to the application of any clause which results in a cap on our liability for payments for terrorism losses.
Application of Other Exclusions	The terms and limitations of any terrorism exclusion, or the inapplicability or omission of a terrorism exclusion, do not serve to create coverage for any loss which would otherwise be excluded under this Coverage Part or Policy, such as losses excluded by the Nuclear Hazard Exclusion or the War And Military Action Exclusion.

Certified Act of Terrorism Exclusion	We will not pay for loss or damage caused directly or indirectly by a "certified act of terrorism". Such loss or damage is excluded regardless of any other cause or event that contributes concurrently or in any sequence to the loss.
Punitive damages exclusion	This insurance does not apply to: TERRORISM PUNITIVE DAMAGES Damages arising, directly or indirectly, out of a "certified act of terrorism" that are awarded as punitive damages.

Application of Other Exclusions Provision

All of the TRIA property and liability terrorism coverage endorsements are subject to the underlying coverage policy provisions. In other words, the exclusions in the underlying policy prevail.

Nuclear Hazard

An Application of Other Exclusions provision is added to all Fast Track TRIA endorsements that include property coverages to clarify that terrorism endorsements do not create property coverage for Nuclear Hazard, War or Military Action, or any loss that would be otherwise excluded.

Application of Other Exclusions	The terms and limitations of any terrorism exclusion, or the inapplicability or omission of a terrorism exclusion, do not serve to create coverage for any loss which would otherwise be excluded under this Coverage Part or Policy, such as losses excluded by the Nuclear Hazard Exclusion or the War And Military Action Exclusion.

Property vs. Liability Policies   Nuclear hazards are not excluded as comprehensively in commercial liability policies as in commercial property policies. For example, CGL policies contain mandatory nuclear energy exclusions, which are intended to avoid duplicating coverage that is available through the various government nuclear energy association pool policies.

Before 9/11/01, it was generally accepted that this mandatory Nuclear Energy exclusion, along with the war exclusion that is part of all insurance policies, adequately addressed nuclear hazards in commercial liability policies.

The CA policy does not list nuclear hazard as an exclusion under Section II Liability.

Liability Nuclear Hazard Coverage Review   Because property coverages include a comprehensive exclusion for nuclear hazard and liability policies are more hazard-specific, in some cases a policyholder who purchases certified act of terrorism coverage could have some terrorist nuclear hazards excluded under policy property forms and be eligible for coverage under the policy liability forms.

Insurers can create a comprehensive liability nuclear hazard exclusion like the comprehensive commercial property exclusion by using one of the Prior Approval Nuclear Hazard Liability exclusions available for CGL, CA and CU. These nuclear hazard liability exclusions are explained in the *Property and Liability Prior Approval* lesson of this unit.

We will now review the CA Fast Track terrorism coverage acceptance options on a per form basis.

Exception to Terrorism Exclusion for Certified Acts of Terrorism; Cap on Losses from Certified Acts of Terrorism

Covers Certified Acts of Terrorism Only—Exception to Terrorism Exclusion for Certified Acts of Terrorism; Cap on Losses from Certified Acts of Terrorism Form CA 23 63

This endorsement option had to be offered to CA policyholders with midterm policies that had preexisting terrorism exclusions.

This endorsement amends any preexisting terrorism exclusion to provide coverage for certified acts of terrorism only and caps the insurer's responsibility to the amount included within the Terrorism Risk Insurance Act of 2002.

Preexisting Exclusions Are Amended

In addition to providing coverage for certified acts of terrorism, this endorsement option amends any existing war or terrorism exclusion to also provide coverage for acts that meet the certified act of terrorism definition and result in less than $5 million of losses.

The intent of this endorsement is to avoid affording less coverage than would be provided by the initial 01/01/02 terrorism exclusions to midterm policyholders when they accept coverage for certified acts of terrorism.

The initial 01/01/02 terrorism exclusions did not exclude terrorism losses under the aggregate loss threshold of $25 million unless the loss involved the use or release of nuclear, poisonous, or biological chemicals.

Although the CA 23 63 and other certified acts of terrorism coverage endorsements cover certified losses over $5 million and acts that meet the certified act of terrorism that are under $5 million, only certified acts over $5 million are part of the TRIA federal reimbursement program.

Under this form, the insurance carrier with no federal reimbursement covers acts that meet the certified act of terrorism definition that are under $5 million.

Preexisting Exclusions are Amended, Not Removed

Because this form provides an amendment to a preexisting exclusion rather than an exclusion removal, not all acts of terrorism are covered. For example, a domestic terrorist act (such as the 1995 Oklahoma City bombing) would not be covered because it is outside the certified act of terrorism definition.

Common Endorsement Provisions

This endorsement contains the following Provisions:

Amendment to preexisting terrorism exclusion to now cover certified acts of terrorism	With respect to any exclusion of terrorism in this Coverage Form or attached to this Coverage Form by endorsement, such exclusion does not apply to a "certified act of terrorism". That exclusion also does not apply to an act which meets the criteria set forth in Paragraph 2. of the definition of "certified act of terrorism", when such act resulted in aggregate losses of $5 million or less.
Cap on certified act of terrorism coverage	With respect to any one or more "certified acts of terrorism", we will not pay any amounts for which we are not responsible under the terms of the federal Terrorism Risk Insurance Act of 2002 (including subsequent acts of Congress pursuant to the Act) due to the application of any clause which results in a cap on our liability for payments for terrorism losses.
Definition of Certified Act of Terrorism	"Certified act of terrorism" means an act that is certified by the Secretary of the Treasury, in concurrence with the Secretary of State and the Attorney General of the United States, to be an act of terrorism pursuant to the federal Terrorism Risk Insurance Act of 2002. The federal Terrorism Risk Insurance Act of 2002 sets forth the following criteria for a "certified act of terrorism": 1. The act resulted in aggregate losses in excess of $5 million; and 2. The act is a violent act or an act that is dangerous to human life, property or infrastructure and is committed by an individual or individuals acting on behalf of any foreign person or foreign interest, as part of an effort to coerce the civilian population of the United States or to influence the policy or affect the conduct of the United States Government by coercion.
Application of Other Exclusions	The terms and limitations of any terrorism exclusion, or the inapplicability or omission of a terrorism exclusion, do not serve to create coverage for any loss which would otherwise be excluded under this Coverage Part or Policy, such as losses excluded by the Nuclear Hazard Exclusion or the War And Military Action Exclusion.

Real Life Application

Jones Trucking Company has a Commercial Package Policy that includes terrorism coverage for certified acts of terrorism under Commercial Property, Commercial Auto, and Commercial General Liability Coverage forms.

Jones Co. does not always complete extensive background checks on all drivers, and unfortunately has hired a terrorist from a foreign interest group. The terrorist, who has access to the company vehicles, takes one of the company semi trucks without the owner's permission and places a small nuclear bomb into the trailer.

The terrorist, during his off-duty hours, drives the semi into a large metropolitan city and crashes it into a skyscraper. Over $25 million in property damage and 1,000 fatalities ensue.

Does Jones Co. have coverage under its CA for this act?

The claims professionals and the courts would decide claim coverage for this incident. Points that the professional would consider include the following:

When the incident occurred, was the terrorist acting as an insured?

- The terrorist would not meet the policy definition of an insured at the time the incident occurred because he was using the vehicle without the owner's permission and performed the act outside of employment duties.

- The employer did not intend the terrorist to detonate the bomb; therefore, the Expected or Intended exclusion does not apply to the employer.

Was the employer liable?

- Jones Co. is generally not liable for the activities of its employees outside of employment responsibilities; however, the company gave this terrorist access to the company vehicle used to incur the property damages and bodily injury.

- Jones Co. would also most likely be found negligent for improper hiring practices.

This is an excellent example of the need for Terrorism coverage under the Commercial Auto policy. This loss would be covered as a certified act of terrorism if either the Fast Track "Cap on Losses from Certified Acts of Terrorism" or the Prior Approval "Limited Exclusion of Acts of Terrorism (Other Than Certified Acts of Terrorism) Cap on Losses from Certified Acts of Terrorism" forms were attached to the policy.

There would be a possible issue with the underlying CA pollution exclusion in regards to the release of radiation after the explosion, unless Jones Trucking had purchased pollution coverage (Pollution Liability—Broadened Coverage for Covered Autos CA 9948). The physical damage to the autos, both tractor and trailer would be excluded by the underlying nuclear exclusion in Section III Physical Damage.

Liability Nuclear Hazard Exposures

Insurers can avoid nuclear hazard liability exposures like the one presented in the previous hypothetical example by attaching a Prior Approval terrorism nuclear exclusion endorsement to BOP, CG, CA, and CU policies. The prior approval lesson in this unit explains this endorsement option.

Policyholders have new terrorist prevention responsibilities as employers. Whether property or liability insurance coverage for this type of exposure should be available to employers is an issue that will be debated for some time to come.

Coverage for All Acts of Terrorism—Removal of Terrorism Exclusion; Cap on Losses from Certified Acts of Terrorism Form CA 23 64

Our examination of the forms will now continue with the second coverage option that had to be offered to midterm CA policyholders with policies that currently have preexisting terrorism exclusion endorsements.

It removes any preexisting terrorism exclusion but caps the insurer's responsibility for certified acts of terrorism to the amount included within the TRIA.

Only certified acts of terrorism that meet the TRIA terrorism definition and exceed the $5 million aggregate loss requirement are eligible for federal reimbursement to insurers. By removing all preexisting terrorism exclusions, however, this endorsement provides terrorism coverage for all acts of terrorism, subject to the cap applicable to certified acts of terrorism and any other policy provisions.

Common Endorsement Provisions:

Cap on certified act of terrorism coverage	With respect to any one or more "certified acts of terrorism", we will not pay any amounts for which we are not responsible under the terms of the federal Terrorism Risk Insurance Act of 2002 (including subsequent acts of Congress pursuant to the Act) due to the application of any clause which results in a cap on our liability for payments for terrorism losses.
Definition of Certified Act of Terrorism	"Certified act of terrorism" means an act that is certified by the Secretary of the Treasury, in concurrence with the Secretary of State and the Attorney General of the United States, to be an act of terrorism pursuant to the federal Terrorism Risk Insurance Act of 2002. The federal Terrorism Risk Insurance Act of 2002 sets forth the following criteria for a "certified act of terrorism": 1. The act resulted in aggregate losses in excess of $5 million; and 2. The act is a violent act or an act that is dangerous to human life, property or infrastructure and is committed by an individual or individuals acting on behalf of any foreign person or foreign interest, as part of an effort to coerce the civilian population of the United States or to influence the policy or affect the conduct of the United States Government by coercion.

Midterm Policyholder with Terrorism Exclusions

Companies had to offer midterm CA policyholders as of 11/26/02 who had preexisting terrorism exclusions:

Application of Other Exclusions	The terms and limitations of any terrorism exclusion, or the inapplicability or omission of a terrorism exclusion, do not serve to create coverage for any loss which would otherwise be excluded under this Coverage Part or Policy, such as losses excluded by the Nuclear Hazard Exclusion or the War And Military Action Exclusion.

- Option 1. Exception to Terrorism Exclusion for Certified Acts of Terrorism; Cap on Losses from Certified Acts of Terrorism (CA 23 63); and

- Option 2. Removal of Terrorism Exclusion; Cap on Losses from Certified Acts of Terrorism (CA 23 64).

CA policyholders selected one or the other terrorism coverage endorsements or rejected terrorism coverage in writing. If a policyholder rejected both of the above endorsements or failed to pay when due the additional premium for terrorism coverage, the insurer had the option to reinstate the preexisting 01/01/02 War or Terrorism Exclusion that TRIA declared void.

At renewal, policyholders had to choose among the TRIA terrorism coverage and exclusion endorsements available at that time because continued use of the 01/01/02 exclusions are disallowed under TRIA.

Cap on Losses from Certified Acts of Terrorism

New and Renewed Policies—Cap on Losses from Certified Acts of Terrorism Form CA 23 56

This endorsement provides liability coverage for all terrorists acts (subject to attached policy exclusions) but caps the insurer's responsibility for certified acts of terrorism to any amount included within the Terrorism Risk Insurance Act of 2002.

At the time of offer, purchase, or renewal, the policyholder may either accept the terrorism coverage provided by this endorsement and pay the premium when due, or reject the endorsement. If rejected, the insurer will use the Exclusion of Certified Acts of Terrorism endorsement.

Common Endorsement Provisions

Cap on certified act of terrorism coverage	With respect to any one or more "certified acts of terrorism", we will not pay any amounts for which we are not responsible under the terms of the federal Terrorism Risk Insurance Act of 2002 (including subsequent acts of Congress pursuant to the Act) due to the application of any clause which results in a cap on our liability for payments for terrorism losses.

Definition of Certified Act of Terrorism	"Certified act of terrorism" means an act that is certified by the Secretary of the Treasury, in concurrence with the Secretary of State and the Attorney General of the United States, to be an act of terrorism pursuant to the federal Terrorism Risk Insurance Act of 2002. The federal Terrorism Risk Insurance Act of 2002 sets forth the following criteria for a "certified act of terrorism": 1. The act resulted in aggregate losses in excess of $5 million; and 2. The act is a violent act or an act that is dangerous to human life, property or infrastructure and is committed by an individual or individuals acting on behalf of any foreign person or foreign interest, as part of an effort to coerce the civilian population of the United States or to influence the policy or affect the conduct of the United States Government by coercion.
Application of Other Exclusions	The terms and limitations of any terrorism exclusion, or the inapplicability or omission of a terrorism exclusion, do not serve to create coverage for any loss which would otherwise be excluded under this Coverage Part or Policy, such as losses excluded by the Nuclear Hazard Exclusion or the War And Military Action Exclusion.

■ TERRORISM COVERAGE REJECTION FORMS

We have just completed a review of the Fast Track endorsements that midterm, new, and renewal policyholders can use to accept terrorism coverage. Next we will examine the options they have to reject terrorism coverage.

Exclusions for Certified Acts of Terrorism

New and Renewed Policies—Exclusion of certified Acts of Terrorism Only Form CA 23 57

This form option is for new and renewal policyholders who reject terrorism coverage. It excludes any injury or damage arising directly or indirectly out of a certified act of terrorism.

This endorsement may be used on new and renewal policies by an insurer if the policyholder rejects coverage for terrorism as offered in the endorsement Cap on Losses from Certified Acts of Terrorism specific to each line of business.

Losses that do not arise from a certified act of terrorism will continue to be covered by the existing policy with this endorsement attached. For instance, if a terrorist act (as defined) causes less than a total of $5,000,000 of damage, any liability an insured would have resulting from the act would continue to be covered by the attached policy, subject to all other policy provisions.

Midterm Policies

Midterm policyholders as of 11/26/02 that elect to reject terrorism coverage must do so in writing. Any preexisting terrorism exclusions will be reinstated until the next policy renewal at which time the insured must select from the TRIA coverage or exclusion endorsements in effect at that time.

Common Endorsement Provisions:

Definition of Certified Act of Terrorism	"Certified act of terrorism" means an act that is certified by the Secretary of the Treasury, in concurrence with the Secretary of State and the Attorney General of the United States, to be an act of terrorism pursuant to the federal Terrorism Risk Insurance Act of 2002. The federal Terrorism Risk Insurance Act of 2002 sets forth the following criteria for a "certified act of terrorism": 1. The act resulted in aggregate losses in excess of $5 million; and 2. The act is a violent act or an act that is dangerous to human life, property or infrastructure and is committed by an individual or individuals acting on behalf of any foreign person or foreign interest, as part of an effort to coerce the civilian population of the United States or to influence the policy or affect the conduct of the United States Government by coercion.
Application of Other Exclusions	The terms and limitations of any terrorism exclusion, or the inapplicability or omission of a terrorism exclusion, do not serve to create coverage for any loss which would otherwise be excluded under this Coverage Part or Policy, such as losses excluded by the Nuclear Hazard Exclusion or the War And Military Action Exclusion.
Certified Act of Terrorism Exclusion	We will not pay for loss or damage caused directly or indirectly by a "certified act of terrorism". Such loss or damage is excluded regardless of any other cause or event that contributes concurrently or in any sequence to the loss.

Liability Terrorism Coverage Summary Charts

This completes the review of the CA Fast Track TRIA endorsements. The endorsements are effective immediately in all states and offer policyholders the certified acts of terrorism coverage mandated by the TRIA as well as terrorism exclusion options.

It is important that insurance professionals have a comprehensive understanding of these forms to advise CA policyholders of the terrorism coverage options now mandated by the TRIA through 2005.

Additional liability and property reference charts and sample forms for all commercial lines of business are available in the following reference guide:

- Terrorism Coverage for Commercial Lines Reference Guide

If you would like a copy of this guide, call Drabber customer service at 1-800-824-8742 to order a printed copy, which can be a valuable resource upon completion of this course.

■ PRIOR APPROVAL PROPERTY AND LIABILITY FORMS

The discussion thus far has been limited to the Fast Track TRIA endorsements. This lesson is devoted to Prior Approval TRIA endorsements.

The Fast Track TRIA endorsements pertain to terrorism risks associated with certified acts of terrorism. ISO also offers optional exclusion endorsements for:

- other acts of terrorism only; and

- other acts of terrorism and certified acts of terrorism.

In general, the term *other acts of terrorism* is used to distinguish between certified acts of terrorism and all other acts of terrorism.

Other Acts of Terrorism Examples

Examples of other acts of terrorism that could be excluded using the Prior Approval endorsements are:

- domestic acts of terrorism; and

- acts that meet all certified acts of terrorism definition requirements except the $5 million aggregate loss threshold; and

- losses of any damage amount involving nuclear, biological, or chemical acts.

The prior approval forms offer varying degrees of exclusions for these terrorist acts.

Some of the Prior Approval endorsements offer exclusion options similar to the initial 01/01/02 War or Terrorism exclusions.

Limited Exclusion of Acts of Terrorism (Other than Certified Acts of Terrorism); Cap on Losses from Certified Acts of Terrorism

Limited Exclusion Option—Limited Terrorism Exclusion (Other Than Certified Acts Of Terrorism); Cap On Losses From Certified Acts Of Terrorism Form CA 23 58

This form provides coverage for certified acts of terrorism, but it also uses damage thresholds to trigger an exclusion for non-certified acts that are similar to the 01/01/02 War or Terrorism exclusions.

Similar Damage Thresholds

Like the initial 01/01/02 exclusions, this CA Prior Approval endorsement uses a $25 million in damages and 50 people bodily injury threshold to trigger the exclusion for non-certified acts of terrorism and no damage threshold on all acts of biological or chemical terrorism. Underlying policy exclusions such as nuclear hazard continue to apply.

The form does not exclude:

- certified acts of terrorism; and

- non-nuclear/chemical/biological acts of terrorism under the $25 million damage threshold.

Insurers Must Offer Coverage for Certified Acts

Insurers can elect to meet the TRIA required offer to cover certified acts of terrorism with either or both of the following forms:

- The *Limited Exclusion of Acts of Terrorism (Other Than Certified Acts of Terrorism); Cap on Losses from Certified Acts of Terrorism*; or

- The *Cap on Losses from Certified Acts of Terrorism*, which covers both certified and non-certified acts of terrorism.

Exclusion of Punitive Damages Related to a Certified Act of Terrorism

Exclusion of Punitive Damages—Exclusion of Punitive Damages Related to a Certified Act of Terrorism Form CA 23 62

This is also an optional CA Prior Approval endorsement that is available for CA midterm, new, and renewal policies that contain coverage for certified acts of terrorism. Because it is a prior approval form, check with your state to determine form status.

This exclusion includes the following statement:

> *This insurance does not apply to:*
>
> *TERRORISM PUNITIVE DAMAGES*
>
> *Damages arising, directly or indirectly, out of a "certified act of terrorism" that are awarded as punitive damages.*

This endorsement is designed to eliminate the risk of unfair or excessive litigation against American companies following terrorist attacks.

It helps to insure that for-profit and charitable entities will be able to obtain affordable terrorism coverage because it reduces the risk that they will be unfairly sued for the acts of international terrorists. Punitive damages are designed to punish criminal or near-criminal wrong doing, not entities that are victims of terrorism.

Punitive Damages Exclusions Vary by State

The Exclusion of Punitive Damages Related to a Certified Act of Terrorism endorsement is not offered in all states because some states prohibit excluding punitive damages, while others prohibit coverage. As with all Prior Approval forms, check with your state to determine form approval status.

Also note that the TRIA specifically states that punitive damages will not be considered as part of insured losses. In other words, punitive damages will not be included in the calculation of the $5 million certified act loss threshold or the $100 billion annual cap.

Common Endorsement Provisions

Punitive damages exclusion	This insurance does not apply to: TERRORISM PUNITIVE DAMAGES Damages arising, directly or indirectly, out of a "certified act of terrorism" that are awarded as punitive damages.
Definition of Certified Act of Terrorism	"Certified act of terrorism" means an act that is certified by the Secretary of the Treasury, in concurrence with the Secretary of State and the Attorney General of the United States, to be an act of terrorism pursuant to the federal Terrorism Risk Insurance Act of 2002. The federal Terrorism Risk Insurance Act of 2002 sets forth the following criteria for a "certified act of terrorism": 1. The act resulted in aggregate losses in excess of $5 million; and 2. The act is a violent act or an act that is dangerous to human life, property or infrastructure and is committed by an individual or individuals acting on behalf of any foreign person or foreign interest, as part of an effort to coerce the civilian population of the United States or to influence the policy or affect the conduct of the United States Government by coercion.

■ LIABILITY NUCLEAR HAZARD EXCLUSIONS

The following two nuclear hazard Prior Approval endorsement options are available for CA policies.

- *Nuclear, Biological Or Chemical Terrorism Exclusion (Other Than Certified Acts Of Terrorism); Cap on Losses from Certified Acts of Terrorism*, which excludes only nuclear, biological or chemical losses and places a cap on certified losses; or

- *Exclusion Of Certified Acts Of Terrorism; And Other Nuclear, Biological Or Chemical Acts of Terrorism*, which excludes certified acts and nuclear, biological or chemical acts of terrorism.

■ SUMMARY

While insurers must offer coverage for certified acts of terrorism, the Prior Approval forms offer a variety of levels of coverage for terrorism, ranging from what is required to be offered by the TRIA to a flat exclusion for all acts of terrorism.

The Terrorism Prior Approval chart for all liability policies appears on the next page. This chart and other reference charts, along with a sample of all property and liability terrorism endorsements, are included in the following course reference guide:

- *Terrorism Coverage for Commercial Lines Reference Guide*

This guide includes reference charts and sample endorsement forms for all lines covered under the TRIA. If you would like to order this guide, call Dearborn Customer Service at 1-800-824-8742. This is an excellent resource to use after completing this course.

Liability Prior Approval Terrorism Forms Summary
New or Renewal Policies

Name	Description/Purpose	CGL Form #	CA Form #	Umb. Form #
Limited Exclusion of Acts of Terrorism (Other Than Certified Acts of Terrorism); Cap on Losses from Certified Acts of Terrorism	Adds a terrorism exclusion similar to the 1/01/ 02 terrorism exclusions similar to that in place today (the definition of terrorism has changed) with an exception for coverage for certified acts of terrorism.	CG 21 71	CA 23 58	CU 21 31
Nuclear, Biological or Chemical Terrorism Exclusion (Other Than Certified Acts of Terrorism); Cap on Losses from Certain Acts of Terrorism	Excludes only nuclear, biological or chemical losses. Places a cap on certified losses.	CG 21 72	CA 23 59	CU 21 32
Exclusion of Certified Acts of Terrorism and Other Acts of Terrorism	"Total" exclusion of all terrorist acts subject to definition of what triggers the exclusion.	CG 21 75	CG 23 61	CU 21 35
Exclusion of Certified Acts of Terrorism; and Other Nuclear, Biological or Chemical Acts of Terrorism	Excludes certified acts and nuclear, biological or chemical acts of terrorism.	CG 21 74	CA 23 60	CU 21 34
War Liability Exclusion Specific forms per coverage parts	Expanded war exclusion definition.	CG 00 62, 63, 64	N/A	CU 00 02
Exclusion of Punitive Damages Related to a Certified Act of Terrorism For all policies containing coverage for certified acts of terrorism	Excludes damages that are awarded as punitive damages from certified acts of terrorism.	CG 21 76	CA 23 62	CU 21 36

■ **UNIT 6 REVIEW QUESTIONS**

1. Which of the following are examples of terrorism acts that can be excluded using the Prior Approval terrorism endorsements?

   A. Domestic acts of terrorism

   B. Acts that meet all certified acts of terrorism definition requirements except the $5 million aggregate loss threshold

   C. Losses of any damage amount involving nuclear, biological, or chemical acts

   D. All of the above

2. Which of the following is a reason why there are Prior Approval terrorism exclusions for other acts of terrorism that involve nuclear materials for commercial liability policies and not for commercial property policies?

   A. There is a greater exposure for commercial liability policies.

   B. Commercial property policies have a comprehensive nuclear hazard exclusion within their property coverage forms.

   C. There are Prior Approval liability terrorism exclusion options for commercial property policies.

   D. ISO has not yet introduced commercial property nuclear exclusion endorsements

■ **ANSWERS TO UNIT 6 REVIEW QUESTIONS**

1. **D.** All are examples of acts of terrorism that can be excluded using the Prior Approval terrorism endorsements.

2. **B.** All terrorism coverage endorsements are subject to the underlying coverage form exclusions. Commercial property coverage forms have a comprehensive nuclear hazard exclusion. Liability coverage forms, however, have a more limited Nuclear Energy exclusion that was intended primarily to exclude coverage that is required for purchase from Nuclear Energy Liability Insurance Association Pools, which are designed to provide coverage for businesses that have loss exposures due to activities on or near nuclear energy plants. Before 9/11/01, it was generally accepted that the stated nuclear energy exclusions along with the war exclusion adequately eliminated coverage for catastrophic nuclear events.

7

The Garage Policy

T he Insurance Services Office developed the **Garage Coverage Form** (CA 00 05) to provide selected liability and physical damage coverages to meet the special needs of garage risks. The form uses simplified wording and must be combined with the appropriate Declarations Page, supplementary schedule, and endorsements to constitute a Garage Policy.

The Garage Coverage Form consists of six parts:

- Section I—Covered Autos

- Section II—Liability Coverage

- Section III—Garagekeepers Coverage

- Section IV—Physical Damage Coverage

- Section V—Garage Conditions

- Section VI—Definitions

Learning Objectives

This unit will examine each section of the Garage Coverage Form and discuss some recent major revisions to ISO's Garage Program.

When you have completed this unit, you should be able to:

- identify the types of businesses that need and qualify for garage coverage;

- understand the special coverage needs of garage risks;

- explain the coverage options available to meet the needs of garage operations;

- analyze the Garage Coverage Form provisions, conditions, and exclusions;

- discuss the garagekeepers coverage endorsement;

- explain the new ISO Auto Service Risks Program; and

- explain the function of the Garage Coverage Form with other commercial auto policies.

■ ■ ■ ■ ■

■ THE NEED FOR GARAGE POLICY COVERAGE

Companies in the business of selling, servicing, storing, or parking autos have unique insurance needs. To meet the special needs of garages, ISO developed a special Garage Program and the Garage Coverage Form (CA 00 05).

Garage risks, like other businesses, need to protect their automobile exposures. Garage businesses also need liability protection for damage or loss to autos left in their care, custody, or control.

As explained previously in this course, the Business Auto Policy (BAP) provides physical damage coverage and broad liability protection to meet the needs of most commercial insureds. However, garage businesses have additional premises and operations exposures that are not covered under the BAP.

Understanding the Basics

Many insurance professionals do not have direct responsibility for garage, trucker, or motor carrier business. However, as a professional, you should have a basic understanding of the risks involved and coverage available for these types of business.

✓ *Helpful Hint:* The state CE exam for this course covers only basic information about the Garage, Truckers and Motor Carrier Coverage Forms. The test does not include technical questions about automobile symbols or coverage forms.

BAP and CGL May Not Provide Adequate Coverage

The Commercial General Liability Coverage Form (CG 00 01 10 01) provides coverage for most of the premises, products, completed operations, personal injury, advertising, and contractual liability exposures of an organization.

A garage's premises exposure can be addressed with a CGL form. However, the CGL has a "care, custody, and control" exclusion that would eliminate coverage for damage to customers' autos, an exposure that garages need to address. Used alone, the CGL is not suitable for garage risks.

Comparison of Garage Policy to BAP and CGL

Many of the policy provisions found in the Commercial General Liability (CGL) form and/or the Business Auto Policy (BAP) are also found in the Garage Coverage Form.

Simply combining the two forms in a single policy would not completely address the unique exposures of firms engaged in the automobile business, such as damage to customer vehicles. To avoid any coverage gaps that might arise by using only the CGL and BAP forms, ISO created a distinct Garage Coverage Form.

The Garage Coverage Form is a Commercial Auto Form. The form provides liability coverage for bodily injury arising out of the ownership, maintenance, or use of an automobile. It also provides physical damage protection for covered vehicles, including vehicles held for sale.

In addition, the Garage Coverage Form functions as a Commercial General Liability (CGL) form. It provides liability coverage for bodily injury and property damage resulting from the garage's commercial premises and operations.

The form also contains garagekeepers coverage, a specialized coverage for bodily injury or property damage arising out of the garage business operations. The insured may select comprehensive, specified causes of loss, or collision coverage.

Two Types of Auto Business Risks Need Coverage

When the Garage Coverage Form was originally created, ISO intended it to cover businesses engaged in the business of selling, servicing, storing, or parking automobiles. ISO divided these businesses into two categories:

- **Auto dealerships**-Individuals or organizations in the business of selling autos, trucks, motorcycles, or other vehicles

- **Non-dealer** auto service risks-Repair shops, service stations, storage garages, public parking places, and tow truck operators.

Garage Program Does Not Cover Non-Dealer Auto Service Risks

Currently, the Garage Coverage Form only covers auto dealerships defined as individuals or organizations in the business of selling autos, trucks, motorcycles, or other vehicles.

In mid-2001, ISO revised the Garage Program so that it no longer applies to non-dealer auto service risks. This class of business must now be covered by a special combination of forms or by a newly introduced ISO program. Later in this unit we will further explore coverage of non-dealer auto service risks.

Non-dealer auto service risks, such as repair shops, service stations, storage garages, public parking places, and tow truck operators must now be covered by either:

- a combination of the CGL, BAP, and a Garagekeepers Coverage (CA 99 37) endorsement; or

- ISO's Auto Service Risks Program.

Why Are Auto Service Risks No Longer Part of the Garage Program?

Under the Garage Coverage Form, garage operations are defined as the ownership, maintenance, or use of locations for garage business. It also includes covered autos as indicated in the policy and all operations that are necessary or incidental to a garage business.

As garages and service stations began to offer a broad range of services (such as convenience stores that are unrelated to "garage operations" per se) insurers began to question whether these risks were covered under the Garage Program.

ISO determined that the Garage Coverage Form was not intended to provide coverage for this type of auto service risk exposure. However, ISO's Commercial General Liability (CGL) Program can provide coverage for auto service risks. Underwriting guidelines, general rules, and other information are available in the CGL sections of the *Commercial Lines Manual*.

Non-dealer auto service risks and their coverage options will be covered in more detail later in this course.

Garage Coverage Form Addresses Special Needs

The Garage Coverage Form covers three types of garage risk: (1) auto liability, (2) commercial general liability, and (3) physical damage coverages. The form also incorporates premises and operations liability, contractual, and products and completed operations.

A number of endorsements are available to further broaden coverage.

Garage Liability Coverage Similar to CGL Coverage

The Garage Coverage Form provides liability coverage similar to that provided by the CGL and the BAP in two insuring agreements.

- The Garage Operations—Other Than Covered Autos insuring agreement promises to pay all sums an insured must legally pay for damages because of bodily injury or property damages caused by an accident and resulting from garage operations other than the ownership, maintenance, or use of covered autos.

- The Garage Operations—Covered Autos insuring agreement promises to pay all sums an insured must legally pay for damages because of bodily injury or property damages caused by an accident and involving the ownership, maintenance, or use of covered autos.

Liability Coverage Depends on Covered Auto Use

Whether someone is an "insured" under the Garage Coverage Form depends on whether the liability involves covered autos or garage operations involving other than covered autos.

- Garage liability for covered autos is provided for the insured named and anyone else using the auto with the insured's permission, the insured's employees (if the covered auto is owned by an employee), and customers (with certain restrictions).

- Garage liability for garage operations for other than covered autos is provided for the named insured, the insured's partners, employees, and directors or stockholders while acting within the scope of their duties.

Liability Coverage Provided for Garage Products

Liability for products that are made or sold in a garage business are covered under the Garage Coverage Form. The definition of "products" also includes: "...*the providing of or failure to provide warnings or instructions.*"

Complete operations coverage applies in the event of a claim that resulted from property damage to an auto as a result of work the insured performed on the auto.

Garagekeepers Coverage for Autos Left with the Insured

Section III—Garagekeepers Coverage covers the insured's liability for a loss to a covered auto or auto equipment left in the insured's care while the insured is attending, servicing, repairing, parking, or storing the auto in the garage operation.

The Garage Coverage Form includes garagekeepers coverage because the garage liability section of the policy (and the CGL) excludes coverage for autos left in the insured's care, custody, or control.

The insured may elect from three causes of loss: (1) comprehensive, (2) collision, or (3) specified causes of loss (fire, explosion, theft, and mischief or vandalism.

Garage Physical Damage Coverage

The Garage Coverage Form provides the same collision, comprehensive, or specified causes of loss coverages available under the BAP. However, the garage form contains additional exclusions such as loss to a covered auto by false pretense as defined in the form.

Auto dealers physical damage coverage is provided for new or used autos held for sale by the auto dealership. If this coverage is needed, it is usually written on a reporting form basis.

ISO Garage Policy Construction

The Garage Coverage Form is only part of a garage policy. An auto dealership needs a complete garage policy which consists of:

- Garage Declarations (CA 00 06);

- Garage Coverage Form—Auto Dealer's Supplemental Schedule (CA 00 07);

- Garage Coverage Form (CA 00 05); and

- Endorsements.

Because it primarily coverage premises operations, the garage policy is intended to closely align with the Commercial General Liability (CGL) policy.

Next we will briefly cover the forms that typically make up the garage policy.

Dec Page, Supplementary Schedules, and Forms

The garage policy format begins with the Garage Coverage Declarations (CA 00 06). The form lists two important items of information:

- Item One: the insured's name, policy number, and form of business

- Item Two: a schedule of coverages afforded and types of covered autos

The type of coverage afforded for the covered autos is determined by the use of 11 auto symbols ranging from Symbol 21 through 31. Symbols 21 through 29 closely correspond to the Symbols 1 through 9 on the BAP. The similarities and differences are discussed in the next unit.

✓ *Helpful Hint:* The Garage Coverage Form Declarations is on page 306 in the Appendix.

Auto Dealer's Supplementary Schedule

The Declarations Page is completed with the attachment of the Garage Coverage Form—Auto Dealer's Supplemental Schedule (CA 00 07) that provides information about the auto dealer garage risk.

The schedule begins with Item Three, adding additional information to Item One and Two shown on the Declarations Page.

- Item Three: Locations Where You Conduct Garage Operation (lists main and all business locations by address)

- Item Four: Liability Coverage—Premiums (based on the number of employees and non-employees)

- Item Five: Liability Coverage For Your Customers (provides or removes liability for the dealer's customers)

- Item Six: Garagekeepers Coverages and Premiums (includes insurance limits and coverages)

- Item Seven: Physical Damage Coverage — Types Of Covered Autos And Interests In These Autos — Premiums — Reporting Or Nonreporting Basis (indicates physical damage coverage for autos held for sale)

- Item Eight: Medical Payments Coverage (premium schedule for other than those listed in Item Nine)

- Item Nine: Schedule of Covered Autos Which are Furnished to Someone Other Than a Class I or Class II Operators or Which are Insured on a Specified Car Basis (contains rates and premiums for certain covered autos)

✓ **Helpful Hint:** The Garage Coverage Form—Auto Dealers' Supplementary Schedule is on p. 350 in the Appendix.

Endorsements Amend the Policy Coverage

Like many other insurance policies, the coverage in the garage policy may be added, deleted, or amended by a number of endorsements.

Common endorsements include:

- Garage Locations and Operations Medical Payments Coverage (CA 25 05) that pays reasonable medical and funeral expenses for bodily injury caused by an accident related to the garage operations; and

- Dealer's Driver Collision Coverage (CA 25 02) that removes the exclusion for collision loss to covered autos driven or transported more than 50 road miles from point of purchase or distribution to their destination.

Garage Coverage Form Provides Broad Coverage

The major portion of the basic garage policy is the Insurance Services Office's (ISO's) Garage Coverage Form (CA 00 05). This form provides coverage for liability arising from garage operations, medical payments, automobile physical damage, and uninsured or underinsured motorists in a single contract for automobile dealers.

The Garage Coverage Form is divided into six major sections:

- Section I—Covered Autos

- Section II—Liability Coverage

- Section III—Garagekeepers Coverage

- Section IV—Physical Damage Coverage

- Section V—Garage Conditions

- Section VI—Definitions

■ SECTION I—COVERED AUTOS DESCRIBED BY NUMERIC SYMBOLS

The Garage Coverage Form, like the Business Auto Policy, uses coverage symbols to denote covered autos. The 11 coverage symbols and their descriptions appear in Subsection A. Description of Covered Auto Designation Symbols of the Garage Coverage Form.

Like the BAP, the type of coverage afforded for autos is determined by the use of covered auto designation symbols. The appropriate symbols must be included in Item Two of the Declarations Page of the garage policy or on the Garage Coverage Form—Auto Dealer's Supplementary Schedule (CA 00 07)

The BAP Symbols 1 through 9 closely align with the Garage Coverage Form Symbols 21 through 29. However, there are some wording variances between the symbols. The differences between Symbols 7 (BAP) and 27 (Garage Coverage Form) are:

BAP Symbol 7	Only those "autos" described in Item Three of the Declarations for which a premium charge is shown (and for liability Coverage any "trailers" you don't own while attached to any power unit described in Item Three).
Garage Symbol 27	Only those "autos" described in Item Seven of the Non-Dealers and Trailers Dealers' Supplementary Schedule or Item Nine of the Dealers Supplementary Schedule for which a premium charge is shown (and for liability Coverage any "trailers" you don't own while attached to any power unit described in Item Seven or Item Nine).

Symbols Provide Different Coverage

The Garage Coverage Form—Auto Dealer's Supplementary Schedule requires a great deal more information than needed on the BAP Declarations Page.

Under Item Seven, above, which provides physical damage coverage, the insured must select the type of coverage requested, the types of covered autos, and interests in these autos on either a reporting or non-reporting basis.

The vehicles' locations and the limit of insurance for each location must also be selected.

Note: As stated earlier, Non-Dealers and Trailer Dealers are no longer eligible for the Garage Program. However, ISO has not yet revised the definitions of the coverage symbols.

The BAP and Garage symbols are similar in many ways.

Following is a chart showing the descriptions of the covered auto designation symbols. **Variances** are indicated by an asterisk and explained on the following pages.

BAP Symbol	Garage Form Symbol	Description
1	21	Any "Auto"
2	22	Owned "Autos" Only
3	23	Owned Private Passenger "Autos" Only
4	24	Owned "Autos" Other Than Private Passenger "Autos" Only
5	25	Owned "Autos" Subject To No-Fault
6	26	Owned "Autos" Subject To A Compulsory Uninsured Motorists Law
7	27*	Specifically Described "Autos"
8	28	Hired "Autos" Only
9	29*	Nonowned "Autos" Only Garage Form Nonowned "Autos" Only Used in Your Garage Business
	30*	"Autos" Left With You For Service, Repair, Storage, Or Safekeeping
	31*	Dealers "Autos" And "Autos" Held For Sale By Non-Dealers Or Trailer Dealers (Physical Damage Coverages)

NOTE: Although non-dealers and trailer dealers are no longer eligible for the Garage Program, it is likely that ISO will not withdraw or revise the definitions of these coverage symbols until the Auto Service Risk Program is approved in all states.

Garage Policy Adds Three Garage-Related Symbols

As shown in the BAP Symbol vs. Garage Form Symbol Comparison Chart, above, the Garage Coverage Form adds three symbols specific to a garage business—29, 30, and 31—that are not included in the BAP's covered auto section:

- Symbol 29—Nonowned Autos Used in Your Garage Business;

- Symbol 30—Autos Left With You for Service, Care, Storage, or Safekeeping; and

- Symbol 31—Dealers' Autos and Autos Held For Sale by Non-Dealers or Trailer Dealers (Physical Damage Coverage)

Symbol 29 Used for Liability Coverage

Symbol 29—Non-Owned Autos Used in Your Garage Business applies to autos the insured uses, leases, rents, or borrows in connection with the garage business described in the Declarations Page. Symbol 29 is designed solely for liability coverage and may be used alone or with Symbols 22, 23, 24, or 28.

Symbol 29 also covers those autos the insured has used, leased, rented, or borrowed from any employee, a partner (when the insured is a partnership), a member (when the insured is a limited liability company), or a member of an employee's or partner's household.

Symbols Provided Different Coverage   Unlike the BAP Symbol 9 that covers autos for business or personal use, Symbol 29 only covers autos used in the garage business. When autos are used for personal use, no coverage applies under the garage policy.

BAP Symbol 9	Only those "autos" you do not own, lease, hire, rent, or borrow that are used in connection with your business. This includes "autos" owned by your "employees," partners (if you are a partnership), members (if you are a limited liability company) or members of their households but only while used in your business or your personal affairs.
Garage Symbol 27	Any "auto" you do not own, lease, hire, rent, or borrow used in connection with your garage business described in the Declarations. This includes "autos" owned by your "employees" or partners (if you are a partnership), members (if you are a limited liability company) or members of their households but only while used in your garage business.

Symbol 29 Provides Additional Liability Coverage   Employees who have a Personal Auto Policy (PAP) may use their own autos in the garage business. When employees use their owned auto in a "trade, profession, or occupation," they provide their employers with primary protection under the PAP.

If a loss occurs and the employee's PAP limits are found to be inadequate, the addition of Symbol 29 to the employer's garage policy provides employers with non-ownership liability coverage as excess insurance.

If the employee does not have insurance, Symbol 29 provides primary liability coverage for the employer only.

Symbol 29 Protects Employer   Ralph works as a service manager at ABC Auto Dealership. He schedules regular service appointments for customers who have purchased new cars from ABC. With his employer's knowledge and permission, Ralph often provides transportation in his own car when a customer must leave a car for service and needs a ride home.

Real Life Application

On the way to a customer's home, Ralph is involved in an accident that damages several cars and injures the customer. The drivers of the other cars and the customer bring suit against both Ralph and ABC.

1. If Ralph has a PAP and ABC has selected Symbol 29 on its garage policy, what liability protection is provided for ABC?

Symbol 30 Used for Cars Left in Garage

An auto dealer may perform many of the activities normally associated with a garage. For example, owners often return their cars to a dealership for normal maintenance such as oil and filter changes. In addition, the dealer has an ever-changing number of new and used cars that may need service or repair.

Vehicles that customers leave with the garage may be covered with Symbol 30—Autos Left With You for Service, Repair, Storage, or Safekeeping. The definition of *vehicles* includes land motor vehicles, trailers, or semitrailers. Under the garage policy, the definition of a *customer* is extended to include employee or members of their households who pay for the services performed.

Symbol 30 applies only to garagekeepers coverage. A full discussion of this symbol is included in the next lesson.

Symbol 31 Used for Consignment Cars

Symbol 31 is used to cover autos described in Item Seven of the Garage Coverage Form—Auto Dealer's Supplementary Schedule (CA 00 07). These autos are sometimes referred to as consigned autos because they belong to someone other than the dealer who currently has possession of the autos in order to sell them. That auto possession (care, custody, or control) creates an exposure for the dealer.

To cover this exposure, Symbol 31 is placed opposite the desired coverages in the policy Declarations (CA 00 06).

The value of the autos must be shown in Item Seven of the Garage Coverage Form—Auto Dealer's Supplementary Schedule (CA 00 07). The value of each auto is not separately included, but the total value of all the covered autos must be shown.

Autos Acquired after the Policy Inception

When Symbols 21, 22, 24, 25, or 26 are shown in Item Two of the Declarations Page, coverage is provided for newly acquired autos of the type described for each symbol for the remainder of the policy period.

However, when Symbol 27 is shown in Item Two, newly acquired autos are covered only if:

Answer & Rationale

1. ABC Auto Dealership has primary protection under Ralph's PAP. If the loss is determined to be part of the garage operations, ABC also has excess liability protection under its own policy because it selected Symbol 29.

- the insurer already covers all autos the insured owns of that types or if the newly acquired auto replaces an auto the insured previously owned that had that coverage; and

- the insured notifies the insurer within 30 days to advise of the intention to cover the newly acquired auto.

■ SECTION II—LIABILITY COVERAGE COVERS GARAGE OPERATIONS

Section II—Liability Coverage provides coverage for two types of expenses related to garage operations: (1) customer's autos and (2) business-owned autos.

Customer's autos are covered under the Garage Operations—Other Than Covered Autos insuring agreement. Under this insuring agreement, the insurer:

- pays all sums an insured must pay legally as damages because of bodily injury or property damage caused by an accident resulting from garage operations other than the ownership, maintenance, or use of covered autos; and

- has the right and duty to defend any suit asking for these damages.

The insurer's duty to defend or settle ends when the applicable liability coverage limit of insurance shown on the Declarations Page has been exhausted by the payment of judgments or settlements.

> ### ■ *ISO FORM*
>
> **1. "Garage Operations" – Other Than Covered "Autos"**
>
> **a.** We will pay all sums an "insured" legally must pay as damages because of "bodily injury" or "property damage" to which this insurance applies caused by an "accident" and resulting from "garage operations" other than the ownership, maintenance or use of covered "autos".

Garage Operations Adds Covered Pollution Cost

Business-owned autos are covered under the Garage Operations—Covered Autos insuring agreement. The insuring agreements in the BAP and the Garage Coverage Form are the same in substance, except for the first two. In the Garage Coverage Form, the insuring agreements provide that the carrier will pay:

- all sums an insured must pay legally as damages because of bodily injury or property damage caused by an accident resulting from garage operations involving the ownership, maintenance, or use of covered autos; and

- all sums an insured must pay legally as a covered pollution cost or an expense caused by an accident resulting from garage operations involving the ownership, maintenance, or use of covered autos;

However, the other coverage agreements are the same as the BAP's, including the insurer's right to investigate and settle, and its duty to defend the insured, which ends when the liability coverage limit of insurance has been exhausted by payment of judgments or settlements.

> ### ■ ISO FORM
>
> We have the right and duty to defend any "insured" against a "suit" asking for these damages. However, we have no duty to defend any "insured" against a "suit" seeking damages for "bodily injury" or "property damage" to which this insurance does not apply. We may investigate and settle any claim or "suit" as we consider appropriate. Our duty to defend or settle ends when the applicable Liability Coverage Limit of Insurance – "Garage Operations" – Other Than Covered "Autos" has been exhausted by payment of judgments or settlements.

Definition of "Who Is an Insured" Differs Slightly From BAP

The insuring agreement promises to pay damages on behalf on an insured, when the insured is found legally liable. In the Garage Coverage Form, the following are insureds for covered autos:

- you, the insured, for any covered auto;

- any permissive user of a covered auto the insured owns, hires or borrows, except:

   1. the owner or anyone else from whom you hire or borrow a covered auto, but does not apply to trailers;

   2. employees if the covered auto is owned by that employee or member of household;

   3. someone using a covered auto while working in the business of selling, servicing or repairing autos;

   4. customers (with some exceptions);

   5. partners or member of a limited liability company for a covered auto owned by the partner or member or any household member; and

6. anyone liable for the conduct of an insured, but only to the extent of that liability.

■ *ISO FORM*

3. Who Is An Insured

a. The following are "insureds" for covered "autos":

(1) You for any covered "auto".

(2) Anyone else while using with your permission a covered "auto" you own, hire or borrow except:

(a) The owner or anyone else from whom you hire or borrow a covered "auto". This exception does not apply if the covered "auto" is a "trailer" connected to a covered "auto" you own.

(b) Your "employee" if the covered "auto" is owned by that "employee" or a member of his or her household.

(c) Someone using a covered "auto" while he or she is working in a business of selling, servicing, repairing, parking or storing "autos" unless that business is your "garage operations".

(d) Your customers, if your business is shown in the Declarations as an "auto" dealership. However, if a customer of yours:

(i) Has no other available insurance (whether primary, excess or contingent), they are an "insured" but only up to the compulsory or financial responsibility law limits where the covered "auto" is principally garaged.

> **(ii)** Has other available insurance (whether primary, excess or contingent) less than the compulsory or financial responsibility law limits exceed the limit of their other insurance. **(e)**A partner (if you are a partnership), or a member (if you are a limited liability company), for a covered "auto" owned by him or her or a member of his or her household.
>
> **(3)** Anyone liable for the conduct of an "insured" described above but only to the extent of that liability.

Insureds for Customer Autos

For the purposes of garage operations involving customer autos, the only insureds are:

- you (the named insured); and

- your partners, members, employees, directors or shareholders, but only while acting within the scope of their duties.

In other words, anyone else using a covered auto with the insured's permission is not considered an insured under Section II—Liability Coverage.

> ■ *ISO FORM*
>
> **b.** The following are "insureds" for "garage operations" other than covered "autos":
>
> **(1)** You.
>
> **(2)** Your partners (if you are a partnership), members (if you are a limited liability company), "employees", directors or shareholders but only while acting within the scope of their duties.

Coverage Extensions—Supplementary Payments

In addition to the limit of insurance, there are six supplementary payments the insurer pays for the insured. The payments apply to any claim or lawsuit the insurer defends and include:

- all expenses the insurer incurs;

- up to $2,000 for the cost of bail bonds, including bonds for related traffic law violations, required because of an accident the insurer covers (the insurer does not have to furnish these bonds);

- the cost of bonds to release attachments in any suit the insurer defends, but only for bond amounts within the limit of insurance;

- all reasonable expenses the insured incurs for court appearances, depositions, and other legal proceedings, including actual loss of earnings up to $250 a day because of time off work;

- all costs taxed against the insured in any suit; and

- all interest on the full amount of any judgment that accrues after entry of the judgment (the insurer's duty to pay interest ends when it has paid, offered to pay or deposited in court the part of the judgment that is within its limit of insurance).

Out-of-State Coverage Extensions

While a covered auto is away from the state in which it is licensed or garaged, two important coverage extensions are provided. These extensions allow the insurance provided by the garage policy to comply with state responsibility laws, no-fault or other compulsory insurance.

The insurer will:

- increase the limit of insurance for liability coverage to meet the limits specified by a state's compulsory or financial responsibility law (this extension does not apply to the limit or limits specified by any law governing motor carriers of passengers or property); and

- provide the minimum amounts and types of other coverages, such as no fault coverage, required of out-of-state vehicles by the jurisdiction where the covered auto is being used.

> ■ *ISO FORM*
>
> **(1)** Increase the Limit of Insurance for Liability Coverage to meet the limits specified by a compulsory or financial responsibility law of the jurisdiction where the covered "auto" is being used. This extension does not apply to the limit or limits specified by any law governing motor carriers of passengers or property.
>
> **(2)** Provide the minimum amounts and types of other coverages, such as no-fault, required of out-of-state vehicles by the jurisdiction where the covered "auto" is being used.

■ GARAGE COVERAGE EXCLUSIONS

The Garage Coverage Form lists 17 exclusions. Many of the exclusions are similar to those listed in the BAP (which has 13 exclusions), but some exclusions are more restrictive. The differences between the two forms are pointed out in the following pages.

The broad range of exclusions speaks to the broad premises, business operations, and auto liability exposures covered under the Garage Coverage Form. When applicable, the exclusions provide information about how coverage may be "bought back" by endorsement or otherwise covered.

Because BAP exclusions were previously covered in this course, the next several pages address only the Garage Coverage Form exclusions that are not in the BAP or are treated differently from the BAP.

Insured May Use Force to Protect Property

The Expected Or Intended Injury exclusion is sometimes referred to as the intentional acts exclusion. Most bodily injury or property damage that the insured intends or expects to cause is not covered. However, when an insured uses reasonable force to protect or defend persons or property, the policy provides coverage.

The intent of the intentional acts exclusion is to reiterate that the garage policy intends to cover accidents, which are unexpected and unintended events. The exclusion only applies if the injury or damage in question is expected or intended from the standpoint of the insured (not any other party.)

The CGL policy, like the Garage Coverage Form, does not apply this exclusion if the insured must use reasonable bodily force to protect persons or property. The BAP, however, does not address the use of reasonable bodily force.

Currently, there are no ISO endorsements to buy back expected or intended injury coverage.

> ■ *ISO FORM*
>
> ### 1. Expected Or Intended Injury
>
> "Bodily injury" or "property damage" expected or intended from the standpoint of the "insured". But for "garage operations" other than covered "autos" this exclusion does not apply to "bodily injury" resulting from the use of reasonable force to protect persons or property.

Garage Care, Custody, or Control Is Broader

Under the BAP, the Care, Custody, Or Control exclusion eliminates property damage to or the covered pollution cost or expense for property owned or transported by the insured. The exclusion is broader under the Garage Coverage Form.

The Garage Coverage Form also excludes property:

- rented or occupied by the insured;

- loaned to the insured;

- held for sale or being transported by the insured; or

- in the care, custody, or control of the insured.

The CGL, BAP, and Garage Coverage Form(s) all include an exception to this exclusion for liability assumed under sidetrack agreements.

A sidetrack agreement is a contractual **hold-harmless** agreement between a railroad and a property owner pertaining to the use of a sidetrack leading to the property owner's premises. The railroad requires that the property owner assume certain liabilities in exchange for constructing the sidetrack, such as liability for damaged goods or bodily injury resulting from use of the sidetrack.

The contractual liability resulting from a sidetrack agreement is provided automatically under the Insurance Services Office commercial general liability forms.

> ■ *ISO FORM*
>
> ### 6. Care, Custody Or Control
>
> "Property damage" to or "covered pollution cost or expense" involving:
>
> **a.** Property owned, rented or occupied by the "insured";
>
> **b.** Property loaned to the "insured";
>
> **c.** Property held for sale or being transported by the "insured"; or
>
> **d.** Property in the "insured's" care, custody or control.
>
> But this exclusion does not apply to liability assumed under a sidetrack agreement.

Handling of Property Not Specifically Mentioned

The BAP includes a Handling of Property exclusion that eliminates coverage for accidents that occur during the loading or unloading of autos. Bodily injury or property damage that occurs before or after property is moved is excluded.

Neither the CGL nor the Garage Coverage Form mention handling of property. However, under the care, custody, or control exclusion, property being transported by the insured is not covered.

Leased Autos Covered When Rented to Customers

The Garage Cover Form excludes Leased Autos described as any covered auto while leased or rented to others.

However, the exclusion does not apply to a covered auto that the insured rents to a customer while the customer's auto is left with the insured for service or repair.

The BAP does not mention a leased auto exclusion.

> ■ *ISO FORM*
>
> ### 7. Leased Autos
>
> Any covered "auto" while leased or rented to others. But this exclusion does not apply to a covered "auto" you rent to one of your customers while their "auto" is left with you for service or repair.

Liquor Liability Coverage May Be Excluded

Host liquor liability covers individuals or organizations (not engaged in the business of distilling, selling, or distributing alcoholic beverages) that sponsor or host events where liquor is served. Liability coverage is provided for injury or damage caused by an intoxicated person to whom the insured served liquor.

Insureds under the BAP or the Truckers Coverage Form do not have a premises exposure. Therefore, neither form addresses Liquor Liability. Garages, however, have premises exposures that could potentially lead to liability claims.

If the insured serves liquor on the premises and the insured is held liable for bodily injury or property damage, the Garage Coverage Form applies the Liquor Liability exclusion if the premises was used to furnish liquor for a charge, if a license was required for serving liquor, or the liquor was served for financial gain.

Some Host Liquor Liability Provided

Some host liquor liability applies for incidental exposures that arise from serving liquor. For example, if a garage is hosting a party for a group of friends and one has an auto accident after drinking excessively, it is likely that the garage policy will provide a defense and pay damages, if damages are awarded.

The Broadened Coverage—Garages (CA 25 14) endorsement may also be added to cover host liquor liability. The endorsement also provides coverage for personal and advertising injury liability, **fire legal liability**, **incidental medical malpractice**, **non-owned watercraft**, newly acquired businesses, additional persons, and limited worldwide liability coverage.

Miscellaneous Exclusions for Difficult-to-Insure Risks

The remaining Garage Coverage Form exclusions exclude coverage for toxic and environmental hazards (pollution); product and business liability (**defective products**, **recall** expenses, work performed, impaired property, personal and advertising injury); watercraft and aircraft liability; racing and demolition, and war and insurrection.

These exclusions are all contained in the CGL policy, and are in the Garage Policy because of the garage owner's premises and operations exposure.

Because business property insured under a BAP does not have certain exposures, some exclusions are not addressed. For example, leased autos, defective products, and pollution exclusions applicable to garage operations are not listed in the BAP.

Policy Provides an Aggregate Limit of Insurance

The **Aggregate Limit** Of Insurance—Garage Operations—Other Than Covered Autos section limits the amount the insurer will pay for damages involving garage operations other than those involving covered autos.

The following coverages are contained in the CGL. As stated in the Garage Coverage Form's **Limit Of Insurance** section, these coverage may be added to the garage policy by separate endorsement:

- **Personal Injury Liability** Coverage

- **Personal and Advertising Injury Liability** Coverage

- Host Liquor Liability Coverage

- Fire Legal Liability Coverage

- Incidental Medical Malpractice Liability Coverage

- Nonowned Watercraft Coverage

- Broad Form Products Coverage

As stated previously, these coverages may also be added to the Garage Coverage Form with a single endorsement, Broadened Coverages—Garages (CA 25 14).

✓ *Helpful Hint:* Samples of these forms are available in the Appendix.

Section I Does Not Mention Mobile Equipment

You'll recall that the BAP excludes mobile equipment from its definition of an auto under the policy. The BAP includes liability for mobile equipment only when it is being transported or towed by a covered auto.

Under the Garage Coverage Form, an auto is defined as ". . . *a land motor vehicle, 'trailer' or semitrailer."*

There is no mention of mobile equipment in this definition. Therefore, coverage for mobile equipment is implied. However, there is some debate among insurers on this issue and insureds may elect to cover mobile equipment by endorsement under a CGL policy or an inland marine form.

■ GARAGEKEEPERS COVERAGE SECTION III

Auto dealers often work on customer autos which are in the garage's care, custody, or control. Therefore, the auto dealer's garage needs a special type of bailee liability coverage to protect it. Unfortunately, Section II—Liability Coverage of the Garage Coverage Form excludes damage to property in the insured's care, custody, or control.

This important coverage is granted in the insuring agreement of Section III—Garagekeepers Coverage. This section provides needed protection for garage operators against direct damage or legal liability for damage to vehicles in the insured's care, custody, or control.

Garagekeepers Coverage for Customer Vehicles

In the Garagekeepers Coverage insuring agreement, the insurance company agrees to pay the amounts for which the insured becomes liable as a result of damages to a customer's auto or its equipment while it is in the insured's care. Coverage applies while the insured is attending, servicing, repairing, parking, or storing the auto in the insured's garage operations.

Most auto dealers would need garagekeepers coverage if they do any auto service or repair. A premium for the coverage is included as part of the Garage Coverage Form premium.

Insuring Agreement Limits Payment to Legal Liability

A closer look at the Section III—Garagekeepers Coverage insuring agreement reveals a policy condition that may create some problems for the insured when a customer's car is damaged.

The insurer agrees to pay all sums the insured must pay for damages to a customer's vehicle in the insured's care if the insured is found legally liable for the damage and the damage is caused by a covered cause of loss.

When a loss occurs, the vehicle's policy (typically the Personal Auto Policy (PAP)) applies first. There are many instances, however, when the garage wants to maintain goodwill with customers and would opt to repair the damage, without regard for any determination of fault. In these cases, the garage may have to be personally responsible because the Garage Coverage Form would not provide coverage.

> ■ *ISO FORM*
>
> **A. Coverage**
> **1.** We will pay all sums the "insured" legally must pay as damages for "loss" to a "customer's auto" or "customer's auto" equipment left in the "insured's" care while the "insured" is attending, servicing, repairing, parking or storing it in your "garage operations" under:

Three Physical Damage Coverage Options

Section III—Garagekeepers Coverage provides three physical damage coverage options. Selections must be made for each of the insured's locations. The insured may select:

- Comprehensive Coverage—loss to a customer's auto from any cause of loss except the customer's auto's collision with another object;

- Specified Causes of Loss Coverage—damage from fire, lightning, explosion, theft, mischief, or vandalism; or

- Collision Coverage—damage caused by the customer's auto collision with another object or the customer's auto's overturn.

The selections are noted on the Garage Coverage Form—Auto Dealer's Supplementary Schedule (CA 00 07). Any loss is subject to a deductible for each customer's auto and a premium is charged based on the options selected.

Coverage—Insuring Agreements

The garage policy provides coverage for legal liability for property damage, which applies only if the garage is legally liable for damage. If the insured wants additional coverage, the policy can be amended by checking the appropriate box in Item Six of the Auto Dealers' Supplementary Schedule (CA 00 07).

There are two Direct Coverage Options:

- Primary basis, where the garagekeepers coverage becomes primary with respect to a customer's automobile, regardless of the garage's liability; and

- Excess basis, where the garagekeepers coverage responds regardless of liability, on an excess basis over any other collectible insurance.

There is a premium charge for each selection.

■ *ISO FORM*

DIRECT COVERAGE OPTIONS

Indicate below with an "X" which, if any, Direct Coverage Option is selected.

☐ **EXCESS INSURANCE**

If this box is checked, Garagekeepers Coverage remains applicable on a legal liability basis. However, coverage also applies without regard to your or any other "insured's" legal liability for "loss" to a "customer's auto" on an excess basis over any other collectible insurance regardless of whether the other insurance covers your or any other "insured's" interest or the interest of the "customer's auto's" owner.

☐ **PRIMARY INSURANCE**

If this box is checked, Garagekeepers Coverage is changed to apply without regard to your or any other "insured's" legal liability for "loss" to a "customer's auto" and is primary insurance.

Insurer Has the Right and Duty to Defend Suits or Claims

The Section III—Garagekeepers Coverage insuring agreement also states that the insurer reserves the right to investigate, settle, and defend any suit or claim as it deems appropriate.

There is no duty to settle or defend non-covered claims, and the **duty to defend** or settle ends when the Limit of Insurance for that coverage has been exhausted by the payment of judgments or settlements.

Definition of an Insured Different for Loss to Customer Autos

The definition of "Who Is An Insured" as it applies to Section III—Garagekeepers Coverage is relatively brief in comparison to the definition in Section II—Liability Coverage of the Garage Coverage Form.

The definition of *insured* under this section includes the named insured, any partners, members, employees, directors, or shareholders as defined in the policy.

However, coverage for those insureds applies only to loss to a customer's auto or auto equipment.

> ◪ *ISO FORM*
>
> **3. Who Is An Insured**
>
> The following are "insureds" for "loss" to "customer's autos" and "customer's auto" equipment:
>
> **a.** You.
>
> **b.** Your partners (if you are a partnership), or members (if you are a limited liability company), "employees", directors or shareholders while acting within the scope of their duties as such.

Supplementary Payments in Addition to Limit of Insurance

Section III—Garagekeepers Coverage includes supplementary payments in addition to the Limit of Insurance specified in the policy. The insurer agrees to pay:

- all expenses it incurs;

- bond amounts within the Limit of Liability;

- reasonable expenses, including up to $250 a day for loss of earnings, that the insured incurs at the insurer's request;

- costs taxed against the insured; and

- all interest on the full amount of a judgment against the insured.

The insurer's duty to pay interest ends when the insurer has paid, has offered to pay, or has deposited in court the part of the judgment that is within its Limit of Liability.

Liability Coverage Is Not All Inclusive

There are four primary types of damages that are excluded under Section III—Garagekeepers Coverage, Section B. Exclusions. The following exclusions should be carefully reviewed.

1. Contractual Obligations—Liability resulting from any agreement by which the insured accepts responsibility for loss. (There is no insured contract exception to this exclusion.)

2. Theft—Loss due to theft or conversion caused in any way by the insured, the insured's employees, or by the insured's shareholders.

3. Defective Parts—Defective parts or materials.

4. Faulty Work—Faulty work the insured performed.

This section also prohibits payment for loss to certain types of equipment. There is no coverage for loss to tape decks, sound equipment (unless permanently installed), sound reproducing equipment, sound receiving equipment, or any device designed or used to detect speed such as radar or laser detectors and any jamming apparatus intended to elude or disrupt speed measuring equipment.

■ *ISO FORM*

    2. We will not pay for "loss" to any of the following:

      a. Tape decks or other sound reproducing equipment unless permanently installed in a "customer's auto".

      b. Tapes, records or other sound reproducing devices designed for use with sound reproducing equipment.

      c. Sound receiving equipment designed for use as a citizens' band radio, two-way mobile radio or telephone or scanning monitor receiver, including its antennas and other accessories, unless permanently installed in the dash or console opening normally used by the "customer's auto" manufacturer for the installation of a radio.

d. Any device designed or used to detect speed measurement equipment such as radar or laser detectors and any jamming apparatus intended to elude or disrupt speed measurement equipment.

Limit of Insurance and Deductible

In certain cases, Garagekeepers Coverage provides specified limits of insurance and requires the application of a **deductible**.

- The most the insurer is obligated to pay is the Garagekeepers Coverage Limit for each loss at each location is the limit shown on the Declarations Page, less any applicable deductible.

- The maximum deductible stated in the Declarations for Specified Causes of Loss or Comprehensive under Garagekeepers Coverage is the most that will be deducted for all loss in any one event.

- The company reserves the right to pay all or part of a deductible in settlement of a claim or suit. The insured is obligated to reimburse the company for any such deductible payment.

Valet Parking Exposures Need Coverage

Although businesses such as restaurants or hospitals are not eligible for insurance under the Garage Coverage Form, they may have some garage exposures. For example, they may have parking garages or lots for visitors who may be injured while on that property.

The Garagekeepers Coverage (CA 99 37) endorsement may be added to the Business Auto Coverage Form as part of the organization's commercial package policy. This endorsement is explained in more detail on the following pages.

Garage Coverage Form vs. Garagekeepers Coverage Endorsement

For an additional premium, the Garagekeepers Coverage (CA 99 37) endorsement may be added to the BAP, Motor Carrier, or Trucker Coverage Forms.

The CA 99 07 endorsement contains the same coverage wording as Section III—Garagekeepers Coverage in the Garage Coverage Form. However, it also adds a schedule to list both the limit of liability and deductibles for each insured location.

The addresses of the insured garage operations must also be shown on the endorsement. A premium is charged for each location.

Garagekeepers Coverage May Apply as Excess or Primary Coverage

The Garagekeepers Coverage endorsement provides coverage on an excess or primary basis, depending on the insured's needs and wishes. The insured's coverage choice is indicated by an "X" in the appropriate box on the endorsement.

- If the insured selects the Excess Insurance box, Garagekeepers Coverage applies in excess of any primary insurance. Excess liability coverage does not respond to a loss until the amount of the loss exceeds (or exhausts) any existing primary policy limits. It is designed to increase the limits of liability, thereby providing catastrophe coverage. Coverage applies without regard to legal liability for the loss.

- If the insured selects the Primary Insurance box, Garagekeepers Coverage is the primary insurance and applies regardless of any other collectible insurance or the insured's legal liability.

An insured is opening a restaurant with a large parking lot. He wants to purchase a single policy to protect his property and liability exposures.

      2. As an insurance professional, what do you recommend?

Real Life ■
Application

GARAGE COVERAGE SECTIONS IV, V AND VI

Because much of the information in Sections IV, V, and VI of the Garage Coverage is similar to the BAP, it is only briefly covered here. Reading the CA 00 05 form will enhance your understanding of this information.

Section IV applies only to covered autos and pays for loss to a covered auto or its equipment under:

- Comprehensive;

- Specified Causes of Loss; or

- Collision Coverage.

> ■ *ISO FORM*
>
> **A. Coverage**
>   **1.** We will pay for "loss" to a covered "auto"
>   or its equipment under:

Answer & Rationale

    2. Coverage would best be provided by a commercial package policy (CPP) that includes commercial property, CGL, crime, and auto coverages. The Garagekeepers Form (CA 99 37) should be added to the Business Auto Coverage Form to protect against the parking lot liability exposure.

a. Comprehensive Coverage

From any cause except:

(1) The covered "auto's" collision with another object; or

(2) The covered "auto's" overturn.

b. Specified Causes Of Loss Coverage

Caused by:

(1) Fire, lightning or explosion;

(2) Theft;

(3) Windstorm, hail or earthquake;

(4) Flood;

(5) Mischief or vandalism; or

(6) The sinking, burning, collision or derailment of any conveyance transporting the covered "auto".

c. Collision Coverage

Caused by:

(1) The covered "auto's" collision with another object; or

(2) The covered "auto's" overturn.

Additional coverage is provided to covered autos for:

- Towing—Non-Dealers Only; and

- Glass Breakage (Animals, Falling Objects, and Missiles).

The options are the same as in the Business Auto policy, as are the insuring agreements and descriptions of coverage.

■ *ISO FORM*

1. Towing – Non-Dealer Only

If your business is shown in the Declarations as something other than an "auto" dealership, we will pay up to the limit shown in the Declarations for towing and labor costs incurred each time a covered "auto" of the private passenger type is disabled. However the labor must be performed at the place of disablement.

> **2. Glass Breakage – Hitting a Bird or Animal – Falling Objects or Missiles**
>
> If you carry Comprehensive Coverage for the damaged covered "auto", we will pay for the following under Comprehensive Coverage:
>
> **a.** Glass breakage
>
> **b.** "Loss" caused by hitting a bird or animal; and
>
> **c.** "Loss" caused by falling objects or missiles.
>
> However, you have the option of having glass breakage caused by a covered "auto"'s collision or overturn considered a loss under Collision Coverage.

Coverage Extensions Include Transportation Expense

If the insured business is something other than an auto dealership, the policy will pay up to $20 per day to a maximum of $600 for temporary transportation expenses when a covered private passenger type auto is stolen. Only auto dealerships may be covered under the Garage Coverage Form so ISO should soon amend this wording.

Payments are made available 48 hours after the theft and end when the covered auto is returned to use or the insurer pays for the auto theft claim.

Difficult to Insure Perils Are Excluded

All physical damage exclusions found in the BAP are also found in the Garage Coverage Form. For example, war, nuclear hazard, loss to sound producing equipment devices, wear and tear, and road damage to tires are excluded.

In addition, no coverage applies in the Garage Coverage Form for:

- covered autos leased or rented to others (except covered autos rented to customers while their cars are being serviced or repaired);

- covered autos while being prepared for or used in racing, demolition contests, or stunts;

- loss to a covered auto the named insured acquired from a seller without a legal title; and

- loss to a covered auto by trick, scheme, or false pretense.

False pretense, more commonly found in commercial and personal inland marine or crime policies, is the only unique exclusion. Loss of an auto is not covered when an insured voluntarily parts with it because of a trick, scheme, or false pretense. If the insured acquires an auto from a seller who does not possess legal title to the vehicle, no coverage is provided.

Coverage may be added for an additional premium with the False Pretense Coverage (CA 25 03).

> ■ *ISO FORM*
>
> **3. False Pretense**
> We will not pay for "loss" to a covered "auto" caused by or resulting from:
> **a.** Someone causing you to voluntarily part with it by trick or scheme or under false pretenses; or
> **b.** Your acquiring an "auto" from a seller who did not have legal title.

Additional Exclusions for Auto Dealerships

In addition to the exclusions already noted, the Garage Coverage Form does not provide an auto dealership with coverage for:

- the dealer's expected profit;

- loss to a covered auto at a nonscheduled location if the location is not reported to the insurer within 45 days after the location begins its operations;

- loss to a covered auto caused by collision or upset of any vehicle transporting it if the auto is covered for specified causes of loss only; and

- any covered auto under collision coverage while being transported or driven from the point of purchase or distribution to a destination more than 50 road miles (coverage may be added with the Dealers Driveaway Collision Coverage (CA 25 02) endorsement).

Loss and General Conditions

In addition to the Common Policy Conditions that apply, there are five Loss Conditions and eight General Conditions in the Garage policy that apply.

Loss Conditions:

- Appraisal for Physical Damage Loss

- Duties in the Event of Accident, Claim, Suit, or Loss

- Legal Action against the Company

- Loss Payment—Physical Damage

- Transfer of Rights of Recovery

General Conditions:

- Bankruptcy

- Concealment, Misrepresentation, and Fraud

- Liberalization Clause

- No Benefit to Bailee—Physical Damage Coverage

- Other Insurance Clause

- Premium Audit

- Policy Period, Coverage Territory

- Two or More Coverage Forms or Policies applied to the same loss

These are the same Loss and Policy Conditions common to the BAP, the CGL, and all standard commercial policies. These conditions were previously covered in this course.

Garage Operations Definition Is Broad

The definitions in the garage policy are basically the same as in the BAP and CGL; however, there are a few terms with specific significance to the application of the liability coverage, i.e., the definition of garage operations.

As defined in the policy, garage operations means the ownership, maintenance, or use of locations for garage business and that portion of the roads or other accesses that adjoin these locations. Garage operations includes the ownership, maintenance, or use of the autos indicated in Section I of this Coverage Form as covered autos. Garage operations also include all operations necessary or incidental to a garage business.

The definition is quite broad and triggers the same liability exposures that a CGL policy does.

> ▪ **ISO FORM**
>
> **H.** "Garage operations" means the ownership, maintenance or use of locations for garage business and that portion of the roads or other accesses that adjoin these locations. "Garage operations" includes the owner- ship, maintenance or use of the "autos" indicated in Section I of this Coverage Form as covered "autos." "Garage opera- tions" also include all operations neces- sary or incidental to a garage business.

Definition of Auto Differs From BAP

As explained earlier, the definition of an auto in the garage policy includes a land motor vehicle, trailer, or semitrailer. The form does not mention that these items must be designed for travel on public roads, as the BAP does.

The definition section also fails to mention mobile equipment. Because the Garage Coverage Form is less restrictive than the BAP, mobile equipment used in the nec- essary or incidental garage operations is covered.

Endorsements to the Garage Coverage Form

The following endorsements are available under the commercial auto Garage Cov- erage Form:

- **Broad Form** Products Coverage (CA 25 08)

- Dealers Driveaway Collision Coverage (CA 25 02)

- False Pretense Coverage (CA 25 03)

- Medical Payments: *Auto Medical Payments Coverage (CA 99 03) Garage Locations and Operations Medical Coverage (CA 25 05)*

- Personal Injury Liability (CA 25 08)

- Uninsured Motorists Coverage (form numbers vary by state—no sample form available)

- War Exclusion—Garage Coverage Form (CA 00 40)

✓ *Helpful Hints:* Samples of these forms are available in the Appendix under the Garage Endorsements section.

■ **AUTO SERVICE RISKS MARKET**

Garage Program Does Not Cover Auto Service Risks

As explained earlier, ISO's Garage Program once covered two broad categories: dealers or service operations.

- Dealers consist of franchised and non-franchised operations which sell various motor vehicles.

- Service operations include repair shops, service stations, storage garages and public parking places, franchised and non-franchised trailer dealers, and tow truck operators.

ISO revised the Garage Program so that it is no longer appropriate for non-dealer auto service risks. ISO determined that non-dealers or service operations classes are primarily premises/operations exposures. These exposures can be covered by ISO's Commercial General Liability (CGL) Program.

Non-Dealers Need CGL and BAP Coverage

Prior to ISO's filing to withdraw non-dealers from the Garage Program, agents and insurers handled non-dealer garage risks in one of two ways:

1. the Garage Coverage Form (CA 00 05) was added to a commercial package policy (CPP); or

2. the Commercial General Liability Coverage Form (CG 00 01) was used in combination with the Business Auto Coverage Form (CA 00 01) as part of a package policy (the Garagekeepers Coverage (CA 99 37) endorsement was also added to complete the coverage).

Coverage Provided by CGL and BAP

Some insurance professionals will continue to use the CGL in combination with the BAP as part of a Commercial Package Policy (CPP) to insure auto service risks.

A CPP offers some additional protection that was not provided by the Garage Coverage Form. For example, the CGL provides personal and advertising injury for newly acquired organizations, broad legal liability, and a separate aggregate limit for Products and Completed Operations claims.

Additional Endorsements May Be Needed

Limited coverage for operating a customer's auto is provided under the CGL. It covers "... *parking an auto on, or on the ways next to, premises you own, or rent, provided the 'auto' is not owned or rented or loaned by you or the insured.*"

If the CPP coverage option is selected, three important endorsements may be added to the BAP to cover the auto exposures of non-dealer risks. Following is a brief explanation of what each covers.

- Employees As Insureds (CA 99 33)

  This endorsement amends the "Who Is An Insured" provision to include employees as insured while using a covered auto the insured does not own, hire, or borrow in insured's business or personal affairs.

- Garagekeepers Coverage (CA 99 37)

  This endorsement provides coverage of garage operators against direct damage or legal liability for damage to vehicles in the insured's care, custody, or control.

- Physical Damage for Autos Held for Sale (CA 20 78)

  This endorsement provides either comprehensive or specified causes of loss coverage for specifically described vehicles listed on the supplementary schedule

In lieu of the CPP option, insurers may choose to use ISO's new Market Segments to insure auto service risks.

Market Segments Program Covers Auto Service Risks

In 1999, ISO introduced its Market Segments Program with its own policy forms, rules, and loss costs.

Eventually, the program will be expanded to provide separate coverage options for restaurant, supermarket, hotels, motels, inns, self-storage facilities, and landscapers' risks.

ISO Market Segments—Auto Service Risks

The Auto Service Risks Program is the first of the new ISO products. The Auto Service Risks Program is designed for:

- repair shops—risks primarily engaged in the auto repair, including body, fender, radiator, and ignition repair-and paint shops;

- service stations—risks primarily engaged in servicing autos-including car washes and shops that sell and install auto accessories (but not shops that do major engine or body repair); and

- storage garages and other public parking places.

Automobile, motor home, trailer, and motorcycle dealers are not eligible for the Auto Service Risks Market Segment Program.

This section provided a brief overview of the auto service risk market. It is basic information only and it not intended to completely cover this subject.

✓ *Helpful Hints:* Check ISO's *Commercial Lines Manual* (CLM) for rules applicable to your state. For more information about ISO's Market Segments Program, refer to the *Commercial Lines Manual* and applicable state rules. You may also call ISO Customer Service at 1-800-888-4476 for more information.

Auto Service Risks Forms Wrap Around Existing CPP

The coverages and endorsements that form the Auto Service Risks Market Segment Program are designed to wrap around an existing commercial package policy (CPP).

They do not replace basic commercial property or liability coverage forms, but provide additional coverages and enhancements to the underlying coverage forms. For example, mandatory property coverage is provided by the Building And Personal Property Coverage Form (CP 00 10) and the Causes of Loss—Special Form (CP 10 30).

Mandatory liability coverage is provided by the Commercial General Liability Coverage Forms (CG 00 01)—occurrence version or (CG 00 02)—claims-made version.

Special Forms Are Used for Auto Service Risks

The Auto Service Risks basic policy includes:

- Common Policy Conditions (IL 00 17);

- Building And Personal Property Coverage Form (CP 00 01);

- Causes of Loss—Special Form (CP 10 30);

- Commercial Property Conditions Form (CP 00 90);

- Commercial General Liability Forms (CG 00 01) [occurrence version] or (CG 00 02) [claims-made version, where permitted];

- Auto Service Risks Supplemental Schedule (MS AS DS);

- Auto Service Risks Endorsement (MS AS 01); and

- any mandatory endorsements required by state manual rules.

A number of other coverage parts eligible for the commercial package policy (CPP) and optional coverages designed for auto risks may also be included in the package.

✓ *Helpful Hints:* Samples of these forms are available in the Appendix.

Auto Service Risks Endorsement Increases Limits

The **Auto Service Risks** (MS AS 01) allows the limits of insurance for mandatory coverage to be increased to specified limits for:

- Money and Securities;

- Outdoor Signs;

- Employee Dishonesty;

- Valuable Papers;

- Employees' Tools; and

- Accounts Receivable.

Additional Coverage Added by Optional Endorsements

The auto service risk can purchase additional coverage by adding optional endorsements. Endorsements are available for:

- loss or damage to customers' auto (direct primary or legal liability basis);

- customers' and lessors' property;

- mechanical breakdown coverage; and

- hired and non-owned auto liability.

✓ *Helpful Hint:* Check ISO's *Commercial Lines Manual* (CLM) for rules applicable to your state.

Overview Is Provided for Information Only

As stated previously, many insurance professionals do not have direct responsibility for Garage, Truckers' or Motor Carriers' business. However, as a professional, you should have a basic understanding of the risks involved and available coverages for these types of business.

✓ *Helpful Hint:* The state CE exam covers only basic information about the Garage, Truckers' and Motor Carriers' Coverage Forms. The test does not include technical questions about automobile symbols, coverage forms, or the auto service risks market.

■ SUMMARY

Although the Garage policy is versatile because it combines general and auto liability, physical damage coverage, and garagekeepers coverage in one package policy, the cross-line exposures sometimes make the garage risk (and the garage policy) difficult to understand. A careful reading of each coverage form and endorsement is necessary to fully understand the unique loss exposures inherent in this type of risk.

In the next unit of this course, we will discuss the two remaining commercial auto coverage forms—the Truckers Form and the Motor Carrier Form.

■ UNIT 7 REVIEW QUESTIONS

1. The Garage Form is a General Liability Coverage Form.

    A. True
    B. False

2. Which of the following symbols provides the broadest liability protection under the garage policy?

    A. 21
    B. 22
    C. 23
    D. 24

3. The primary reason for buying a garage policy is to provide

    A. liability coverage for owners of auto repair facilities who cannot get coverage elsewhere
    B. coverage for buildings and other structures occupied as garages and service stations
    C. a combination of automobile and general liability coverage for garages.
    D. coverage for the vehicles auto dealers own

4. Each of the following coverage options is available to insure damage to customer vehicles in an insured's care, custody, or control EXCEPT

    A. direct primary
    B. legal liability
    C. direct excess
    D. direct legal

5. The insured can endorse Garagekeepers Coverage onto the Truckers, Business Auto, and Motor Carrier Coverage Forms.

    A. True
    B. False

■ ANSWERS TO UNIT 7 REVIEW QUESTIONS

1. **B.** False. The Garage Coverage Form is a Commercial Auto Form, but it also functions as a CGL because of the commercial premises and operations exposures. It is primarily an auto policy and mimics the coverages also available under the Business Auto Coverage Form.

2. **A.** The broadest coverage available under the garage policy is Symbol 21, Any "Auto."

3. **D.** The garage policy combines the liability and auto coverage for auto deliverships only. Coverage is no longer available under the Garage Coverage Form for garages that service or repair autos but are not dealerships.

4. **D.** An insured who wishes to purchase coverage for damage to customer automobiles in his care, custody or control may do so on a direct primary, direct excess, or legal liability basis.

5. **A.** True. The coverage can be added on by endorsement to any of the commercial auto coverage forms. It is already included in the Garage Coverage form, but only applies if a premium charge is shown in the Declarations.

8

Other Commercial Auto Forms

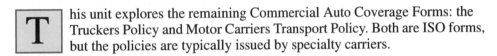

T his unit explores the remaining Commercial Auto Coverage Forms: the Truckers Policy and Motor Carriers Transport Policy. Both are ISO forms, but the policies are typically issued by specialty carriers.

This unit will examine how these forms fit with existing monoline or multi-line policies to tailor coverage to specific business needs.

✓ **Helpful Hints:** The state CE exam for this course consists mainly of BAP coverage questions. The exam covers only basic information about the Garage, Truckers, and Motor Carrier forms.

When you have completed this unit, you should be able to:

Learning Objectives

- distinguish the Truckers Policy from the BAP, Garage, and Motor Carrier Policies;

- recognize and apply the major coverages and exclusions in the Truckers Policy and the Motor Carrier Transport Policy;

- explain Trailer Interchange coverage;

- discuss applicable endorsements; and

- explain the use of Truckers and Motor Carrier Transport coverage with existing policies.

■ ■ ■ ■ ■

■ TRUCKERS COVERAGE FORM

The Truckers Coverage Form (CA 00 12) is similar in format to the Business Auto Coverage Form and has many of the same coverages and policy provisions.

The Truckers Coverage Form provides insurance for a person, firm, or corporation in the business of transporting goods, materials, or commodities for hire for another. When a person or organization transports people rather than property, the Motor Carrier Coverage Form (CA 00 20) is used.

Truckers coverage can be purchased as a stand-alone policy, or it can be added by endorsement to the Business Auto Coverage Form as part of a package policy. When issued as a stand-alone policy, the form is attached to a Truckers Declarations (CA 0014).

This unit will highlight the unique characteristics of the Truckers policy as well as the Motor Carrier policy, which is the remaining commercial auto coverage form.

Basic Understanding of Coverage Is Needed

Many insurance professionals do not have direct responsibility for garage, **truckers**, or motor carriers business. However, as a professional, you should have a basic understanding of the risks involved and available coverages for these types of business.

✓ **Helpful Hints:** The state CE exam covers only basic information about the Garage, Truckers, and Motor Carrier Coverage Forms. The exam does not include technical questions about automobile symbols or coverage forms.

Trucking Industry Is Regulated

Railroad companies dominated the movement of goods both locally and cross-country until the late 1920s and early 1930s when the trucking industry became a viable means of hauling freight. With the rise of trucking, many problems arose between major freight lines and railroad companies.

The Interstate Commerce Commission (ICC) was created in the 1800s by the federal government to regulate the railroad industry and was empowered to regulate the trucking industry. It established rates and tariffs and established a set of safety standards, which included the number of hours truckers could drive.

Despite the ICC's efforts, the trucking industry was burdened with financial instability. In the early years, many poorly financed companies went bankrupt. In response, Congress passed the Motor Carrier Act of 1935 to restrict entry into the business to financially stable companies. The act also required trucking firms to purchase minimum limits of liability.

Some Carriers Not Eligible

Not all truckers require truckers coverage and some are not eligible to use this coverage.

Private carriers who haul their own property and public or private passenger liveries are not eligible. These entities can be insured under a BAP using Symbol 4. This Symbol is used to cover trucks, truck tractors, buses, taxies, motorcycles, trailers, and emergency vehicles.

Some Policy Features Different From BAP

Like the Business Auto Coverage Form, the Truckers Coverage Form provides both liability and physical damage coverages. The coverage is the same as that provided under the BAP with two exceptions:

1. Coverage is available for trailers owned by others and in the insured's possession.

2. Trailers may be covered when they are in the possession of others.

Truckers often borrow or switch their trailers with other truckers in order to carry cargo on return trips to minimize returning with empty trailers or rigs. These trailer interchange agreements are common in the trucking industry. The truckers policy provides coverage for this arrangement, but the BAP does not.

Bobtail Operations May Be Covered

Assume a owner-operator of a truck makes a one-way trip hauling a company's products using its semitrailer. After making the delivery, the driver returns without the semitrailer attached. The use of a tracker without its tailer (or tail) is called a "bobtail operation."

The trucker is no longer covered under the Truckers Coverage Form because no goods are being hauled. Liability coverage may be added with a Truckers Insurance for Non-Trucking Use Endorsement (CA 23 09) to cover the nontrucking use of the vehicle.

Identical in Structure to Garage Coverage Form

The Truckers Coverage Form policy is almost identical to the Garage Coverage Form. Both offer key business coverage in Section III which was tailored to meet each business's needs.

- The Garage Coverage Form contains Section III—Garagekeepers Coverage to provide physical damage coverage for customer autos in the care, custody, and control of the garage while being serviced, stored, or repaired.

- The Truckers Coverage Form contains Section III—Trailer Interchange Coverage to cover physical damage to trailers and equipment specific to the trucking industry.

Trailer Interchange Coverage Provides Liability Coverage

The Trucking industry revolves around the interchange of trailers used to transport property "for hire" for another. **Trailer interchange agreements** are an arrangement whereby one trucker transfers a trailer containing a shipment to a second trucker for continued transportation.

Section III—Trailer Interchange Coverage provides coverage for the legal liability of truckers for loss or damage to non-owned trailers and equipment that are in the insured's possession under a written trailer interchange agreement.

Sections Similar to Garage Coverage Form

Like the Garage Coverage Form, there are six sections to the Truckers Coverage Form (CA 00 12), as follows:

- Section I—Covered Autos

- Section II—Liability Coverage

- Section III—Trailer Interchange Coverage

- Section IV—Physical Damage Coverage

- Section V—Truckers Conditions

- Section VI—Definitions

If the coverage is written as a stand-alone policy, the Truckers Coverage Form is added to the Truckers Declarations Form (CA 00 14).

Covered Auto Symbols

The Truckers Coverage Form, like the Garage and Business Auto Coverage Forms, uses coverage symbols to denote covered autos. The symbols are shown on the policy's Declarations Page.

The covered auto designation symbols are contained in Section I—Covered Autos of the policy and range from Symbol 41 to 50.

■ **ISO FORM**		
Symbol	**Description Of Covered Auto Designation Symbols**	
41	Any "Autos"	
42	Owned "Autos" Only	Only the "autos" you own (and for Liability Coverage any "trailers" you don't own while connected to a power unit you own). This includes those "autos" you acquire ownership of after the policy begins.
43	Owned Commercial "Autos" Only	Only those trucks, tractors and "trailers" you own (and for Liability Coverage any "trailers" you don't own while connected to a power unit you own). This includes those trucks, tractors and "trailers" you acquire ownership of after the policy begins.

Section I—Covered Autos Provides Description

The truckers policy uses similar covered auto categories as the BAP and Garage policy, except for coverage Symbols 48 and 49, which are specific to the trucking industry.

- 41—Any Auto

- 42—Owned Autos Only

- 43—Owned Commercial Autos Only

- 44—Owned Autos Subject to No-Fault Rules

- 45—Owned Autos Subject to a Compulsory Uninsured Motorist Law

- 46—Specifically Described Autos

- 47—Hired Autos Only

- 48—Trailers in Your Possession under a Written Trailer or Equipment Interchange Agreement

- 49—Your Trailers in the Possession of Anyone Else Under a Written Trailer Interchange Agreement

- 50—Nonowned Autos Only

As we have already discussed the use of coverage symbols, this section will summarize the key symbols.

Newly Acquired Autos Covered with Some Restrictions

For Symbols 41,42, 43, 44, or 45, coverage is provided for autos the insured acquires of the type described for the remainder of the policy period.

Under Symbol 46, newly acquired autos are covered if:

- all autos the insured owns already are covered or if it replaces an auto the insured previously owned that had that coverage; and

- the insured notifies the insurer within 30 days of his desire to cover the newly acquired auto.

> ■ **ISO FORM**
>
> 1. If Symbols **41, 42, 43, 44** or **45** are entered next to a coverage in Item Two of the Declarations, then you have coverage for "autos" that you acquire of the type described for the remainder of the policy period.
>
> 2. But, if Symbol **46** is entered next to a coverage in Item Two of the Declarations, an "auto" you acquire will be a covered "auto" for that coverage only if:
>
>   a. We already cover all "autos" that you own for that coverage or it replaces an "auto" you previously owned that had that coverage; and
>
>   b. You tell us within 30 days after you acquire it that you want us to cover it for that coverage.

Symbol 48 Covers Nonowned Trailers

Symbol 48 provides coverage for trailer interchange agreements. If this symbol is used, the insured has coverage for liability that the trucker assumes when a trailer or equipment interchange agreement is signed.

Symbol 48 covers trailers in the named insured's possession that are not owned. The symbol is used only for one of three interchange coverages:

- comprehensive;

- specified causes of loss; or

- collision.

Symbol 49 Covers Owned Trailers

Symbol 49 provides coverage trailers owned by the named insured but in the possession of others under a written trailer interchange agreement.

Symbol 49 may be used under the insured's physical damage coverage (discussed later).

Symbol 50 Covers Nonowned Autos

Symbol 50 provides coverage for autos used in the insured's business but are not owned, leased, hired, rented, or borrowed by the insured.

The category would include autos owned by employees or partners or members of their households while being used in the named insured's business or personal affairs.

Section II—Insuring Agreements

Under the Section II—Liability insuring agreements, the insurer agrees to pay all sums an insured must pay legally as damages because of bodily injury or property damage or covered pollution expense or costs caused by an accident and resulting from the ownership, maintenance, or use of covered autos.

The insurance company has the right and duty to defend any suit asking for these damages but has no duty to defend any insured against a suit seeking damages for bodily injury or property damage or covered pollution expense or cost to which the policy does not apply.

The carrier reserves the right to investigate and settle any claim or suit as it deems appropriate; however, the duty to defend or settle ends when the Liability Coverage Limit of Insurance has been exhausted by payment of judgments or settlements.

> ■ *ISO FORM*
>
> **A. Coverage**
> We will pay all sums an "insured" legally must pay as damages because of "bodily injury" or "property damage" to which this insurance applies, caused by an "accident" and resulting from the ownership, maintenance or use of a covered "auto".

"Who Is An Insured" Provides Broad Coverage

The following are insureds for covered autos:

- The insured, for any covered auto

- Any permissive user of a covered auto the insured owns, hires, or borrows, except the owner, employees, someone using a covered auto in the auto service industry, anyone while moving property to or from a covered auto, or partners for covered private passenger autos they own

- The owner or anyone else from whom you hire or borrow a covered auto that is a trailer while the trailer is connected to another covered auto that is a power unit, or if not connected, that is being used exclusively in your business as a trucker and is being used pursuant to operating rights granted to you by a public authority

- The owner or anyone else from whom you hire or borrow a covered auto that is not a trailer vehicle, and the covered auto is being used exclusively in your business as a trucker under grant of right by public authority

- Anyone liable for the conduct of an insured, but only to the extent of that liability

Who Is Not an Insured—Truckers and Agents

Under the Truckers Coverage Form, none of the following are considered to be an insured.

Any trucker or his agents or employees, other than the insured and its employees:

- if the trucker is subject to motor carrier insurance requirements and meets them by a means other than auto liability insurance; and

- if the trucker is not insured for hired autos under an auto liability insurance form that insures on a primary basis the owners of the autos and their agents and employees while the autos are being used exclusively in the truckers business and pursuant to operating rights granted to the trucker by a public authority.

Air, Rail, or Water Carriers and Agents Not Covered

Also excluded under the form are:

Any rail, water or air carrier or its employees or agents, other than you and your employees, for a trailer, if bodily injury or property damage occurs while the trailer is detached from a covered auto you are using and:

- is being transported by the carrier; or

- is being loaded on or unloaded from any unit of transportation by the carrier.

Supplementary Payments Add Additional Coverage

The supplementary payments are exactly the same as in the Garage and BAP coverage forms as follows.

- Up to $2,000 for the cost of bail bonds, including bonds for related traffic law violations, required because of an accident the insurer covers. (The insurer does not have to furnish these bonds.)

- The cost of bonds to release attachments in any suit the insurer defends, but only for bond amounts within the limit of insurance. (Attachment is a statutory legal remedy whereby one party may prevent removal of property belonging to another party, pending determination of a court action.)

- All reasonable expenses the insured incurs for court appearances, depositions, and other legal proceedings, including actual loss of earnings up to $250 a day because of time off work.

- All costs taxed against the insured in any suit.

- All interest on the full amount of any judgment that accrues after entry of the judgment. (The insurer's duty to pay interest ends when it has paid, offered to pay or deposited in court the part of the judgment that is within its limit of insurance.)

Out-of-State Coverage Extensions Meet Compulsory Law

While a covered auto is away from the state where it is licensed, the company will:

- increase the limit of insurance for liability coverage to meet the limits specified by a state's compulsory or financial responsibility law; and

- provide the minimum amounts and types of other coverages required of out-of-state vehicles by the jurisdiction where the covered auto is being used.

■ *ISO FORM*

(1) Increase the Limit of Insurance for Liability Coverage to meet the limit specified by a compulsory or financial responsibility law of the jurisdiction where the covered "auto" is being used. This extension does not apply to the limit or limits specified by any law governing motor carriers of passengers or property.

(2) Provide the minimum amounts and types of other coverages, such as no-fault, required of out-of-state vehicles by the jurisdiction where the covered "auto" is being used.

Coverage Exclusions for Difficult-to-Insure Exposures

The Truckers Coverage Form contains 13 exclusions, as follows:

- Expected or Intended Injury

- Contractual

- Workers Compensation

- Employee Indemnification and Employer's Liability

- Fellow Employee

- Care, Custody, or Control

- Handling of Property

- Movement of Property by a Mechanical Device

- Operations

- Completed Operations

- Pollution

- War

- Racing

Since these are the same exclusions contained in the Business Auto Policy and Garage policies, they will not be discussed in any detail in this lesson.

Limits of Insurance Shown on Declarations Page

Regardless of the number of covered autos, insureds, premiums paid, claims made or vehicles involved in the accident, the most the company will pay is the amount shown on the Declarations Page.

> ■ *ISO FORM*
>
> **C. Limit Of Insurance**
> Regardless of the number of covered "autos", "insureds", premiums paid, claims made or vehicles involved in the "accident", the most we will pay for the total of all damages and "covered pollution cost or expense" combined, resulting from any one "accident" is the Limit of Insurance for Liability Coverage shown in the Declarations.

The insured may select the comprehensive coverage, specified causes of loss, or collision coverage option. The company pays all sums the insured legally must pay as damages for loss to non-owned trailers or equipment under:

Comprehensive Coverage—for any cause except:

- the trailer's collision with another object; or

- the trailer's overturn.

Specified Causes of Loss Coverage—for losses caused by:

- fire, lightning, or explosion;

- theft;

- windstorm, hail, or earthquake;

- flood;

- mischief or vandalism; or

- the sinking, burning, collision, or derailment of any conveyance transporting the trailer.

Collision Coverage—for losses caused by:

- the trailer's collision with another object; or

- the trailer's overturn.

The carrier reserves the right to investigate, settle, and defend any suit or claim as it deems appropriate. There is no duty to settle or defend non-covered claims, and the duty to defend or settle ends when the Limit of Insurance for that coverage has been exhausted by the payment of judgments or settlements.

Exclusions for Catastrophic Loss

There are three primary coverage exclusions:

- Nuclear Hazard And War;

- **Loss of Use**; and

- Wear and Tear, blowouts or road damage to tires, and mechanical breakdown.

Limit of Insurance and Deductible

The most the carrier is obligated to pay for any one trailer is the least of the following amounts minus any applicable deductible shown in the Declarations:

- The actual cash value of the damaged or stolen property at the time of the loss.

- The cost of repairing or replacing the damaged or stolen property with other property of like kind and quality.

- The limit of insurance shown in the Declarations.

Section IV—Physical Damage Coverage A

Section IV applies only to covered autos, and pays for loss to a covered auto or its equipment under:

- Comprehensive;

- Specified Causes of Loss;

- Collision Coverage.

Additional coverage is provided to covered autos for:

- Towing—Private Passenger Autos; and

- Glass Breakage (Animals, Falling Objects, and Missiles).

The options are the same as in the Garage and Business Auto policies, with the same insuring agreements and description of coverage.

Extensions of Coverage—Transportation Expense

The policy will pay up to $20 per day to a maximum of $600 for temporary transportation expenses due to a total theft of a covered auto of the private passenger type.

Payments are made available 48 hours after the theft and end when the covered auto is returned to use or the insurer pays for the auto theft claim.

Exclusions Are Similar to BAP

No physical damage coverage is allowed for loss resulting from any of the following:

- Nuclear hazards

- War or military action

- Wear and tear, freezing, mechanical breakdown, blowouts, or road damage to tires

- Diminution in value of a covered auto

Additionally, the company will not pay for loss to any of the following:

- Covered autos in the possession of others

- Under writer trailer interchange agreements

- Covered autos involved in racing and demolition

- Tape decks, sound equipment, electronic, and similar devices, whether or not permanently installed

- Jamming devices, accessories to any electronic equipment

Some Conditions Only Apply to Losses

There are five loss conditions in the Truckers policy:

1. Appraisal for Physical Damage Loss

2. Duties in the Event of Accident, Claim, Suit, or Loss

3. Legal Action against the Company

4. Loss Payment—Physical Damage

5. Transfer of Rights of Recovery Against Others to Us

These loss conditions were previously discussed in the BAP sections.

General Conditions Apply to the Entire Policy

There are eight general conditions in the Truckers Coverage Form that apply to the entire contract:

1. Bankruptcy

2. Concealment, Misrepresentation, Fraud

3. Liberalization Clause

4. No Benefit to Bailee—Physical Damage Coverage

5. Other Insurance Clause

6. Premium Audit

7. Policy Period, Coverage Territory

8. Two or More Coverage Forms or Policies Applied to the Same Loss

These Conditions common to all policies and are specifically found in the BAP, Garage, and CGL policies. These Conditions were discussed in depth in the Business Auto Conditions and will not be covered again in this section.

Definitions Included for Trailers and Truckers

The definitions in the Truckers policy are very similar to the BAP, Garage, and CGL policies; however, there are a few terms with specific significance, i.e., the definition of trailer and trucker.

- The term *trailer* is intended to include:

  semitrailer or a dilly used to convert a semitrailer into a trailer. But for Trailer Interchange Coverage only, "trailer" also includes a container.

- The term *trucker* means:

  any person or organization engaged in the business of transporting property by "auto" for hire.

Endorsements May be Added to Modify Coverage

Truckers coverage can be endorsed onto the Business Auto policy, under ISO Form CA 23 20 10 01, Truckers Endorsement. This only applies to Business Auto Coverage Form.

The following endorsements are also available:

CA 23 17 09 00—Truckers—Uniform Intermodal Interchange Endorsement Form UIEE—1 (which can be used with the Business Auto, Motor Carrier, and Truckers Coverage forms).

CA 23 09 02 99—Truckers—Insurance for Non-Trucking Use (only applies to Business Auto Coverage Form).

These are only a few of the many endorsements available to be used with the Truckers policy and other commercial auto coverage forms to either restrict or expand coverage.

■ MOTOR CARRIER COVERAGE FORM

The Motor Carrier Coverage Form (CA 00 20) is used for a person or organization providing transportation by auto in the furtherance of a commercial enterprise. In other words, the policy covers anyone involved in the auto transportation industry (including the transport of people), rather than the transport of property for hire, which is the focus of the trucking industry.

The policy is exactly the same as the Truckers Coverage Form, including Section III -Trailer Interchange Coverage. There are, however, some minor differences are in the coverage symbols, "Who Is An Insured" section, "Other Insurance" condition, and Definitions section.

Thus, this lesson will only point out these minor differences, since the remainder of the Motor Carrier coverage form is identical to the Truckers Coverage form.

Section I—Covered Autos Difference

The Motor Carrier Coverage Form uses the identical categories in the Truckers coverage form, except coverage Symbol 63—Owned Private Passenger Autos is added.

- 61—Any Auto

- 62—Owned Autos Only

- 63—Owned Private Passenger Autos Only

- 64—Owned Commercial Autos Only

- 65—Owned Autos Subject to No-Fault Rules

- 66—Owned Autos Subject to a Compulsory Uninsured Motorist Law

- 67—Specifically Described Autos

- 68—Hired Autos Only

- 69—Trailers in Your Possession under a Written Trailer or Equipment Interchange Agreement

- 70—Your Trailers in the Possession of Anyone Else Under a Written Trailer Interchange Agreement

- 71—Nonowned Autos Only

Declarations Page Added to Create Policy

If a stand-alone policy is needed, the Motor Carrier Coverage Form is attached to the Motor Carrier Coverage Form Declarations (CA 00 19).

The appropriate auto symbols are included on the Dec Page to indicate desired coverage.

Symbol 63—Owned Private Passenger Autos

Technically, the Truckers Policy could cover owned private passenger auto with the use of Symbol 41—Any Autos. It is unlikely, however, that a trucking company would need to cover private passenger autos since it is in the business of transporting property and would need trucks to do so.

On the other hand, a motor carrier might use only private passenger vehicles such as vans or limousines to transport people. Therefore, Symbol 63 might be commonly used.

■ *ISO FORM*	
Symbol	**Description Of Covered Auto Designation Symbols**
63	Owned Private Passenger Type "Autos" Only	Only the "private passenger type" "autos" you own. This includes those "private passenger type" "autos" that you acquire ownership of after the policy begins.

Eliminates Coverage for Personally Owned Autos

Under the "Who Is An Insured" section, the Truckers Form excludes coverage for employees, agents or partners when they are using a private passenger-type auto that they or a family member owns. If the vehicle were a truck, rather than a private passenger car, coverage would apply.

The Motor Carrier Form in the "Who Is An Insured" section excludes coverage for any employee, agent, or partner who is driving any auto that they or a member of their household owns.

> ■ *ISO FORM*
>
> **(2)** Your "employee" or agent if the covered "auto" is owned by that "employee" or agent or a member of his or her household.

"Other Insurance" Applies to Autos Hired or Borrowed from Insured

The General Conditions section of the Motor Carrier Coverage Form contains an "Other Insurance" provision. Unlike the Trucker Carrier Form that is primary for covered autos, the Motor Carrier Form adds some additional provisions.

When the insured lends or hires a covered auto to another party or carrier, the Motor Carrier Form is:

- primary if the written agreement requires the insured to hold the other motor carrier harmless; or

- excess over other collectible insurance if the other carrier does not require the insured to agree to hold it harmless.

> ■ **ISO FORM**
>
> **a.** While any covered "auto" is hired or borrowed from you by another "motor carrier", this Coverage Form's liability coverage is:
>
> **(1)** Primary if a written agreement between you as the lessor and the other "motor carrier" as the lessee requires you to hold the lessee harmless.
>
> **(2)** Excess over any other collectible insurance if a written agreement between you as the lessor and the other "motor carrier" as the lessee does not require you to hold the lessee harmless.

"Other Insurance" Applies to Autos Hired or Borrowed by Insured

When the insured hires or borrows a covered auto from another party or carrier, the Motor Carrier Form is:

- primary if the written agreement does not require the insured to hold the other motor carrier harmless and the borrowed auto is used exclusively in the business as an auto for hire; or

- excess over other collectible insurance if a written agreement with the other carrier requires the insured to agree to hold it harmless.

Note that the coverage application is reversed when the insured borrows or hires the auto.

> ■ **ISO FORM**
>
> **b.** While any covered "auto" is hired or borrowed by you from another "motor carrier" this Coverage Form's liability coverage is:
>
> **(1)** Primary if a written agreement between the other "motor carrier" as the lessor and you as the lessee does not require the lessor to hold you harmless, and then only while the covered "auto" is used exclusively in your business as a "motor carrier" for hire.

> **(2)** Excess over any other collectible insurance if a written agreement between the other "motor carrier" as the lessor and you as the lessee requires the lessor to hold you harmless.

Section VI—Definitions: Motor Carrier Defined

The Definitions sections of the Truckers Coverage Form and Motor Carrier Coverage Form contain the most noteworthy difference between the two forms.

The Truckers Coverage Form, defines *trucker* as:

> *any person or organization engaged in the business of transporting property by "auto" for hire.*

The Motor Carrier Coverage Form, defines *motor carrier* as:

> *a person or organization providing transportation by "auto" in the furtherance of a commercial enterprise.*

> ■ *ISO FORM*
>
> **L.** "Motor Carrier" means a person or organization providing transportation by "auto" in the furtherance of a commercial enterprise.

Not All Motor Carriers Are Truckers

It is important to note that the definitions of *trucker* and *motor carrier* explain who is eligible for coverage.

The motor carrier definition is broader than the trucker definition and includes those who are in the business of transporting people or property.

By extension, all truckers are motor carriers because they transport property, but all motor carrier are not truckers because they transport people.

■ SUMMARY

The Truckers Coverage Form and the Motor Carrier Coverage Form are very similar in structure and substance, to the Business Auto policy and the Garage policy. The only differences are in the coverage symbol categories, some of the insuring agreements for the truckers policy, and the addition of some definitions.

The transportation and cargo industries are regulated by state and federal laws. For this reason, the coverage is offered primarily by specialty carriers.

■ **UNIT 8 REVIEW QUESTIONS**

1. Of the following coverage symbols in the Truckers policy, which are used to denote coverage for trailers in the possession of the insured under the terms of a written trailer or equipment interchange agreement?

   A. 41 and 42

   B. 44 and 45

   C. 46 and 47

   D. 48 and 49

2. Which of the following is not insured under a Truckers policy?

   A. Permissive users of covered autos

   B. Named insured for any covered auto

   C. Air carriers for damage to detached trailers

   D. Owners of a trailer connected to a covered auto that is a power unit

3. The truckers policy has to pay its liability limits more than once if more than one person is involved in an accident covered under the policy.

   A. True

   B. False

4. Glass Breakage is one of the risks insured against under Section IV of the Truckers Policy.

   A. True

   B. False

5. The Truckers Coverage Form can only be endorsed onto which of the following policies?

   A. CGL

   B. PAP

   C. Garage

   D. BAP

6. The Motor Carrier Policy is identical to the Truckers Policy in all of its features, except coverage symbols and definitions?

   A. True

   B. False

■ ANSWERS TO UNIT 8 REVIEW QUESTIONS

1. **D.** Symbols 48 and 49 are specific to coverage for trailers in the insured's possession, or in the possession of someone else under the terms of either a written trailer or equipment interchange agreement.

2. **C.** Air, water, and rail carriers are specifically excluded if property damage or bodily injury occurs while the trailer is detached from a covered auto the insured is using and is being transported by the carrier, or is being loaded on or unloaded from any unit of transportation by the carrier.

3. **B.** False. Regardless of the number or claimants, claims or insureds, the most the policy will pay for any one accident is the Limit of Insurance for Liability Coverage shown in the Declarations.

4. **A.** True. Glass Breakage is provided as part of the comprehensive coverage, if selected by the named insured on the Declarations.

5. **D.** The Truckers Coverage Form can only be endorsed onto the Business Auto Policy. The CGL is a commercial liability not auto form, the PAP is a personal auto, not commercial auto policy, and the GARAGE coverage form, although a commercial auto form, cannot be used for trucking operations.

6. **A.** True. The only difference is coverage symbol usage and the addition of *motor carrier* to the definitions.

9

Rating the Business Auto Policy

T his unit covers the rating procedures for the Business Auto Policy and will discuss the method for classifying auto risks and identifying the appropriate risk factors to apply. It is intended to provide a basic orientation to the process for rating the Business Auto Policy and does not cover the more advanced topics such as Zone-Rated (long haul) risks, experience, or schedule rating.

While many companies use computers to rate Business Auto Policies, an understanding of the rating system can be an aid to the underwriting and sales/marketing processes.

The rates used in this lesson are for example purposes only. Because each state has its own insurance regulations, ISO has filed exceptions to its countrywide rules in each state. However, for the purposes of this unit, we will be using the countrywide rules. You should refer to your state exception pages for differences, if any. In addition, each insurer is free to file its own rules and rates. Therefore, be sure you check with company exception pages as well when rating an actual policy.

✓ *Helpful Hints:* The tables referred to throughout this unit are available in the Appendix. You must refer to these tables in order to complete the problems and answer the questions in this unit.

Throughout this unit you will have the opportunity to answer problems using these tables. The answers to these rating problems appear at the end of the unit.

When you have completed this unit, you should be able to:

Learning Objectives

- explain the key elements for rating commercial auto policies;

- identify primary and secondary rating factors;

- determine the premium for Business Auto Liability and Physical Damage coverages;

- determine the premium for Hired Auto coverage; and

- determine the premium for Non-Owned Auto coverage.

■ ■ ■ ■ ■

Do You Know These Key Terms?

Before we tackle the ISO rating rules, you should be familiar with some of the terms that are used. The definitions are found in the glossary starting on page 219.

- Base Premium

- Business Use Class

- Fleet

- GCW

- GVW

- Primary Rating Factor

- Radius Class

- Secondary Rating Factor

- Service Use

- Retail Use

- Commercial Use

■ DETERMINING THE PREMIUM

The Steps in Classifying the Risk

There are six steps to rating most trucks, tractors, and trailers for the Commercial Auto Policy:

Step 1	Determine the Primary Rating Factor
Step 2	+ Determine the Secondary Rating Factor
Step 3	Combined Primary and Secondary Rating Factors
Step 4	× Base Premium
Step 5	× Increased Limits Factor
Step 6	× Fleet Factor (if applicable)
Final Premium	

Now let's look at each step.

Step 1—Primary Rating Factors

Determine the **primary rating factor** based on the vehicle's size, use, and radius of use.

The first step in rating any insurance policy is to classify the risk. The process of classifying commercial autos is similar to the process used for private passenger vehicles. Both base the primary rating factor on the use of the vehicle and its radius of operation. Commercial auto rating adds the additional element of vehicle size.

All of these characteristics are captured in a sample section of the Primary Rating Factors table showing only light trucks:

Size Class	Bus. Use Class		Radius					
			Up to 50 miles		51-200 Miles		Over 200 Miles	
			Liability	Phys. Dam	Liability	Phys. Dam	Liability	Phys. Dam
Light Trucks (0-10,000 lbs. GWV)	Service	Factor Code	1.00 014- -	1.00 014- -	1.10 015- -	1.05 015- -	1.15 016- -	1.00 016- -
	Retail	Factor Code	1.60 024- -	1.20 024- -	1.65 025- -	1.50 025- -	1.70 026- -	1.65 026- -
	Commercial	Factor Code	1.30 034- -	1.15 034- -	1.55 035- -	1.40 035- -	1.60 036- -	1.70 036- -

Remember, "rates reflect exposure?" Refer to p. 237 in the Appendix to view the complete table.

Notice how the factors increase as mileage goes up, and as the size of the vehicle increases.

Let's look at the table in a little more detail.

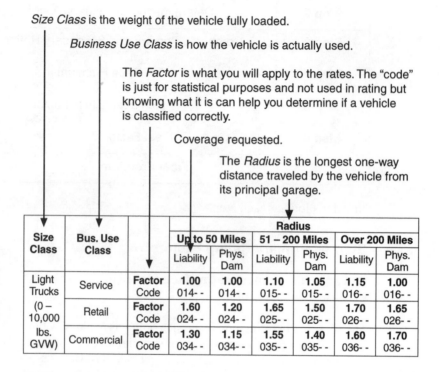

Size Class is the weight of the vehicle fully loaded.

Business Use Class is how the vehicle is actually used.

The *Factor* is what you will apply to the rates. The "code" is just for statistical purposes and not used in rating but knowing what it is can help you determine if a vehicle is classified correctly.

Coverage requested.

The *Radius* is the longest one-way distance traveled by the vehicle from its principal garage.

Size Class	Bus. Use Class		Radius					
			Up to 50 Miles		51 – 200 Miles		Over 200 Miles	
			Liability	Phys. Dam	Liability	Phys. Dam	Liability	Phys. Dam
Light Trucks (0 – 10,000 lbs. GVW)	Service	Factor Code	1.00 014- -	1.00 014- -	1.10 015- -	1.05 015- -	1.15 016- -	1.00 016- -
	Retail	Factor Code	1.60 024- -	1.20 024- -	1.65 025- -	1.50 025- -	1.70 026- -	1.65 026- -
	Commercial	Factor Code	1.30 034- -	1.15 034- -	1.55 035- -	1.40 035- -	1.60 036- -	1.70 036- -

A *light truck* (**1**) that is used to deliver furniture from the *store* (**2**) to the buyer's house and travels less than 50 miles *one-way* (**3**) would have a *primary liability* (**4**) factor of *1.60* (**5**) and primary physical damage factor of *1.20*.

Size Class	Bus. Use Class		Radius					
			(3) Up to 50 miles		51-200 Miles		Over 200 Miles	
			(4) Liability	(6) Phys. Dam	Liability	Phys. Dam	Liability	Phys. Dam
(1) Light Trucks (0-10,000 lbs. GWV)	Service	Factor Code	1.00 014- -	1.00 014- -	1.10 015- -	1.05 015- -	1.15 016- -	1.00 016- -
	(2) Retail	Factor Code	(5) 1.60 024- -	(7) 1.20 024- -	1.65 025- -	1.50 025- -	1.70 026- -	1.65 026- -
	Commercial	Factor Code	1.30 034- -	1.15 034- -	1.55 035- -	1.40 035- -	1.60 036- -	1.70 036- -

How these factors are applied to the rates will be discussed shortly. But first, let's practice classifying autos using the tables in the Appendix. The answers to the following problems are found at the end of this unit.

1. What are the primary factors for a truck that weighs 25,000 lbs. fully loaded, is used to haul equipment to the job site and back, and has a 100 mile radius of operation?

   Liability _____?

   Physical Damage _____?

Need a hint?

Size Class	Bus. Use Class		Radius					
			Up to 50 Miles		51 – 200 Miles		Over 200 Miles	
			Liability	Phys. Dam	Liability	Phys. Dam	Liability	Phys. Dam
Light Trucks (0 – 10,000 lbs. GVW)	Service	Factor Code	1.00 014- -	1.00 014- -	1.10 015- -	_(100-mile radius of operation)_		1.00 6- -
	Retail	Factor Code	1.60 024- -	1.20 024- -	1.65 025- -	025- -	026- -	.65 026- -
	truck that weighs 25,000 lbs. fully loaded	actor Code	1.30 034- -	1.15 034- -	1.55 035- -	1.40 035- -	1.60 036- -	1.70 036- -
Medium Trucks (10,001 – 20,000 lbs. GVW)	Retail	actor Code	1.05	.85	1.20	1.00	ZONE RATED	
		act Cod	_haul equipment to the job site and back_		1.70	1.25		
	Commercial	Fact Cod			1.60	1.20		
Heavy Trucks (20,001 – 45,000 lbs. GVW)	Service	Factor Code	1.10	.75	1.35	.85		
	Retail	Factor Code	1.70	1.15	1.75	1.35		
	Commercial	Factor Code	1.80	1.00	2.25	1.20		

2. What are the primary factors for a 12,000 lb. truck, fully loaded, that is to delivery office supplies to businesses within a 50-mile radius?

   Liability _____?

   Physical Damage _____?

Determine the secondary rating factor based on the insured's industry.

Step 2—Secondary Rating Factors

Secondary rating factors adjust the rates for the insured's type of industry. By nature of their operations, some industries have a greater or lesser exposure to loss. Secondary factors are grouped into the following classifications. Definitions of each classification are found in the Glossary beginning on page 219.

- Truckers

- Food Delivery

- Specialized Delivery

- Waste Disposal

- Farmers

- Dump and Transit Mix Trucks and Trailers

- Contractors

- Not Otherwise Specified

Study the Secondary Rating Factor table (Table 2 on page 238 in the Appendix) and note the definitions of the eight categories of industries. It is important to accurately classify the industry as the factors range from a factor reduction of .15 to a factor increase of .95.

3. What is the Secondary Rating Factor for a truck used by a meat store to make deliveries to customer?

    _____?

4. What is the Secondary Rating Factor for a vehicle to pick up garbage from individual households?

    _____?

Step 3—Combined Rating Factors

Add the Primary and Secondary Rating Factors together.

So, a vehicle with a Primary Rating Factor of 1.35 and a Secondary Rating Factor of +0.50 would have a combined rating factor of 1.85.

This is fairly easy provided you remember the definitions for the primary and secondary categories.

5. What are the combined rating factors for an extra-heavy truck used in the construction business to haul cement to the job sites within a 50-mile radius? Refer to the Appendix ratings tables beginning on page 237 to view the tables necessary to answer this question.

- Primary Rating Factor Table

- Secondary Rating Factor Table

Liability _____?

Physical Damage _____?

6. What are the combined rating factors for a light truck used by a construction supervisor to manage job sites within a 100-mile radius?

    • Primary Rating Factor Table

    • Secondary Rating Factor Table

Liability _____?

Physical Damage _____?

Step 4—Base Premiums

In Step 3 we combined the Primary and Secondary rating factors by adding them together. In Step 4 we multiply the base premium by that combined factor.

To find the base premium you must first identify the territory where the vehicle(s) are primarily garaged. Each state has multiple territories, each reflecting the loss exposure in that particular community.

Refer to Table 6 on page 240 in the Appendix to view a portion of a territory rate page for liability.

The rate page contains basic rates for Medical Payments and Personal Injury Protection. For the purpose of this lesson, however, we will only deal with the Liability rates.

A commercial vehicle with a combined rating factor of 1.35 would have an adjusted Base Premium of $946:

$701 × 1.35 = $946.35 or $946 rounded

TERRITORY XXX LIAB, MED, PAY, PIP									
LIABILITY Subline Code (611) Limits Identifier Code (1)	MEDICAL PAYMENTS Subline Code (620) Limit Per Person				PERSONAL INJURY PROTECTION Subline Code (615)				
Limit of Liab. $25,000	500	1000	2000	5000	Base Limits				
	Limit Codes								
05	01	03	04	06	01				
RULE 23. TRUCKS, TRACTORS AND TRAILERS CLASSIFICATIONS									
					All Autos				
$701	$3.00	$4.00	$5.00	$8.00			$37		

Note that premiums are always rounded down below $ .50 and up beyond that.

Note, also, that this premium is for basic limits, $25,000, which is the state's minimum financial responsibility limits in our example.

7. Given the rates in the tables below, what is the adjusted liability premium for a 15,000-pound truck used to deliver goods to retail stores within a 200 mile radius?

Refer to the Appendix to view the following tables necessary to answer this question:

- Primary Rating Factor Table

- Secondary Rating Factor Table

- Territory Rate Page

The table with the Physical Damage rates looks somewhat like the Liability rates table but there is one major difference: additional adjustment factors are needed.

PHYSICAL DAMAGE Original Cost of New Range $15,001-20,000			
Coverage Codes	**Specified Causes of Loss**	**Full Comp**	**$100 Ded. Coll.**
RULE 23. TRUCKS, TRACTORS, AND TRAILERS CLASSIFICATIONS •Not used in Dumping Operations •Local and Immediate—All Vehicles •Long Distance—Light Trucks and Trailers Used WIth Light Trucks	$55	$115	$338

First, as you can see at the top of the table, the rates shown are only for vehicles that cost between $15,000-$20,000 new. Obviously, many vehicles cost more or less than that and the rates need to be adjusted to reflect it.

Additionally, vehicles depreciate over time. The rates for a used vehicle need to be adjusted to reflect the original cost new.

To adjust the rates to reflect the original cost new of the vehicle, a factor is selected from the Original Cost New Factors table.

Price Range	Comprehensive and Specified Causes of Loss*	Collision
$0-4500	0.40	0.36
4501-6000	0.50	0.46
6001-8000	0.62	0.62
8001-10000	0.76	0.75
10001-15000	0.90	0.86
15001-20000	1.00	1.00
20001-25000	1.10	1.06
25001-40000	1.20	1.27
40001-65000	1.36	1.82
65001-90000	1.60	2.18
Over 90000	2.00	2.55

Next, a factor is selected from the Age Group Factors table to adjust the rates for the vehicle's age.

Age Group	Comprehensive and Specified Causes of Loss*	Collision
1	1.00	1.00
2	1.00	1.00
3	1.00	1.00
4	0.90	0.85
5	0.85	0.75
6	0.70	0.65

8. What are the adjusted Comprehensive and $100 deductible Collision base premium for a heavy truck with a cost new $68,000 and Age Group 4?

Refer to the tables above, or in the Appendix, to identify the specific factors.

9. What is the fully developed Physical Damage premium for a heavy truck-tractor, commercial use, frozen food manufacturer, 50-mile radius, cost new = $52,000, and Age Group 3? Use the following tables:

- Primary Rating Factor Table

- Secondary Rating Factor Table

- Physical Damage Base Premium

- Original Cost New Factors

- Age Group Factors

Comprehensive _____?

$100 Ded. Collision _____?

10. What is the fully developed Physical Damage premium for a light truck, retail use, furniture store, 200-mile radius, cost new = $15,000, Age Group 2. Use the following tables:

- Primary Rating Factor Table

- Secondary Rating Factor Table

- Physical Damage Base Premium

- Original Cost New Factors

- Age Group Factors

Comprehensive _____?

$100 Ded. Collision _____?

Step 5—Increased Limits Factors

If the basic $25,000 liability limit is not enough, the following may suffice.

State rate pages only show the liability rates for basic limits but most insureds will want limits considerably higher. This is achieved by applying an increased limits factor to the base rate. Refer to the Appendix Table 7, Increased Limits Factors on page 241.

This table contains increased limit factors for only the Combined Single Limit options for the vehicle size classes. For Split Limit coverage, refer to the specific insurer's own rate pages. This sample table is an abbreviation of the actual ISO Increased Limits Table, which includes many more limit options and Zone-Rated Vehicles.

The increased limits factor is found in the following manner.

You want $300,000 liability for your 12,000 lb. truck.

$300,000 liability
12,000 lb. truck

Increased Limits Factors			
Combined Single Limit of Liability (000's)	Light and **Medium Trucks**	Heavy Trucks and Truck-Tractors	Extra-Heavy Trucks and Truck-Tractors
25	1.00	1.00	1.00
50	1.26	1.25	1.25
100	1.54	1.52	1.56
250	1.95	1.93	2.09
300	2.05	2.03	2.20
500	2.31	2.31	2.56
1000	2.63	2.74	3.16

The increased limits factor is 2.05.

Here is an example of the calculation:

The adjusted liability premium for a $300,000 Business Auto Policy is $2,490 for a heavy truck, retail use for wholesale parts delivery, in a 150-mile radius. Use the following tables:

- Primary Rating Factor Table

- Secondary Rating Factor Table

- Territory Rate Page

- Increased Limits Factors

Base Prem.	×	Primary + Secondary Factors	×	Increased Limits Factor	=	Adjusted Prem.
$701	×	(1.75 + 0.00)	×	2.03	=	$2,490

11. What is the adjusted premium for a $500,000 Business Auto policy? The vehicle is a medium truck used by a farmer to haul produce to market up to 100 miles away? Use the following tables:

- Primary Rating Factor Table

- Secondary Rating Factor Table

- Territory Rate Page

- Increased Limits Factors

Step 6—Fleet Factor

How do you determine if the account to be rated is fleet or not fleet?

A **fleet** account is one that has five or more powered units (whether commercial or private passenger type vehicles). A trailer is not a powered unit and is not counted.

Physical damage Base Premiums will have a different fleet factor than the liability Base Premiums:

Fleet Factors	
Liability	1.10
Physical Damage	
Collision	.90
Other than Collision	.70

Why are the physical damage factors lower than the liability?

- Fleets have a greater risk of liability loss because they have more vehicles and therefore more over-the-road exposure. In addition, fleet accounts tend to be larger insureds and attract higher lawsuits.

- On the other hand, fleet accounts are more likely to have safety training programs, driver training programs, and regular maintenance schedules.

12. Quote the Liability premium for a $100,000 Business Auto policy. The insured company owns three private passenger vehicles and three trucks. One vehicle is a 5,000 lb. GVW truck, used by a highway contractor to supervise road construction over a 250-mile radius. Use the following tables:

   - Primary Rating Factor Table

   - Secondary Rating Factor Table

   - Territory Rate Page

   - Increased Limits Factors

   - Fleet Factors

13. Quote the Physical Damage premiums, full Comprehensive, and $100 deductible Collision for the same contractor's vehicle (5,000 GVW, commercial use, 250-mile radius). The vehicle cost new is $13,000, Age Group 6. Use the following tables:

- Primary Rating Factor Table

- Secondary Rating Factor Table

- Physical Damage Base Premium

- Original Cost New Factors

- Age Group Factors

- Territory Rate Page

- Increased Limits Factors

- Fleet Factors

Comprehensive _____?

$100 Ded. Collision _____?

An Additional Commercial Auto Coverage—Hired Autos

An earlier unit discussed the fact that coverage for Hired Autos is obtained by showing Symbols 1 or 8 on the policy. Whichever symbol is used, the same rating method applies. Hired Auto coverage is rated on the amount the insured spends to lease autos during the year.

To determine the rate for the coverage, simple take the rate for Hired Autos from the state rate pages and multiply it by the appropriate increased limits factor for the amount of desired coverage.

Below is a calculation for $300,000 Limit, Light Weight Autos.

Est. Cost of Hire	×	Hired Auto Rate (per $100)	×	Increased Limit Factor	=	Annual Premium
$7,000	×	.89	×	2.05	=	$128

If, as it often happens, the insured does not know how much will be spent on leased autos, the coverage can be written on an "if any" basis, in which case the minimum premium is charged (subject to the increased limits factor). The insured's policy is audited at the end of the year and a final premium is made based on the actual cost of leased vehicles.

An Additional Commercial Auto Coverage—Non-Owned Autos

For Non-Owned Auto coverage, the premium is derived from a non-owned auto rate table based on the number of employees at all of the insured's locations.

Non-Owned Auto Rates

# of Employees	$25,000 Limit
0 - 25	$34
26 - 100	$80
101 - 500	$175
501 -1000	$275
Over 1,000	$617

What is the annual premium for an insured with 400 employees who chooses $300,000 coverage?

Non-Owned Auto Rate	×	Increased Limit Factor*	=	Annual Premium
$175	×	2.05	=	$359

*The increased limit factor used in this example assumes that the employees are driving private passenger-type vehicles, which is normally the case.

Note: Auto garages, partnerships, and volunteer organizations use a different rating approach that will not be covered in this lesson.

■ SUMMARY

This unit covered the key elements for rating a commercial vehicle. Those elements are the vehicle's:

- size;

- use;

- radius of operation;

- cost new;

- age group; and

- fleet status.

Additionally, you learned how to develop the premium for Liability and Physical Damage coverages and the rating procedure for Non-Owned and Hired Auto coverages.

A fundamental concept of insurance is that rates reflect exposure. Therefore, an understanding of the rating process for any line of coverage helps you understand the underwriting concerns that are associated with that risk.

■ COURSE SUMMARY

The commercial auto coverage program was developed by ISO in the late 70s to address the emerging commercial business market with multiple vehicle exposures in one business.

With the use of coverage symbols to denote covered autos by specific category on the policy Declarations, it became easy to select and tailor coverage on the basis of vehicle type and use and to restrict liability coverage to specific exposures.

The Business Auto Coverage Form is the most commonly used of the Commercial Auto forms, followed by the Garage Coverage form, because of its versatility. ISO also developed the Truckers and Motor Carrier Transport forms to tailor coverage to specific industry practices, subject to state and federal regulation of trucking and transport of cargo. For this reason, these policies are offered primarily through specialty carriers.

■ ANSWERS TO UNIT 9 RATING PROBLEMS

1. Liability = 1.35

Physical Damage = .85

A truck that weighs 25,000 lbs fully loaded is considered a "Heavy Truck". Hauling equipment to the job site and back falls in the "Service" class. The 100 mile radius falls in the "51-200 mile" Radius category.

2. Liability = 1.35; Physical Damage = .95

A truck that weighs 12,000 lbs fully loaded is considered a "Medium Truck". Delivering office supplies to businesses falls in the "Commercial" class. The 50 mile radius falls in the "Up to 50 miles" Radius category.

3. Not Otherwise Classified - +0.00.

The Food Delivery classification is used for food manufacturers or wholesalers such as a truck delivering meat to customers.

4. +0.50.

A vehicle used to pick up garbage is classified as Waste Disposal.

5. Liability - 2.35; Physical Damage - 1.00

The calculation for liability: 2.50 - 0.15 = 2.35

The calculation for physical damage: 1.15 - 0.15 = 1.00

Even though the vehicle is owned by a contractor, it takes the "dump and transit mix trucks" classification because that is how it is used.

6. Liability -1.55; Physical Damage - 1.40

The calculation for liability: 1.55 + 0.00 = 1.55

The calculation for physical damage: 1.40 + 0.00 = 1.40

Remember, the "service" classification is reserved for vehicles us to haul equipment/employees to a job site and remain there for the majority of the day. Therefore, the "commercial" use class would apply here.

7. $1,122

The calculation is $701 × 1.60 = $1,121.60 (round up). Remember, the "retail" classification is reserved for vehicles delivering to individual households.

8. Comprehensive - $166; Collision - $626

	Base Premium	×	Cost New Factor	×	Age Group Factor	=	Adjusted Base Premium
Comprehensive	$115	×	1.6	×	.90	=	$166
$100 Ded. Collision	$338	×	2.18	×	.85	=	$626

9. $1,234

	Base Premium	×	Cost New Factor	×	Age Group Factor	×	Primary + Secondary Factors	=	Adjusted Prem.
Comp.	$115	×	1.36	×	1.00	×	(1.25 + .35)	=	$250
$100 Ded. Collision	$338	×	1.82	×	1.00	×	(1.25 + .35)	=	$984
									Total = $1,234

10. $651

	Base Premium	×	Cost New Factor	×	Age Group Factor	×	Primary + Secondary Factors	=	Adjusted Prem.
Comp.	$115	×	.90	×	1.00	×	(1.65 + .00)	=	$171
$100 Ded. Collision	$338	×	.86	×	1.00	×	(1.65 + .00)	=	$480
									Total = $651

11. $1,781

Base Premium	×	Primary + Secondary Factors	×	Increased Limits Factor	=	Adjusted Prem.
$701	×	(1.60 − .50)	×	2.31	=	$1,781

12. $1,900

Remember, the vehicles do not have to be all of one type to be considered a fleet. They can be five or more powered units of any type.

Base Prem.	×	Primary + Secondary Factors	×	Increased Limits Factor	×	Fleet Factor	=	Adjusted Prem.
$701	×	(1.60 + 0.00)	×	1.54	×	1.10	=	$1,900

13. $375

	Base Prem.	×	Cost New Factor	×	Age Group Factor	×	Primary + Secondary Factors	×	Fleet Factors	=	Adjusted Prem.
Comp.	$115	×	.90	×	.70	×	(1.70 + .00)		.70	=	$86
$100 Ded. Coll.	$338	×	.86	×	.65	×	(1.70 + .00)		.90	=	$289
										Total =	**$375**

····· **Review Test**

IMPORTANT INFORMATION REGARDING THIS REVIEW TEST

This exam was designed for review purposes and may be used to fulfill your training and firm element requirements. *This exam has not been approved for insurance continuing education and cannot be used for this purpose.* If you need insurance continuing education credit for this course, a different exam is required.

Contact Dearborn at 1-800-423-4723.

1. What is the correct coverage form for a limo company with an airport service?

   A. Business Auto Coverage Form
   B. Garage Coverage Form
   C. Commercial Property Coverage Form
   D. Commercial Liability Coverage Form

2. Tanya is the underwriter for New Ways Insurance Company and wonders how she is going to underwrite a new fleet auto account. What factors should she consider?

   A. Loss history
   B. Accident history
   C. Driver training and safety
   D. All of the above

3. Your insured purchases a mini-van that will sometimes be used for business purposes and wants to add it to the business BAP. Which coverage symbol would you use to add the mini-van to the insured's BAP?

   A. Symbol 1—Any Auto
   B. Symbol 2—Owned Autos Only
   C. Symbol 3—Owned Private Passenger Autos Only
   D. Symbol 4—Owned Autos Other than Private Passenger Autos Only

4. The insured uses an auto covered under an unendorsed BAP to move a table from an apartment. As the table is moved out the door, it knocks over an expensive lamp and shatters the chandelier bulb. The property damage to the lamp is probably

   A. covered under the BAP because the insured was at fault
   B. covered under the BAP because the table was not yet on the covered auto
   C. not covered under the BAP
   D. covered under the owner's personal liability policy

5. Coverage Symbols 5 and 6 are used for

   A. non-compulsory coverage in any state
   B. mandatory No-Fault and Uninsured Motorist Coverage
   C. optional No-Fault and Uninsured Motorist Coverage
   D. owned autos only

6. As a general rule, the definition of auto does not include

   A. mobile equipment
   B. semi-trailer
   C. trailer
   D. motorcycle

7. Coverage Symbol 3 is used for

   A. any auto
   B. private passenger vehicles only
   C. owned autos only
   D. owned private passenger autos only

8. Coverage Symbol 1 offers the broadest coverage under the business auto form because

   A. any auto is a covered auto
   B. coverage applies to owned, non-owned, borrowed or hired vehicles
   C. all coverage symbols are included in Symbol 1
   D. all of the above

9. Under the Insuring Agreements for Section II—Liability, the insurance company has a duty to pay all

   A. damages, and all pollution claims
   B. claims and defend all suits
   C. sums the insured becomes legally obligated to pay as damages for property damage or bodily injury caused by an accident involving a covered auto
   D. all of the above

10. The BAP's Physical Damage Coverage options include

    A. comprehensive
    B. collision or overturn
    C. towing
    D. all of the above

11. Your insured's vehicle is covered under the BAP with Specified Causes of Loss Coverage for physical damage coverage. The insured hits an icy spot and the car flips over, causing $4,000 in damages. How much does the BAP pay?

    A. $4,000
    B. $3,900 ($4,000 less a standard $100 deductible)
    C. $0
    D. None of the above

12. The insured runs a designer paint store and sponsors two cars at NASCAR. He is putting the last-minute paint touches on his newest derby car on the way to competition. Just before arriving at the racetrack, the trailer transporting the racecar overturns and damages the derby car. The insured files a claim for the front-end damage to the derby car. Is the physical damage to the derby car covered under the Physical Damage Coverage of the Business Auto Policy?

    A. No, because Section I—Covered Autos (even with Symbol 1) does not include non-owned autos.
    B. No, because even if that car was not racing, the prep paintwork still triggers the racing and demolition exclusion under Section III—Physical Damage.
    C. No, because the loading and unloading exclusion under the Property Damage provisions of Section II—Liability Coverage applies.
    D. Yes, because the overturn of the trailer, a covered auto, includes the overturn of any car it is transporting.

13. One of your insured's employees uses a company car to make a delivery and to also give a friend a ride home. The employee causes an accident in which both he and the friend are injured. Assuming your insured has properly endorsed this policy, which section of the policy will cover the emergency room fees for the injured parties?

    A. Uninsured Motorists Coverage
    B. Underinsured Motorists Coverage
    C. Medical Payments
    D. Deductible Liability Insurance

14. Which of the following is the same between a personal auto policy and a business auto policy?

    A. Number of units each policy covers
    B. Types of vehicles each policy covers
    C. Coverage of no-fault benefits
    D. Use of covered auto symbols

15. One of the reasons an auto dealership should purchase a garage policy is to provide

    A. liability coverage for owners of repair facilities who cannot get coverage elsewhere
    B. coverage for building and other structures occupied as service stations
    C. a combination of automobile and general liability coverage
    D. coverage for catastrophic loss

16. For which of the following reasons might some commercial insureds NOT wish to include medical payments and uninsured motorists coverage in their business auto policies?

    A. They are unconcerned about injuries to the passengers in their vehicles.
    B. Because only employees drive certain vehicles, they are covered by workers compensation.
    C. They do not feel a social responsibility to the passengers in commercial vehicles.
    D. They are covered for injuries to passenger under the bodily injury portions of their coverage.

17. Which of the following is specifically excluded in Section IV—Physical Damage Coverage of the Garage Policy?

    A. False pretense
    B. Personal and advertising injury
    C. Employees
    D. Bodily injury to trespassers

18. In the Garage Coverage Form, the garage-keepers coverage specifically excludes

    A. theft or conversion by employees or shareholders
    B. wrongful hiring and firing practices of the employer
    C. pollution-related exposures
    D. mischief or vandalism

19. Each of the following options is available to insure damage to customer vehicles in an insured's care, custody, or control EXCEPT

    A. direct primary
    B. legal liability
    C. direct excess
    D. direct legal

20. Of the following coverage Symbols in the Truckers policy, which are used to denote coverage for trailers in the possession of the insured under the terms of a written trailer or equipment interchange agreement?

    A. 41 and 42 only
    B. 44 and 45 only
    C. 46 and 47 only
    D. 48 and 49 only

21. Who of the following is NOT insured under a Truckers policy?

    A. Permissive users of covered autos
    B. Named insured for any covered auto
    C. Rail carrier for bodily injury while detached trailer was being offloaded from train
    D. Owners of a trailer connected to covered auto that is a power unit

22. An endorsement to the BAP that broadens the definition of covered auto is

    A. Additional Insured—Lessor
    B. Mobile Equipment
    C. Rental Reimbursement
    D. State Amount

23. The BAP's definition of autos would include all of the following EXCEPT

   A. self-propelled vehicles with permanently attached air compressors or generators
   B. self-propelled vehicles designed primarily for snow removal
   C. cherry-pickers mounted on trailers
   D. self-propelled vehicles with permanently attached lighting or well servicing equipment

24. Which of the following statements is the best summary of the Motor Carrier Coverage Form?

   A. It covers anyone involved in the cash and carry industry.
   B. It applies to a person or organization engaged in transportation by auto in the furtherance of a commercial enterprise.
   C. It applies only to the trucking industry.
   D. It applies to air, rail, and water carriers.

25. Which of the following statements regarding the BAP pollution coverage is TRUE?

   A. BAP pollution coverage is very broad.
   B. BAP pollution coverage is very limited.
   C. Pollutants transported by the insured are covered.
   D. Pollutants handled for movement into, onto, or from the covered auto are covered.

Answers to Review Test

1. A	6. A	11. C	16. B	21. C
2. D	7. D	12. B	17. A	22. B
3. C	8. D	13. C	18. A	23. C
4. C	9. C	14. C	19. D	24. B
5. B	10. D	15. C	20. D	25. B

..... **Glossary**

A

accident Continuous or repeated exposure to the same conditions.

ACORD form Standardized forms utilized extensively by the insurance industry for application, supplements, and all manner of forms.

actual cash value Replacement cost less depreciation.

ACV Actual cash value; replacement cost less depreciation.

adjusting losses The process through which the insurance company goes when a claim has been filed. The process begins when the first report is made and ends when the claim is paid or denied.

aggregate limit The maximum coverage under a liability policy during a specified period of time (usually one year or the policy period) regardless of the number of separate losses that may occur. Losses paid under coverages subject to aggregate limits reduce the amounts available for future losses.

Any Auto A symbol definition on the ISO form. Any auto literally means any auto.

appraisal Process whereby an individual requests a current market price on an item. The individual determining the price is usually an expert who specifically handles property of the type under examination.

arbitrator Individual who mediates between parties to a dispute.

assumed liability When an individual assumes liability for another individual or entity, they become the responsible party who will assume full responsibility for the acts of another.

auto dealership Individual or organization in the business of selling autos, trucks, motorcycles, or other vehicles. A franchised dealer has an agreement to sell a particular make or makes of auto; a non-franchised dealer is normally a used car dealer.

automobile   Motor vehicle designed for use on public roads; includes a land motor vehicle, trailer, or semi-trailer. Mobile equipment is not considered an automobile.

bailee   Person who accepts responsibility for the goods of others.

base premium   Insurer's rates unadjusted for increased limits or loss experience.

B

BI   Bodily injury, harm to a person. Includes injury, sickness, disease, or death.

bodily injury   BI, harm to a person. Includes injury, sickness, disease, or death.

Broad Form Products Coverage   An ISO endorsement that covers Products Liability on the Broad Form which includes more coverage than the Limited Form.

Business Use Class   Identifies whether the vehicle in question is subject to Service, Retail, or Commercial rating use.

C

care, custody, and control   A bailee takes the property of others into their care, custody, and control which creates insurance issues. These classes of property are generally excluded.

cash flow   The amount of cash generated from operations that flows through a business. An important factor as it identifies whether an entity is generating little or no cash as that will make it difficult (if not impossible) to continue operations.

CGL   Commercial General Liability; the ISO form that broadly covers premises and operation, fire legal liability, medical payments, products and completed operations, and advertising liability. It may cover some or all these situations and can be endorsed to cover all manner of insurable liability.

classification   System designed by ISO to categorize the many vehicle types to develop insurance rates.

co-insurance penalty   An individual or entity that does not carry the proper amount of insurance will be penalized in the event of loss. The purpose of the penalty is to encourage insureds to carry insurance to value.

collision   Physical damage coverage used when an automobile is overturned or upset.

Commercial Auto Insurance   ISO program that includes BAP, Garage Coverage Form, Truckers Coverage Form, and Motor Carrier Coverage Form.

Commercial General Liability   CGL, the ISO form that broadly covers premises and operation, fire legal liability, medical payments, products and completed operations, and advertising liability. It may cover some or all these situations and can be endorsed to cover all manner of insurable liability.

Commercial Package Policy (CPP)   A standardized package policy developed by ISO for insuring commercial loss exposures. The package consists of Common Declarations, Common Conditions, and specific coverage parts.

commercial use   Rating category that includes all uses of commercial vehicles other than those specifically included in the Service or Retail categories.

completed operations   Work that has been completed and is considered delivered when it is put to its intended use.

comprehensive   Type of physical damage protection that generally covers all losses other than collision.

compulsory insurance laws   State laws that require all citizens of a particular state to carry certain levels of insurance.

compulsory uninsured motorist laws   State laws that mandate all citizens of a particular state carry certain minimum levels of uninsured motorist coverage.

conditions   Requirements imposed on an individual who is a party to a contract. The Conditions outline the responsibilities of both parties to a contract.

contract   The four elements are offer and acceptance, legal purpose, consideration, and competent parties. Provided it meets these four criteria, a contact can be for almost anything.

contract carrier   Trucker that carriers the goods of others on a contract basis; they enter into agreements with individuals to haul their property from one point to another. Unlike a common carrier, contract carriers do not travel across regular routes.

contractors   Secondary rating industry category for autos used by residential or commercial contractors, including excavation and street or roadwork.

coverage territory   Geographical area where the policy is effective. Coverage can be worldwide or restricted to a specific area.

covered autos   Autos or vehicles covered by a certain policy. The autos covered are governed by the symbols selected on the Declarations Page of the Commercial Auto Policy.

covered peril   Cause of loss that is included in the insurance policy. Note: not all perils are covered.

CPP   Commercial Package Policy; a standardized package policy developed by ISO for insuring commercial loss exposures. The package consists of Common Declarations, Common Conditions, and specific coverage parts.

D

Declarations   Ordinarily the first page of any policy that specify who is insured, for what, and for how long.

deductible   Amount the insured is responsible for paying in the event of loss.

defective products   Products with an inherent defect that will prevent them from fulfilling their primary function.

Definitions   Section of every insurance policy that outlines the specific definition of certain words and terms used in the policy.

dump and transit mix trucks and trailers   Secondary rating industry category for autos used in dumping operations and mixers hauling cement or similar products.

duties in event of loss   Section of an insurance policy that outlines the responsibility of the insured and insurer in the event of a loss.

duty to defend   Section of an insurance policy that details the duty of the insurer to defend in suits brought against the insured.

E

employee   Person who works under the exclusive direction and control of another; includes leased workers, but generally not temporary workers.

employee indemnification   Process of protecting the employee from damage, loss, or injury. , This coverage is generally excluded from most insurance policies as it is intended to be covered by workers compensation and employers liability coverage.

employer's liability   Form of coverage ordinarily purchased with workers compensation. This protects the insured from suits brought by employees hurt during the course of their employment.

endorsements   Items that change an insurance contract and are attached as separate documents that become part of the contract.

examination of your books and records   Clause in an insurance contract giving the insurer the right to examine your books and records to ensure you are paying a premium that reflects the actual risk.

Exclusions   Items excluded from coverage.

expected or intended injury   Intended or expected losses.

extensions   Found in most policies and offer additional coverage to the insured. Generally include supplementary payments and out-of-state coverages.

F

Farmers Secondary rating industry category for autos used by farmers in connection with farm operations.

Fast Track Certain policy endorsements that TRIA exempted from review by state insurance departments. These endorsements are available for immediate use by insurers.

financial responsibility Minimum amount of insurance a particular state requires to be carried (e.g., Connecticut requires all registered motor vehicles to carry a minimum of 20,000/40,000 of liability coverage).

fire legal liability Coverage that will pay for damage to the area of a particular property occupied by the insured if the acts of the insured cause a fire. If an insured leases space, they generally do not carry property coverage and, in the event of loss, would not have coverage to rebuild their damaged work area.

first named insured Individual named first in the policy who receives all bills and notices, as well as serving as the primary contact with the insurance company.

fleet ISO classification that reduces premiums for five or more powered units (whether commercial or private passenger type vehicles).

food delivery Secondary rating industry category for autos used by food manufacturers to transport raw and finished products or autos used in wholesale distribution of food.

G

Garage Coverage Form Type of insurance policy designed for auto dealers in the business of servicing, selling, repairing, storing, or parking vehicles.

garagekeepers insurance Type of coverage found in the Garage Coverage Form (and Garagekeepers Coverage endorsement) that allows an insured to insure vehicles owned by others that are in their custody .

GCW Gross Combined Weight; weight of the combined tractor-trailer unit fully loaded; truck, trailer, and cargo.

GLW Gross Loaded Weight; maximum loaded weight for a truck-tractor and the semi-trailer(s) for which the truck-tractor was designed (as specified by the manufacturer).

GVW Gross vehicle weight; weight of a vehicle including the cargo.

H

hazards Event increases the chance of loss.

hired autos Leased, borrowed, or rented autos.

hold-harmless   Agreement between two parties whereby one of the parties will assume the liability of the other in the event of loss.

host liquor liability   A host may incur liability for serving alcohol to others who subsequently harm themselves or others. Liquor liability is generally excluded from most coverage forms and so is a valuable coverage to be added to an insurance policy for a premium.

I

incidental medical malpractice liability   Liability for a location that has a medical professional on staff or who comes into the facility on a regular basis. The professional should carry their own medical malpractice insurance, but that coverage will not protect the insured from losses that may arise from their negligence. This coverage can be added to an existing policy for a premium.

indemnification   To protect against damage, loss, or injury.

Insurance Services Office, Inc.   ISO; a company that writes standardized insurance policies and endorsements and also publishes the definitive source on all lines of insurance.

insured contracts   Contracts covered by the insurance policy. Many classes of contacts are excluded.

ISO   Insurance Services Office; a company that writes standardized insurance policies and endorsements and also publishes the definitive source on all lines of insurance.

L

land motor vehicle   Any type of vehicle designed for use on land; includes mobile equipment.

legal liability   Person or entity that is legally liable has been found liable in a court. The determination is blatantly obvious and the insurance company makes the finding without court assistance.

legally obligated   Person or entity is legally obligated to act or not to act by contract or law.

liability coverage   Provides valuable protection against bodily injury or property damages arising from many covered causes of loss.

liberalization   General condition found in the insurance policy that states if coverage is broadened for a class of insureds, the broader coverage would apply to existing insureds.

license agreement   Legal contact between parties that allows one party to use the idea, technology, or concept of another for a fee.

limit of insurance   Amount the insurance company will pay for a certain type of loss.

loss history   Insurance companies generate loss runs that detail loss dates, types, and amounts paid. Generally required by an insurance company before they will quote on a new program of insurance.

loss of use   Interference with an individual or entity's beneficial use of their property due to a covered cause of loss.

M

medical payments   Provides first party benefits regardless to fault; a prompt source of funds.

member   Owner of a limited liability type company.

mid-term   Category that applies to policies in force as of 11/26/02. Reference to this category of policyholders expired on 11/26/03 with regard to the terrorism exclusions.

mono-line policy   Policy that only covers one type of loss exposure (e.g., an auto or property policy).

Motor Carrier Coverage Form   Commercial auto form created to cover risks that may have trucking and business auto on one coverage form.

N

named insured   Individual listed in the policy who has certain rights and responsibilities due to their status as a named insured.

no benefit to bailee   Clause which states that a bailee cannot profit from the loss of property that does not belong to the insured.

non-dealer   Garage operations such as repair shops, service stations, storage garages, public parking places, and tow truck operators. Under the CLM, dealers of mobile homes or commercial trailers also fall within this category.

non-fleet   Part of the ISO classification system that signifies the policy has less than four autos.

non-owned   Leased, borrowed, or rented autos.

non-owned watercraft coverage   If the insured rents a watercraft for a company party and injury results, there is no coverage under the CGL or BAP unless endorsed with this type of coverage. This coverage is for the vicarious liability that may arise as a result of using a watercraft.

nonprofit   Organization established under the Internal Revenue Code such as a church, charity, or other humanitarian organization that is exempt from paying federal income taxes.

Not Otherwise Specified   Secondary rating industry category for autos used for any purpose other than already described in another industry category. This category includes logging and lumbering operations.

O

out-of-state extensions   Insurance is regulated at the state level and each state has their own laws and regulation. When an individual or entity travels from state to state, they may not carry the proper level of insurance. This extension automatically adjusts their insurance to ensure compliance with the state laws of the states travelled through.

owned automobile   For automobile liability purposes, any automobile owned by the insured, including non-owned trailers while attached to an owned automobile.

P

PAP   Personal Auto Policy; designed to cover individuals and families for their use of automobiles.

partner   Individual who has an ownership interest in a company or business.

PD   Property damage; damage to the property of others; distinct from bodily injury.

peril   Cause of loss.

personal and advertising liability   Provides coverage for acts that may arise from personal or advertising activities. A company may inadvertently make false statements or claims in their advertising that leads to harm; they would be covered under this class of liability coverage.

Personal Auto Policy   PAP; designed to cover individuals and families for their use of automobiles.

personal injury liability   Coverage for acts such as libel, slander, and false arrest.

Personal Injury Protection   PIP; provides benefits for funeral expenses and lost wages in the event an individual is involved in an auto accident. An optional coverage that can be endorsed to a policy. In some states this is a mandatory coverage.

physical damage coverage   Coverage for damaged vehicles. Includes comprehensive, collision, and other coverages.

PIP   Personal Injury Protection; provides benefits for funeral expenses and lost wages in the event an individual is involved in an auto accident. An optional coverage that can be endorsed to a policy. In some states this is a mandatory coverage.

policy period   Period of time covered under the policy. Usually one year, but can be any time-frame agreed to between the insured and insurer.

premium audit   Process by which the insurance company assesses whether they are collecting the correct premium. The company will ask for proof regarding various aspects of the insured's business (i.e. sales, payroll, number of employees, number of autos, etc.).

primary rating factor   Reflects both the vehicle's size and how it is used, two elements that have obvious implications for loss experience.

products recall   Process whereby a company recalls all of a certain class of products that have been found defective or to cause harm.

property damage   Damage to or loss of use of tangible property.

R

radius class   Divides the exposure into three groups: up to 50 miles, 51-200 miles, and over 200 miles. The more time a vehicle spends on the road, the greater the risk of accident.

radius of operations   Factor used in rating commercial trucks based on the distance travelled from the principal garage location. Risks are assumed to be greater for trucks traveling long distances (usually more than 50 miles) because of driver fatigue and higher speeds than for those confined to a small area. It is customary to measure the radius by a straight line rather than by road miles.

reporting   Method of communicating the amount or number of individual units that should be insured to the insurance company. The number of cars on a lot from month to month.

retail use   Rating category that includes vehicles used for retail pick-up or delivery to households.

revenue   Sales; the total amount of units sold multiplied by the selling price.

risk   Chance of loss.

risk management   Process whereby an insured systematically evaluates their loss exposures and devises and implements plans to deal with losses should they arise.

S

scheduled credits   Credits to reduce premiums available to business that meet certain characteristics.

secondary rating factor   A key element of loss exposure is the industry in which the vehicle is used. Some industries have better loss experience than others.

semi-trailer   Trailers equipped with a fifth wheel coupling to be used with a truck-tractor rig and have a load capacity over 2,000 pounds.

service use   Rating category that includes vehicles primarily used to carry employees or equipment to and from the job site, remaining there for the majority of the working day.

social insurance   Government insurance programs such as social security, unemployment, and welfare.

specialized delivery   Secondary rating industry category for autos used for deliveries subject to time and similar constraints such as armored cars, magazines, newspapers, and mail.

subrogation clause   Clause in a policy that explains the right of a person to assume a legal claim of another; the right of a person who has paid a liability or obligation of another to be indemnified by that person; an insurer's substitution in place of the insured in regard to a claim against a third party for indemnification of a loss paid by the insurer.

supplementary payments   Payments that are made in addition to the limits of liability. The cost of defending a suit is ordinarily a supplementary payment.

symbols   Classes of vehicles that have been developed by ISO to rate commercial auto policies.

T

tort   Private wrong, as opposed to a criminal wrong.

trailer   Any trailer with load capacity of over 2,000 pounds that is not considered a semi-trailer.

Trailer Interchange Agreements   Agreement between truckers that enable them to switch trailers and provide for continuous insurance. This is valuable coverage that allows truckers to more efficiently run their businesses.

Transfer of Your Rights and Duties Under this Policy   More commonly referred to as subrogation. When the insurer makes payment to the insured, the right to recover from other parties is transferred to the insurer.

truckers   Secondary rating industry category for autos used to haul or transport goods, materials, or commodities for others (except moving operations).

Truckers Coverage Form   Special variation of the commercial auto program designed to cover the needs of those engaged in the trucking business.

U

underwriting guidelines   Criteria established by individual companies to determine what types of risks they will insure. These guidelines outline the rules of submitting business and the types of businesses that are eligible for coverage

utility trailer   Any trailer or semi-trailer that has a load capacity of 2,000 pounds or less.

V

variance   Waiver that allows an individual or entity to deviate from established zoning laws.

vicarious liability   Concept that an employer is responsible for the acts of its employees and agents. If an employee hurts someone in the course of work, it is assumed that the employer knew of these actions and is liable for the acts of the employee.

W

waste disposal   Secondary rating industry category for autos transporting salvage and waste material for disposal or resale.

Who is an Insured   Section of an insurance policy that stipulates who is covered. Usual classes of insureds include named insureds, permitted users, and anyone liable for the acts of others.

Y

your work   May be a part of a larger work, but is distinct as your own. Generally, coverage for your work is not covered.

■■■■■ **Appendix**

e have made the following charts, rating tables, and ISO forms available for you.

■ ■ ■ ■ ■

■ **CHARTS**

- BAP 2001 Versus 1997 Comparison Chart

- BAP/Garage Form Symbol Comparison Chart

- Garage Risks Coverage Options

■ **RATING TABLES**

- Unit 10—Rating the Business Auto Policy

■ **ISO FORMS**

- Business Auto Coverage Forms

- Business Auto Physical Damage Coverage Form

- Garage Coverage Form

- Truckers Coverage Form

- Motor Carrier Coverage Form

- Business Auto Declarations

- Motor Carrier Coverage Form Declarations

- Common Policy Conditions

- Common Policy Declarations

- War Exclusion

- Drive Other Car Coverage – Broadened Coverage For Named Individuals

- Employees as Insureds

- Individual Named Insured

- Lessor – Additional Insured and Loss Payee

- Loss Payable Clause

- Mobile Equipment

- Rental Reimbursement Coverage

- Tapes, Records and Discs Coverage

- Auto Medical Payment Coverage

- Broad Form Coverage Products Coverage

- Broadened Coverage – Garages

- Dealers Driveway Collision Coverage

- Garage Coverage Form – Auto Dealers' Supplementary Schedule

- Garage Locations and Operations Medical Payments and Coverage

- Garagekeepers Coverage

- Personal Injury Liability Coverage – Garages

BAP 2001 VERSUS 1997 COMPARISON CHART

The October 2001 Edition of the Business Auto Coverage Form (CA 00 01) increases the amounts paid for some coverages, adds a new exclusion, and expands coverage in some areas. The forms should be compared side-by-side to fully understand these changes.

July 1997 Edition	October 2001 Edition
Section III – Physical Damage Coverage	**Section III – Physical Damage Coverage**
Coverage Extensions: • $15 per day to a $450 maximum for temporary transportation • No coverage for Loss of Use Expenses	*Coverage Extensions:* • $20 per day to a $600 maximum for temporary transportation • Adds coverage for Loss of Use Expenses – pays based on option selected (other than collision, specified causes of loss, or collision) – pays $20 per day to a maximum of $600. *Exclusions:* • Adds "diminution in value," which means the actual or perceived loss in market or resale value as a result of a direct and accidental loss. *Limit of Insurance:* • Adds adjustment for depreciation and physical damage when a total loss occurs. • Adds statement that insured will not pay for the amount of betterment.
Section IV – Business Auto Conditions *Premium Audit:* • Does not provide a due date *Policy Period, Coverage Territory:* • Coverage territory limited to the United States of America, its territories and possessions; Puerto Rico; and Canada.	**Section IV – Business Auto Conditions** *Premium Audit:* • Adds "due date" definition for the final premium as the date shown as the due date on the bill. *Policy Period, Coverage Territory:* • Expands coverage to anywhere in the world if (1) a covered auto is leased, hired rented or borrowed without a driver for 30 days or less; and (2) the insured is found legally liable in a lawsuit in the U.S., its possessions and territories, Puerto Rico or Canada or in a settlement to which the insurer agrees.
Section V – Definitions • No definition of "diminution in value"	**Section V – Definitions** • Adds "diminution in value" which means the actual or perceived loss in market value or resale value which results from a direct and accidental loss.

BAP / GARAGE FORM SYMBOL COMPARISON CHART

Differences in the names and descriptions align with the terms and form names of the underlying coverage provisions. *The Garage Form differences are shown in bold italics.*

BAP Symbol	Garage Form Symbol		Description Of Covered Auto Designation Symbols
1	21	Any "Auto"	
2	22	Owned "Autos" Only	Only those "autos" you own (and for Liability Coverage any "trailers" you don't own while attached to power units you own). This includes those "autos" you acquire ownership of after the policy begins.
3	23	Owned Private Passenger "Autos" Only	Only the private passenger "autos" you own. This includes those private passenger "autos" you acquire ownership of after the policy begins.
4	24	Owned "Autos" Other Than Private Passenger "Autos" Only	Only those "autos" you own that are not of the private passenger type (and for Liability Coverage any "trailers" you don't own while attached to power units you own). This includes those "autos" not of the private passenger type you acquire ownership of after the policy begins.
5	25	Owned "Autos" Subject To No-Fault	Only those "autos" you own that are required to have No-Fault benefits in the state where they are licensed or principally garaged. This includes those "autos" you acquire ownership of after the policy begins provided they are required to have No-Fault benefits in the state where they are licensed or principally garaged.
6	26	Owned "Autos" Subject To A Compulsory Uninsured Motorists Law	Only those "autos" you own that because of the law in the state where they are licensed or principally garaged are required to have and cannot reject Uninsured Motorists Coverage. This includes those "autos" you acquire ownership of after the policy begins provided they are subject to the same state uninsured motorists requirement.
7	27	Specifically Described "Autos"	Only those "autos" described in Item Three of the Declarations for which a premium charge is shown (and for Liability Coverage any "trailers" you don't own while attached to any power unit described in Item Three). Garage Form Description *Only those "autos" described in Item Seven of the Non-Dealers' and Trailer Dealers' Supplementary Schedule or Item Nine of the Dealers' Supplementary Schedule for which a premium charge is shown (and for Liability Coverage any "trailers" you don't own while attached to a power unit described in Item Seven or Item Nine).***
8	28	Hired "Autos" Only	Only those "autos" you lease, hire, rent or borrow. This does not include any "auto" you lease, hire, rent, or borrow from any of your "employees", partners (if you are a partnership), members (if you are a limited liability company) or members of their households.

9	29	Nonowned "Autos" Only	Only those "autos" you do not own, lease, hire, rent or borrow that are used in connection with your business. This includes "autos" owned by your "employees", partners (if you are a partnership), members (if you are a limited liability company), or members of their households but only while used in your business or your personal affairs.
		Garage Form *Nonowned "Autos" Only Used in Your Garage Business*	Garage Form Description *Any "auto" you do not own, lease, hire, rent or borrow used in connection with your garage business described in the Declarations. This includes "autos" owned by your "employees" or partners (if you are a partnership), members (if you are a limited liability company), or members of their households while used in your garage business.*
BAP Symbol	**Garage Form Symbol**	**Description Of Covered Auto Designation Symbols**	**BAP Symbol**
	30	*"Autos" Left With You For Service, Repair, Storage Or Safekeeping*	*Any customer's land motor vehicle or trailer or semitrailer while left with you for service, repair, storage or safekeeping. Customers include your "employees", and members of their households, who pay for the services performed.*
	31	*Dealers "Autos" And "Autos" Held For Sale By Non-Dealers Or Trailer Dealers (Physical Damage Coverages)*	*Any "autos" and the interests in these "autos" described in Item Seven of the Dealers' Supplementary Schedule or Item Nine of the Non-Dealers' and Trailer Dealers' Supplementary Schedule.***

**NOTE: The Auto Service Risk Program is not available in all states. Prior to the creation of this Program, Non-Dealers and Trailer Dealers could be covered under the Garage Program. It is likely that ISO will not withdraw or revise these coverage symbols until the Program is approved in all states.

GARAGE RISKS COVERAGE OPTIONS

The ISO Garage Program was streamlined in 2001 to exclude "service operations" that primarily present premises/operations exposures. Auto dealerships and auto service risks are now covered differently.

Auto Dealerships

Individuals or organizations in the business or selling autos, trucks, motorcycles or other vehicles

Garage Coverage Form (CA 00 05)
Provides coverage for liability arising from garage operations, medical payments, automobile physical damage, and uninsured or underinsured motorists in a single contract: • Section I – Covered Autos   • Section IV – Physical Damage Coverage • Section II – Liability Coverage   • Section V – Garage Conditions • Section III – Garagekeepers Coverage   • Section VI - Definitions

Auto Service Risks

Repair shops, service stations, storage garages, public parking places, and tow truck operators.

CGL + BAP + Garagekeepers Coverage
Commercial General Liability (CG 00 01 or CG 00 02) • Covers loss exposures arising from an organization's premises and operations, its products or its work. • Covers various other offenses that may result in claims or lawsuits, such as liable slander, false arrest, or invasion of privacy • Available as an occurrence form (CG 00 01) or a claims-made form (CG 00 02), providing an extended reporting period **Business Auto Policy** (CA 00 01) • Provides selected liability and physical damage coverages on vehicles used for commercial purposes. • Form uses simplified wording and must be combined with the appropriate declarations, conditions and endorsements to constitute a commercial vehicle policy. **Garagekeepers Coverage** (CA 99 37) • Coverage of garage operators against direct damage or legal liability for damage to vehicles in the insured's care, custody, or control. .

<u>OR</u>

ISO's Market Segments Program - Auto Service Risks
• Addresses specific coverage needs of auto service risks • Offers wrap-around endorsements that modify one of more of ISO's monoline coverage forms • Endorsements for money and securities, employees' tools, computer equipment, above- and below-ground fuel tanks and fuel pumps • Optional coverage for loss or damage to customers' autos and property, mechanical breakdown coverage, and hired and nonowned auto liability

RATING TABLES

Unit 10 – Rating The Business Auto Policy

Table 1: Primary Rating Factors

Size Class	Bus. Use Class		Radius					
			Up to 50 Miles		51 – 200 Miles		Over 200 Miles	
			Liability	Phys. Dam	Liability	Phys. Dam	Liability	Phys. Dam
Light Trucks (0 – 10,000 lbs. G.V.W.)	Service	Factor Code	1.00 014- -	1.00 014- -	1.10 015- -	1.05 015- -	1.15 016- -	1.00 016- -
	Retail	Factor Code	1.60 024- -	1.20 024- -	1.65 025- -	1.50 025- -	1.70 026- -	1.65 026- -
	Commercial	Factor Code	1.30 034- -	1.15 034- -	1.55 035- -	1.40 035- -	1.60 036- -	1.70 036- -
Medium Trucks (10,001 – 20,000 lbs. G.V.W.)	Service	Factor Code	1.05	.85	1.20	1.00	ZONE RATED	
	Retail	Factor Code	1.65	1.00	1.70	1.25		
	Commercial	Factor Code	1.35	.95	1.60	1.20		
Heavy Trucks (20,001 – 45,000 lbs. G.V.W.)	Service	Factor Code	1.10	.75	1.35	.85		
	Retail	Factor Code	1.70	1.15	1.75	1.35		
	Commercial	Factor Code	1.80	1.00	2.25	1.20		
Extra-Heavy Trucks (over 45,000 lbs. G.V.W.)		Factor Code	2.50	1.15	3.00	1.35		
Heavy Truck-Tractors (0 – 45,000 lbs. G.C.W.)	Service	Factor Code	1.50	1.05	1.55	1.15		
	Retail	Factor Code	2.40	1.45	2.45	1.65		
	Commercial	Factor Code	2.10	1.25	2.60	1.45		
Extra-Heavy Truck-Tractors (Over 45,000 lbs. G.C.W.)		Factor Code	2.60	1.25	3.75	1.45		

Table 2: Secondary Rating Factors

Industry	Trailer Types and Zone-Rated Autos	All Other Autos	Secondary Code
1. **Truckers:** Autos used to haul or transport goods, materials or commodities for others (except moving operations)	0.00	+0.95	21
2. **Food Delivery:** Autos used by food manufacturers to transport raw and finished products or used in wholesale distribution of food	0.00	+0.35	31
3. **Specialized Delivery:** For deliveries subject to time and similar constraints such as armored cars, magazines, newspapers, mail, etc.	0.00	+0.40	41
4. **Waste Disposal:** Autos transporting salvage and waste material for disposal or resale.	0.00	+0.50	51
5. **Farmers:** Autos used by farmers in connection with farm operations	0.00	-0.50	61
6. **Dump and Transit Mix Trucks and Trailers:** Autos used in dumping operations and mixers hauling cement or similar products	0.00	-0.15	71
7. **Contractors:** Autos used in by residential or commercial contractors including excavation and street or road work	0.00	+0.00	81
8. **Not Otherwise Specified:** Autos used for any purpose other than one already described above. This category includes logging and lumbering operations.	0.00	+0.00	91

Table 3: Physical Damage Base Premium

PHYSICAL DAMAGE **Original Cost New Range** **$15,001 – 20,000**			
Coverage Codes	**Specified Causes Of Loss**	**Full Comp.**	**$100 Ded. Coll.**
RULE 23. TRUCKS, TRACTORS AND TRAILERS CLASSIFICATIONS - Not Used In Dumping Operations - Local And Intermediate – All Vehicles - Long Distance – Light Trucks And Trailers Used With Light Trucks	$ 55	$ 115	$ 338

Table 4: Original Cost New Factors

Price Range	Comprehensive and Specified Causes of Loss*	Collision
$ 0 – 4500	0.40	0.36
4501 – 6000	0.50	0.46
6001 – 8000	0.62	0.62
8001 – 10000	0.76	0.75
10001 – 15000	0.90	0.86
15001 – 20000	1.00	1.00
20001 – 25000	1.10	1.06
25001 – 40000	1.20	1.27
40001 – 65000	1.36	1.82
65001 - 90000	1.60	2.18
Over 90000	2.00	2.55

Table 5: Age Group Factors

Age Group*	Comprehensive and Specified Causes of Loss	Collision
1	1.00	1.00
2	1.00	1.00
3	1.00	1.00
4	0.90	0.85
5	0.85	0.75
6	0.70	0.65

Table 6: Territory Rate Page

TERRITORY XXX				
LIAB, MED PAY, PIP				
LIABILTY Subline Code (611) Limits Identifier Code (1)	**MEDICAL PAYMENTS** Subline Code (620) Limit Per Prson			**PERSONAL INJURY PROTECTION** Subline Code (615)
Limit of Liab. $25,000	500 1000 2000 5000			Base Limits
	Limit Codes			
05	01 03 04 06			01
RULE 23. TRUCKS, TRACTORS AND TRAILERS CLASSIFICATIONS All Autos				
$ 701	$ $ $ $ 3.00 4.00 5.00 8.00			$ 37

Table 7: Increased Limits Factors

Combined Single Limit of Liability (000's)	Light and Medium Trucks	Heavy Trucks and Truck-Tractors	Extra-Heavy Trucks and Truck-Tractors
25	1.00	1.00	1.00
50	1.26	1.25	1.25
100	1.54	1.52	1.56
250	1.95	1.93	2.09
300	2.05	2.03	2.20
500	2.31	2.31	2.56
1000	2.63	2.74	3.16

Table 8: Fleet Factors

Liability	1.10
Physical Damage	
Collision	.90
Other Than Collision	.70

Table 9: Non-Owned Auto Rates

Non-Owned Auto Rates	
# of Employees	$25,000 Limit
0 - 25	$ 34
26 - 100	$ 80
101 - 500	$ 175
501 – 1,000	$ 275
Over 1,000	$ 617

COMMERCIAL AUTO
CA 00 01 10 01

BUSINESS AUTO COVERAGE FORM

Various provisions in this policy restrict coverage. Read the entire policy carefully to determine rights, duties and what is and is not covered.

Throughout this policy the words "you" and "your" refer to the Named Insured shown in the Declarations. The words "we", "us" and "our" refer to the Company providing this insurance.

Other words and phrases that appear in quotation marks have special meaning. Refer to Section **V** – Definitions.

SECTION I – COVERED AUTOS

Item Two of the Declarations shows the "autos" that are covered "autos" for each of your coverages. The following numerical symbols describe the "autos" that may be covered "autos". The symbols entered next to a coverage on the Declarations designate the only "autos" that are covered "autos".

A. Description Of Covered Auto Designation Symbols

Symbol	Description Of Covered Auto Designation Symbols	
1	Any "Auto"	
2	Owned "Autos" Only	Only those "autos" you own (and for Liability Coverage any "trailers" you don't own while attached to power units you own). This includes those "autos" you acquire ownership of after the policy begins.
3	Owned Private Passenger "Autos" Only	Only the private passenger "autos" you own. This includes those private passenger "autos" you acquire ownership of after the policy begins.
4	Owned "Autos" Other Than Private Passenger "Autos" Only	Only those "autos" you own that are not of the private passenger type (and for Liability Coverage any "trailers" you don't own while attached to power units you own). This includes those "autos" not of the private passenger type you acquire ownership of after the policy begins.
5	Owned "Autos" Subject To No-Fault	Only those "autos" you own that are required to have No-Fault benefits in the state where they are licensed or principally garaged. This includes those "autos" you acquire ownership of after the policy begins provided they are required to have No-Fault benefits in the state where they are licensed or principally garaged.
6	Owned "Autos" Subject To A Compulsory Uninsured Motorists Law	Only those "autos" you own that because of the law in the state where they are licensed or principally garaged are required to have and cannot reject Uninsured Motorists Coverage. This includes those "autos" you acquire ownership of after the policy begins provided they are subject to the same state uninsured motorists requirement.
7	Specifically Described "Autos"	Only those "autos" described in Item Three of the Declarations for which a premium charge is shown (and for Liability Coverage any "trailers" you don't own while attached to any power unit described in Item Three).
8	Hired "Autos" Only	Only those "autos" you lease, hire, rent or borrow. This does not include any "auto" you lease, hire, rent, or borrow from any of your "employees", partners (if you are a partnership), members (if you are a limited liability company) or members of their households.
9	Nonowned "Autos" Only	Only those "autos" you do not own, lease, hire, rent or borrow that are used in connection with your business. This includes "autos" owned by your "employees", partners (if you are a partnership), members (if you are a limited liability company), or members of their households but only while used in your business or your personal affairs.

B. Owned Autos You Acquire After The Policy Begins

1. If Symbols **1, 2, 3, 4, 5** or **6** are entered next to a coverage in Item Two of the Declarations, then you have coverage for "autos" that you acquire of the type described for the remainder of the policy period.

2. But, if Symbol **7** is entered next to a coverage in Item Two of the Declarations, an "auto" you acquire will be a covered "auto" for that coverage only if:

   a. We already cover all "autos" that you own for that coverage or it replaces an "auto" you previously owned that had that coverage; and

   b. You tell us within 30 days after you acquire it that you want us to cover it for that coverage.

C. Certain Trailers, Mobile Equipment And Temporary Substitute Autos

If Liability Coverage is provided by this Coverage Form, the following types of vehicles are also covered "autos" for Liability Coverage:

1. "Trailers" with a load capacity of 2,000 pounds or less designed primarily for travel on public roads.

2. "Mobile equipment" while being carried or towed by a covered "auto".

3. Any "auto" you do not own while used with the permission of its owner as a temporary substitute for a covered "auto" you own that is out of service because of its:

   a. Breakdown;

   b. Repair;

   c. Servicing;

   d. "Loss"; or

   e. Destruction.

SECTION II – LIABILITY COVERAGE

A. Coverage

We will pay all sums an "insured" legally must pay as damages because of "bodily injury" or "property damage" to which this insurance applies, caused by an "accident" and resulting from the ownership, maintenance or use of a covered "auto".

We will also pay all sums an "insured" legally must pay as a "covered pollution cost or expense" to which this insurance applies, caused by an "accident" and resulting from the ownership, maintenance or use of covered "autos". However, we will only pay for the "covered pollution cost or expense" if there is either "bodily injury" or "property damage" to which this insurance applies that is caused by the same "accident".

We have the right and duty to defend any "insured" against a "suit" asking for such damages or a "covered pollution cost or expense". However, we have no duty to defend any "insured" against a "suit" seeking damages for "bodily injury" or "property damage" or a "covered pollution cost or expense" to which this insurance does not apply. We may investigate and settle any claim or "suit" as we consider appropriate. Our duty to defend or settle ends when the Liability Coverage Limit of Insurance has been exhausted by payment of judgments or settlements.

1. **Who Is An Insured**

   The following are "insureds":

   a. You for any covered "auto".

   b. Anyone else while using with your permission a covered "auto" you own, hire or borrow except:

   (1) The owner or anyone else from whom you hire or borrow a covered "auto". This exception does not apply if the covered "auto" is a "trailer" connected to a covered "auto" you own.

   (2) Your "employee" if the covered "auto" is owned by that "employee" or a member of his or her household.

   (3) Someone using a covered "auto" while he or she is working in a business of selling, servicing, repairing, parking or storing "autos" unless that business is yours.

   (4) Anyone other than your "employees", partners (if you are a partnership), members (if you are a limited liability company), or a lessee or borrower or any of their "employees", while moving property to or from a covered "auto".

   (5) A partner (if you are a partnership), or a member (if you are a limited liability company) for a covered "auto" owned by him or her or a member of his or her household.

 CA 00 01 10 01 □

c. Anyone liable for the conduct of an "insured" described above but only to the extent of that liability.

2. Coverage Extensions

a. Supplementary Payments

In addition to the Limit of Insurance, we will pay for the "insured":

(1) All expenses we incur.

(2) Up to $2,000 for cost of bail bonds (including bonds for related traffic law violations) required because of an "accident" we cover. We do not have to furnish these bonds.

(3) The cost of bonds to release attachments in any "suit" against the "insured" we defend, but only for bond amounts within our Limit of Insurance.

(4) All reasonable expenses incurred by the "insured" at our request, including actual loss of earnings up to $250 a day because of time off from work.

(5) All costs taxed against the "insured" in any "suit" against the "insured" we defend.

(6) All interest on the full amount of any judgment that accrues after entry of the judgment in any "suit" against the "insured" we defend, but our duty to pay interest ends when we have paid, offered to pay or deposited in court the part of the judgment that is within our Limit of Insurance.

b. Out-Of-State Coverage Extensions

While a covered "auto" is away from the state where it is licensed we will:

(1) Increase the Limit of Insurance for Liability Coverage to meet the limits specified by a compulsory or financial responsibility law of the jurisdiction where the covered "auto" is being used. This extension does not apply to the limit or limits specified by any law governing motor carriers of passengers or property.

(2) Provide the minimum amounts and types of other coverages, such as no-fault, required of out-of-state vehicles by the jurisdiction where the covered "auto" is being used.

We will not pay anyone more than once for the same elements of loss because of these extensions.

B. Exclusions

This insurance does not apply to any of the following:

1. Expected Or Intended Injury

"Bodily injury" or "property damage" expected or intended from the standpoint of the "insured".

2. Contractual

Liability assumed under any contract or agreement.

But this exclusion does not apply to liability for damages:

a. Assumed in a contract or agreement that is an "insured contract" provided the "bodily injury" or "property damage" occurs subsequent to the execution of the contract or agreement; or

b. That the "insured" would have in the absence of the contract or agreement.

3. Workers' Compensation

Any obligation for which the "insured" or the "insured's" insurer may be held liable under any workers' compensation, disability benefits or unemployment compensation law or any similar law.

4. Employee Indemnification And Employer's Liability

"Bodily injury" to:

a. An "employee" of the "insured" arising out of and in the course of:

(1) Employment by the "insured"; or

(2) Performing the duties related to the conduct of the "insured's" business; or

b. The spouse, child, parent, brother or sister of that "employee" as a consequence of Paragraph a. above.

This exclusion applies:

(1) Whether the "insured" may be liable as an employer or in any other capacity; and

(2) To any obligation to share damages with or repay someone else who must pay damages because of the injury.

But this exclusion does not apply to "bodily injury" to domestic "employees" not entitled to workers' compensation benefits or to liability assumed by the "insured" under an "insured contract". For the purposes of the Coverage Form, a domestic "employee" is a person engaged in household or domestic work performed principally in connection with a residence premises.

5. Fellow Employee

"Bodily injury" to any fellow "employee" of the "insured" arising out of and in the course of the fellow "employee's" employment or while performing duties related to the conduct of your business.

6. Care, Custody Or Control

"Property damage" to or "covered pollution cost or expense" involving property owned or transported by the "insured" or in the "insured's" care, custody or control. But this exclusion does not apply to liability assumed under a sidetrack agreement.

7. Handling Of Property

"Bodily injury" or "property damage" resulting from the handling of property:

a. Before it is moved from the place where it is accepted by the "insured" for movement into or onto the covered "auto"; or

b. After it is moved from the covered "auto" to the place where it is finally delivered by the "insured".

8. Movement Of Property By Mechanical Device

"Bodily injury" or "property damage" resulting from the movement of property by a mechanical device (other than a hand truck) unless the device is attached to the covered "auto".

9. Operations

"Bodily injury" or "property damage" arising out of the operation of any equipment listed in Paragraphs **6.b.** and **6.c.** of the definition of "mobile equipment".

10. Completed Operations

"Bodily injury" or "property damage" arising out of your work after that work has been completed or abandoned.

In this exclusion, your work means:

a. Work or operations performed by you or on your behalf; and

b. Materials, parts or equipment furnished in connection with such work or operations.

Your work includes warranties or representations made at any time with respect to the fitness, quality, durability or performance of any of the items included in Paragraphs **a.** or **b.** above.

Your work will be deemed completed at the earliest of the following times:

(1) When all of the work called for in your contract has been completed.

(2) When all of the work to be done at the site has been completed if your contract calls for work at more than one site.

(3) When that part of the work done at a job site has been put to its intended use by any person or organization other than another contractor or subcontractor working on the same project.

Work that may need service, maintenance, correction, repair or replacement, but which is otherwise complete, will be treated as completed.

11. Pollution

"Bodily injury" or "property damage" arising out of the actual, alleged or threatened discharge, dispersal, seepage, migration, release or escape of "pollutants":

a. That are, or that are contained in any property that is:

(1) Being transported or towed by, handled, or handled for movement into, onto or from, the covered "auto";

(2) Otherwise in the course of transit by or on behalf of the "insured"; or

(3) Being stored, disposed of, treated or processed in or upon the covered "auto";

b. Before the "pollutants" or any property in which the "pollutants" are contained are moved from the place where they are accepted by the "insured" for movement into or onto the covered "auto"; or

c. After the "pollutants" or any property in which the "pollutants" are contained are moved from the covered "auto" to the place where they are finally delivered, disposed of or abandoned by the "insured".

Paragraph **a.** above does not apply to fuels, lubricants, fluids, exhaust gases or other similar "pollutants" that are needed for or result from the normal electrical, hydraulic or mechanical functioning of the covered "auto" or its parts, if:

(1) The "pollutants" escape, seep, migrate, or are discharged, dispersed or released directly from an "auto" part designed by its manufacturer to hold, store, receive or dispose of such "pollutants"; and

(2) The "bodily injury", "property damage" or "covered pollution cost or expense" does not arise out of the operation of any equipment listed in Paragraphs **6.b.** and **6.c.** of the definition of "mobile equipment".

CA 00 01 10 01

Paragraphs **b.** and **c.** above of this exclusion do not apply to "accidents" that occur away from premises owned by or rented to an "insured" with respect to "pollutants" not in or upon a covered "auto" if:

(1) The "pollutants" or any property in which the "pollutants" are contained are upset, overturned or damaged as a result of the maintenance or use of a covered "auto"; and

(2) The discharge, dispersal, seepage, migration, release or escape of the "pollutants" is caused directly by such upset, overturn or damage.

12. War

"Bodily injury" or "property damage" due to war, whether or not declared, or any act or condition incident to war. War includes civil war, insurrection, rebellion or revolution. This exclusion applies only to liability assumed under a contract or agreement.

13. Racing

Covered "autos" while used in any professional or organized racing or demolition contest or stunting activity, or while practicing for such contest or activity. This insurance also does not apply while that covered "auto" is being prepared for such a contest or activity.

C. Limit Of Insurance

Regardless of the number of covered "autos", "insureds", premiums paid, claims made or vehicles involved in the "accident", the most we will pay for the total of all damages and "covered pollution cost or expense" combined, resulting from any one "accident" is the Limit of Insurance for Liability Coverage shown in the Declarations.

All "bodily injury", "property damage" and "covered pollution cost or expense" resulting from continuous or repeated exposure to substantially the same conditions will be considered as resulting from one "accident".

No one will be entitled to receive duplicate payments for the same elements of "loss" under this Coverage Form and any Medical Payments Coverage Endorsement, Uninsured Motorists Coverage Endorsement or Underinsured Motorists Coverage Endorsement attached to this Coverage Part.

SECTION III – PHYSICAL DAMAGE COVERAGE

A. Coverage

1. We will pay for "loss" to a covered "auto" or its equipment under:

a. Comprehensive Coverage

From any cause except:

(1) The covered "auto's" collision with another object; or

(2) The covered "auto's" overturn.

b. Specified Causes Of Loss Coverage

Caused by:

(1) Fire, lightning or explosion;

(2) Theft;

(3) Windstorm, hail or earthquake;

(4) Flood;

(5) Mischief or vandalism; or

(6) The sinking, burning, collision or derailment of any conveyance transporting the covered "auto".

c. Collision Coverage

Caused by:

(1) The covered "auto's" collision with another object; or

(2) The covered "auto's" overturn.

2. Towing

We will pay up to the limit shown in the Declarations for towing and labor costs incurred each time a covered "auto" of the private passenger type is disabled. However, the labor must be performed at the place of disablement.

3. Glass Breakage – Hitting A Bird Or Animal – Falling Objects Or Missiles

If you carry Comprehensive Coverage for the damaged covered "auto", we will pay for the following under Comprehensive Coverage:

a. Glass breakage;

b. "Loss" caused by hitting a bird or animal; and

c. "Loss" caused by falling objects or missiles.

However, you have the option of having glass breakage caused by a covered "auto's" collision or overturn considered a "loss" under Collision Coverage.

4. Coverage Extensions

a. Transportation Expenses

We will pay up to $20 per day to a maximum of $600 for temporary transportation expense incurred by you because of the total theft of a covered "auto" of the private passenger type. We will pay only for those covered "autos" for which you carry either Comprehensive or Specified Causes of Loss Coverage. We will pay for temporary transportation expenses incurred during the period beginning 48 hours after the theft and ending, regardless of the policy's expiration, when the covered "auto" is returned to use or we pay for its "loss".

b. Loss Of Use Expenses

For Hired Auto Physical Damage, we will pay expenses for which an "insured" becomes legally responsible to pay for loss of use of a vehicle rented or hired without a driver, under a written rental contract or agreement. We will pay for loss of use expenses if caused by:

(1) Other than collision only if the Declarations indicate that Comprehensive Coverage is provided for any covered "auto";

(2) Specified Causes Of Loss only if the Declarations indicate that Specified Causes Of Loss Coverage is provided for any covered "auto"; or

(3) Collision only if the Declarations indicate that Collision Coverage is provided for any covered "auto".

However, the most we will pay for any expenses for loss of use is $20 per day, to a maximum of $600.

B. Exclusions

1. We will not pay for "loss" caused by or resulting from any of the following. Such "loss" is excluded regardless of any other cause or event that contributes concurrently or in any sequence to the "loss".

a. Nuclear Hazard

(1) The explosion of any weapon employing atomic fission or fusion; or

(2) Nuclear reaction or radiation, or radioactive contamination, however caused.

b. War Or Military Action

(1) War, including undeclared or civil war;

(2) Warlike action by a military force, including action in hindering or defending against an actual or expected attack, by any government, sovereign or other authority using military personnel or other agents; or

(3) Insurrection, rebellion, revolution, usurped power or action taken by governmental authority in hindering or defending against any of these.

2. We will not pay for "loss" to any covered "auto" while used in any professional or organized racing or demolition contest or stunting activity, or while practicing for such contest or activity. We will also not pay for "loss" to any covered "auto" while that covered "auto" is being prepared for such a contest or activity.

3. We will not pay for "loss" caused by or resulting from any of the following unless caused by other "loss" that is covered by this insurance:

a. Wear and tear, freezing, mechanical or electrical breakdown.

b. Blowouts, punctures or other road damage to tires.

4. We will not pay for "loss" to any of the following:

a. Tapes, records, discs or other similar audio, visual or data electronic devices designed for use with audio, visual or data electronic equipment.

b. Any device designed or used to detect speed measuring equipment such as radar or laser detectors and any jamming apparatus intended to elude or disrupt speed measurement equipment.

c. Any electronic equipment, without regard to whether this equipment is permanently installed, that receives or transmits audio, visual or data signals and that is not designed solely for the reproduction of sound.

d. Any accessories used with the electronic equipment described in Paragraph **c.** above.

 CA 00 01 10 01 □

Exclusions **4.c.** and **4.d.** do not apply to:

a. Equipment designed solely for the reproduction of sound and accessories used with such equipment, provided such equipment is permanently installed in the covered "auto" at the time of the "loss" or such equipment is removable from a housing unit which is permanently installed in the covered "auto" at the time of the "loss", and such equipment is designed to be solely operated by use of the power from the "auto's" electrical system, in or upon the covered "auto"; or

b. Any other electronic equipment that is:

(1) Necessary for the normal operation of the covered "auto" or the monitoring of the covered "auto's" operating system; or

(2) An integral part of the same unit housing any sound reproducing equipment described in **a.** above and permanently installed in the opening of the dash or console of the covered "auto" normally used by the manufacturer for installation of a radio.

5. We will not pay for "loss" to a covered "auto" due to "diminution in value".

C. Limit Of Insurance

1. The most we will pay for "loss" in any one "accident" is the lesser of:

a. The actual cash value of the damaged or stolen property as of the time of the "loss"; or

b. The cost of repairing or replacing the damaged or stolen property with other property of like kind and quality.

2. An adjustment for depreciation and physical condition will be made in determining actual cash value in the event of a total "loss".

3. If a repair or replacement results in better than like kind or quality, we will not pay for the amount of the betterment.

D. Deductible

For each covered "auto", our obligation to pay for, repair, return or replace damaged or stolen property will be reduced by the applicable deductible shown in the Declarations. Any Comprehensive Coverage deductible shown in the Declarations does not apply to "loss" caused by fire or lightning.

SECTION IV – BUSINESS AUTO CONDITIONS

The following conditions apply in addition to the Common Policy Conditions:

A. Loss Conditions

1. **Appraisal For Physical Damage Loss**

If you and we disagree on the amount of "loss", either may demand an appraisal of the "loss". In this event, each party will select a competent appraiser. The two appraisers will select a competent and impartial umpire. The appraisers will state separately the actual cash value and amount of "loss". If they fail to agree, they will submit their differences to the umpire. A decision agreed to by any two will be binding. Each party will:

a. Pay its chosen appraiser; and

b. Bear the other expenses of the appraisal and umpire equally.

If we submit to an appraisal, we will still retain our right to deny the claim.

2. **Duties In The Event Of Accident, Claim, Suit Or Loss**

We have no duty to provide coverage under this policy unless there has been full compliance with the following duties:

a. In the event of "accident", claim, "suit" or "loss", you must give us or our authorized representative prompt notice of the "accident" or "loss". Include:

(1) How, when and where the "accident" or "loss" occurred;

(2) The "insured's" name and address; and

(3) To the extent possible, the names and addresses of any injured persons and witnesses.

b. Additionally, you and any other involved "insured" must:

(1) Assume no obligation, make no payment or incur no expense without our consent, except at the "insured's" own cost.

(2) Immediately send us copies of any request, demand, order, notice, summons or legal paper received concerning the claim or "suit".

(3) Cooperate with us in the investigation or settlement of the claim or defense against the "suit".

(4) Authorize us to obtain medical records or other pertinent information.

(5) Submit to examination, at our expense, by physicians of our choice, as often as we reasonably require.

c. If there is "loss" to a covered "auto" or its equipment you must also do the following:

(1) Promptly notify the police if the covered "auto" or any of its equipment is stolen.

(2) Take all reasonable steps to protect the covered "auto" from further damage. Also keep a record of your expenses for consideration in the settlement of the claim.

(3) Permit us to inspect the covered "auto" and records proving the "loss" before its repair or disposition.

(4) Agree to examinations under oath at our request and give us a signed statement of your answers.

3. Legal Action Against Us

No one may bring a legal action against us under this Coverage Form until:

a. There has been full compliance with all the terms of this Coverage Form; and

b. Under Liability Coverage, we agree in writing that the "insured" has an obligation to pay or until the amount of that obligation has finally been determined by judgment after trial. No one has the right under this policy to bring us into an action to determine the "insured's" liability.

4. Loss Payment – Physical Damage Coverages

At our option we may:

a. Pay for, repair or replace damaged or stolen property;

b. Return the stolen property, at our expense. We will pay for any damage that results to the "auto" from the theft; or

c. Take all or any part of the damaged or stolen property at an agreed or appraised value.

If we pay for the "loss", our payment will include the applicable sales tax for the damaged or stolen property.

5. Transfer Of Rights Of Recovery Against Others To Us

If any person or organization to or for whom we make payment under this Coverage Form has rights to recover damages from another, those rights are transferred to us. That person or organization must do everything necessary to secure our rights and must do nothing after "accident" or "loss" to impair them.

B. General Conditions

1. Bankruptcy

Bankruptcy or insolvency of the "insured" or the "insured's" estate will not relieve us of any obligations under this Coverage Form.

2. Concealment, Misrepresentation Or Fraud

This Coverage Form is void in any case of fraud by you at any time as it relates to this Coverage Form. It is also void if you or any other "insured", at any time, intentionally conceal or misrepresent a material fact concerning:

a. This Coverage Form;

b. The covered "auto";

c. Your interest in the covered "auto"; or

d. A claim under this Coverage Form.

3. Liberalization

If we revise this Coverage Form to provide more coverage without additional premium charge, your policy will automatically provide the additional coverage as of the day the revision is effective in your state.

4. No Benefit To Bailee – Physical Damage Coverages

We will not recognize any assignment or grant any coverage for the benefit of any person or organization holding, storing or transporting property for a fee regardless of any other provision of this Coverage Form.

5. Other Insurance

a. For any covered "auto" you own, this Coverage Form provides primary insurance. For any covered "auto" you don't own, the insurance provided by this Coverage Form is excess over any other collectible insurance. However, while a covered "auto" which is a "trailer" is connected to another vehicle, the Liability Coverage this Coverage Form provides for the "trailer" is:

(1) Excess while it is connected to a motor vehicle you do not own.

(2) Primary while it is connected to a covered "auto" you own.

b. For Hired Auto Physical Damage Coverage, any covered "auto" you lease, hire, rent or borrow is deemed to be a covered "auto" you own. However, any "auto" that is leased, hired, rented or borrowed with a driver is not a covered "auto".

c. Regardless of the provisions of Paragraph **a.** above, this Coverage Form's Liability Coverage is primary for any liability assumed under an "insured contract".

 CA 00 01 10 01

d. When this Coverage Form and any other Coverage Form or policy covers on the same basis, either excess or primary, we will pay only our share. Our share is the proportion that the Limit of Insurance of our Coverage Form bears to the total of the limits of all the Coverage Forms and policies covering on the same basis.

6. Premium Audit

a. The estimated premium for this Coverage Form is based on the exposures you told us you would have when this policy began. We will compute the final premium due when we determine your actual exposures. The estimated total premium will be credited against the final premium due and the first Named Insured will be billed for the balance, if any. The due date for the final premium or retrospective premium is the date shown as the due date on the bill. If the estimated total premium exceeds the final premium due, the first Named Insured will get a refund.

b. If this policy is issued for more than one year, the premium for this Coverage Form will be computed annually based on our rates or premiums in effect at the beginning of each year of the policy.

7. Policy Period, Coverage Territory

Under this Coverage Form, we cover "accidents" and "losses" occurring:

a. During the policy period shown in the Declarations; and

b. Within the coverage territory.

The coverage territory is:

a. The United States of America;

b. The territories and possessions of the United States of America;

c. Puerto Rico;

d. Canada; and

e. Anywhere in the world if:

(1) A covered "auto" of the private passenger type is leased, hired, rented or borrowed without a driver for a period of 30 days or less; and

(2) The "insured's" responsibility to pay damages is determined in a "suit" on the merits, in the United States of America, the territories and possessions of the United States of America, Puerto Rico, or Canada or in a settlement we agree to.

We also cover "loss" to, or "accidents" involving, a covered "auto" while being transported between any of these places.

8. Two Or More Coverage Forms Or Policies Issued By Us

If this Coverage Form and any other Coverage Form or policy issued to you by us or any company affiliated with us apply to the same "accident", the aggregate maximum Limit of Insurance under all the Coverage Forms or policies shall not exceed the highest applicable Limit of Insurance under any one Coverage Form or policy. This condition does not apply to any Coverage Form or policy issued by us or an affiliated company specifically to apply as excess insurance over this Coverage Form.

SECTION V – DEFINITIONS

A. "Accident" includes continuous or repeated exposure to the same conditions resulting in "bodily injury" or "property damage".

B. "Auto" means a land motor vehicle, "trailer" or semitrailer designed for travel on public roads but does not include "mobile equipment".

C. "Bodily injury" means bodily injury, sickness or disease sustained by a person including death resulting from any of these.

D. "Covered pollution cost or expense" means any cost or expense arising out of:

1. Any request, demand, order or statutory or regulatory requirement; or

2. Any claim or "suit" by or on behalf of a governmental authority demanding

that the "insured" or others test for, monitor, clean up, remove, contain, treat, detoxify or neutralize, or in any way respond to, or assess the effects of "pollutants".

"Covered pollution cost or expense" does not include any cost or expense arising out of the actual, alleged or threatened discharge, dispersal, seepage, migration, release or escape of "pollutants":

a. That are, or that are contained in any property that is:

(1) Being transported or towed by, handled, or handled for movement into, onto or from the covered "auto";

(2) Otherwise in the course of transit by or on behalf of the "insured";

(3) Being stored, disposed of, treated or processed in or upon the covered "auto";

b. Before the "pollutants" or any property in which the "pollutants" are contained are moved from the place where they are accepted by the "insured" for movement into or onto the covered "auto"; or

c. After the "pollutants" or any property in which the "pollutants" are contained are moved from the covered "auto" to the place where they are finally delivered, disposed of or abandoned by the "insured".

Paragraph **a.** above does not apply to fuels, lubricants, fluids, exhaust gases or other similar "pollutants" that are needed for or result from the normal electrical, hydraulic or mechanical functioning of the covered "auto" or its parts, if:

(1) The "pollutants" escape, seep, migrate, or are discharged, dispersed or released directly from an "auto" part designed by its manufacturer to hold, store, receive or dispose of such "pollutants"; and

(2) The "bodily injury", "property damage" or "covered pollution cost or expense" does not arise out of the operation of any equipment listed in Paragraphs **6.b.** or **6.c.** of the definition of "mobile equipment".

Paragraphs **b.** and **c.** above do not apply to "accidents" that occur away from premises owned by or rented to an "insured" with respect to "pollutants" not in or upon a covered "auto" if:

(1) The "pollutants" or any property in which the "pollutants" are contained are upset, overturned or damaged as a result of the maintenance or use of a covered "auto"; and

(2) The discharge, dispersal, seepage, migration, release or escape of the "pollutants" is caused directly by such upset, overturn or damage.

E. "Diminution in value" means the actual or perceived loss in market value or resale value which results from a direct and accidental "loss".

F. "Employee" includes a "leased worker". "Employee" does not include a "temporary worker".

G. "Insured" means any person or organization qualifying as an insured in the Who Is An Insured provision of the applicable coverage. Except with respect to the Limit of Insurance, the coverage afforded applies separately to each insured who is seeking coverage or against whom a claim or "suit" is brought.

H. "Insured contract" means:

1. A lease of premises;

2. A sidetrack agreement;

3. Any easement or license agreement, except in connection with construction or demolition operations on or within 50 feet of a railroad;

4. An obligation, as required by ordinance, to indemnify a municipality, except in connection with work for a municipality;

5. That part of any other contract or agreement pertaining to your business (including an indemnification of a municipality in connection with work performed for a municipality) under which you assume the tort liability of another to pay for "bodily injury" or "property damage" to a third party or organization. Tort liability means a liability that would be imposed by law in the absence of any contract or agreement;

6. That part of any contract or agreement entered into, as part of your business, pertaining to the rental or lease, by you or any of your "employees", of any "auto". However, such contract or agreement shall not be considered an "insured contract" to the extent that it obligates you or any of your "employees" to pay for "property damage" to any "auto" rented or leased by you or any of your "employees".

An "insured contract" does not include that part of any contract or agreement:

a. That indemnifies a railroad for "bodily injury" or "property damage" arising out of construction or demolition operations, within 50 feet of any railroad property and affecting any railroad bridge or trestle, tracks, roadbeds, tunnel, underpass or crossing; or

b. That pertains to the loan, lease or rental of an "auto" to you or any of your "employees", if the "auto" is loaned, leased or rented with a driver; or

c. That holds a person or organization engaged in the business of transporting property by "auto" for hire harmless for your use of a covered "auto" over a route or territory that person or organization is authorized to serve by public authority.

I. "Leased worker" means a person leased to you by a labor leasing firm under an agreement between you and the labor leasing firm, to perform duties related to the conduct of your business. "Leased worker" does not include a "temporary worker".

J. "Loss" means direct and accidental loss or damage.

K. "Mobile equipment" means any of the following types of land vehicles, including any attached machinery or equipment:

1. Bulldozers, farm machinery, forklifts and other vehicles designed for use principally off public roads;

2. Vehicles maintained for use solely on or next to premises you own or rent;

3. Vehicles that travel on crawler treads;

4. Vehicles, whether self-propelled or not, maintained primarily to provide mobility to permanently mounted:

    a. Power cranes, shovels, loaders, diggers or drills; or

    b. Road construction or resurfacing equipment such as graders, scrapers or rollers.

5. Vehicles not described in Paragraphs **1.**, **2.**, **3.**, or **4.** above that are not self-propelled and are maintained primarily to provide mobility to permanently attached equipment of the following types:

    a. Air compressors, pumps and generators, including spraying, welding, building cleaning, geophysical exploration, lighting and well servicing equipment; or

    b. Cherry pickers and similar devices used to raise or lower workers.

6. Vehicles not described in Paragraphs **1.**, **2.**, **3.** or **4.** above maintained primarily for purposes other than the transportation of persons or cargo. However, self-propelled vehicles with the following types of permanently attached equipment are not "mobile equipment" but will be considered "autos":

    a. Equipment designed primarily for:

        (1) Snow removal;

        (2) Road maintenance, but not construction or resurfacing; or

        (3) Street cleaning;

    b. Cherry pickers and similar devices mounted on automobile or truck chassis and used to raise or lower workers; and

    c. Air compressors, pumps and generators, including spraying, welding, building cleaning, geophysical exploration, lighting or well servicing equipment.

L. "Pollutants" means any solid, liquid, gaseous or thermal irritant or contaminant, including smoke, vapor, soot, fumes, acids, alkalis, chemicals and waste. Waste includes materials to be recycled, reconditioned or reclaimed.

M. "Property damage" means damage to or loss of use of tangible property.

N. "Suit" means a civil proceeding in which:

1. Damages because of "bodily injury" or "property damage"; or

2. A "covered pollution cost or expense",

to which this insurance applies, are alleged.

"Suit" includes:

    a. An arbitration proceeding in which such damages or "covered pollution costs or expenses" are claimed and to which the "insured" must submit or does submit with our consent; or

    b. Any other alternative dispute resolution proceeding in which such damages or "covered pollution costs or expenses" are claimed and to which the insured submits with our consent.

O. "Temporary worker" means a person who is furnished to you to substitute for a permanent "employee" on leave or to meet seasonal or short-term workload conditions.

P. "Trailer" includes semitrailer.

COMMERCIAL AUTO
CA 00 10 10 01

BUSINESS AUTO
PHYSICAL DAMAGE COVERAGE FORM

Various provisions in this policy restrict coverage. Read the entire policy carefully to determine rights, duties and what is and is not covered.

Throughout this policy the words "you" and "your" refer to the Named Insured shown in the Declarations. The words "we", "us" and "our" refer to the Company providing this insurance.

Other words and phrases that appear in quotation marks have special meaning. Refer to Section **IV** – Definitions.

SECTION I – COVERED AUTOS

Item Two of the Declarations shows the "autos" that are covered "autos" for each of your coverages. The following numerical symbols describe the "autos" that may be covered "autos". The symbols entered next to a coverage on the Declarations designate the only "autos" that are covered "autos".

A. Description Of Covered Auto Designation Symbols

Symbol		Description Of Covered Auto Designation Symbols
1	Owned "Autos" Only	Only those "autos" you own. This includes those "autos" you acquire ownership of after the policy begins.
2	Owned Private Passenger "Autos" Only	Only the private passenger "autos" you own. This includes those private passenger "autos" you acquire ownership of after the policy begins.
3	Owned "Autos" Other Than Private Passenger "Autos" Only	Only those "autos" you own that are not of the private passenger type. This includes those "autos" not of the private passenger type you acquire ownership of after the policy begins.
4	Specifically Described "Autos"	Only those "autos" described in Item Three of the Declarations for which a premium charge is shown.
5	Hired "Autos" Only	Only those "autos" you lease, hire, rent or borrow. This does not include any "auto" you lease, hire, rent or borrow from any of your "employees", partners (if you are a partnership), members (if you are a limited liability company), or members of their households.

B. Owned Autos You Acquire After The Policy Begins

1. If Symbols **1**, **2** or **3** are entered next to a coverage in Item Two of the Declarations, then you have coverage for "autos" that you acquire of the type described for the remainder of the policy period.

2. But, if Symbol **4** is entered next to a coverage in Item Two of the Declarations, an "auto" you acquire will be a covered "auto" for that coverage only if:

a. We already cover all "autos" that you own for that coverage or it replaces an "auto" you previously owned that had that coverage; and

b. You tell us within 30 days after you acquire it that you want us to cover it for that coverage.

  □

SECTION II – PHYSICAL DAMAGE COVERAGE

A. Coverage

1. We will pay for "loss" to a covered "auto" or its equipment under:

   a. Comprehensive Coverage

   From any cause except:

   (1) The covered "auto's" collision with another object; or

   (2) The covered "auto's" overturn.

   b. Specified Causes Of Loss Coverage

   Caused by:

   (1) Fire, lightning or explosion;

   (2) Theft;

   (3) Windstorm, hail or earthquake;

   (4) Flood;

   (5) Mischief or vandalism; or

   (6) The sinking, burning, collision or derailment of any conveyance transporting the covered "auto".

   c. Collision Coverage

   Caused by:

   (1) The covered "auto's" collision with another object; or

   (2) The covered "auto's" overturn.

2. **Towing**

   We will pay up to the limit shown in the Declarations for towing and labor costs incurred each time a covered "auto" of the private passenger type is disabled. However, the labor must be performed at the place of disablement.

3. **Glass Breakage – Hitting A Bird Or Animal – Falling Objects Or Missiles**

   If you carry Comprehensive Coverage for the damaged covered "auto", we will pay for the following under Comprehensive Coverage:

   a. Glass breakage;

   b. "Loss" caused by hitting a bird or animal; and

   c. "Loss" caused by falling objects or missiles.

   However, you have the option of having glass breakage caused by a covered "auto's" collision or overturn considered a "loss" under Collision Coverage.

4. **Coverage Extensions**

   a. Transportation Expenses

   We will also pay up to $20 per day to a maximum of $600 for temporary transportation expense incurred by you because of the total theft of a covered "auto" of the private passenger type. We will pay only for those covered "autos" for which you carry either Comprehensive or Specified Causes of Loss Coverage. We will pay for temporary transportation expenses incurred during the period beginning 48 hours after the theft and ending, regardless of the policy's expiration, when the covered "auto" is returned to use or we pay for its "loss".

   b. Loss Of Use Expenses

   For Hired Auto Physical Damage, we will pay expenses for which an insured becomes legally responsible to pay for loss of use of a vehicle rented or hired without a driver, under a written rental contract or agreement. We will pay for loss of use expenses if caused by:

   (1) Other than collision only if the Declarations indicate that Comprehensive Coverage is provided for any covered "auto";

   (2) Specified Causes Of Loss only if the Declarations indicate that Specified Causes Of Loss Coverage is provided for any covered "auto"; or

   (3) Collision only if the Declarations indicate that Collision Coverage is provided for any covered "auto".

   However, the most we will pay for any expenses for loss of use is $20 per day, to a maximum of $600.

B. Exclusions

1. We will not pay for "loss" caused by or resulting from any of the following. Such "loss" is excluded regardless of any other cause or event that contributes concurrently or in any sequence to the "loss".

   a. Nuclear Hazard

   (1) The explosion of any weapon employing atomic fission or fusion; or

   (2) Nuclear reaction or radiation, or radioactive contamination, however caused.

CA 00 10 10 01   □

b. **War Or Military Action**

(1) War, including undeclared or civil war;

(2) Warlike action by a military force, including action in hindering or defending against an actual or expected attack, by any government, sovereign or other authority using military personnel or other agents; or

(3) Insurrection, rebellion, revolution, usurped power or action taken by governmental authority in hindering or defending against any of these.

2. We will not pay for "loss" to any of the following:

a. Tapes, records, discs or other similar audio, visual or data electronic devices designed for use with audio, visual or data electronic equipment.

b. Any device designed or used to detect speed measuring equipment such as radar or laser detectors and any jamming apparatus intended to elude or disrupt speed measurement equipment.

c. Any electronic equipment, without regard to whether this equipment is permanently installed, that receives or transmits audio, visual or data signals and that is not designed solely for the reproduction of sound.

d. Any accessories used with the electronic equipment described in Paragraph c. above.

Exclusions 2.c. and 2.d. do not apply to:

a. Equipment designed solely for the reproduction of sound and accessories used with such equipment, provided such equipment is permanently installed in the covered "auto" at the time of the "loss" or such equipment is removable from a housing unit which is permanently installed in the covered "auto" at the time of the "loss", and such equipment is designed to be solely operated by use of the power from the "auto's" electrical system, in or upon the covered "auto"; or

b. Any other electronic equipment that is:

(1) Necessary for the normal operation of the covered "auto" or the monitoring of the covered "auto's" operating system; or

(2) An integral part of the same unit housing any sound reproducing equipment described in a. above and permanently installed in the opening of the dash or console of the covered "auto" normally used by the manufacturer for installation of a radio.

3. We will not pay for "loss" caused by or resulting from any of the following unless caused by other "loss" that is covered by this insurance:

(1) Wear and tear, freezing, mechanical or electrical breakdown.

(2) Blowouts, punctures or other road damage to tires.

4. We will not pay for "loss" to any covered "auto" while used in any professional or organized racing or demolition contest or stunting activity, or while practicing for such contest or activity. We will also not pay for "loss" to any covered "auto" while that covered "auto" is being prepared for such a contest or activity.

5. We will not pay for "loss" to a covered "auto" due to "diminution in value".

C. Limit Of Insurance

1. The most we will pay for "loss" in any one "accident" is the lesser of:

a. The actual cash value of the damaged or stolen property as of the time of the "loss"; or

b. The cost of repairing or replacing the damaged or stolen property with other property of like kind and quality.

2. An adjustment for depreciation and physical condition will be made in determining actual cash value in the event of a total "loss".

3. If a repair or replacement results in better than like kind or quality, we will not pay for the amount of the betterment.

D. Deductible

For each covered "auto", our obligation to pay for, repair, return or replace damaged or stolen property will be reduced by the applicable deductible shown in the Declarations. Any Comprehensive Coverage deductible shown in the Declarations does not apply to "loss" caused by fire or lightning.

SECTION III – BUSINESS AUTO CONDITIONS

The following conditions apply in addition to the Common Policy Conditions:

A. Loss Conditions

1. Appraisal

If you and we disagree on the amount of "loss", either may demand an appraisal of the "loss". In this event, each party will select a competent appraiser. The two appraisers will select a competent and impartial umpire. The appraisers will state separately the actual cash value and amount of "loss". If they fail to agree, they will submit their differences to the umpire. A decision agreed to by any two will be binding. Each party will:

a. Pay its chosen appraiser; and

b. Bear the other expenses of the appraisal and umpire equally.

If we submit to an appraisal, we will still retain our right to deny the claim.

2. Duties In The Event Of Loss

We have no duty to provide coverage under this policy unless there has been full compliance with the following duties:

a. In the event of "loss", you must give us or our authorized representative prompt notice of the "loss". Include:

(1) How, when and where the "loss" occurred;

(2) To the extent possible, the names and addresses of any injured persons and witnesses.

b. Additionally, you must:

(1) Assume no obligation, make no payment or incur no expense without our consent, except at your own cost.

(2) Cooperate with us in the investigation or settlement of the claim or defense against the suit.

(3) Promptly notify the police if the covered "auto" or any of its equipment is stolen.

(4) Take all reasonable steps to protect the covered "auto" from further damage. Also keep a record of your expenses for consideration in the settlement of the claim.

(5) Permit us to inspect the covered "auto" and records proving the "loss" before its repair or disposition.

(6) Agree to examination under oath at our request and give us a signed statement of your answers.

3. Legal Action Against Us

No one may bring a legal action against us under this Coverage Form until there has been full compliance with all the terms of this Coverage Form.

4. Loss Payment

At our option we may:

a. Pay for, repair or replace damaged or stolen property;

b. Return the stolen property, at our expense. We will pay for any damage that results to the "auto" from the theft; or

c. Take all or any part of the damaged or stolen property at an agreed or appraised value.

If we pay for the "loss", our payment will include the applicable sales tax for the damaged or stolen property.

5. Transfer Of Rights Of Recovery Against Others To Us

If any person or organization to or for whom we make payment under this Coverage Form has rights to recover damages from another, those rights are transferred to us. That person or organization must do everything necessary to secure our rights and must do nothing after "loss" to impair them.

B. General Conditions

1. Bankruptcy

Bankruptcy or insolvency of the Named Insured or the Named Insured's estate will not relieve us of any obligations under this Coverage Form.

2. Concealment, Misrepresentation Or Fraud

This Coverage Form is void in any case of fraud by you at any time as it relates to this Coverage Form. It is also void if you or any other insured, at any time, intentionally conceal or misrepresent a material fact concerning:

a. This Coverage Form;

b. The covered "auto";

c. Your interest in the covered "auto"; or

d. A claim under this Coverage Form.

3. Liberalization

If we revise this Coverage Form to provide more coverage without additional premium charge, your policy will automatically provide the additional coverage as of the day the revision is effective in your state.

CA 00 10 10 01 □

4. No Benefit To Bailee

We will not recognize any assignment or grant any coverage for the benefit of any person or organization holding, storing or transporting property for a fee regardless of any other provision of this Coverage Form.

5. Other Insurance

a. For any covered "auto" you own, this Coverage Form provides primary insurance. For any covered "auto" you don't own, the insurance provided by this Coverage Form is excess over any other collectible insurance.

b. For Hired Auto Physical Damage Coverage, any covered "auto" you lease, hire, rent or borrow is deemed to be a covered "auto" you own. However, any "auto" that is leased, hired, rented or borrowed with a driver is not a covered "auto".

c. When this Coverage Form and any other Coverage Form or policy covers on the same basis, either excess or primary, we will pay only our share. Our share is the proportion that the Limit of Insurance of our Coverage Form bears to the total of the limits of all the Coverage Forms and policies covering on the same basis.

6. Premium Audit

a. The estimated premium for this Coverage Form is based on the exposures you told us you would have when this policy began. We will compute the final premium due when we determine your actual exposures. The estimated total premium will be credited against the final premium due and the first Named Insured will be billed for the balance, if any. The due date for the final premium or retrospective premium is the date shown as the due date on the bill. If the estimated total premium exceeds the final premium due, the first Named Insured will get a refund.

b. If this policy is issued for more than one year, the premium for this Coverage Form will be computed annually based on our rates or premiums in effect at the beginning of each year of the policy.

7. Policy Period, Coverage Territory

Under this Coverage Form, we cover "losses" occurring:

a. During the policy period shown in the Declarations; and

b. Within the coverage territory.

The coverage territory is:

a. The United States of America;

b. The territories and possessions of the United States of America;

c. Puerto Rico;

d. Canada; and

e. Anywhere in the world if:

(1) A covered "auto" of the private passenger type is leased, hired, rented or borrowed without a driver for a period of 30 days or less; and

(2) The insured's responsibility to pay damages is determined in a suit on the merits, in the United States of America, the territories and possessions of the United States of America, Puerto Rico, or Canada or in a settlement we agree to.

We also cover "loss" to, a covered "auto" while being transported between any of these places.

SECTION IV – DEFINITIONS

A. "Auto" means a land motor vehicle, trailer or semitrailer designed for travel on public roads.

B. "Loss" means direct and accidental loss or damage.

C. "Diminution in value" means the actual or perceived loss in market value or resale value which results from a direct and accidental "loss".

D. "Employee" includes a "leased worker". "Employee" does not include a "temporary worker".

E. "Leased worker" means a person leased to you by a labor leasing firm under an agreement between you and the labor leasing firm, to perform duties related to the conduct of your business. "Leased worker" does not include a "temporary worker".

F. "Temporary worker" means a person who is furnished to you to substitute for a permanent "employee" on leave or to meet seasonal or short-term workload conditions.

COMMERCIAL AUTO
CA 00 05 10 01

GARAGE COVERAGE FORM

Various provisions in this policy restrict coverage. Read the entire policy carefully to determine rights, duties and what is and is not covered.

Throughout this policy the words "you" and "your" refer to the Named Insured shown in the Declarations. The words "we", "us" and "our" refer to the Company providing this insurance.

Other words and phrases that appear in quotation marks have special meaning. Refer to Section **VI** – Definitions.

SECTION I – COVERED AUTOS

Item Two of the Declarations shows the "autos" that are covered "autos" for each of your coverages. The following numerical symbols describe the "autos" that may be covered "autos". The symbols entered next to a coverage on the Declarations designate the only "autos" that are covered "autos".

A. Description Of Covered Auto Designation Symbols

Symbol		Description Of Covered Auto Designation Symbols
21	Any "Auto"	
22	Owned "Autos" Only	Only those "autos" you own (and for Liability Coverage any "trailers" you don't own while attached to power units you own). This includes those "autos" you acquire ownership of after the policy begins.
23	Owned Private Passenger "Autos" Only	Only the private passenger "autos" you own. This includes those private passenger "autos" you acquire ownership of after the policy begins.
24	Owned "Autos" Other Than Private Passenger "Autos" Only	Only those "autos" you own that are not of the private passenger type (and for Liability Coverage any "trailers" you don't own while attached to power units you own). This includes those "autos" not of the private passenger type you acquire ownership of after the policy begins.
25	Owned "Autos" Subject To No-Fault	Only those "autos" you own that are required to have No-Fault benefits in the state where they are licensed or principally garaged. This includes those "autos" you acquire ownership of after the policy begins provided they are required to have No-Fault benefits in the state where they are licensed or principally garaged.
26	Owned "Autos" Subject To A Compulsory Uninsured Motorists Law	Only those "autos" you own that because of the law in the state where they are licensed or principally garaged are required to have and cannot reject Uninsured Motorists Coverage. This includes those "autos" you acquire ownership of after the policy begins provided they are subject to the same state uninsured motorists requirement.
27	Specifically Described "Autos"	Only those "autos" described in Item Seven of the Non-Dealers' and Trailer Dealers' Supplementary Schedule or Item Nine of the Dealers' Supplementary Schedule for which a premium charge is shown (and for Liability Coverage any "trailers" you don't own while attached to a power unit described in Item Seven or Item Nine).
28	Hired "Autos" Only	Only those "autos" you lease, hire, rent or borrow. This does not include any "auto" you lease, hire, rent, or borrow from any of your "employees", partners, (if you are a partnership), members (if you are a limited liability company) or members of their households.
29	Non-Owned "Autos" Used In Your Garage Business	Any "auto" you do not own, lease, hire, rent or borrow used in connection with your garage business described in the Declarations. This includes "autos" owned by your "employees" or partners (if you are a partnership), members (if you are a limited liability company), or members of their households while used in your garage business.

Symbol		Description Of Covered Auto Designation Symbols
30	"Autos" Left With You For Service, Repair, Storage Or Safekeeping	Any customer's land motor vehicle or trailer or semitrailer while left with you for service, repair, storage or safekeeping. Customers include your "employees", and members of their households, who pay for the services performed.
31	Dealers "Autos" And "Autos" Held For Sale By Non-Dealers Or Trailer Dealers (Physical Damage Coverages)	Any "autos" and the interests in these "autos" described in Item Seven of the Dealers' Supplementary Schedule or Item Nine of the Non-Dealers' and Trailer Dealers' Supplementary Schedule.

B. Owned Autos You Acquire After The Policy Begins

1. If Symbols **21, 22, 23, 24, 25,** or **26** are entered next to a coverage in Item Two of the Declarations, then you have coverage for "autos" that you acquire of the type described for the remainder of the policy period.

2. But, if Symbol **27** is entered next to a coverage in Item Two of the Declarations, an "auto" you acquire will be a covered "auto" for that coverage only if:

   a. We already cover all "autos" that you own for that coverage or it replaces an "auto" you previously owned that had that coverage; and

   b. You tell us within 30 days after you acquire it that you want us to cover it for that coverage.

C. Certain Trailers And Temporary Substitute Autos

If Liability coverage is provided by this Coverage Form, the following types of vehicles are also covered "autos" for Liability Coverage:

1. "Trailers" with a load capacity of 2,000 pounds or less designed primarily for travel on public roads.

2. Any "auto" you do not own while used with the permission of its owner as a temporary substitute for a covered "auto" you own that is out of service because of its:

   a. Breakdown;

   b. Repair;

   c. Servicing;

   d. "Loss"; or

   e. Destruction.

SECTION II – LIABILITY COVERAGE

A. Coverage

1. **"Garage Operations" – Other Than Covered "Autos"**

   a. We will pay all sums an "insured" legally must pay as damages because of "bodily injury" or "property damage" to which this insurance applies caused by an "accident" and resulting from "garage operations" other than the ownership, maintenance or use of covered "autos".

   We have the right and duty to defend any "insured" against a "suit" asking for these damages. However, we have no duty to defend any "insured" against a "suit" seeking damages for "bodily injury" or "property damage" to which this insurance does not apply. We may investigate and settle any claim or "suit" as we consider appropriate. Our duty to defend or settle ends when the applicable Liability Coverage Limit of Insurance – "Garage Operations" – Other Than Covered "Autos" has been exhausted by payment of judgments or settlements.

   b. This insurance applies to "bodily injury" and "property damage" only if:

   (1) The "accident" occurs in the coverage territory;

   (2) The "bodily injury" or "property damage" occurs during the policy period; and

© ISO Properties, Inc., 2000

(3) Prior to the policy period, no "insured" listed under **Who Is An Insured** and no "employee" authorized by you to give or receive notice of an "accident" or claim, knew that the "bodily injury" or "property damage" had occurred, in whole or in part. If such a listed "insured" or authorized "employee" knew, prior to the policy period, that the "bodily injury" or "property damage" occurred, then any continuation, change or resumption of such "bodily injury" or "property damage" during or after the policy period will be deemed to have been known prior to the policy period.

c. "Bodily injury" or "property damage" which occurs during the policy period and was not, prior to the policy period, known to have occurred by any "insured" listed under **Who Is An Insured** or any "employee" authorized by you to give or receive notice of an "accident" or claim, includes any continuation, change or resumption of that "bodily injury" or "property damage" after the end of the policy period.

d. "Bodily injury" or "property damage" will be deemed to have been known to have occurred at the earliest time when any "insured" listed under **Who Is An Insured** or any "employee" authorized by you to give or receive notice of an "accident" or claim:

(1) Reports all, or any part, of the "bodily injury" or "property damage" to us or any other insurer;

(2) Receives a written or verbal demand or claim for damages because of the "bodily injury" or "property damage"; or

(3) Becomes aware by any other means that "bodily injury" or "property damage" has occurred or has begun to occur.

2. "Garage Operations" – Covered "Autos"

We will pay all sums an "insured" legally must pay as damages because of "bodily injury" or "property damage" to which this insurance applies, caused by an "accident" and resulting from "garage operations" involving the ownership, maintenance or use of covered "autos".

We will also pay all sums an "insured" legally must pay as a "covered pollution cost or expense" to which this insurance applies, caused by an "accident" and resulting from "garage operations" involving the ownership, maintenance or use of covered "autos". However, we will only pay for the "covered pollution cost or expense" if there is either "bodily injury" or "property damage" to which this insurance applies that is caused by the same "accident".

We have the right and duty to defend any "insured" against a "suit" asking for such damages or a "covered pollution cost or expense". However, we have no duty to defend any "insured" against a "suit" seeking damages for "bodily injury" or "property damage" or a "covered pollution cost or expense" to which this insurance does not apply. We may investigate and settle any claim or "suit" as we consider appropriate. Our duty to defend or settle ends when the Liability Coverage Limit of Insurance – "Garage Operations" – Covered "Autos" has been exhausted by payment of judgments or settlements.

3. Who Is An Insured

a. The following are "insureds" for covered "autos":

(1) You for any covered "auto".

(2) Anyone else while using with your permission a covered "auto" you own, hire or borrow except:

(a) The owner or anyone else from whom you hire or borrow a covered "auto". This exception does not apply if the covered "auto" is a "trailer" connected to a covered "auto" you own.

(b) Your "employee" if the covered "auto" is owned by that "employee" or a member of his or her household.

(c) Someone using a covered "auto" while he or she is working in a business of selling, servicing, repairing, parking or storing "autos" unless that business is your "garage operations".

(d) Your customers, if your business is shown in the Declarations as an "auto" dealership. However, if a customer of yours:

(i) Has no other available insurance (whether primary, excess or contingent), they are an "insured" but only up to the compulsory or financial responsibility law limits where the covered "auto" is principally garaged.

(ii) Has other available insurance (whether primary, excess or contingent) less than the compulsory or financial responsibility law limits where the covered "auto" is principally garaged, they are an "insured" only for the amount by which the compulsory or financial responsibility law limits exceed the limit of their other insurance.

(e) A partner (if you are a partnership), or a member (if you are a limited liability company), for a covered "auto" owned by him or her or a member of his or her household.

(3) Anyone liable for the conduct of an "insured" described above but only to the extent of that liability.

b. The following are "insureds" for "garage operations" other than covered "autos":

(1) You.

(2) Your partners (if you are a partnership), members (if you are a limited liability company), "employees", directors or shareholders but only while acting within the scope of their duties.

4. **Coverage Extensions**

a. **Supplementary Payments**

In addition to the Limit of Insurance, we will pay for the "insured":

(1) All expenses we incur.

(2) Up to $2,000 for the cost of bail bonds (including bonds for related traffic law violations) required because of an "accident" we cover. We do not have to furnish these bonds.

(3) The cost of bonds to release attachments in any "suit" against the "insured" we defend, but only for bond amounts within our Limit of Insurance.

(4) All reasonable expenses incurred by the "insured" at our request, including actual loss of earnings up to $250 a day because of time off from work.

(5) All costs taxed against the "insured" in any "suit" against the "insured" we defend.

(6) All interest on the full amount of any judgment that accrues after entry of the judgment in any "suit" against the "insured" we defend; but our duty to pay interest ends when we have paid, offered to pay or deposited in court the part of the judgment that is within our Limit of Insurance.

b. **Out-Of-State Coverage Extensions**

While a covered "auto" is away from the state where it is licensed we will:

(1) Increase the Limit of Insurance for Liability Coverage to meet the limits specified by a compulsory or financial responsibility law of the jurisdiction where the covered "auto" is being used. This extension does not apply to the limit or limits specified by any law governing motor carriers of passengers or property.

(2) Provide the minimum amounts and types of other coverages, such as no-fault, required of out-of-state vehicles by the jurisdiction where the covered "auto" is being used.

We will not pay anyone more than once for the same elements of loss because of these extensions.

B. **Exclusions**

This insurance does not apply to any of the following:

1. **Expected Or Intended Injury**

"Bodily injury" or "property damage" expected or intended from the standpoint of the "insured". But for "garage operations" other than covered "autos" this exclusion does not apply to "bodily injury" resulting from the use of reasonable force to protect persons or property.

2. **Contractual**

Liability assumed under any contract or agreement. But this exclusion does not apply to liability for damages:

a. Assumed in a contract or agreement that is an "insured contract" provided the "bodily injury" or "property damage" occurs subsequent to the execution of the contract or agreement; or

b. That the "insured" would have in the absence of the contract or agreement.

3. **Workers' Compensation**

Any obligation for which the "insured" or the "insured's" insurer may be held liable under any workers' compensation, disability benefits or unemployment compensation law or any similar law.

4. Employee Indemnification And Employer's Liability

"Bodily injury" to:

a. An "employee" of the "insured" arising out of and in the course of:

(1) Employment by the "insured"; or

(2) Performing the duties related to the conduct of the "insured's" business; or

b. The spouse, child, parent, brother or sister of that "employee" as a consequence of Paragraph **a.** above.

c. A person arising out of any:

(1) Refusal to employ that person;

(2) Termination of that person's employment; or

(3) Employment-related practices, policies, acts or omissions, such as coercion, demotion, evaluation, reassignment, discipline, defamation, harassment, humiliation or discrimination directed at that person; or

d. The spouse, child, parent, brother or sister of that person as a consequence of "bodily injury" to that person at whom any of the employment-related practices described in Paragraphs **(1)**, **(2)** or **(3)** above are directed.

This exclusion applies:

(1) Whether the "insured" may be liable as an employer or in any other capacity; and

(2) To any obligation to share damages with or repay someone else who must pay damages because of the injury.

But this exclusion does not apply to "bodily injury" to domestic "employees" not entitled to workers' compensation benefits or to liability assumed by the "insured" under an "insured contract". For the purposes of the Coverage Form, a domestic "employee" is a person engaged in household or domestic work performed principally in connection with a residence premises.

5. Fellow Employee

"Bodily injury" to any fellow "employee" of the "insured" arising out of and in the course of the fellow "employee's" employment or while performing duties related to the conduct of your business.

6. Care, Custody Or Control

"Property damage" to or "covered pollution cost or expense" involving:

a. Property owned, rented or occupied by the "insured";

b. Property loaned to the "insured";

c. Property held for sale or being transported by the "insured"; or

d. Property in the "insured's" care, custody or control.

But this exclusion does not apply to liability assumed under a sidetrack agreement.

7. Leased Autos

Any covered "auto" while leased or rented to others. But this exclusion does not apply to a covered "auto" you rent to one of your customers while their "auto" is left with you for service or repair.

8. Pollution Exclusion Applicable To "Garage Operations" – Other Than Covered "Autos"

a. "Bodily injury" or "property damage" arising out of the actual, alleged or threatened discharge, dispersal, seepage, migration, release or escape of "pollutants":

(1) At or from any premises, site or location that is or was at any time owned or occupied by, or rented or loaned to, any "insured";

(2) At or from any premises, site or location that is or was at any time used by or for any "insured" or others for the handling, storage, disposal, processing or treatment of waste;

(3) At or from any premises, site or location on which any "insured" or any contractors or subcontractors working directly or indirectly on any "insured's" behalf are performing operations:

(a) To test for, monitor, clean up, remove, contain, treat, detoxify or neutralize, or in any way respond to, or assess the effects of the "pollutants"; or

(b) If the "pollutants" are brought on or to the premises, site or location in connection with such operations by such "insured", contractor or subcontractor; or

(4) That are or were at any time transported, handled, stored, treated, disposed of, or processed as waste by or for any "insured" or any person or organization for whom you may be legally responsible.

Paragraphs **a.(1)** and **a.(3)(b)** do not apply to "bodily injury" or "property damage" arising out of heat, smoke or fumes from a hostile fire. A hostile fire means one that becomes uncontrollable, or breaks out from where it was intended to be.

Paragraph **a.(1)** does not apply to "bodily injury" if sustained within a building and caused by smoke, fumes, vapor or soot from equipment used to heat that building.

Paragraph **a.(3)(b)** does not apply to "bodily injury" or "property damage" sustained within a building and caused by the release of gases, fumes or vapors from material brought into that building in connection with operations being performed by you or on your behalf by a contractor or subcontractor.

b. Any loss, cost or expense arising out of any:

(1) Request, demand, order or statutory or regulatory requirement that any "insured" or others test for, monitor, clean up, remove, contain, treat, detoxify or neutralize, or in any way respond to, or assess the effects of "pollutants";

(2) Claim or suit by or on behalf of a governmental authority for damages because of testing for, monitoring, cleaning up, removing, containing, treating, detoxifying or neutralizing, or in any way responding to or assessing the effects of "pollutants".

However, this paragraph does not apply to liability for damages because of "property damage" that the "insured" would have in the absence of such request, demand, order or statutory or regulatory requirement, or such claim or "suit" by or on behalf of a governmental authority.

9. Pollution Exclusion Applicable To "Garage Operations" – Covered "Autos"

"Bodily injury" or "property damage" arising out of the actual, alleged or threatened discharge, dispersal, seepage, migration, release or escape of "pollutants":

a. That are, or that are contained in any property that is:

(1) Being transported or towed by, handled, or handled for movement into, onto or from, the covered "auto";

(2) Otherwise in the course of transit by or on behalf of the "insured"; or

(3) Being stored, disposed of, treated or processed in or upon the covered "auto";

b. Before the "pollutants" or any property in which the "pollutants" are contained are moved from the place where they are accepted by the "insured" for movement into or onto the covered "auto"; or

c. After the "pollutants" or any property in which the "pollutants" are contained are moved from the covered "auto" to the place where they are finally delivered, disposed of or abandoned by the "insured".

Paragraph **a.** above does not apply to fuels, lubricants, fluids, exhaust gases or other similar "pollutants" that are needed for or result from the normal electrical, hydraulic or mechanical functioning of the covered "auto" or its parts, if the "pollutants" escape, seep, migrate, or are discharged, dispersed or released directly from an "auto" part designed by its manufacturer to hold, store, receive or dispose of such "pollutants".

Paragraphs **b.** and **c.** above of this exclusion do not apply to "accidents" that occur away from premises owned by or rented to an "insured" with respect to "pollutants" not in or upon a covered "auto" if:

(1) The "pollutants" or any property in which the "pollutants" are contained are upset, overturned or damaged as a result of the maintenance or use of a covered "auto"; and

(2) The discharge, dispersal, seepage, migration, release or escape of the "pollutants" is caused directly by such upset, overturn or damage.

10. Racing

Covered "autos" while used in any professional or organized racing or demolition contest or stunting activity, or while practicing for such contest or activity. This insurance also does not apply while that covered "auto" is being prepared for such a contest or activity.

11. Watercraft Or Aircraft

Any watercraft or aircraft except watercraft while ashore on premises where you conduct "garage operations".

12. Defective Products

"Property damage" to any of your "products", if caused by a defect existing in your "products" or any part of your "products", at the time it was transferred to another.

13. Work You Performed

"Property damage" to "work you performed" if the "property damage" results from any part of the work itself or from the parts, materials or equipment used in connection with the work.

14. Loss Of Use

Loss of use of other property not physically damaged if caused by:

a. A delay or failure by you or anyone acting on your behalf to perform a contract or agreement in accordance with its terms.

b. A defect, deficiency, inadequacy or dangerous condition in your "products" or "work you performed". But this exclusion, **14.b.**, does not apply if the loss of use was caused by sudden and accidental damage to or destruction of your "products" or "work you performed" after they have been put to their intended use.

15. Products Recall

Damages claimed for any loss, cost or expense incurred by you or others for the loss of use, withdrawal, recall, inspection, repair, replacement, adjustment, removal or disposal of your "products" or "work you performed" or other property of which they form a part, if such product, work or property is withdrawn or recalled from the market or from use by any person or organization because of a known or suspected defect, deficiency, inadequacy or dangerous condition in it.

16. War

"Bodily injury" or "property damage" due to war, whether or not declared, or any act or condition incident to war. War includes civil war, insurrection, rebellion or revolution. This exclusion applies only to liability assumed under a contract or agreement.

17. Liquor Liability

"Bodily injury" or "property damage" for which an "insured" may be held liable by reason of:

a. Causing or contributing to the intoxication of any person;

b. The furnishing of alcoholic beverages to a person under the legal drinking age or under the influence of alcohol; or

c. Any statute, ordinance or regulation relating to the sale, gift, distribution or use of alcoholic beverages.

This exclusion applies only if you use the premises in part for the following purposes:

(1) Serving or furnishing alcoholic beverages for a charge whether or not such activity:

(a) Requires a license; or

(b) Is for the purpose of financial gain or livelihood; or

(2) Serving or furnishing alcoholic beverages without a charge, if a license is required for such activity.

C. Limit Of Insurance

1. Aggregate Limit Of Insurance – "Garage Operations" – Other Than Covered "Autos"

For "garage operations" other than the ownership, maintenance or use of covered "autos", the following applies:

Regardless of the number of "insureds", claims made or "suits" brought or persons or organizations making claims or bringing "suits", the most we will pay for the sum of all damages involving "garage operations" other than "auto" is the Aggregate Limit of Insurance – "Garage Operations" – Other Than Covered "Autos" for Liability Coverage shown in the Declarations.

Damages payable under the Aggregate Limit of Insurance – "Garage Operations" – Other Than Covered "Autos" consist of damages resulting from "garage operations", other than the ownership, maintenance or use of the "autos" indicated in Section I of this Coverage Form as covered "autos", including the following coverages, if provided by endorsement:

a. "Personal injury" liability coverage;

b. "Personal and advertising injury" liability coverage;

c. Host liquor liability coverage;

d. Fire legal liability coverage;

e. Incidental medical malpractice liability coverage;

f. Non-owned watercraft coverage;

g. Broad form products coverage.

Damages payable under the Each "Accident" Limit of Insurance – "Garage Operations" – Other Than Covered "Autos" are not payable under the Each "Accident" Limit of Insurance – "Garage Operations" – Covered "Autos".

Subject to the above, the most we will pay for all damages resulting from all "bodily injury" and "property damage" resulting from any one "accident" is the Each "Accident" Limit of Insurance – "Garage Operations" – Other Than Covered "Autos" for Liability Coverage shown in the Declarations.

All "bodily injury" and "property damage" resulting from continuous or repeated exposure to substantially the same conditions will be considered as resulting from one "accident".

The Aggregate Limit of Insurance – "Garage Operations" Other Than Covered "Autos" applies separately to each consecutive annual period and to any remaining period of less than 12 months, starting with the beginning of the policy period shown in the Declarations, unless the policy period is extended after issuance for an additional period of less than 12 months. In that case, the additional period will be deemed part of the last preceding period for purposes of determining the Aggregate Limit of Insurance – "Garage Operations" – Other Than Covered "Autos".

2. Limit Of Insurance – "Garage Operations" – Covered "Autos"

For "accidents" resulting from "garage operations" involving the ownership, maintenance or use of covered "autos", the following applies:

Regardless of the number of covered "autos", "insureds", premiums paid, claims made or vehicles involved in the "accident", the most we will pay for the total of all damages and "covered pollution cost or expense" combined, resulting from any one "accident" involving a covered "auto" is the Each "Accident" Limit of Insurance – "Garage Operations" – Covered "Autos" for Liability Coverage shown in the Declarations.

Damages and "covered pollution cost or expense" payable under the Each "Accident" Limit of Insurance – "Garage Operations" – Covered "Autos" are not payable under the Each "Accident" Limit of Insurance – "Garage Operations" – Other Than Covered "Autos".

All "bodily injury", "property damage" and "covered pollution cost or expense" resulting from continuous or repeated exposure to substantially the same conditions will be considered as resulting from one "accident".

No one will be entitled to receive duplicate payments for the same elements of "loss" under this Coverage Form and any Medical Payments Coverage endorsement, Uninsured Motorists Coverage endorsement or Underinsured Motorists Coverage endorsement attached to this Coverage Part.

D. Deductible

We will deduct $100 from the damages in any "accident" resulting from "property damage" to an "auto" as a result of "work you performed" on that "auto".

SECTION III – GARAGEKEEPERS COVERAGE

A. Coverage

1. We will pay all sums the "insured" legally must pay as damages for "loss" to a "customer's auto" or "customer's auto" equipment left in the "insured's" care while the "insured" is attending, servicing, repairing, parking or storing it in your "garage operations" under:

    a. Comprehensive Coverage

    From any cause except:

    (1) The "customer's auto's" collision with another object; or

    (2) The "customer's auto's" overturn.

    b. Specified Causes Of Loss Coverage

    Caused by:

    (1) Fire, lightning or explosion;

    (2) Theft; or

    (3) Mischief or vandalism.

    c. Collision Coverage

    Caused by:

    (1) The "customer's auto's" collision with another object; or

    (2) The "customer's auto's" overturn.

2. We have the right and duty to defend any "insured" against a "suit" asking for these damages. However, we have no duty to defend any "insured" against a "suit" seeking damages for any loss to which this insurance does not apply. We may investigate and settle any claim or "suit" as we consider appropriate. Our duty to defend or settle ends for a coverage when the Limit of Insurance for that coverage has been exhausted by payment of judgments or settlements.

3. **Who Is An Insured**

    The following are "insureds" for "loss" to "customer's autos" and "customer's auto" equipment:

    a. You.

    b. Your partners (if you are a partnership), members (if you are a limited liability company), "employees", directors or shareholders while acting within the scope of their duties as such.

4. **Coverage Extensions**

    The following applies as Supplementary Payments. In addition to the Limit of Insurance, we will pay for the "insured":

    a. All expenses we incur.

b. The cost of bonds to release attachments in any "suit" against the "insured" we defend, but only for bond amounts within our Limit of Insurance.

c. All reasonable expenses incurred by the "insured" at our request, including actual loss of earnings up to $250 a day because of time off from work.

d. All costs taxed against the "insured" in any "suit" against the "insured" we defend.

e. All interest on the full amount of any judgment that accrues after entry of the judgment in any "suit" against the "insured" we defend; but our duty to pay interest ends when we have paid, offered to pay or deposited in court the part of the judgment that is within our Limit of Insurance.

B. Exclusions

1. This insurance does not apply to any of the following:

   a. **Contractual Obligations**

   Liability resulting from any agreement by which the "insured" accepts responsibility for "loss".

   b. **Theft**

   "Loss" due to theft or conversion caused in any way by you, your "employees" or by your shareholders.

   c. **Defective Parts**

   Defective parts or materials.

   d. **Faulty Work**

   Faulty "work you performed".

2. We will not pay for "loss" to any of the following:

   a. Tape decks or other sound reproducing equipment unless permanently installed in a "customer's auto".

   b. Tapes, records or other sound reproducing devices designed for use with sound reproducing equipment.

   c. Sound receiving equipment designed for use as a citizens' band radio, two-way mobile radio or telephone or scanning monitor receiver, including its antennas and other accessories, unless permanently installed in the dash or console opening normally used by the "customer's auto" manufacturer for the installation of a radio.

   d. Any device designed or used to detect speed measuring equipment such as radar or laser detectors and any jamming apparatus intended to elude or disrupt speed measuring equipment.

C. Limit Of Insurance And Deductible

1. Regardless of the number of "customer's autos", "insureds", premiums paid, claims made or "suits" brought, the most we will pay for each "loss" at each location is the Garagekeepers Coverage Limit of Insurance shown in the Declarations for that location minus the applicable deductibles for "loss" caused by collision; and

   a. Theft or mischief or vandalism; or

   b. All perils.

2. The maximum deductible stated in the Declarations for Garagekeepers Coverage Comprehensive or Specified Causes of Loss Coverage is the most that will be deducted for all "loss" in any one event caused by:

   a. Theft or mischief or vandalism; or

   b. All perils.

3. Sometimes to settle a claim or "suit", we may pay all or any part of the deductible. If this happens you must reimburse us for the deductible or that portion of the deductible that we paid.

SECTION IV – PHYSICAL DAMAGE COVERAGE

A. Coverage

1. We will pay for "loss" to a covered "auto" or its equipment under:

   a. **Comprehensive Coverage**

   From any cause except:

   (1) The covered "auto's" collision with another object; or

   (2) The covered "auto's" overturn.

   b. **Specified Causes Of Loss Coverage**

   Caused by:

   (1) Fire, lightning or explosion;

   (2) Theft;

   (3) Windstorm, hail or earthquake;

   (4) Flood;

   (5) Mischief or vandalism; or

   (6) The sinking, burning, collision or derailment of any conveyance transporting the covered "auto".

   c. **Collision Coverage**

   Caused by:

   (1) The covered "auto's" collision with another object; or

   (2) The covered "auto's" overturn.

2. Towing – Non-Dealers Only

If your business is shown in the Declarations as something other than an "auto" dealership, we will pay up to the limit shown in the Declarations for towing and labor costs incurred each time a covered "auto" of the private passenger type is disabled. However, the labor must be performed at the place of disablement.

3. Glass Breakage – Hitting A Bird Or Animal – Falling Objects Or Missiles

If you carry Comprehensive Coverage for the damaged covered "auto", we will pay for the following under Comprehensive Coverage:

a. Glass breakage;

b. "Loss" caused by hitting a bird or animal; and

c. "Loss" caused by falling objects or missiles.

However, you have the option of having glass breakage caused by a covered "auto's" collision or overturn considered a "loss" under Collision Coverage.

4. Coverage Extension

a. Transportation Expenses

If your business is shown in the Declarations as something other than an "auto" dealership, we will pay up to $20 per day to a maximum of $600 for temporary transportation expense incurred by you because of the total theft of a covered "auto" of the private passenger type. We will pay only for those covered "autos" for which you carry either Comprehensive or Specified Causes of Loss Coverage. We will pay for temporary transportation expenses incurred during the period beginning 48 hours after the theft and ending, regardless of the policy's expiration, when the covered "auto" is returned to use or we pay for its "loss".

b. Loss Of Use Expenses

For Hired Auto Physical Damage, we will pay expenses for which an "insured" becomes legally responsible to pay for loss of use of a vehicle rented or hired without a driver, under a written rental contract or agreement. We will pay for loss of use expenses if caused by:

(1) Other than collision only if the Declarations indicate that Comprehensive Coverage is provided for any covered "auto";

(2) Specified Causes Of Loss only if the Declarations indicate that Specified Causes Of Loss Coverage is provided for any covered "auto"; or

(3) Collision only if the Declarations indicate that Collision Coverage is provided for any covered "auto".

However, the most we will pay for any expenses for loss of use is $20 per day, to a maximum of $600.

B. Exclusions

1. We will not pay for "loss" caused by or resulting from any of the following. Such "loss" is excluded regardless of any other cause or event that contributes concurrently or in any sequence to the "loss".

a. Nuclear Hazard

(1) The explosion of any weapon employing atomic fission or fusion; or

(2) Nuclear reaction or radiation, or radioactive contamination, however caused.

b. War Or Military Action

(1) War, including undeclared or civil war;

(2) Warlike action by a military force, including action in hindering or defending against an actual or expected attack, by any government, sovereign or other authority using military personnel or other agents; or

(3) Insurrection, rebellion, revolution, usurped power or action taken by governmental authority in hindering or defending against any of these.

2. We will not pay for "loss" to any of the following:

a. Any covered "auto" leased or rented to others unless rented to one of your customers while their "auto" is left with you for service or repair.

b. Any covered "auto" while used in any professional or organized racing or demolition contest or stunting activity, or while practicing for such contest or activity. We will also not pay for "loss" to any covered "auto" while that covered "auto" is being prepared for such contest or activity.

c. Tapes, records, discs or other similar audio, visual or data electronic devices designed for use with audio, visual or data electronic equipment.

d. Any device designed or used to detect speed measuring equipment such as radar or laser detectors and any jamming apparatus intended to elude or disrupt speed measurement equipment.

 CA 00 05 10 01 ☐

e. Any electronic equipment, without regard to whether this equipment is permanently installed, that receives or transmits audio, visual or data signals and that is not designed solely for the reproduction of sound.

f. Any accessories used with the electronic equipment described in Paragraph **e.** above.

Exclusions **2.e.** and **2.f.** do not apply to:

a. Equipment designed solely for the reproduction of sound and accessories used with such equipment, provided such equipment is permanently installed in the covered "auto" at the time of the "loss" or such equipment is removable from a housing unit which is permanently installed in the covered "auto" at the time of the "loss", and such equipment is designed to be solely operated by use of the power from the "auto's" electrical system, in or upon the covered "auto"; or

b. Any other electronic equipment that is:

(1) Necessary for the normal operation of the covered "auto" or the monitoring of the covered "auto's" operating system; or

(2) An integral part of the same unit housing any sound reproducing equipment described in **a.** above and permanently installed in the opening of the dash or console of the covered "auto" normally used by the manufacturer for installation of a radio.

3. False Pretense

We will not pay for "loss" to a covered "auto" caused by or resulting from:

a. Someone causing you to voluntarily part with it by trick or scheme or under false pretenses; or

b. Your acquiring an "auto" from a seller who did not have legal title.

4. If your business is shown in the Declarations as an "auto" dealership, we will not pay for:

a. Your expected profit, including loss of market value or resale value.

b. "Loss" to any covered "auto" displayed or stored at any location not shown in Item Three of the Declarations if the "loss" occurs more than 45 days after your use of the location begins.

c. Under the Collision Coverage, "loss" to any covered "auto" while being driven or transported from the point of purchase or distribution to its destination if such points are more than 50 road miles apart.

d. Under the Specified Causes of Loss Coverage, "loss" to any covered "auto" caused by or resulting from the collision or upset of any vehicle transporting it.

5. We will not pay for "loss" to a covered "auto" due to "diminution in value".

6. Other Exclusions

We will not pay for "loss" caused by or resulting from any of the following unless caused by other "loss" that is covered by this insurance:

a. Wear and tear, freezing, mechanical or electrical breakdown;

b. Blowouts, punctures or other road damage to tires.

C. Limits Of Insurance

1. The most we will pay for "loss" to any one covered "auto" is the lesser of:

a. The actual cash value of the damaged or stolen property as of the time of "loss"; or

b. The cost of repairing or replacing the damaged or stolen property with other property of like kind and quality.

2. An adjustment for depreciation and physical condition will be made in determining actual cash value in the event of a total "loss".

3. If a repair or replacement results in better than like kind or quality, we will not pay for the amount of the betterment.

4. For those businesses shown in the Declarations as "auto" dealerships, the following provisions also apply:

a. Regardless of the number of covered "autos" involved in the "loss", the most we will pay for all "loss" at any one location is the amount shown in the Auto Dealers Supplementary Schedule for that location. Regardless of the number of covered "autos" involved in the "loss", the most we will pay for all "loss" in transit is the amount shown in the Auto Dealers Supplementary Schedule for "loss" in transit.

b. Quarterly Or Monthly Reporting Premium Basis

If, on the date of your last report, the actual value of the covered "autos" at the "loss" location exceeds what you last reported, when a "loss" occurs we will pay only a percentage of what we would otherwise be obligated to pay. We will determine this percentage by dividing your total reported value for the involved location by the value you actually had on the date of your last report.

If the first report due is delinquent on the date of "loss", the most we will pay will not exceed 75 percent of the Limit of Insurance shown in the Auto Dealers Supplementary Schedule for the applicable location.

c. Non-Reporting Premium Basis

If, when "loss" occurs, the total value of your covered "autos" exceeds the Limit of Insurance shown in the Declarations, we will pay only a percentage of what we would otherwise be obligated to pay. We will determine this percentage by dividing the limit by the total values you actually had when "loss" occurred.

D. Deductible

For each covered "auto", our obligation to pay for, repair, return or replace damaged or stolen property will be reduced by the applicable deductible shown in the Declarations provided that:

1. "Auto" Dealers Only Special Deductible Provisions

If your business is shown in the Declarations as an "auto" dealership:

a. The Comprehensive or Specified Causes of Loss Coverage deductible applies only to "loss" caused by:

(1) Theft or mischief or vandalism; or

(2) All perils.

b. Regardless of the number of covered "autos" damaged or stolen, the per "loss" deductible for Comprehensive or Specified Causes of Loss Coverage shown in the Declarations is the maximum deductible applicable for all "loss" in any one event caused by:

(1) Theft or mischief or vandalism; or

(2) All perils.

2. Non-Dealers Only Special Deductible Provisions

If your business is shown in the Declarations as something other than an "auto" dealership, the Comprehensive Coverage deductible does not apply to "loss" caused by fire or lightning.

SECTION V – GARAGE CONDITIONS

The following conditions apply in addition to the Common Policy Conditions:

A. Loss Conditions

1. Appraisal For Physical Damage Loss

If you and we disagree on the amount of "loss", either may demand an appraisal of the "loss". In this event, each party will select a competent appraiser. The two appraisers will select a competent and impartial umpire.

The appraisers will state separately the actual cash value and amount of "loss". If they fail to agree, they will submit their differences to the umpire. A decision agreed to by any two will be binding. Each party will:

a. Pay its chosen appraiser; and

b. Bear the other expenses of the appraisal and umpire equally.

If we submit to an appraisal, we will still retain our right to deny the claim.

2. Duties In The Event Of Accident, Claim, Suit Or Loss

We have no duty to provide coverage under this policy unless there has been full compliance with the following duties:

a. In the event of "accident", claim, "suit" or "loss", you must give us or our authorized representative prompt notice of the accident or "loss". Include:

(1) How, when and where the "accident" or "loss" occurred;

(2) The "insured's" name and address; and

(3) To the extent possible, the names and addresses of any injured persons and witnesses.

b. Additionally, you and any other involved "insured" must:

(1) Assume no obligation, make no payment or incur no expense without our consent, except at the "insured's" own cost.

(2) Immediately send us copies of any request, demand, order, notice, summons or legal paper received concerning the claim or "suit".

(3) Cooperate with us in the investigation or settlement of the claim or defense against the "suit".

(4) Authorize us to obtain medical records or other pertinent information.

(5) Submit to examination at our expense, by physicians of our choice, as often as we reasonably require.

c. If there is "loss" to a covered "auto" or its equipment you must also do the following:

(1) Promptly notify the police if the covered "auto" or any of its equipment is stolen.

(2) Take all reasonable steps to protect the covered "auto" from further damage. Also keep a record of your expenses for consideration in the settlement of the claim.

(3) Permit us to inspect the covered "auto" and records proving the "loss" before its repair or disposition.

(4) Agree to examinations under oath at our request and give us a signed statement of your answers.

3. Legal Action Against Us

No one may bring a legal action against us under this Coverage Form until:

a. There has been full compliance with all the terms of this Coverage Form; and

b. Under Liability Coverage, we agree in writing that the "insured" has an obligation to pay or until the amount of that obligation has finally been determined by judgment after trial. No one has the right under this policy to bring us into an action to determine the "insured's" liability.

4. Loss Payment – Physical Damage Coverages

At our option we may:

a. Pay for, repair or replace damaged or stolen property;

b. Return the stolen property, at our expense. We will pay for any damage that results to the "auto" from the theft; or

c. Take all or any part of the damaged or stolen property at an agreed or appraised value.

If we pay for the "loss", our payment will include the applicable sales tax for the damaged or stolen property.

5. Transfer Of Rights Of Recovery Against Others To Us

If any person or organization to or for whom we make payment under this Coverage Form has rights to recover damages from another, those rights are transferred to us. That person or organization must do everything necessary to secure our rights and must do nothing after "accident" or "loss" to impair them.

B. General Conditions

1. Bankruptcy

Bankruptcy or insolvency of the "insured" or the "insured's" estate will not relieve us of any obligations under this Coverage Form.

2. Concealment, Misrepresentation Or Fraud

This Coverage Form is void in any case of fraud by you at any time as it relates to this Coverage Form. It is also void if you or any other "insured", at any time, intentionally conceal or misrepresent a material fact concerning:

a. This Coverage Form;

b. The covered "auto";

c. Your interest in the covered "auto"; or

d. A claim under this Coverage Form.

3. Liberalization

If we revise this Coverage Form to provide more coverage without additional premium charge, your policy will automatically provide the additional coverage as of the day the revision is effective in your state.

4. No Benefit To Bailee – Physical Damage Coverages

We will not recognize any assignment or grant any coverage for the benefit of any person or organization holding, storing or transporting property for a fee regardless of any other provision of this Coverage Form.

5. Other Insurance

a. For any covered "auto" you own, this Coverage Form provides primary insurance. For any covered "auto" you don't own, the insurance provided by this Coverage Form is excess over any other collectible insurance. However, while a covered "auto" which is a "trailer" is connected to another vehicle, the Liability Coverage this Coverage Form provides for the "trailer" is:

(1) Excess while it is connected to a motor vehicle you do not own.

(2) Primary while it is connected to a covered "auto" you own.

b. For Hired Auto Physical Damage Coverage, any covered "auto" you lease, hire, rent or borrow is deemed to be a covered "auto" you own. However, any "auto" that is leased, hired, rented or borrowed with a driver is not a covered "auto".

c. Regardless of the provisions of Paragraph **a.** above, this Coverage Form's Liability coverage is primary for any liability assumed under an "insured contract".

d. When this Coverage Form and any other Coverage Form or policy covers on the same basis, either excess or primary, we will pay only our share. Our share is the proportion that the Limit of Insurance of our Coverage Form bears to the total of the limits of all the Coverage Forms and policies covering on the same basis.

6. Premium Audit

a. The estimated premium for this Coverage Form is based on the exposures you told us you would have when this policy began. We will compute the final premium due when we determine your actual exposures. The estimated total premium will be credited against the final premium due and the first Named Insured will be billed for the balance, if any. The due date for the final premium or retrospective premium is the date shown as the due date on the bill. If the estimated total premium exceeds the final premium due, the first Named Insured will get a refund.

b. If this policy is issued for more than one year, the premium for this Coverage Form will be computed annually based on our rates or premiums in effect at the beginning of each year of the policy.

7. Policy Period, Coverage Territory

Under this Coverage Form, we cover:

a. "Bodily injury", "property damage" and "losses" occurring; and

b. "Covered pollution cost or expense" arising out of "accidents" occurring

during the policy period shown in the Declarations and within the coverage territory.

The coverage territory is:

a. The United States of America;

b. The territories and possessions of the United States of America;

c. Puerto Rico;

d. Canada; and

e. Anywhere in the world if:

(1) A covered "auto" of the private passenger type is leased, hired, rented or borrowed without a driver for a period of 30 days or less; and

(2) The "insured's" responsibility to pay damages is determined in a "suit" on the merits, in the United States of America, the territories and possessions of the United States of America, Puerto Rico, or Canada or in a settlement we agree to.

We also cover "bodily injury", "property damage", "covered pollution cost or expense" and "losses" while a covered "auto" is being transported between any of these places.

The coverage territory is extended to anywhere in the world if the "bodily injury" or "property damage" is caused by one of your "products" which is sold for use in the United States of America, its territories or possessions, Puerto Rico or Canada. The original "suit" for damages resulting from such "bodily injury" or "property damage" must be brought in one of these places.

8. Two Or More Coverage Forms Or Policies Issued By Us

If this Coverage Form and any other Coverage Form or policy issued to you by us or any company affiliated with us apply to the same "accident", the aggregate maximum Limit of Insurance under all the Coverage Forms or policies shall not exceed the highest applicable Limit of Insurance under any one Coverage Form or policy. This condition does not apply to any Coverage Form or policy issued by us or an affiliated company specifically to apply as excess insurance over this Coverage Form.

SECTION VI – DEFINITIONS

A. "Accident" includes continuous or repeated exposure to the same conditions resulting in "bodily injury" or "property damage".

B. "Auto" means a land motor vehicle, "trailer" or semitrailer.

C. "Bodily injury" means bodily injury, sickness or disease sustained by a person including death resulting from any of these.

D. "Covered pollution cost or expense" means any cost or expense arising out of:

1. Any request, demand, order or statutory or regulatory requirement; or

2. Any claim or "suit" by or on behalf of a governmental authority demanding

that the "insured" or others test for, monitor, clean up, remove, contain, treat, detoxify or neutralize, or in any way respond to, or assess the effects of "pollutants".

"Covered pollution cost or expense" does not include any cost or expense arising out of the actual, alleged or threatened discharge, dispersal, seepage, migration, release or escape of "pollutants":

a. That are, or that are contained in any property that is:

(1) Being transported or towed by, handled, or handled for movement into, onto or from the covered "auto";

(2) Otherwise in the course of transit by or on behalf of the "insured";

(3) Being stored, disposed of, treated or processed in or upon the covered "auto"; or

b. Before the "pollutants" or any property in which the "pollutants" are contained are moved from the place where they are accepted by the "insured" for movement into or onto the covered "auto"; or

c. After the "pollutants" or any property in which the "pollutants" are contained are moved from the covered "auto" to the place where they are finally delivered, disposed of or abandoned by the "insured".

Paragraph **a.** above does not apply to fuels, lubricants, fluids, exhaust gases or other similar "pollutants" that are needed for or result from the normal electrical, hydraulic or mechanical functioning of the covered "auto" or its parts, if the "pollutants" escape, seep, migrate, or are discharged, dispersed or released directly from an "auto" part designed by its manufacturer to hold, store, receive or dispose of such "pollutants".

Paragraphs **b.** and **c.** above do not apply to "accidents" that occur away from premises owned by or rented to an "insured" with respect to "pollutants" not in or upon a covered "auto" if:

(1) The "pollutants" or any property in which the "pollutants" are contained are upset, overturned or damaged as a result of the maintenance or use of a covered "auto"; and

(2) The discharge, dispersal, seepage, migration, release or escape of the "pollutants" is caused directly by such upset, overturn or damage.

E. "Customer's auto" means a customer's land motor vehicle, "trailer" or semitrailer. It also includes any "customer's auto" while left with you for service, repair, storage or safekeeping. Customers include your "employees", and members of their households who pay for services performed.

F. "Diminution in value" means the actual or perceived loss in market value or resale value which results from a direct and accidental "loss".

G. "Employee" includes a "leased worker". "Employee" does not include a "temporary worker".

H. "Garage operations" means the ownership, maintenance or use of locations for garage business and that portion of the roads or other accesses that adjoin these locations. "Garage operations" includes the ownership, maintenance or use of the "autos" indicated in Section I of this Coverage Form as covered "autos". "Garage operations" also include all operations necessary or incidental to a garage business.

I. "Insured" means any person or organization qualifying as an insured in the Who Is an Insured provision of the applicable coverage. Except with respect to the Limit of Insurance, the coverage afforded applies separately to each insured who is seeking coverage or against whom a claim or "suit" is brought.

J. "Insured contract" means:

1. A lease of premises;

2. A sidetrack agreement;

3. Any easement or license agreement, except in connection with construction or demolition operations on or within 50 feet of a railroad;

4. An obligation, as required by ordinance, to indemnify a municipality, except in connection with work for a municipality;

5. That part of any other contract or agreement pertaining to your garage business (including an indemnification of a municipality in connection with work performed for a municipality) under which you assume the tort liability of another to pay for "bodily injury" or "property damage" to a third party or organization. Tort liability means a liability that would be imposed by law in the absence of any contract or agreement;

6. An elevator maintenance agreement;

7. That part of any contract or agreement entered into, as part of your garage business, pertaining to the rental or lease, by you or any of your "employees", of any "auto". However, such contract or agreement shall not be considered an "insured contract" to the extent that it obligates you or any of your "employees" to pay "property damage" to any "auto" rented or leased by you or any of your "employees".

An "insured contract" does not include that part of any contract or agreement:

1. That indemnifies an architect, engineer or surveyor for injury or damage arising out of:

a. Preparing, approving or failing to prepare or approve maps, drawings, opinions, reports, surveys, change orders, designs or specifications; or

b. Giving directions or instructions, or failing to give them, if that is the primary cause of the injury or damage.

2. That indemnifies any person or organization for damage by fire to premises rented or loaned to you.

3. That pertains to the loan, lease or rental of an "auto", to you or any of your "employees" if the "auto" is loaned, leased or rented with a driver.

4. That holds a person or organization engaged in the business of transporting property by "auto" for hire harmless for your use of a covered "auto" over a route or territory that person or organization is authorized to serve by public authority.

5. That indemnifies a railroad for "bodily injury" or "property damage" arising out of construction or demolition operations, within 50 feet of any railroad property and affecting any railroad bridge or trestle, tracks, roadbeds, tunnel, underpass or crossing.

K. "Leased worker" means a person leased to you by a labor leasing firm under an agreement between you and the labor leasing firm, to perform duties related to the conduct of your business. "Leased worker" does not include a "temporary worker".

L. "Loss" means direct and accidental loss or damage. But for Garagekeepers Coverage only, "loss" also includes any resulting loss of use.

M. "Pollutants" means any solid, liquid, gaseous or thermal irritant or contaminant, including smoke, vapor, soot, fumes, acids, alkalis, chemicals and waste. Waste includes materials to be recycled, reconditioned or reclaimed.

N. "Products" includes:

a. The goods or products you made or sold in a garage business; and

b. The providing of or failure to provide warnings or instructions.

O. "Property damage" means damage to or loss of use of tangible property.

P. "Suit" means a civil proceeding in which:

1. Damages because of "bodily injury" or "property damage"; or

2. A "covered pollution cost or expense",

to which this insurance applies, are claimed.

"Suit" includes:

a. An arbitration proceeding in which such damages or "covered pollution costs or expenses" are claimed and to which the "insured" must submit or does submit with our consent; or

b. Any other alternative dispute resolution proceeding in which such damages or "covered pollution costs or expenses" are claimed and to which the insured submits with our consent.

Q. "Temporary worker" means a person who is furnished to you to substitute for a permanent "employee" on leave or to meet seasonal or short-term workload conditions.

R. "Trailer" includes semitrailer.

S. "Work you performed" includes:

a. Work that someone performed on your behalf; and

b. The providing of or failure to provide warnings or instructions.

 CA 00 05 10 01 ☐

COMMERCIAL AUTO
CA 00 12 10 01

TRUCKERS COVERAGE FORM

Various provisions in this policy restrict coverage. Read the entire policy carefully to determine rights, duties and what is and is not covered.

Throughout this policy the words "you" and "your" refer to the Named Insured shown in the Declarations. The words "we", "us" and "our" refer to the Company providing this insurance.

Other words and phrases that appear in quotation marks have special meaning. Refer to Section **VI** – Definitions.

SECTION I – COVERED AUTOS

Item Two of the Declarations shows the "autos" that are covered "autos" for each of your coverages. The following numerical symbols describe the "autos" that may be covered "autos". The symbols entered next to a coverage on the Declarations designate the only "autos" that are covered "autos".

A. Description Of Covered Auto Designation Symbols

Symbol		Description Of Covered Auto Designation Symbols
41	Any "Autos"	
42	Owned "Autos" Only	Only the "autos" you own (and for Liability Coverage any "trailers" you don't own while connected to a power unit you own). This includes those "autos" you acquire ownership of after the policy begins.
43	Owned Commercial "Autos" Only	Only those trucks, tractors and "trailers" you own (and for Liability Coverage any "trailers" you don't own while connected to a power unit you own). This includes those trucks, tractors and "trailers" you acquire ownership of after the policy begins.
44	Owned "Autos" Subject To No-Fault	Only those "autos" you own that are required to have No-Fault benefits in the state where they are licensed or principally garaged. This includes those "autos" you acquire ownership of after the policy begins provided they are subject to the No-Fault law in the state where they are licensed or principally garaged.
45	Owned "Autos" Subject To A Compulsory Uninsured Motorists Law	Only those "autos" you own that, because of the law in the state where they are licensed or principally garaged, are required to have and cannot reject Uninsured Motorists Coverage. This includes those "autos" you acquire ownership of after the policy begins provided they are subject to the same state uninsured motorists requirement.
46	Specifically Described "Autos"	Only those "autos" described in Item Three of the Declarations for which a premium charge is shown (and for Liability Coverage any "trailers" you don't own while attached to any power unit described in Item Three).
47	Hired "Autos" Only	Only those "autos" you lease, hire, rent or borrow. This does not include any "private passenger type auto" you lease, hire, rent or borrow from any member of your household, any of your "employees", partners (if you are a partnership), members (if you are a limited liability company), or agents or members of their households.
48	"Trailers" In Your Possession Under A Written Trailer Or Equipment Interchange Agreement	Only those "trailers" you do not own while in your possession under a written "trailer" or equipment interchange agreement in which you assume liability for "loss" to the "trailers" while in your possession.

Symbol		Description Of Covered Auto Designation Symbols
49	Your "Trailers" In The Posses-sion Of Anyone Else Under A Written Trailer Interchange Agreement	Only those "trailers" you own or hire while in the possession of anyone else under a written "trailer" interchange agreement. When Symbol "49" is entered next to a Physical Damage Coverage in Item Two of the Declarations, the Physical Damage Coverage exclusion relating to "loss" to a "trailer" in the possession of anyone else does not apply to that coverage.
50	Nonowned "Autos" Only	Only those "autos" you do not own, lease, hire, rent or borrow that are used in connection with your business. This includes "private passenger type autos" owned by your "employees", partners (if you are a partnership), members (if you are a limited liability company), or members of their households but only while used in your business or your personal affairs.

B. **Owned Autos You Acquire After The Policy Begins**

1. If Symbols **41, 42, 43, 44** or **45** are entered next to a coverage in Item Two of the Declarations, then you have coverage for "autos" that you acquire of the type described for the remainder of the policy period.

2. But, if Symbol **46** is entered next to a coverage in Item Two of the Declarations, an "auto" you acquire will be a covered "auto" for that coverage only if:

    a. We already cover all "autos" that you own for that coverage or it replaces an "auto" you previously owned that had that coverage; and

    b. You tell us within 30 days after you acquire it that you want us to cover it for that coverage.

C. **Certain Trailers, Mobile Equipment And Temporary Substitute Autos**

If Liability Coverage is provided by this Coverage Form, the following types of vehicles are also covered "autos" for Liability Coverage:

1. "Trailers" with a load capacity of 2,000 pounds or less designed primarily for travel on public roads.

2. "Mobile equipment" while being carried or towed by a covered "auto".

3. Any "auto" you do not own while used with the permission of its owner as a temporary substitute for a covered "auto" you own that is out of service because of its:

    a. Breakdown;

    b. Repair;

    c. Servicing;

    d. "Loss"; or

    e. Destruction.

SECTION II – LIABILITY COVERAGE

A. **Coverage**

We will pay all sums an "insured" legally must pay as damages because of "bodily injury" or "property damage" to which this insurance applies, caused by an "accident" and resulting from the ownership, maintenance or use of a covered "auto".

We will also pay all sums an "insured" legally must pay as a "covered pollution cost or expense" to which this insurance applies, caused by an "accident" and resulting from the ownership, maintenance or use of covered "autos". However, we will only pay for the "covered pollution cost or expense" if there is either "bodily injury" or "property damage" to which this insurance applies that is caused by the same "accident".

We have the right and duty to defend any "insured" against a "suit" asking for such damages or a "covered pollution cost or expense". However, we have no duty to defend any "insured" against a "suit" seeking damages for "bodily injury" or "property damage" or a "covered pollution cost or expense" to which this insurance does not apply. We may investigate and settle any claim or "suit" as we consider appropriate. Our duty to defend or settle ends when the Liability Coverage Limit of Insurance has been exhausted by payment of judgments or settlements.

1. **Who Is An Insured**

    The following are "insureds":

    a. You for any covered "auto".

    b. Anyone else while using with your permission a covered "auto" you own, hire or borrow except:

        (1) The owner or anyone else from whom you hire or borrow a covered "private passenger type auto".

 CA 00 12 10 01 □

(2) Your "employee" or agent if the covered "auto" is a "private passenger type auto" and is owned by that "employee" or agent or a member of his or her household.

(3) Someone using a covered "auto" while he or she is working in a business of selling, servicing, repairing, parking or storing "autos" unless that business is yours.

(4) Anyone other than your "employees", partners (if you are a partnership), members (if you are a limited liability company), a lessee or borrower or any of their "employees", while moving property to or from a covered "auto".

(5) A partner (if you are a partnership), or a member (if you are a limited liability company), for a covered "private passenger type auto" owned by him or her or a member of his or her household.

c. The owner or anyone else from whom you hire or borrow a covered "auto" that is a "trailer" while the "trailer" is connected to another covered "auto" that is a power unit, or, if not connected:

(1) Is being used exclusively in your business as a "trucker"; and

(2) Is being used pursuant to operating rights granted to you by a public authority.

d. The owner or anyone else from whom you hire or borrow a covered "auto" that is not a "trailer" while the covered "auto":

(1) Is being used exclusively in your business as a "trucker"; and

(2) Is being used pursuant to operating rights granted to you by a public authority.

e. Anyone liable for the conduct of an "insured" described above but only to the extent of that liability.

However, none of the following is an "insured":

a. Any "trucker" or his or her agents or "employees", other than you and your "employees":

(1) If the "trucker" is subject to motor carrier insurance requirements and meets them by a means other than "auto" liability insurance.

(2) If the "trucker" is not insured for hired "autos" under an "auto" liability insurance form that insures on a primary basis the owners of the "autos" and their agents and "employees" while the "autos" are being used exclusively in the "truckers" business and pursuant to operating rights granted to the "trucker" by a public authority.

b. Any rail, water or air carrier or its "employees" or agents, other than you and your "employees", for a "trailer" if "bodily injury" or "property damage" occurs while the "trailer" is detached from a covered "auto" you are using and:

(1) Is being transported by the carrier; or

(2) Is being loaded on or unloaded from any unit of transportation by the carrier.

2. Coverage Extensions

a. Supplementary Payments

In addition to the Limit of Insurance, we will pay for the "insured":

(1) All expenses we incur.

(2) Up to $2,000 for the cost of bail bonds (including bonds for related traffic law violations) required because of an "accident" we cover. We do not have to furnish these bonds.

(3) The cost of bonds to release attachments in any "suit" against the "insured" we defend, but only for bond amounts within our Limit of Insurance.

(4) All reasonable expenses incurred by the "insured" at our request, including actual loss of earnings up to $250 a day because of time off from work.

(5) All costs taxed against the "insured" in any "suit" against the "insured" we defend.

(6) All interest on the full amount of any judgment that accrues after entry of the judgment in any "suit" against the "insured" we defend; but our duty to pay interest ends when we have paid, offered to pay or deposited in court the part of the judgment that is within our Limit of Insurance.

b. **Out-Of-State Coverage Extensions**

While a covered "auto" is away from the state where it is licensed we will:

(1) Increase the Limit of Insurance for Liability Coverage to meet the limit specified by a compulsory or financial responsibility law of the jurisdiction where the covered "auto" is being used. This extension does not apply to the limit or limits specified by any law governing motor carriers of passengers or property.

(2) Provide the minimum amounts and types of other coverages, such as no-fault, required of out-of-state vehicles by the jurisdiction where the covered "auto" is being used.

We will not pay anyone more than once for the same elements of loss because of these extensions.

B. **Exclusions**

This insurance does not apply to any of the following:

1. **Expected Or Intended Injury**

"Bodily injury" or "property damage" expected or intended from the standpoint of the "insured".

2. **Contractual**

Liability assumed under any contract or agreement. But this exclusion does not apply to liability for damages:

a. Assumed in a contract or agreement that is an "insured contract" provided the "bodily injury" or "property damage" occurs subsequent to the execution of the contract or agreement; or

b. That the "insured" would have in the absence of the contract or agreement.

3. **Workers' Compensation**

Any obligation for which the "insured" or the "insured's" insurer may be held liable under any workers' compensation, disability benefits or unemployment compensation law or any similar law.

4. **Employee Indemnification And Employer's Liability**

"Bodily injury" to:

a. An "employee" of the "insured" arising out of and in the course of:

(1) Employment by the "insured"; or

(2) Performing the duties related to the conduct of the "insured's" business; or

b. The spouse, child, parent, brother or sister of that "employee" as a consequence of Paragraph **a.** above.

This exclusion applies:

(1) Whether the "insured" may be liable as an employer or in any other capacity; and

(2) To any obligation to share damages with or repay someone else who must pay damages because of the injury.

But this exclusion does not apply to "bodily injury" to domestic "employees" not entitled to workers' compensation benefits or to liability assumed by the "insured" under an "insured contract". For the purposes of the Coverage Form, a domestic "employee" is a person engaged in household or domestic work performed principally in connection with a residence premises.

5. **Fellow Employee**

"Bodily injury" to any fellow "employee" of the "insured" arising out of and in the course of the fellow "employee's" employment or while performing duties related to the conduct of your business.

6. **Care, Custody Or Control**

"Property damage" to or "covered pollution cost or expense" involving property owned or transported by the "insured" or in the "insured's" care, custody or control. But this exclusion does not apply to liability assumed under a sidetrack agreement.

7. **Handling Of Property**

"Bodily injury" or "property damage" resulting from the handling of property:

a. Before it is moved from the place where it is accepted by the "insured" for movement into or onto the covered "auto"; or

b. After it is moved from the covered "auto" to the place where it is finally delivered by the "insured".

8. **Movement Of Property By Mechanical Device**

"Bodily injury" or "property damage" resulting from the movement of property by a mechanical device (other than a hand truck) unless the device is attached to the covered "auto".

9. **Operations**

"Bodily injury" or "property damage" arising out of the operation of any equipment listed in Paragraphs **6.b.** and **6.c.** of the definition of "mobile equipment".

 CA 00 12 10 01 □

10. Completed Operations

"Bodily injury" or "property damage" arising out of your work after that work has been completed or abandoned.

In the exclusion, your work means:

a. Work or operations performed by you or on your behalf; and

b. Materials, parts or equipment furnished in connection with such work or operations.

Your work includes warranties or representations made at any time with respect to the fitness, quality, durability or performance of any of the items included in Paragraphs **a.** or **b.** above.

Your work will be deemed completed at the earliest of the following times:

(1) When all of the work called for in your contract has been completed.

(2) When all of the work to be done at the site has been completed if your contract calls for work at more than one site.

(3) When that part of the work done at a job site has been put to its intended use by any person or organization other than another contractor or subcontractor working on the same project.

Work that may need service, maintenance, correction, repair or replacement, but which is otherwise complete, will be treated as completed.

11. Pollution

"Bodily injury" or "property damage" arising out of the actual, alleged or threatened discharge, dispersal, seepage, migration, release or escape of "pollutants":

a. That are, or that are contained in any property that is:

(1) Being transported or towed by, handled, or handled for movement into, onto or from, the covered "auto";

(2) Otherwise in the course of transit by or on behalf of the "insured"; or

(3) Being stored, disposed of, treated or processed in or upon the covered "auto";

b. Before the "pollutants" or any property in which the "pollutants" are contained are moved from the place where they are accepted by the "insured" for movement into or onto the covered "auto"; or

c. After the "pollutants" or any property in which the "pollutants" are contained are moved from the covered "auto" to the place where they are finally delivered, disposed of or abandoned by the "insured".

Paragraph **a.** above does not apply to fuels, lubricants, fluids, exhaust gases or other similar "pollutants" that are needed for or result from the normal electrical, hydraulic or mechanical functioning of the covered "auto" or its parts, if:

(1) The "pollutants" escape, seep, migrate, or are discharged, dispersed or released directly from an "auto" part designed by its manufacturer to hold, store, receive or dispose of such "pollutants"; and

(2) The "bodily injury", "property damage" or "covered pollution cost or expense" does not arise out of the operation of any equipment listed in Paragraphs **6.b.** and **6.c.** of the definition of "mobile equipment".

Paragraphs **b.** and **c.** above of this exclusion do not apply to "accidents" that occur away from premises owned by or rented to an "insured" with respect to "pollutants" not in or upon a covered "auto" if:

(1) The "pollutants" or any property in which the "pollutants" are contained are upset, overturned or damaged as a result of the maintenance or use of a covered "auto"; and

(2) The discharge, dispersal, seepage, migration, release or escape of the "pollutants" is caused directly by such upset, overturn or damage.

12. War

"Bodily injury" or "property damage" due to war, whether or not declared, or any act or condition incident to war. War includes civil war, insurrection, rebellion or revolution. This exclusion applies only to liability assumed under a contract or agreement.

13. Racing

Covered "autos" while used in any professional or organized racing or demolition contest or stunting activity, or while practicing for such contest or activity. This insurance also does not apply while that covered "auto" is being prepared for such a contest or activity.

C. Limit Of Insurance

Regardless of the number of covered "autos", "insureds", premiums paid, claims made or vehicles involved in the "accident", the most we will pay for the total of all damages and "covered pollution cost or expense" combined, resulting from any one "accident" is the Limit of Insurance for Liability Coverage shown in the Declarations.

All "bodily injury", "property damage" and "covered pollution cost or expense" resulting from continuous or repeated exposure to substantially the same conditions will be considered as resulting from one "accident".

No one will be entitled to receive duplicate payments for the same elements of "loss" under this Coverage Form and any Medical Payments Coverage endorsement, Uninsured Motorists Coverage endorsement or Underinsured Motorists Coverage endorsement attached to this Coverage Part.

SECTION III – TRAILER INTERCHANGE COVERAGE

A. Coverage

1. We will pay all sums you legally must pay as damages because of "loss" to a "trailer" you don't own or its equipment under:

   a. Comprehensive Coverage

   From any cause except:

   (1) The "trailer's" collision with another object; or

   (2) The "trailer's" overturn.

   b. Specified Causes Of Loss Coverage

   Caused by:

   (1) Fire, lightning or explosion;

   (2) Theft;

   (3) Windstorm, hail or earthquake;

   (4) Flood;

   (5) Mischief or vandalism; or

   (6) The sinking, burning, collision or derailment of any conveyance transporting the "trailer".

   c. Collision Coverage

   Caused by:

   (1) The "trailer's" collision with another object; or

   (2) The "trailer's" overturn.

2. We have the right and duty to defend any "insured" against a "suit" asking for these damages. However, we have no duty to defend any "insured" against a "suit" seeking damages for any "loss" to which this insurance does not apply. We may investigate and settle any claim or "suit" as we consider appropriate. Our duty to defend or settle ends for a coverage when the Limit of Insurance for that coverage has been exhausted by payment of judgments or settlements.

3. **Coverage Extensions**

   The following applies as Supplementary Payments. In addition to the Limit of Insurance, we will pay for you:

   a. All expenses we incur.

   b. The cost of bonds to release attachments, but only for bond amounts within our Limit of Insurance.

   c. All reasonable expenses incurred at our request, including actual loss of earnings up to $250 a day because of time off from work.

   d. All costs taxed against the "insured" in any "suit" against the "insured" we defend.

   e. All interest on the full amount of any judgment that accrues after entry of the judgment; but our duty to pay interest ends when we have paid, offered to pay, or deposited in court the part of the judgment that is within our Limit of Insurance.

B. Exclusions

1. We will not pay for "loss" caused by or resulting from any of the following. Such "loss" is excluded regardless of any other cause or event that contributes concurrently or in any sequence to the "loss".

   a. Nuclear Hazard

   (1) The explosion of any weapon employing atomic fission or fusion; or

   (2) Nuclear reaction or radiation, or radioactive contamination, however caused.

   b. War Or Military Action

   (1) War, including undeclared or civil war;

   (2) Warlike action by a military force, including action in hindering or defending against an actual or expected attack, by any government, sovereign or other authority using military personnel or other agents; or

   (3) Insurrection, rebellion, revolution, usurped power or action taken by governmental authority in hindering or defending against any of these.

2. We will not pay for loss of use.

3. We will not pay for "loss" caused by or resulting from any of the following unless caused by other "loss" that is covered by this insurance:

   a. Wear and tear, freezing, mechanical or electrical breakdown.

   b. Blowouts, punctures or other road damage to tires.

C. Limit Of Insurance And Deductible

The most we will pay for "loss" to any one "trailer" is the least of the following amounts minus any applicable deductible shown in the Declarations:

1. The actual cash value of the damaged or stolen property at the time of the "loss".

2. The cost of repairing or replacing the damaged or stolen property with other property of like kind and quality.

3. The Limit of Insurance shown in the Declarations.

SECTION IV – PHYSICAL DAMAGE COVERAGE

A. Coverage

1. We will pay for "loss" to a covered "auto" or its equipment under:

   a. Comprehensive Coverage

   From any cause except:

   (1) The covered "auto's" collision with another object; or

   (2) The covered "auto's" overturn.

   b. Specified Causes Of Loss Coverage

   Caused by:

   (1) Fire, lightning or explosion;

   (2) Theft;

   (3) Windstorm, hail or earthquake;

   (4) Flood;

   (5) Mischief or vandalism; or

   (6) The sinking, burning, collision or derailment of any conveyance transporting the covered "auto".

   c. Collision Coverage

   Caused by:

   (1) The covered "auto's" collision with another object; or

   (2) The covered "auto's" overturn.

2. **Towing – Private Passenger Autos**

   We will pay up to the limit shown in the Declarations for towing and labor costs incurred each time a covered "auto" of the "private passenger type" is disabled. However, the labor must be performed at the place of disablement.

3. **Glass Breakage – Hitting A Bird Or Animal – Falling Objects Or Missiles**

   If you carry Comprehensive Coverage for the damaged covered "auto", we will pay for the following under Comprehensive Coverage:

   a. Glass breakage;

b. "Loss" caused by hitting a bird or animal; and

c. "Loss" caused by falling objects or missiles.

However, you have the option of having glass breakage caused by a covered "auto's" collision or overturn considered a "loss" under Collision Coverage.

4. **Coverage Extension**

   a. Transportation Expenses

   We will also pay up to $20 per day to a maximum of $600 for temporary transportation expense incurred by you because of the total theft of a covered "auto" of the "private passenger type". We will pay only for those covered "autos" for which you carry either Comprehensive or Specified Causes of Loss Coverage. We will pay for temporary transportation expenses incurred during the period beginning 48 hours after the theft and ending, regardless of the policy's expiration, when the covered "auto" is returned to use or we pay for its "loss".

   b. Loss Of Use Expenses

   For Hired Auto Physical Damage, we will pay expenses for which an "insured" becomes legally responsible to pay for loss of use of a vehicle rented or hired without a driver, under a written rental contract or agreement. We will pay for loss of use expenses if caused by:

   (1) Other than collision only if the Declarations indicate that Comprehensive Coverage is provided for any covered "auto";

   (2) Specified Causes Of Loss only if the Declarations indicate that Specified Causes Of Loss Coverage is provided for any covered "auto"; or

   (3) Collision only if the Declarations indicate that Collision Coverage is provided for any covered "auto".

   However, the most we will pay for any expenses for loss of use is $20 per day, to a maximum of $600.

B. Exclusions

1. We will not pay for "loss" caused by or resulting from any of the following. Such "loss" is excluded regardless of any other cause or event that contributes concurrently or in any sequence to the "loss".

   a. Nuclear Hazard

   (1) The explosion of any weapon employing atomic fission or fusion; or

   (2) Nuclear reaction or radiation, or radioactive contamination, however caused.

b. **War Or Military Action**

   (1) War, including undeclared or civil war;

   (2) Warlike action by a military force, including action in hindering or defending against an actual or expected attack, by any government, sovereign or other authority using military personnel or other agents; or

   (3) Insurrection, rebellion, revolution, usurped power or action taken by governmental authority in hindering or defending against any of these.

2. We will not pay for "loss" to any of the following:

  a. Any covered "auto" while in anyone else's possession under a written trailer interchange agreement. But this exclusion does not apply to a loss payee; however, if we pay the loss payee, you must reimburse us for our payment.

  b. Any covered "auto" while used in any professional or organized racing or demolition contest or stunting activity, or while practicing for such contest or activity. We will also not pay for "loss" to any covered "auto" while that covered "auto" is being prepared for any such contest or activity.

  c. Tapes, records, discs or other similar audio, visual or data electronic devices designed for use with audio, visual or data electronic equipment.

  d. Any device designed or used to detect speed measuring equipment such as radar or laser detectors and any jamming apparatus intended to elude or disrupt speed measurement equipment.

  e. Any electronic equipment, without regard to whether this equipment is permanently installed, that receives or transmits audio, visual or data signals and that is not designed solely for the reproduction of sound.

  f. Any accessories used with the electronic equipment described in Paragraph e. above.

Exclusions 2.e. and 2.f. do not apply to:

  a. Equipment designed solely for the reproduction of sound and accessories used with such equipment, provided such equipment is permanently installed in the covered "auto" at the time of the "loss" or such equipment is removable from a housing unit which is permanently installed in the covered "auto" at the time of the "loss", and such equipment is designed to be solely operated by use of the power from the "auto's" electrical system, in or upon the covered "auto"; or

  b. Any other electronic equipment that is:

   (1) Necessary for the normal operation of the covered "auto" or the monitoring of the covered "auto's" operating system; or

   (2) An integral part of the same unit housing any sound reproducing equipment described in a. above and permanently installed in the opening of the dash or console of the covered "auto" normally used by the manufacturer for installation of a radio.

3. We will not pay for "loss" caused by or resulting from any of the following unless caused by other "loss" that is covered by this insurance:

  a. Wear and tear, freezing, mechanical or electrical breakdown.

  b. Blowouts, punctures or other road damage to tires.

4. We will not pay for "loss" to a covered "auto" due to "diminution in value".

C. **Limits Of Insurance**

1. The most we will pay for "loss" in any one "accident" is the lesser of:

  a. The actual cash value of the damaged or stolen property as of the time of "loss"; or

  b. The cost of repairing or replacing the damaged or stolen property with other property of like kind and quality.

2. An adjustment for depreciation and physical condition will be made in determining actual cash value in the event of a total "loss".

3. If a repair or replacement results in better than like kind or quality, we will not pay for the amount of the betterment.

CA 00 12 10 01 □

D. Deductible

For each covered "auto", our obligation to pay for, repair, return or replace damaged or stolen property will be reduced by the applicable deductible shown in the Declarations. Any Comprehensive Coverage deductible shown in the Declarations does not apply to "loss" caused by fire or lightning.

SECTION V – TRUCKERS CONDITIONS

The following conditions apply in addition to the Common Policy Conditions:

A. Loss Conditions

1. **Appraisal For Physical Damage Loss**

   If you and we disagree on the amount of "loss", either may demand an appraisal of the "loss". In this event, each party will select a competent appraiser. The two appraisers will select a competent and impartial umpire. The appraisers will state separately the actual cash value and amount of "loss". If they fail to agree, they will submit their differences to the umpire. A decision agreed to by any two will be binding. Each party will:

   a. Pay its chosen appraiser; and

   b. Bear the other expenses of the appraisal and umpire equally.

   If we submit to an appraisal, we will still retain our right to deny the claim.

2. **Duties In The Event Of Accident, Claim, Suit Or Loss**

   We have no duty to provide coverage under this policy unless there has been full compliance with the following duties:

   a. In the event of "accident", claim, "suit" or "loss", you must give us or our authorized representative prompt notice of the accident or "loss". Include:

   (1) How, when and where the "accident" or "loss" occurred;

   (2) The "insured's" name and address; and

   (3) To the extent possible, the names and addresses of any injured persons and witnesses.

   b. Additionally, you and any other involved "insured" must:

   (1) Assume no obligation, make no payment or incur no expense without our consent, except at the "insured's" own cost.

   (2) Immediately send us copies of any request, demand, order, notice, summons or legal paper received concerning the claim or "suit".

   (3) Cooperate with us in the investigation or settlement of the claim or defense against the "suit".

   (4) Authorize us to obtain medical records or other pertinent information.

   (5) Submit to examination at our expense, by physicians of our choice, as often as we reasonably require.

   c. If there is a "loss" to a covered "auto" or its equipment you must also do the following:

   (1) Promptly notify the police if the covered "auto" or any of its equipment is stolen.

   (2) Take all reasonable steps to protect the covered "auto" from further damage. Also keep a record of your expenses for consideration in the settlement of the claim.

   (3) Permit us to inspect the covered "auto" and records proving the "loss" before its repair or disposition.

   (4) Agree to examination under oath at our request and give us a signed statement of your answers.

3. **Legal Action Against Us**

   No one may bring a legal action against us under this Coverage Form until:

   a. There has been full compliance with all the terms of this Coverage Form; and

   b. Under Liability Coverage, we agree in writing that the "insured" has an obligation to pay or until the amount of that obligation has finally been determined by judgment after trial. No one has the right under this policy to bring us into an action to determine the "insured's" liability.

4. **Loss Payment – Physical Damage Coverages**

   At our option we may:

   a. Pay for, repair or replace damaged or stolen property;

   b. Return the stolen property at our expense. We will pay for any damage that results to the "auto" from the theft; or

   c. Take all or any part of the damaged or stolen property at an agreed or appraised value.

   If we pay for the "loss", our payment will include the applicable sales tax for the damaged or stolen property.

5. Transfer Of Rights Of Recovery Against Others To Us

If any person or organization to or for whom we make payment under this Coverage Form has rights to recover damages from another, those rights are transferred to us. That person or organization must do everything necessary to secure our rights and must do nothing after "accident" or "loss" to impair them.

B. General Conditions

1. Bankruptcy

Bankruptcy or insolvency of the "insured" or the "insured's" estate will not relieve us of any obligation under this Coverage Form.

2. Concealment, Misrepresentation Or Fraud

This Coverage Form is void in any case of fraud by you at any time as it relates to this Coverage Form. It is also void if you or any other "insured", at any time, intentionally conceal or misrepresent a material fact concerning:

a. This Coverage Form;

b. The covered "auto";

c. Your interest in the covered "auto"; or

d. A claim under this Coverage Form.

3. Liberalization

If we revise this Coverage Form to provide more coverage without additional premium charge, your policy will automatically provide the additional coverage as of the day the revision is effective in your state.

4. No Benefit To Bailee – Physical Damage Coverages

We will not recognize any assignment or grant any coverage for the benefit of any person or organization holding, storing or transporting property for a fee regardless of any other provision of this Coverage Form.

5. Other Insurance – Primary And Excess Insurance Provisions

a. This Coverage Form's Liability Coverage is primary for any covered "auto" while hired or borrowed by you and used exclusively in your business as a "trucker" and pursuant to operating rights granted to you by a public authority. This Coverage Form's Liability Coverage is excess over any other collectible insurance for any covered "auto" while hired or borrowed from you by another "trucker". However, while a covered "auto" which is a "trailer" is connected to a power unit, this Coverage Form's Liability Coverage is:

(1) On the same basis, primary or excess, as for the power unit if the power unit is a covered "auto".

(2) Excess if the power unit is not a covered "auto".

b. Any Trailer Interchange Coverage provided by this Coverage Form is primary for any covered "auto".

c. Except as provided in Paragraphs **a.** and **b.** above, this Coverage Form provides primary insurance for any covered "auto" you own and excess insurance for any covered "auto" you don't own.

d. For Hired Auto Physical Damage Coverage, any covered "auto" you lease, hire, rent or borrow is deemed to be a covered "auto" you own. However, any "auto" that is leased, hired, rented or borrowed with a driver is not a covered "auto".

e. Regardless of the provisions of Paragraphs **a.**, **b.** and **c.** above, this Coverage Form's Liability Coverage is primary for any liability assumed under an "insured contract".

f. When this Coverage Form and any other Coverage Form or policy covers on the same basis, either excess or primary, we will pay only our share. Our share is the proportion that the Limit of Insurance of our Coverage Form bears to the total of the limits of all the Coverage Forms and policies covering on the same basis.

6. Premium Audit

a. The estimated premium for this Coverage Form is based on the exposures you told us you have when this policy began. We will compute the final premium due when we determine your actual exposures. The estimated total premium will be credited against the final premium due and the first Named Insured will be billed for the balance, if any. The due date for the final premium or retrospective premium is the date shown as the due date on the bill. If the estimated total premium exceeds the final premium due, the first Named Insured will get a refund.

b. If this policy is issued for more than one year, the premium for this Coverage Form will be computed annually based on our rates or premiums in effect at the beginning of each year of the policy.

7. Policy Period, Coverage Territory

Under this Coverage Form, we cover "accidents" and "losses" occurring:

a. During the policy period shown in the Declarations; and

© ISO Properties, Inc., 2000

CA 00 12 10 01

b. Within the coverage territory.

The coverage territory is:

a. The United States of America;

b. The territories and possessions of the United States of America;

c. Puerto Rico;

d. Canada; and

e. Anywhere in the world if:

(1) A covered "auto" of the "private passenger" type is leased, hired, rented or borrowed without a driver for a period of 30 days or less; and

(2) The "insured's" responsibility to pay damages is determined in a "suit" on the merits, in the United States of America, the territories and possessions of the United States of America, Puerto Rico, or Canada or in a settlement we agree to.

We also cover "loss" to, or "accidents" involving, a covered "auto" while being transported between any of these places.

8. **Two Or More Coverage Forms Or Policies Issued By Us**

If this Coverage Form and any other Coverage Form or policy issued to you by us or any company affiliated with us apply to the same "accident", the aggregate maximum Limit of Insurance under all the Coverage Forms or policies shall not exceed the highest applicable Limit of Insurance under any one Coverage Form or policy. This condition does not apply to any Coverage Form or policy issued by us or an affiliated company specifically to apply as excess insurance over this Coverage Form.

SECTION VI – DEFINITIONS

A. "Accident" includes continuous or repeated exposure to the same conditions resulting in "bodily injury" or "property damage".

B. "Auto" means a land motor vehicle, "trailer" or semitrailer designed for travel on public roads but does not include "mobile equipment".

C. "Bodily injury" means bodily injury, sickness or disease sustained by a person including death resulting from any of these.

D. "Covered pollution cost or expense" means any cost or expense arising out of:

1. Any request, demand, order or statutory or regulatory requirement; or

2. Any claim or "suit" by or on behalf of a governmental authority demanding,

that the "insured" or others test for, monitor, clean up, remove, contain, treat, detoxify or neutralize, or in any way respond to, or assess the effects of "pollutants".

"Covered pollution cost or expense" does not include any cost or expense arising out of the actual, alleged or threatened discharge, dispersal, seepage, migration, release or escape of "pollutants":

a. That are, or that are contained in any property that is:

(1) Being transported or towed by, handled, or handled for movement into, onto or from the covered "auto";

(2) Otherwise in the course of transit by or on behalf of the "insured";

(3) Being stored, disposed of, treated or processed in or upon the covered "auto";

b. Before the "pollutants" or any property in which the "pollutants" are contained are moved from the place where they are accepted by the "insured" for movement into or onto the covered "auto"; or

c. After the "pollutants" or any property in which the "pollutants" are contained are moved from the covered "auto" to the place where they are finally delivered, disposed of or abandoned by the "insured".

Paragraph a. above does not apply to fuels, lubricants, fluids, exhaust gases or other similar "pollutants" that are needed for or result from the normal electrical, hydraulic or mechanical functioning of the covered "auto" or its parts, if:

(1) The "pollutants" escape, seep, migrate, or are discharged, dispersed or released directly from an "auto" part designed by its manufacturer to hold, store, receive or dispose of such "pollutants"; and

(2) The "bodily injury", "property damage" or "covered pollution cost or expense" does not arise out of the operation of any equipment listed in Paragraphs **6.b.** or **6.c.** of the definition of "mobile equipment".

Paragraphs b. and c. above do not apply to "accidents" that occur away from premises owned by or rented to an "insured" with respect to "pollutants" not in or upon a covered "auto" if:

(1) The "pollutants" or any property in which the "pollutants" are contained are upset, overturned or damaged as a result of the maintenance or use of a covered "auto"; and

(2) The discharge, dispersal, seepage, migration, release or escape of the "pollutants" is caused directly by such upset, overturn or damage.

E. "Diminution in value" means the actual or perceived loss in market value or resale value which results from a direct and accidental "loss".

F. "Employee" includes a "leased worker". "Employee" does not include a "temporary worker".

G. "Insured" means any person or organization qualifying as an insured in the Who Is An Insured provision of the applicable coverage. Except with respect to the Limit of Insurance, the coverage afforded applies separately to each insured who is seeking coverage or against whom a claim or "suit" is brought.

H. "Insured Contract" means:

1. A lease of premises;

2. A sidetrack agreement;

3. Any easement or license agreement, except in connection with construction or demolition operations on or within 50 feet of a railroad;

4. An obligation, as required by ordinance, to indemnify a municipality, except in connection with work for a municipality;

5. That part of any other contract or agreement pertaining to your business (including an indemnification of a municipality in connection with work performed for a municipality) under which you assume the tort liability of another to pay for "bodily injury" or "property damage" to a third party or organization. Tort liability means a liability that would be imposed by law in the absence of any contract or agreement;

6. That part of any contract or agreement, entered into, as part of your business, pertaining to the rental or lease, by you or any of your "employees", of any "auto". However, such contract or agreement shall not be considered an "insured contract" to the extent that it obligates you or any of your "employees" to pay for "property damage" to any "auto" rented or leased by you or any of your "employees".

An "insured contract" does not include that part of any contract or agreement:

a. That indemnifies a railroad for "bodily injury" or "property damage" arising out of construction or demolition operations, within 50 feet of any railroad property and affecting any railroad bridge or trestle, tracks, roadbeds, tunnel, underpass or crossing; or

b. That pertains to the loan, lease or rental of an "auto" to you or any of your "employees", if the "auto" is loaned, leased or rented with a driver; or

c. That holds a person or organization engaged in the business of transporting property by "auto" for hire harmless for your use of a covered "auto" over a route or territory that person or organization is authorized to serve by public authority.

I. "Leased worker" means a person leased to you by a labor leasing firm under an agreement between you and the labor leasing firm, to perform duties related to the conduct of your business. "Leased worker" does not include a "temporary worker".

J. "Loss" means direct and accidental loss or damage.

K. "Mobile equipment" means any of the following types of land vehicles, including any attached machinery or equipment:

1. Bulldozers, farm machinery, forklifts and other vehicles designed for use principally off public roads;

2. Vehicles maintained for use solely on or next to premises you own or rent;

3. Vehicles that travel on crawler treads;

4. Vehicles, whether self-propelled or not, maintained primarily to provide mobility to permanently mounted:

a. Power cranes, shovels, loaders, diggers or drills; or

b. Road construction or resurfacing equipment such as graders, scrapers or rollers;

5. Vehicles not described in Paragraphs **1.**, **2.**, **3.** or **4.** above that are not self-propelled and are maintained primarily to provide mobility to permanently attached equipment of the following types:

a. Air compressors, pumps and generators, including spraying, welding, building cleaning, geophysical exploration, lighting and well servicing equipment; or

b. Cherry pickers and similar devices used to raise or lower workers.

6. Vehicles not described in Paragraphs **1.**, **2.**, **3.** or **4.** above maintained primarily for purposes other than the transportation of persons or cargo. However, self-propelled vehicles with the following types of permanently attached equipment are not "mobile equipment" but will be considered "autos":

a. Equipment designed primarily for:

(1) Snow removal;

(2) Road maintenance, but not construction or resurfacing; or

(3) Street cleaning;

© ISO Properties, Inc., 2000 CA 00 12 10 01 ▢

b. Cherry pickers and similar devices mounted on automobile or truck chassis and used to raise or lower workers; and

c. Air compressors, pumps and generators, including spraying, welding, building cleaning, geophysical exploration, lighting or well servicing equipment.

L. "Pollutants" means any solid, liquid, gaseous or thermal irritant or contaminant, including smoke, vapor, soot, fumes, acids, alkalis, chemicals and waste. Waste includes materials to be recycled, reconditioned or reclaimed.

M. "Private passenger type" means a private passenger or station wagon type "auto" and includes an "auto" of the pickup or van type if not used for business purposes.

N. "Property damage" means damage to or loss of use of tangible property.

O. "Suit" means a civil proceeding in which:

1. Damages because of "bodily injury" or "property damage"; or

2. A "covered pollution cost or expense",

to which this insurance applies, are alleged.

"Suit" includes:

a. An arbitration proceeding in which such damages or "covered pollution costs or expenses" are claimed and to which the "insured" must submit or does submit with our consent; or

b. Any other alternative dispute resolution proceeding in which such damages or "covered pollution costs or expenses" are claimed and to which the "insured" submits with our consent.

P. "Trailer" includes semitrailer or a dolly used to convert a semitrailer into a trailer. But for Trailer Interchange Coverage only, "trailer" also includes a container.

Q. "Trucker" means any person or organization engaged in the business of transporting property by "auto" for hire.

R. "Temporary worker" means a person who is furnished to you to substitute for a permanent "employee" on leave or to meet seasonal or short-term workload conditions.

COMMERCIAL AUTO
CA 00 20 10 01

MOTOR CARRIER COVERAGE FORM

Various provisions in this policy restrict coverage. Read the entire policy carefully to determine rights, duties and what is and is not covered.

Throughout this policy the words "you" and "your" refer to the Named Insured shown in the Declarations. The words "we", "us" and "our" refer to the Company providing this insurance.

Other words and phrases that appear in quotation marks have special meaning. Refer to Section **VI** – Definitions.

SECTION I – COVERED AUTOS

Item Two of the Declarations shows the "autos" that are covered "autos" for each of your coverages. The following numerical symbols describe the "autos" that may be covered "autos". The symbols entered next to a coverage on the Declarations designate the only "autos" that are covered "autos".

A. Description Of Covered Auto Designation Symbols

Symbol		Description Of Covered Auto Designation Symbols
61	Any "Auto"	
62	Owned "Autos" Only	Only the "autos" you own (and for Liability Coverage any "trailers" you don't own while connected to a power unit you own). This includes those "autos" you acquire ownership of after the policy begins.
63	Owned Private Passenger Type "Autos" Only	Only the "private passenger type" "autos" you own. This includes those "private passenger type" "autos" that you acquire ownership of after the policy begins.
64	Owned Commercial "Autos" Only	Only those trucks, tractors and "trailers" you own (and for Liability Coverage any "trailers" you don't own while connected to a power unit you own). This includes those trucks, tractors and "trailers" you acquire ownership of after the policy begins.
65	Owned "Autos" Subject To No-Fault	Only those "autos" you own that are required to have No-Fault benefits in the state where they are licensed or principally garaged. This includes those "autos" you acquire ownership of after the policy begins provided they are subject to the No-Fault law in the state where they are licensed or principally garaged.
66	Owned "Autos" Subject To A Compulsory Uninsured Motorists Law	Only those "autos" you own that, because of the law in the state where they are licensed or principally garaged, are required to have and cannot reject Uninsured Motorists Coverage. This includes those "autos" you acquire ownership of after the policy begins provided they are subject to the same state uninsured motorists requirement.
67	Specifically Described "Autos"	Only those "autos" described in Item Three of the Declarations for which a premium charge is shown (and for Liability Coverage any "trailers" you don't own while attached to any power unit described in Item Three).
68	Hired "Autos" Only	Only those "autos" you lease, hire, rent or borrow. This does not include any "private passenger type" "auto" you lease, hire, rent or borrow from any member of your household, any of your "employees", partners (if you are a partnership), members (if you are a limited liability company), or agents or members of their households.
69	"Trailers" In Your Possession Under A Written Trailer Or Equipment Interchange Agreement	Only those "trailers" you do not own while in your possession under a written "trailer" or equipment interchange agreement in which you assume liability for "loss" to the "trailers" while in your possession.

Symbol		Description Of Covered Auto Designation Symbols
70	Your "Trailers" In The Possession Of Anyone Else Under A Written Trailer Interchange Agreement	Only those "trailers" you own or hire while in the possession of anyone else under a written "trailer" interchange agreement. When Symbol "70" is entered next to a Physical Damage Coverage in Item Two of the Declarations, the Physical Damage Coverage exclusion relating to "loss" to a "trailer" in the possession of anyone else does not apply to that coverage.
71	Nonowned "Autos" Only	Only those "autos" you do not own, lease, hire, rent or borrow that are used in connection with your business. This includes "private passenger type" "autos" owned by your "employees" or partners (if you are a partnership), members (if you are a limited liability company), or members of their households but only while used in your business or your personal affairs.

B. Owned Autos You Acquire After The Policy Begins

1. If Symbols **61, 62, 63, 64, 65** or **66** are entered next to a coverage in Item Two of the Declarations, then you have coverage for "autos" that you acquire of the type described for the remainder of the policy period.

2. But, if Symbol **67** is entered next to a coverage in Item Two of the Declarations, an "auto" you acquire will be a covered "auto" for that coverage only if:

   a. We already cover all "autos" that you own for that coverage or it replaces an "auto" you previously owned that had that coverage; and

   b. You tell us within 30 days after you acquire it that you want us to cover it for that coverage.

C. Certain Trailers, Mobile Equipment And Temporary Substitute Autos

If Liability Coverage is provided by this Coverage Form, the following types of vehicles are also covered "autos" for Liability Coverage:

1. "Trailers" with a load capacity of 2,000 pounds or less designed primarily for travel on public roads.

2. "Mobile equipment" while being carried or towed by a covered "auto".

3. Any "auto" you do not own while used with the permission of its owner as a temporary substitute for a covered "auto" you own that is out of service because of its:

   a. Breakdown;

   b. Repair;

   c. Servicing;

   d. "Loss"; or

   e. Destruction.

SECTION II – LIABILITY COVERAGE

A. Coverage

We will pay all sums an "insured" legally must pay as damages because of "bodily injury" or "property damage" to which this insurance applies, caused by an "accident" and resulting from the ownership, maintenance or use of a covered "auto".

We will also pay all sums an "insured" legally must pay as a "covered pollution cost or expense" to which this insurance applies, caused by an "accident" and resulting from the ownership, maintenance or use of covered "autos". However, we will only pay for the "covered pollution cost or expense" if there is either "bodily injury" or "property damage" to which this insurance applies that is caused by the same "accident".

We will have the right and duty to defend any "insured" against a "suit" asking for such damages or a "covered pollution cost or expense". However, we have no duty to defend any "insured" against a "suit" seeking damages for "bodily injury" or "property damage" or a "covered pollution cost or expense" to which this insurance does not apply. We may investigate and settle any claim or "suit" as we consider appropriate. Our duty to defend or settle ends when the Liability Coverage Limit of Insurance has been exhausted by payment of judgments or settlements.

1. **Who Is An Insured**

   The following are "insureds":

   a. You for any covered "auto".

   b. Anyone else while using with your permission a covered "auto" you own, hire or borrow except:

      (1) The owner, or any "employee", agent or driver of the owner, or anyone else from whom you hire or borrow a covered "auto".

© ISO Properties, Inc., 2000

CA 00 20 10 01 ☐

(2) Your "employee" or agent if the covered "auto" is owned by that "employee" or agent or a member of his or her household.

(3) Someone using a covered "auto" while he or she is working in a business of selling, servicing, repairing, parking or storing "autos" unless that business is yours.

(4) Anyone other than your "employees", partners (if you are a partnership), members (if you are a limited liability company), a lessee or borrower of a covered "auto" or any of their "employees", while moving property to or from a covered "auto".

(5) A partner (if you are a partnership), or member (if you are a limited liability company) for a covered "auto" owned by him or her or a member of his or her household.

c. The owner or anyone else from whom you hire or borrow a covered "auto" that is a "trailer" while the "trailer" is connected to another covered "auto" that is a power unit, or, if not connected, is being used exclusively in your business.

d. The lessor of a covered "auto" that is not a "trailer" or any "employee", agent or driver of the lessor while the "auto" is leased to you under a written agreement if the written agreement between the lessor and you does not require the lessor to hold you harmless and then only when the leased "auto" is used in your business as a "motor carrier" for hire.

e. Anyone liable for the conduct of an "insured" described above but only to the extent of that liability.

However, none of the following is an "insured":

a. Any "motor carrier" for hire or his or her agents or "employees", other than you and your "employees":

(1) If the "motor carrier" is subject to motor carrier insurance requirements and meets them by a means other than "auto" liability insurance.

(2) If the "motor carrier" is not insured for hired "autos" under an "auto" liability insurance form that insures on a primary basis the owners of the "autos" and their agents and "employees" while the "autos" are leased to that "motor carrier" and used in his or her business.

However, Paragraph **a.** above does not apply if you have leased an "auto" to the for-hire "motor carrier" under a written lease agreement in which you have held that "motor carrier" harmless.

b. Any rail, water or air carrier or its "employees" or agents, other than you and your "employees", for a "trailer" if "bodily injury" or "property damage" or a "covered pollution cost or expense" occurs while the "trailer" is detached from a covered "auto" you are using and:

(1) Is being transported by the carrier; or

(2) Is being loaded on or unloaded from any unit of transportation by the carrier.

2. Coverage Extensions

a. Supplementary Payments

In addition to the Limit of Insurance, we will pay for the "insured":

(1) All expenses we incur.

(2) Up to $2,000 for the cost of bail bonds (including bonds for related traffic law violations) required because of an "accident" we cover. We do not have to furnish these bonds.

(3) The cost of bonds to release attachments in any "suit" against the "insured" we defend, but only for bond amounts within our Limit of Insurance.

(4) All reasonable expenses incurred by the "insured" at our request, including actual loss of earnings up to $250 a day because of time off from work.

(5) All costs taxed against the "insured" in any "suit" against the "insured" we defend.

(6) All interest on the full amount of any judgment that accrues after entry of the judgment in any "suit" against the "insured" we defend; but our duty to pay interest ends when we have paid, offered to pay or deposited in court the part of the judgment that is within our Limit of Insurance.

b. Out Of State Coverage Extensions

While a covered "auto" is away from the state where it is licensed we will:

(1) Increase the Limit of Insurance for Liability Coverage to meet the limit specified by a compulsory or financial responsibility law of the jurisdiction where the covered "auto" is being used. This extension does not apply to the limit or limits specified by any law governing "motor carriers" of passengers or property.

(2) Provide the minimum amounts and types of other coverages, such as no-fault, required of out-of-state vehicles by the jurisdiction where the covered "auto" is being used.

We will not pay anyone more than once for the same elements of "loss" because of these extensions.

B. Exclusions

This insurance does not apply to any of the following:

1. Expected Or Intended Injury

"Bodily injury" or "property damage" expected or intended from the standpoint of the "insured".

2. Contractual

Liability assumed under any contract or agreement. But this exclusion does not apply to liability for damages:

a. Assumed in a contract or agreement that is an "insured contract" provided the "bodily injury" or "property damage" occurs subsequent to the execution of the contract or agreement; or

b. That the "insured" would have in the absence of the contract or agreement.

3. Workers' Compensation

Any obligation for which the "insured" or the "insured's" insurer may be held liable under any workers' compensation, disability benefits or unemployment compensation law or any similar law.

4. Employee Indemnification And Employer's Liability

"Bodily injury" to:

a. An "employee" of the "insured" arising out of and in the course of:

(1) Employment by the "insured"; or

(2) Performing the duties related to the conduct of the "insured's" business or

b. The spouse, child, parent, brother or sister of that "employee" as a consequence of Paragraph **a.** above.

This exclusion applies:

(1) Whether the "insured" may be liable as an employer or in any other capacity; and

(2) To any obligation to share damages with or repay someone else who must pay damages because of the injury.

But this exclusion does not apply to "bodily injury" to domestic "employees" not entitled to workers' compensation benefits or to liability assumed by the "insured" under an "insured contract". For the purposes of the Coverage Form, a domestic "employee" is a person engaged in household or domestic work performed principally in connection with a residence premises.

5. Fellow Employee

"Bodily injury" to any fellow "employee" of the "insured" arising out of and in the course of the fellow "employee's" employment or while performing duties related to the conduct of your business.

6. Care, Custody Or Control

"Property damage" to or "covered pollution cost or expense" involving property owned or transported by the "insured" or in the "insured's" care, custody or control. But this exclusion does not apply to liability assumed under a sidetrack agreement.

7. Handling Of Property

"Bodily injury" or "property damage" resulting from the handling of property:

a. Before it is moved from the place where it is accepted by the "insured" for movement into or onto the covered "auto"; or

b. After it is moved from the covered "auto" to the place where it is finally delivered by the "insured".

8. Movement Of Property By Mechanical Device

"Bodily injury" or "property damage" resulting from the movement of property by a mechanical device (other than a hand truck) unless the device is attached to the covered "auto".

9. Operations

"Bodily injury" or "property damage" arising out of the operation of any equipment listed in Paragraphs **6.b.** and **6.c.** of the definition of "mobile equipment".

10. Completed Operations

"Bodily injury" or "property damage" arising out of "your work" after that work has been completed or abandoned.

© ISO Properties, Inc., 2000 CA 00 20 10 01 □

In the exclusion, your work means:

a. Work or operations performed by you or on your behalf; and

b. Materials, parts or equipment furnished in connection with such work or operations.

Your work includes warranties or representations made at any time with respect to the fitness, quality, durability or performance of any of the items included in Paragraphs **a.** or **b.** above.

Your work will be deemed completed at the earliest of the following times:

(1) When all of the work called for in your contract has been completed.

(2) When all of the work to be done at the site has been completed if your contract calls for work at more than one site.

(3) When that part of the work done at a job site has been put to its intended use by any person or organization other than another contractor or subcontractor working on the same project.

Work that may need service, maintenance, correction, repair or replacement, but which is otherwise complete, will be treated as completed.

11. Pollution

"Bodily injury" or "property damage" arising out of the actual, alleged or threatened discharge, dispersal, seepage, migration, release or escape of "pollutants":

a. That are, or that are contained in any property that is:

(1) Being transported or towed by, handled, or handled for movement into, onto or from, the covered "auto";

(2) Otherwise in the course of transit by or on behalf of the "insured"; or

(3) Being stored, disposed of, treated or processed in or upon the covered "auto";

b. Before the "pollutants" or any property in which the "pollutants" are contained are moved from the place where they are accepted by the "insured" for movement into or onto the covered "auto"; or

c. After the "pollutants" or any property in which the "pollutants" are contained are moved from the covered "auto" to the place where they are finally delivered, disposed of or abandoned by the "insured".

Paragraph **a.** above does not apply to fuels, lubricants, fluids, exhaust gases or other similar "pollutants" that are needed for or result from the normal electrical, hydraulic or mechanical functioning of the covered "auto" or its parts, if:

(1) The "pollutants" escape, seep, migrate, or are discharged, dispersed or released directly from an "auto" part designed by its manufacturer to hold, store, receive or dispose of such "pollutants"; and

(2) The "bodily injury", "property damage" or "covered pollution cost or expense" does not arise out of the operation of any equipment listed in Paragraphs **6.b.** and **6.c.** of the definition of "mobile equipment".

Paragraphs **b.** and **c.** above of this exclusion do not apply to "accidents" that occur away from premises owned by or rented to an "insured" with respect to "pollutants" not in or upon a covered "auto" if:

(1) The "pollutants" or any property in which the "pollutants" are contained are upset, overturned or damaged as a result of the maintenance or use of a covered "auto"; and

(2) The discharge, dispersal, seepage, migration, release or escape of the "pollutants" is caused directly by such upset, overturn or damage.

12. War

"Bodily injury" or "property damage" due to war, whether or not declared, or any act or condition incident to war. War includes civil war, insurrection, rebellion or revolution. This exclusion applies only to liability assumed under a contract or agreement.

13. Racing

Covered "autos" while used in any professional or organized racing or demolition contest or stunting activity, or while practicing for such contest or activity. This insurance also does not apply while that covered "auto" is being prepared for such a contest or activity.

C. Limit Of Insurance

Regardless of the number of covered "autos", "insureds", premiums paid, claims made or vehicles involved in the "accident", the most we will pay for the total of all damages and "covered pollution cost or expense" combined, resulting from any one "accident" is the Limit of Insurance for Liability Coverage shown in the Declarations.

All "bodily injury", "property damage" and "covered pollution cost or expense" resulting from continuous or repeated exposure to substantially the same conditions will be considered as resulting from one "accident".

No one will be entitled to receive duplicate payments for the same elements of "loss" under this Coverage Form and any Medical Payments Coverage endorsement, Uninsured Motorists Coverage endorsement or Underinsured Motorists Coverage endorsement attached to this Coverage Part.

SECTION III – TRAILER INTERCHANGE COVERAGE

A. Coverage

1. We will pay all sums you legally must pay as damages because of "loss" to a "trailer" you don't own or its equipment under:

   a. Comprehensive Coverage

   From any cause except:

   (1) The "trailer's" collision with another object; or

   (2) The "trailer's" overturn.

   b. Specified Causes Of Loss Coverage

   Caused by:

   (1) Fire, lightning or explosion;

   (2) Theft;

   (3) Windstorm, hail or earthquake;

   (4) Flood;

   (5) Mischief or vandalism; or

   (6) The sinking, burning, collision or derailment of any conveyance transporting the "trailer".

   c. Collision Coverage

   Caused by:

   (1) The "trailer's" collision with another object; or

   (2) The "trailer's" overturn.

2. We have the right and duty to defend any "insured" against a "suit" asking for these damages. However, we have no duty to defend any "insured" against a "suit" seeking damages for any "loss" to which this insurance does not apply. We may investigate and settle any claim or "suit" as we consider appropriate. Our duty to defend or settle ends for a coverage when the Limit of Insurance for that coverage has been exhausted by payment of judgments or settlements.

3. **Coverage Extensions**

   The following applies as Supplementary Payments. In addition to the Limit of Insurance, we will pay for you:

   a. All expenses we incur.

   b. The cost of bonds to release attachments, but only for bond amounts within our Limit of Insurance.

   c. All reasonable expenses incurred at our request, including actual loss of earnings up to $250 a day because of time off from work.

   d. All costs taxed against the "insured" in any "suit" against the "insured" we defend.

   e. All interest on the full amount of any judgment that accrues after entry of the judgment; but our duty to pay interest ends when we have paid, offered to pay, or deposited in court the part of the judgment that is within our Limit of Insurance.

B. Exclusions

1. We will not pay for "loss" caused by or resulting from any of the following. Such "loss" is excluded regardless of any other cause or event that contributes concurrently or in any sequence to the "loss".

   a. Nuclear Hazard

   (1) The explosion of any weapon employing atomic fission or fusion; or

   (2) Nuclear reaction or radiation, or radioactive contamination, however caused.

   b. War Or Military Action

   (1) War, including undeclared or civil war;

   (2) Warlike action by a military force, including action in hindering or defending against an actual or expected attack, by any government, sovereign or other authority using military personnel or other agents; or

   (3) Insurrection, rebellion, revolution, usurped power or action taken by governmental authority in hindering or defending against any of these.

2. We will not pay for loss of use.

3. **Other Exclusions**

   We will not pay for "loss" caused by or resulting from any of the following unless caused by other "loss" that is covered by this insurance:

   a. Wear and tear, freezing, mechanical or electrical breakdown.

   b. Blowouts, punctures or other road damage to tires.

C. Limit Of Insurance And Deductible

The most we will pay for "loss" to any one "trailer" is the least of the following amounts minus any applicable deductible shown in the Declarations:

1. The actual cash value of the damaged or stolen property at the time of the "loss".

2. The cost of repairing or replacing the damaged or stolen property with other property of like kind and quality.

3. The Limit of Insurance shown in the Declarations.

SECTION IV – PHYSICAL DAMAGE COVERAGE

A. Coverage

1. We will pay for "loss" to a covered "auto" or its equipment under:

a. Comprehensive Coverage

From any cause except:

(1) The covered "auto's" collision with another object; or

(2) The covered "auto's" overturn.

b. Specified Causes Of Loss Coverage

Caused by:

(1) Fire, lightning or explosion;

(2) Theft;

(3) Windstorm, hail or earthquake;

(4) Flood;

(5) Mischief or vandalism; or

(6) The sinking, burning, collision or derailment of any conveyance transporting the covered "auto".

c. Collision Coverage

Caused by:

(1) The covered "auto's" collision with another object; or

(2) The covered "auto's" overturn.

2. Towing – Private Passenger Type Autos

We will pay up to the limit shown in the Declarations for towing and labor costs incurred each time a covered "auto" of the "private passenger type" is disabled. However, the labor must be performed at the place of disablement.

3. Glass Breakage – Hitting A Bird Or Animal – Falling Objects Or Missiles

If you carry Comprehensive Coverage for the damaged covered "auto", we will pay for the following under Comprehensive Coverage:

a. Glass breakage;

b. "Loss" caused by hitting a bird or animal; and

c. "Loss" caused by falling objects or missiles.

However, you have the option of having glass breakage caused by a covered "auto's" collision or overturn considered a "loss" under Collision Coverage.

4. Coverage Extension

a. Transportation Expenses

We will also pay up to $20 per day to a maximum of $600 for temporary transportation expense incurred by you because of the total theft of a covered "auto" of the "private passenger type". We will pay only for those covered "autos" for which you carry either Comprehensive or Specified Causes of Loss Coverage. We will pay for temporary transportation expenses incurred during the period beginning 48 hours after the theft and ending, regardless of the policy's expiration, when the covered "auto" is returned to use or we pay for its "loss".

b. Loss Of Use Expenses

For Hired Auto Physical Damage, we will pay expenses for which an "insured" becomes legally responsible to pay for loss of use of a vehicle rented or hired without a driver, under a written rental contract or agreement. We will pay for loss of use expenses if caused by:

(1) Other than collision only if the Declarations indicate that Comprehensive Coverage is provided for any covered "auto";

(2) Specified Causes Of Loss only if the Declarations indicate that Specified Causes Of Loss Coverage is provided for any covered "auto"; or

(3) Collision only if the Declarations indicate that Collision Coverage is provided for any covered "auto".

However, the most we will pay for any expenses for loss of use is $20 per day, to a maximum of $600.

B. Exclusions

1. We will not pay for "loss" caused by or resulting from any of the following. Such "loss" is excluded regardless of any other cause or event that contributes concurrently or in any sequence to the "loss".

a. Nuclear Hazard

(1) The explosion of any weapon employing atomic fission or fusion; or

(2) Nuclear reaction or radiation, or radioactive contamination, however caused.

b. War Or Military Action

(1) War, including undeclared or civil war;

(2) Warlike action by a military force, including action in hindering or defending against an actual or expected attack, by any government, sovereign, or other authority using military personnel or other agents; or

(3) Insurrection, rebellion, revolution, usurped power or action taken by governmental authority in hindering or defending against any of these.

2. We will not pay for "loss" to any of the following:

a. Any covered "auto" while in anyone else's possession under a written "trailer" interchange agreement. But this exclusion does not apply to a loss payee; however, if we pay the loss payee, you must reimburse us for our payment.

b. Any covered "auto" while used in any professional or organized racing or demolition contest or stunting activity, or while practicing for such contest or activity. We will also not pay for "loss" to any covered "auto" while that covered "auto" is being prepared for such a contest or activity.

c. Tapes, records, discs or similar audio, visual or data electronic devices designed for use with audio, visual or data electronic equipment.

d. Any device designed or used to detect speed measuring equipment such as radar or laser detectors and any jamming apparatus intended to elude or disrupt speed measurement equipment.

e. Any electronic equipment, without regard to whether this equipment is permanently installed, that receives or transmits audio, visual or data signals and that is not designed solely for the reproduction of sound.

f. Any accessories used with the electronic equipment described in Paragraph **e.** above.

Exclusions **2.e.** and **2.f.** do not apply to:

a. Equipment designed solely for the reproduction of sound and accessories used with such equipment, provided such equipment is permanently installed in the covered "auto" or such equipment is removable from a housing unit which is permanently installed in the "auto", and such equipment is designed to be solely operated by use of the power from the "auto's" electrical system, in or upon the covered "auto"; or

b. Any other electronic equipment that is:

(1) Necessary for the normal operation of the "auto" or the monitoring of the "auto's" operating system; or

(2) An integral part of the same unit housing any sound reproducing equipment described in **a.** above and permanently installed in the opening of the dash or console of the covered "auto" normally used by the manufacturer for installation of a radio.

3. We will not pay for "loss" caused by or resulting from any of the following unless caused by other "loss" that is covered by this insurance:

a. Wear and tear, freezing, mechanical or electrical breakdown.

b. Blowouts, punctures or other road damage to tires.

4. We will not pay for "loss" to a covered "auto" due to "diminution in value".

C. Limits Of Insurance

1. The most we will pay for "loss" in any one "accident" is the lesser of:

a. The actual cash value of the damaged or stolen property as of the time of "loss"; or

b. The cost of repairing or replacing the damaged or stolen property with other property of like kind and quality.

2. An adjustment for depreciation and physical condition will be made in determining actual cash value in the event of a total "loss".

3. If a repair or replacement results in better than like kind or quality, we will not pay for the amount of the betterment.

D. Deductible

For each covered "auto", our obligation to pay for, repair, return or replace damaged or stolen property will be reduced by the applicable deductible shown in the Declarations. Any Comprehensive Coverage deductible shown in the Declarations does not apply to "loss" caused by fire or lightning.

© ISO Properties, Inc., 2000   CA 00 20 10 01   □

SECTION V – MOTOR CARRIER CONDITIONS

The following conditions apply in addition to the Common Policy Conditions:

A. Loss Conditions

1. Appraisal For Physical Damage Loss

If you and we disagree on the amount of "loss", either may demand an appraisal of the "loss". In this event, each party will select a competent appraiser. The two appraisers will select a competent and impartial umpire. The appraisers will state separately the actual cash value and amount of "loss". If they fail to agree, they will submit their differences to the umpire. A decision agreed to by any two will be binding. Each party will:

a. Pay its chosen appraiser; and

b. Bear the other expenses of the appraisal and umpire equally.

If we submit to an appraisal, we will still retain our right to deny the claim.

2. Duties In The Event Of Accident, Claim, Suit Or Loss

We have no duty to provide coverage under this policy unless there has been full compliance with the following duties:

a. In the event of "accident", claim, "suit" or "loss", you must give us or our authorized representative prompt notice of the "accident" or "loss". Include:

(1) How, when and where the "accident" or "loss" occurred;

(2) The "insured's" name and address; and

(3) To the extent possible, the names and addresses of any injured persons and witnesses.

b. Additionally, you and any other involved "insured" must:

(1) Assume no obligation, make no payment or incur no expense without our consent, except at the "insured's" own cost.

(2) Immediately send us copies of any request, demand, order, notice, summons or legal paper received concerning the claim or "suit".

(3) Cooperate with us in the investigation or settlement of the claim or defense against the "suit".

(4) Authorize us to obtain medical records or other pertinent information.

(5) Submit to examination at our expense, by physicians of our choice, as often as we reasonably require.

c. If there is a "loss" to a covered "auto" or its equipment you must also do the following:

(1) Promptly notify the police if the covered "auto" or any of its equipment is stolen.

(2) Take all reasonable steps to protect the covered "auto" from further damage. Also keep a record of your expenses for consideration in the settlement of the claim.

(3) Permit us to inspect the covered "auto" and records proving the "loss" before its repair or disposition.

(4) Agree to examination under oath at our request and give us a signed statement of your answers.

3. Legal Action Against Us

No one may bring a legal action against us under this Coverage Form until:

a. There has been full compliance with all the terms of this Coverage Form; and

b. Under Liability Coverage, we agree in writing that the "insured" has an obligation to pay or until the amount of that obligation has finally been determined by judgment after trial. No one has the right under this policy to bring us into an action to determine the "insured's" liability.

4. Loss Payment – Physical Damage Coverages

At our option we may:

a. Pay for, repair or replace damaged or stolen property;

b. Return the stolen property at our expense. We will pay for any damage that results to the "auto" from the theft; or

c. Take all or any part of the damaged or stolen property at an agreed or appraised value.

If we pay for the "loss", our payment will include the applicable sales tax for the damaged or stolen property.

5. Transfer Of Rights Of Recovery Against Others To Us

If any person or organization to or for whom we make payment under this Coverage Form has rights to recover damages from another, those rights are transferred to us. That person or organization must do everything necessary to secure our rights and must do nothing after "accident" or "loss" to impair them.

B. General Conditions

1. Bankruptcy

Bankruptcy or insolvency of the "insured" or the "insured's" estate will not relieve us of any obligation under this Coverage Form.

2. Concealment, Misrepresentation Or Fraud

This Coverage Form is void in any case of fraud by you at any time as it relates to this Coverage Form. It is also void if you or any other "insured", at any time, intentionally conceal or misrepresent a material fact concerning:

a. This Coverage Form;

b. The covered "auto";

c. Your interest in the covered "auto"; or

d. A claim under this Coverage Form.

3. Liberalization

If we revise this Coverage Form to provide more coverage without additional premium charge, your policy will automatically provide the additional coverage as of the day the revision is effective in your state.

4. No Benefit To Bailee – Physical Damage Coverages

We will not recognize any assignment or grant any coverage for the benefit of any person or organization holding, storing or transporting property for a fee regardless of any other provision of this Coverage Form.

5. Other Insurance – Primary And Excess Insurance Provisions

a. While any covered "auto" is hired or borrowed from you by another "motor carrier", this Coverage Form's liability coverage is:

(1) Primary if a written agreement between you as the lessor and the other "motor carrier" as the lessee requires you to hold the lessee harmless.

(2) Excess over any other collectible insurance if a written agreement between you as the lessor and the other "motor carrier" as the lessee does not require you to hold the lessee harmless.

b. While any covered "auto" is hired or borrowed by you from another "motor carrier" this Coverage Form's liability coverage is:

(1) Primary if a written agreement between the other "motor carrier" as the lessor and you as the lessee does not require the lessor to hold you harmless, and then only while the covered "auto" is used exclusively in your business as a "motor carrier" for hire.

(2) Excess over any other collectible insurance if a written agreement between the other "motor carrier" as the lessor and you as the lessee requires the lessor to hold you harmless.

c. While a covered "auto" which is a "trailer" is connected to a power unit, this Coverage Form's Liability Coverage is:

(1) Provided on the same basis, either primary or excess, as the liability coverage provided for the power unit if the power unit is a covered "auto".

(2) Excess if the power unit is not a covered "auto".

d. Any Trailer Interchange Coverage provided by this Coverage Form is primary for any covered "auto".

e. Except as provided in Paragraphs a., b., c. and d. above, this Coverage Form provides primary insurance for any covered "auto" you own and excess insurance for any covered "auto" you don't own.

f. For Hired Auto Physical Damage Coverage, any covered "auto" you lease, hire, rent or borrow is deemed to be a covered "auto" you own. However, any "auto" that is leased, hired, rented or borrowed with a driver is not a covered "auto".

g. Regardless of the provisions of Paragraphs a., b., c., d. and e. above, this Coverage Form's Liability Coverage is primary for any liability assumed under an "insured contract".

h. When this Coverage Form and any other Coverage Form or policy covers on the same basis, either excess or primary, we will pay only our share. Our share is the proportion that the Limit of Insurance of our Coverage Form bears to the total of the limits of all the Coverage Forms and policies covering on the same basis.

6. Premium Audit

a. The estimated premium for this Coverage Form is based on the exposures you told us you have when this policy began. We will compute the final premium due when we determine your actual exposures. The estimated total premium will be credited against the final premium due and the first Named Insured will be billed for the balance, if any. The due date for the final premium or retrospective premium is the date shown as the due date on the bill. If the estimated total premium exceeds the final premium due, the first Named Insured will get a refund.

© ISO Properties, Inc., 2000

b. If this policy is issued for more than one year, the premium for this Coverage Form will be computed annually based on our rates or premiums in effect at the beginning of each year of the policy.

7. Policy Period, Coverage Territory

Under this Coverage Form, we cover "accidents" and "losses" occurring:

a. During the policy period shown in the Declarations; and

b. Within the coverage territory.

The coverage territory is:

a. The United States of America;

b. The territories and possessions of the United States of America;

c. Puerto Rico;

d. Canada; and

e. Anywhere in the world if:

(1) A covered "auto" of the "private passenger type" is leased, hired, rented or borrowed without a driver for a period of 30 days or less; and

(2) The "insured's" responsibility to pay damages is determined in a "suit" on the merits, in the United States of America, the territories and possessions of the United States of America, Puerto Rico, or Canada or in a settlement we agree to.

We also cover "loss" to, or "accidents" involving, a covered "auto" while being transported between any of these places.

8. Two Or More Coverage Forms Or Policies Issued By Us

If this Coverage Form and any other Coverage Form or policy issued to you by us or any company affiliated with us apply to the same "accident", the aggregate maximum Limit of Insurance under all the Coverage Forms or policies shall not exceed the highest applicable Limit of Insurance under any one Coverage Form or policy. This condition does not apply to any Coverage Form or policy issued by us or an affiliated company specifically to apply as excess insurance over this Coverage Form.

SECTION VI – DEFINITIONS

A. "Accident" includes continuous or repeated exposure to the same conditions resulting in "bodily injury" or "property damage".

B. "Auto" means a land motor vehicle, "trailer" or semitrailer designed for travel on public roads but does not include "mobile equipment".

C. "Bodily injury" means bodily injury, sickness or disease sustained by a person including death resulting from any of these.

D. "Covered pollution cost or expense" means any cost or expense arising out of:

1. Any request, demand, order or statutory or regulatory requirement; or

2. Any claim or "suit" by or on behalf of a governmental authority demanding that the "insured" or others test for, monitor, clean up, remove, contain, treat, detoxify or neutralize, or in any way respond to, or assess the effects of "pollutants".

"Covered pollution cost or expense" does not include any cost or expense arising out of the actual, alleged or threatened discharge, dispersal, seepage, migration, release or escape of "pollutants":

a. That are, or that are contained in any property that is:

(1) Being transported or towed by, handled, or handled for movement into, onto or from the covered "auto";

(2) Otherwise in the course of transit by or on behalf of the "insured";

(3) Being stored, disposed of, treated or processed in or upon the covered "auto";

b. Before the "pollutants" or any property in which the "pollutants" are contained are moved from the place where they are accepted by the "insured" for movement into or onto the covered "auto"; or

c. After the "pollutants" or any property in which the "pollutants" are contained are moved from the covered "auto" to the place where they are finally delivered, disposed of or abandoned by the "insured".

Paragraph **a.** above does not apply to fuels, lubricants, fluids, exhaust gases or other similar "pollutants" that are needed for or result from the normal electrical, hydraulic or mechanical functioning of the covered "auto" or its parts, if:

(1) The "pollutants" escape, seep, migrate, or are discharged, dispersed or released directly from an "auto" part designed by its manufacturer to hold, store, receive or dispose of such "pollutants"; and

(2) The "bodily injury", "property damage" or "covered pollution cost or expense" does not arise out of the operation of any equipment listed in Paragraphs **6.b.** or **6.c.** of the definition of "mobile equipment".

Paragraphs **b.** and **c.** above do not apply to "accidents" that occur away from premises owned by or rented to an "insured" with respect to "pollutants" not in or upon a covered "auto" if:

(1) The "pollutants" or any property in which the "pollutants" are contained are upset, overturned or damaged as a result of the maintenance or use of a covered "auto"; and

(2) The discharge, dispersal, seepage, migration, release or escape of the "pollutants" is caused directly by such upset, overturn or damage.

E. "Diminution in value" means the actual or perceived loss in market value or resale value which results from a direct and accidental "loss".

F. "Employee" includes a "leased worker". "Employee" does not include a "temporary worker".

G. "Insured" means any person or organization qualifying as an insured in the Who Is An Insured provision of the applicable coverage. Except with respect to the Limit of Insurance, the coverage afforded applies separately to each insured who is seeking coverage or against whom a claim or "suit" is brought.

H. "Insured contract" means:

1. A lease of premises;

2. A sidetrack agreement;

3. Any easement or license agreement, except in connection with construction or demolition operations on or within 50 feet of a railroad;

4. An obligation, as required by ordinance, to indemnify a municipality, except in connection with work for a municipality;

5. That part of any other contract or agreement pertaining to your business (including an indemnification of a municipality in connection with work performed for a municipality) under which you assume the tort liability of another to pay for "bodily injury" or "property damage" to a third party or organization. Tort liability means a liability that would be imposed by law in the absence of any contract or agreement;

6. That part of any other contract or agreement, entered into, as part of your business, pertaining to the rental or lease, by you or any of your "employees", of any "auto". However, such contract or agreement shall not be considered an "insured contract" to the extent that it obligates you or any of your "employees" to pay for "property damage" to any "auto" rented or leased by you or any of your "employees".

An "insured contract" does not include that part of any contract or agreement:

a. That indemnifies a railroad for "bodily injury" or "property damage" arising out of construction or demolition operations, within 50 feet of any railroad property and affecting any railroad bridge or trestle, tracks, roadbeds, tunnel, underpass or crossing; or

b. That pertains to the loan, lease or rental of an "auto" to you or any of your employees, if the "auto" is loaned, leased or rented with a driver; or

c. That holds a person or organization engaged in the business of transporting property by "auto" for hire harmless for your use of a covered "auto" unless the covered "auto" is used in your business as a "motor carrier" for hire as in Section **II**, Paragraph **A.1.d.** of the Who Is An Insured provision.

I. "Leased worker" means a person leased to you by a labor leasing firm under an agreement between you and the labor leasing firm, to perform duties related to the conduct of your business. "Leased worker" does not include a "temporary worker".

J. "Loss" means direct and accidental loss or damage.

K. "Mobile equipment" means any of the following types of land vehicles, including any attached machinery or equipment:

1. Bulldozers, farm machinery, forklifts and other vehicles designed for use principally off public roads;

2. Vehicles maintained for use solely on or next to premises you own or rent;

3. Vehicles that travel on crawler treads;

4. Vehicles, whether self-propelled or not, maintained primarily to provide mobility to permanently mounted:

a. Power cranes, shovels, loaders, diggers or drills; or

b. Road construction or resurfacing equipment such as graders, scrapers or rollers;

5. Vehicles not described in Paragraphs **1.**, **2.**, **3.** or **4.** above that are not self-propelled and are maintained primarily to provide mobility to permanently attached equipment of the following types:

a. Air compressors, pumps and generators, including spraying, welding, building cleaning, geophysical exploration, lighting and well servicing equipment; or

b. Cherry pickers and similar devices used to raise or lower workers.

© ISO Properties, Inc., 2000

6. Vehicles not described in Paragraphs **1.**, **2.**, **3.** or **4.** above maintained primarily for purposes other than the transportation of persons or cargo. However, self-propelled vehicles with the following types of permanently attached equipment are not "mobile equipment" but will be considered "autos":

a. Equipment designed primarily for:

(1) Snow removal;

(2) Road maintenance, but not construction or resurfacing; or

(3) Street cleaning;

b. Cherry pickers and similar devices mounted on automobile or truck chassis and used to raise or lower workers; and

c. Air compressors, pumps and generators, including spraying, welding, building cleaning, geophysical exploration, lighting or well servicing equipment.

L. "Motor Carrier" means a person or organization providing transportation by "auto" in the furtherance of a commercial enterprise.

M. "Pollutants" means any solid, liquid, gaseous or thermal irritant or contaminant, including smoke, vapor, soot, fumes, acids, alkalis, chemicals and waste. Waste includes materials to be recycled, reconditioned or reclaimed.

N. "Private passenger type" means a private passenger or station wagon type "auto" and includes an "auto" of the pick-up or van type if not used for business purposes.

O. "Property damage" means damage to or loss of use of tangible property.

P. "Suit" means a civil proceeding in which:

1. Damages because of "bodily injury" or "property damage" or

2. A "covered pollution cost or expense",

to which this insurance applies, are alleged.

"Suit" includes:

a. An arbitration proceeding in which such damages or "covered pollution costs or expenses" are claimed and to which the "insured" must submit or does submit with our consent; or

b. Any other alternative dispute resolution proceeding in which such damages or "covered pollution costs or expenses" are claimed and to which the "insured" submits with our consent.

Q. "Temporary worker" means a person who is furnished to you to substitute for a permanent "employee" on leave or to meet seasonal or short-term workload conditions.

R. "Trailer" includes a semitrailer or a dolly used to convert a semitrailer into a trailer. But for Trailer Interchange Coverage only, "trailer" also includes a container.

COMMERCIAL AUTO
CA DS 03 02 04

BUSINESS AUTO DECLARATIONS

POLICY NO.: _____

COMPANY NAME AREA	PRODUCER NAME AREA

ITEM ONE
NAMED INSURED: _____
MAILING ADDRESS: _____

POLICY PERIOD: From _____ to _____ at 12:01 A.M. Standard Time at your mailing address shown above.

PREVIOUS POLICY NUMBER: _____

FORM OF BUSINESS:
☐ CORPORATION ☐ LIMITED LIABILITY COMPANY ☐ INDIVIDUAL
☐ PARTNERSHIP ☐ OTHER _____

IN RETURN FOR THE PAYMENT OF THE PREMIUM, AND SUBJECT TO ALL THE TERMS OF THIS POLICY, WE AGREE WITH YOU TO PROVIDE THE INSURANCE AS STATED IN THIS POLICY.

PREMIUM FOR ENDORSEMENTS	$
*ESTIMATED TOTAL PREMIUM	$

*This policy may be subject to final audit.

Premium shown is payable:	$		at inception.				
AUDIT PERIOD (IF APPLICABLE)	☐ ANNUALLY	☐ SEMI-ANNUALLY	☐ QUARTERLY	☐ MONTHLY

ENDORSEMENTS ATTACHED TO THIS POLICY:

   IL 00 17 – Common Policy Conditions (IL 01 46 in Washington)
   IL 00 21 – Broad Form Nuclear Exclusion (Not Applicable in New York)

   _____
   _____
   _____

COUNTERSIGNED _____ BY _____
                           (Date)   (Authorized Representative)

NOTE

OFFICERS' FACSIMILE SIGNATURES MAY BE INSERTED HERE, ON THE POLICY COVER OR ELSEWHERE AT THE COMPANY'S OPTION.

CA DS 03 02 04   © ISO Properties, Inc., 2004   Page 1 of 6   ☐

POLICY NUMBER: _____

ITEM TWO

SCHEDULE OF COVERAGES AND COVERED AUTOS

This policy provides only those coverages where a charge is shown in the premium column below. Each of these coverages will apply only to those "autos" shown as covered "autos". "Autos" are shown as covered "autos" for a particular coverage by the entry of one or more of the symbols from the Covered Autos Section of the Business Auto Coverage Form next to the name of the coverage.

COVERAGES	COVERED AUTOS (Entry of one or more of the symbols from the Covered Autos Section of the Business Auto Coverage Form shows which autos are covered autos.)	LIMIT THE MOST WE WILL PAY FOR ANY ONE ACCIDENT OR LOSS	PREMIUM
LIABILITY		$	$
PERSONAL INJURY PROTECTION (or equivalent No-fault Coverage)		SEPARATELY STATED IN EACH P.I.P. ENDORSEMENT MINUS $ DED.	$
ADDED PERSONAL INJURY PROTECTION (or equivalent added No-fault Coverage)		SEPARATELY STATED IN EACH ADDED P.I.P. ENDORSEMENT.	$
PROPERTY PROTECTION INSURANCE (Michigan only)		SEPARATELY STATED IN THE P.P.I. ENDORSEMENT MINUS $ DED. FOR EACH ACCIDENT.	$
AUTO MEDICAL PAYMENTS		$	$
MEDICAL EXPENSE AND INCOME LOSS BENEFITS (Virginia only)		SEPARATELY STATED IN EACH MEDICAL EXPENSE AND INCOME LOSS BENEFITS ENDORSEMENT.	$
UNINSURED MOTORISTS		$	$
UNDERINSURED MOTORISTS (When not included in Uninsured Motorists Coverage)		$	$
PHYSICAL DAMAGE COMPREHENSIVE COVERAGE		ACTUAL CASH VALUE OR COST OF REPAIR, WHICHEVER IS LESS, MINUS $ DED. FOR EACH COVERED AUTO, BUT NO DEDUCTIBLE APPLIES TO LOSS CAUSED BY FIRE OR LIGHTNING. See ITEM FOUR For Hired Or Borrowed "Autos".	$
PHYSICAL DAMAGE SPECIFIED CAUSES OF LOSS COVERAGE		ACTUAL CASH VALUE OR COST OF REPAIR, WHICHEVER IS LESS, MINUS $ DED. FOR EACH COVERED AUTO FOR LOSS CAUSED BY MISCHIEF OR VANDALISM. See ITEM FOUR For Hired Or Borrowed "Autos".	$
PHYSICAL DAMAGE COLLISION COVERAGE		ACTUAL CASH VALUE OR COST OF REPAIR, WHICHEVER IS LESS, MINUS $ DED. FOR EACH COVERED AUTO. See ITEM FOUR For Hired Or Borrowed "Autos".	$
PHYSICAL DAMAGE TOWING AND LABOR		$ For Each Disablement Of A Private Passenger "Auto".	$
			$
		PREMIUM FOR ENDORSEMENTS	$
		*ESTIMATED TOTAL PREMIUM	$

*This policy may be subject to final audit.

POLICY NUMBER: _____

ITEM THREE

SCHEDULE OF COVERED AUTOS YOU OWN

Covered Auto No.	DESCRIPTION — Year, Model, Trade Name, Body Type Serial Number (S) Vehicle Identification Number (VIN)	PURCHASED — Original Cost New	PURCHASED — Actual Cost & NEW (N) USED (U)	TERRITORY — Town & State Where The Covered Auto Will Be Principally Garaged
1		$	$	
2		$	$	
3		$	$	
4		$	$	
5		$	$	

Covered Auto No.	CLASSIFICATION — Radius Of Operation	Business Use s=service r=retail c=commercial	Size GVW, GCW Or Vehicle Seating Capacity	Age Group	Primary Rating Factor — Liab.	Primary Rating Factor — Phy. Dam.	Secondary Rating Factor	Code	EXCEPT For Towing, All Physical Damage Loss Is Payable To You And The Loss Payee Named Below As Interests May Appear At The Time Of The Loss.
1									
2									
3									
4									
5									

COVERAGES – PREMIUMS, LIMITS AND DEDUCTIBLES (Absence of a deductible or limit entry in any column below means that the limit or deductible entry in the corresponding ITEM TWO column applies instead.)

Covered Auto No.	LIABILITY — Limit	LIABILITY — Premium	PERSONAL INJURY PROTECTION — Limit Stated In Each P.I.P. End. Minus Deductible Shown Below	PERSONAL INJURY PROTECTION — Premium	ADDED P.I.P. — Limit Stated In Each Added P.I.P. End. Premium	PROPERTY PROTECTION (Michigan Only) — Limit Stated In P.P.I. End. Minus Deductible Shown Below	PROPERTY PROTECTION (Michigan Only) — Premium
1	$	$	$	$	$	$	$
2	$	$	$	$	$	$	$
3	$	$	$	$	$	$	$
4	$	$	$	$	$	$	$
5	$	$	$	$	$	$	$
Total Premium		$		$	$		$

POLICY NUMBER: _____

ITEM THREE

SCHEDULE OF COVERED AUTOS YOU OWN (Cont'd)

Covered Auto No.	COVERAGES – PREMIUMS, LIMITS AND DEDUCTIBLES (Absence of a deductible or limit entry in any column below means that the limit or deductible entry in the corresponding ITEM TWO column applies instead.)			
	AUTO MEDICAL PAYMENTS		MEDICAL EXPENSE AND INCOME LOSS BENEFITS (Virginia Only)	
	Limit	Premium	Limit Stated In Each Medical Expense And Income Loss Endorsement For Each Person	Premium
1	$	$	$	$
2	$	$	$	$
3	$	$	$	$
4	$	$	$	$
5	$	$	$	$
Total Premium		$		$

Covered Auto No.	COVERAGES – PREMIUMS, LIMITS AND DEDUCTIBLES (Absence of a deductible or limit entry in any column below means that the limit or deductible entry in the corresponding ITEM TWO column applies instead.)							
	COMPREHENSIVE		SPECIFIED CAUSES OF LOSS		COLLISION		TOWING & LABOR	
	Limit Stated In ITEM TWO Minus Deductible Shown Below	Premium	Limit Stated In Item TWO Minus Deductible Shown Below	Premium	Limit Stated In Item TWO Minus Deductible Shown Below	Premium	Limit Per Disablement	Premium
1	$	$	$	$	$	$	$	$
2	$	$	$	$	$	$	$	$
3	$	$	$	$	$	$	$	$
4	$	$	$	$	$	$	$	$
5	$	$	$	$	$	$	$	$
Total Premium		$		$		$		$

ITEM FOUR

SCHEDULE OF HIRED OR BORROWED COVERED AUTO COVERAGE AND PREMIUMS

LIABILITY COVERAGE – RATING BASIS, COST OF HIRE				
STATE	ESTIMATED COST OF HIRE FOR EACH STATE	RATE PER EACH $100 COST OF HIRE	FACTOR (If Liability Coverage Is Primary)	PREMIUM
	$	$		$
			TOTAL PREMIUM	$

Cost of hire means the total amount you incur for the hire of "autos" you don't own (not including "autos" you borrow or rent from your partners or "employees" or their family members). Cost of hire does not include charges for services performed by motor carriers of property or passengers.

POLICY NUMBER: _____

PHYSICAL DAMAGE COVERAGE

COVERAGES	LIMIT OF INSURANCE THE MOST WE WILL PAY DEDUCTIBLE	ESTIMATED ANNUAL COST OF HIRE	RATE PER EACH $100 ANNUAL COST OF HIRE	PREMIUM
COMPREHENSIVE	ACTUAL CASH VALUE OR COST OF REPAIR, WHICHEVER IS LESS, MINUS $ ___ DED. FOR EACH COVERED AUTO, BUT NO DEDUCTIBLE APPLIES TO LOSS CAUSED BY FIRE OR LIGHTNING.	$	$	$
SPECIFIED CAUSES OF LOSS	ACTUAL CASH VALUE OR COST OF REPAIR, WHICHEVER IS LESS, MINUS $ ___ DED. FOR EACH COVERED AUTO FOR LOSS CAUSED BY MISCHIEF OR VANDALISM.	$	$	$
COLLISION	ACTUAL CASH VALUE OR COST OF REPAIR, WHICHEVER IS LESS, MINUS $ ___ DED. FOR EACH COVERED AUTO.	$	$	$
			TOTAL PREMIUM	$

ITEM FIVE

SCHEDULE FOR NON-OWNERSHIP LIABILITY

NAMED INSURED'S BUSINESS	RATING BASIS	NUMBER	PREMIUM
Other Than A Social Service Agency	Number Of Employees		$
	Number Of Partners		$
Social Service Agency	Number Of Employees		$
	Number Of Volunteers		$
		TOTAL	$

POLICY NUMBER: _____

ITEM SIX

SCHEDULE FOR GROSS RECEIPTS OR MILEAGE BASIS – LIABILITY COVERAGE – PUBLIC AUTO OR LEASING RENTAL CONCERNS

ESTIMATED YEARLY ☐ Gross Receipts ☐ Mileage	RATES ☐ Per $100 Of Gross Receipts ☐ Per Mile		PREMIUMS	
	LIABILITY COVERAGE	AUTO MEDICAL PAYMENTS	LIABILITY COVERAGE	AUTO MEDICAL PAYMENTS
	$	$	$	$
	$	$	$	$
	$	$	$	$
	$	$	$	$
		TOTAL PREMIUMS	$	$
		MINIMUM PREMIUMS	$	$

When used as a premium basis:

FOR PUBLIC AUTOS

Gross Receipts means the total amount to which you are entitled for transporting passengers, mail or merchandise during the policy period regardless of whether you or any other carrier originate the transportation. Gross Receipts does not include:

    A. Amounts you pay to railroads, steamship lines, airlines and other motor carriers operating under their own ICC or PUC permits.

    B. Advertising revenue.

    C. Taxes which you collect as a separate item and remit directly to a governmental division.

    D. C.O.D. collections for cost of mail or merchandise including collection fees.

Mileage means the total live and dead mileage of all revenue producing units operated during the policy period.

FOR RENTAL OR LEASING CONCERNS

Gross receipts means the total amount to which you are entitled for the leasing or rental of "autos" during the policy period and includes taxes except those taxes which you collect as a separate item and remit directly to a governmental division.

Mileage means the total of all live and dead mileage developed by all the "autos" you leased or rented to others during the policy period.

GARAGE COVERAGE FORM DECLARATIONS

ITEM ONE

NAMED INSURED _____   POLICY NO. _____

FORM OF BUSINESS:

☐ CORPORATION   ☐ INDIVIDUAL

☐ PARTNERSHIP   ☐ OTHER _____

ITEM TWO

SCHEDULE OF COVERAGES AND COVERED AUTOS

This policy provides only those coverages where a charge is shown in the premium column below. Each of these coverages will apply only to those "autos" shown as covered "autos." "Autos" are shown as covered "autos" for a particular coverage by the entry of one or more of the symbols from the COVERED AUTO Section of the Garage Coverage Form next to the name of the coverage. Entry of a symbol next to LIABILITY provides coverage for "garage operations."

COVERAGES	COVERED AUTOS (Entry of one or more of the symbols from the COVERED AUTO Section of the Garage Coverage Form shows which autos are covered autos)	LIMIT			PREMIUM
LIABILITY		Each "Accident" "Garage Operations"		Aggregate - "Garage Operations"	
		"Auto" Only	Other Than "Auto" Only	Other Than "Auto" Only	
		$	$	$	
PERSONAL INJURY PROTECTION (or equivalent No-fault Coverage)		SEPARATELY STATED IN EACH P.I.P. ENDORSEMENT MINUS $ Ded.			
ADDED PERSONAL INJURY PROTECTION (or equivalent Added No-fault Coverage)		SEPARATELY STATED IN EACH ADDED P.I.P. ENDORSEMENT			
PROPERTY PROTECTION INSURANCE (Michigan only)		SEPARATELY STATED IN THE P.P.I. ENDORSEMENT MINUS $ Ded. FOR EACH ACCIDENT			
MEDICAL PAYMENTS		$			
UNINSURED MOTORISTS		$			
UNDERINSURED MOTORISTS (When not included in Uninsured Motorists Coverage)		$			

Table continued on next page.

CA 00 06 12 90   Copyright, Insurance Services Office, Inc., 1990   Page 1 of 3   ☐

GARAGE COVERAGE FORM DECLARATIONS (Continued)

COVERAGES	COVERED AUTOS (Entry of one or more of the symbols from the COVERED AUTO Section of the Garage Coverage Form shows which autos are covered autos)	LIMIT	PREMIUM
GARAGEKEEPERS COMPREHENSIVE COVERAGE		$ EACH LOCATION MINUS $ Ded. FOR EACH COVERED AUTO FOR LOSS	
GARAGEKEEPERS SPECIFIED CAUSES OF LOSS COVERAGE		CAUSED BY THEFT OR MISCHIEF OR VANDALISM SUBJECT TO $ MAXIMUM DEDUCTIBLE FOR ALL SUCH LOSS IN ANY ONE EVENT	
GARAGEKEEPERS COLLISION COVERAGE		$ EACH LOCATION MINUS $ Ded. FOR EACH COVERED AUTO	
PHYSICAL DAMAGE COMPREHENSIVE COVERAGE		ACTUAL CASH VALUE OR COST OF REPAIR. WHICHEVER IS LESS MINUS $ Ded. FOR EACH COVERED AUTO. BUT NO DEDUCTIBLE APPLIES TO LOSS CAUSED BY FIRE OR LIGHTNING See Supplementary Schedule for dealers "autos" and "autos" held for sale by trailer dealers and non-dealers	
PHYSICAL DAMAGE SPECIFIED CAUSES OF LOSS COVERAGE		ACTUAL CASH VALUE OR COST OF REPAIR. WHICHEVER IS LESS MINUS $25 Ded. FOR EACH COVERED AUTO FOR LOSS CAUSED BY MISCHIEF OR VANDALISM. See Supplementary Schedule for dealers "autos" and "autos" held for sale by trailer dealers and non-dealers.	
PHYSICAL DAMAGE COLLISION COVERAGE		ACTUAL CASH VALUE OR COST OF REPAIR. WHICHEVER IS LESS MINUS $ Ded. FOR EACH COVERED AUTO. See Supplementary Schedule for dealers "autos" and "autos" held for sale by trailer dealers and non-dealers.	
PHYSICAL DAMAGE TOWING AND LABOR (Not Available in California)		$ for each disablement of a private passenger "auto"	
		PREMIUM FOR ENDORSEMENTS	
		ESTIMATED TOTAL PREMIUM	

     Copyright, Insurance Services Office, Inc., 1990   CA 00 06 12 90   ☐

GARAGE COVERAGE FORM DECLARATIONS (Continued)

ENDORSEMENT ATTACHED TO THIS COVERAGE FORM:
IL 00 21 - Broad Form Nuclear Exclusion (Not Applicable in New York)

_____

_____

_____

THIS DECLARATION MUST BE COMPLETED BY THE ATTACHMENT OF A SUPPLEMENTARY SCHEDULE

CA 00 06 12 90   Copyright, Insurance Services Office, Inc., 1990   Page 3 of 3 ☐

TRUCKERS DECLARATIONS

POLICY NO. _____

COMPANY NAME AREA	PRODUCER NAME AREA

ITEM ONE

NAMED INSURED _____

MAILING ADDRESS: _____

_____

POLICY PERIOD: From _____ to _____ at

12:01 A.M. Standard Time at your mailing address shown above.

FORM OF BUSINESS:
- ☐ CORPORATION
- ☐ PARTNERSHIP
- ☐ INDIVIDUAL
- ☐ OTHER _____

IN RETURN FOR THE PAYMENT OF THE PREMIUM, AND SUBJECT TO ALL THE TERMS OF THIS POLICY, WE AGREE WITH YOU TO PROVIDE THE INSURANCE AS STATED IN THIS POLICY.

Premium shown is payable: $_____ at inception.

ENDORSEMENTS ATTACHED TO THIS POLICY: IL 00 21 - Broad Form Nuclear Exclusion (Not Applicable in New York)

_____

_____

COUNTERSIGNED _____ BY _____

(Date) (Authorized Representative)

NOTE: OFFICERS' FACSIMILE SIGNATURES MAY BE INSERTED HERE, ON THE POLICY COVER OR ELSEWHERE AT THE COMPANY'S OPTION.

TRUCKERS DECLARATIONS (Continued)

ITEM TWO

SCHEDULE OF COVERAGES AND COVERED AUTOS

This policy provides only those coverages where a charge is shown in the premium column below. Each of these coverages will apply only to those "autos" shown as covered "autos". "Autos" are shown as covered "autos" for a particular coverage by the entry of one or more of the symbols from the COVERED AUTO Section of the Truckers Coverage Form next to the name of the coverage.

COVERAGES	COVERED AUTOS (Entry of one or more of the symbols from the COVERED AUTO Section of the Truckers Coverage Form shows which autos are covered autos)	LIMIT THE MOST WE WILL PAY FOR ANY ONE ACCIDENT OR LOSS	PREMIUM
LIABILITY		$	
PERSONAL INJURY PROTECTION (or equivalent No-Fault Coverage)		SEPARATELY STATED IN EACH PIP ENDORSEMENT MINUS $ Ded.	
ADDED PERSONAL INJURY PROTECTION (or equivalent Added No-Fault Coverage)		SEPARATELY STATED IN EACH ADDED PIP ENDORSEMENT	
PROPERTY PROTECTION INSURANCE (Michigan only)		SEPARATELY STATED IN THE P.P.I. ENDORSEMENT MINUS $ Ded. FOR EACH ACCIDENT	
MEDICAL PAYMENTS		$	
UNINSURED MOTORISTS		$	
UNDERINSURED MOTORISTS (When Not included in Uninsured Motorists Coverage)		$	
TRAILER INTERCHANGE COMPREHENSIVE COVERAGE		ACTUAL CASH VALUE, COST OF REPAIR OR $ WHICHEVER IS LESS	
TRAILER INTERCHANGE SPECIFIED CAUSES OF LOSS COVERAGE		ACTUAL CASH VALUE, COST OF REPAIR OR $ WHICHEVER IS LESS, MINUS $25 Ded. FOR EACH COVERED AUTO FOR LOSS CAUSED BY MISCHIEF OR VANDALISM	

Table continues on next page.

Copyright, Insurance Services Office, Inc., 1993   CA 00 14 12 93 □

TRUCKERS DECLARATIONS (Continued)

ITEM TWO (Continued)

COVERAGES	COVERED AUTOS (Entry of one or more of the symbols from the COVERED AUTO Section of the Truckers Coverage Form shows which autos are covered autos)	LIMIT THE MOST WE WILL PAY FOR ANY ONE ACCIDENT OR LOSS	PREMIUM
TRAILER INTERCHANGE COLLISION COVERAGE		ACTUAL CASH VALUE, COST OF REPAIR OR $ WHICHEVER IS LESS, MINUS $ Ded. FOR EACH COVERED AUTO	
PHYSICAL DAMAGE COMPREHENSIVE COVERAGE		ACTUAL CASH VALUE OR COST OF REPAIR, WHICHEVER IS LESS, MINUS $ Ded. FOR EACH COVERED AUTO. BUT NO DEDUCTIBLE APPLIES TO LOSS CAUSED BY FIRE OR LIGHTNING	
PHYSICAL DAMAGE SPECIFIED CAUSES OF LOSS COVERAGE		ACTUAL CASH VALUE OR COST OF REPAIR, WHICHEVER IS LESS, MINUS $25 Ded. FOR EACH COVERED AUTO FOR LOSS CAUSED BY MISCHIEF OR VANDALISM	
PHYSICAL DAMAGE COLLISION COVERAGE		ACTUAL CASH VALUE OR COST OF REPAIR, WHICHEVER IS LESS MINUS $ Ded. FOR EACH COVERED AUTO	
PHYSICAL DAMAGE TOWING AND LABOR (Not Available in California)		$ for each disablement of a private passenger auto	
		PREMIUM FOR ENDORSEMENTS	
		ESTIMATED TOTAL PREMIUM	

TRUCKERS DECLARATIONS (Continued)

ITEM THREE

SCHEDULE OF COVERED AUTOS YOU OWN

Covered Auto No.	DESCRIPTION		PURCHASED		TERRITORY
	Year, Model, Trade Name, Body Type Serial Number (S) Vehicle Identification Number (VIN)		Original Cost New	Actual Cost & NEW (N) USED (U)	Town & State Where the Covered Auto will be principally garaged
1					
2					
3					
4					
5					

Covered Auto No.	CLASSIFICATION								EXCEPT FOR Towing, all physical damage loss is payable to you and the loss payee named below as interests may appear at the time of the loss
	Radius of Operation	Business use s=service r=retail c=commercial	Size GVW,GCW or Vehicle Seating Capacity	Age Group	Primary Rating Factor		Secondary Rating Factor	Code	
					Liab	Phy Dam.			
1									
2									
3									
4									
5									

Table continues on next page.

SAMPLE

CA 00 14 12 93 ☐

TRUCKERS DECLARATIONS (Continued)

ITEM THREE (Continued)

Covered Auto No.	COVERAGES - PREMIUMS, LIMITS AND DEDUCTIBLES (Absence of a deductible or limit entry in any column below means that the limit or deductible entry in the corresponding ITEM TWO column applies instead)									
	LIABILITY		PERSONAL INJURY PROTECTION		ADDED P.I.P.		PROP. PROT. (Mich. only)		AUTO. MED. PAY	
	Limit	Premium	Limit stated in each P.I.P. End. minus deductible shown below	Premium	Limit stated in each Added P.I.P. End. Premium		Limit stated in P.P.I. End. minus deductible shown below	Premium	Limit	Premium
1										
2										
3										
4										
5										
Total Premium										

Covered Auto No.	COVERAGES - PREMIUMS, LIMITS AND DEDUCTIBLES (Absence of a deductible or limit entry in any column below means that the limit or deductible entry in the corresponding ITEM TWO column applies instead)							
	COMPREHENSIVE		SPECIFIED CAUSES OF LOSS		COLLISION		TOWING & LABOR	
	Limit stated in ITEM TWO minus deductible shown below	Premium	Limit stated in ITEM TWO Premium		Limit stated in ITEM TWO minus deductible shown below	Premium	Limit Per Disablement	Premium
1								
2								
3								
4								
5								
Total Premium								

CA 00 14 12 93   Copyright, Insurance Services Office, Inc., 1993   Page 5 of 8

TRUCKERS DECLARATIONS (Continued)

ITEM FOUR

SCHEDULE OF HIRED OR BORROWED COVERED AUTO COVERAGE AND PREMIUMS.

LIABILITY COVERAGE - RATING BASIS, COST OF HIRE - AUTOS USED IN YOUR TRUCKING OPERATIONS

ESTIMATED COST OF HIRE	RATE PER EACH $100 COST OF HIRE	TOTAL ESTIMATED PREMIUM

LIABILITY COVERAGE - RATING BASIS, COST OF HIRE - AUTOS NOT USED IN YOUR TRUCKING OPERATIONS

STATE	ESTIMATED COST OF HIRE FOR EACH STATE	RATE PER EACH $100 COST OF HIRE	FACTOR (if liab. Cov. is primary)	PREMIUM
			TOTAL PREMIUM	

PHYSICAL DAMAGE COVERAGE

COVERAGES	LIMIT OF INSURANCE THE MOST WE WILL PAY DEDUCTIBLE	ESTIMATED ANNUAL COST OF HIRE	RATE PER EACH $100 ANNUAL COST OF HIRE	PREMIUM
COMPREHENSIVE	ACTUAL CASH VALUE, COST OF REPAIRS OR $　　WHICHEVER IS LESS, MINUS $　　Ded. FOR EACH COVERED AUTO BUT NO DEDUCTIBLE APPLIES TO LOSS CAUSED BY FIRE OR LIGHTNING			
SPECIFIED CAUSES OF LOSS	ACTUAL CASH VALUE, COST OF REPAIRS OR $　　WHICHEVER IS LESS, MINUS $25 Ded. FOR EACH COVERED AUTO FOR LOSS CAUSED BY MISCHIEF OR VANDALISM			
COLLISION	ACTUAL CASH VALUE, COST OF REPAIRS OR $　　WHICHEVER IS LESS, MINUS $　　Ded. FOR EACH COVERED AUTO			
		TOTAL PREMIUM		

Cost of Hire means:

(a) The total dollar amount of costs you incurred for the hire of automobiles (includes trailers and semi-trailers), and if not included therein,

(b) The total remunerations of all operators and drivers helpers, of hired automobiles whether hired with a driver by lessor or an employee of the lessee, or any other third party, and,

(c) The total dollar amount of any other costs (i.e. repair, maintenance, fuel, etc.) directly associated with operating the hired automobiles whether such costs are absorbed by the insured, paid to the lessor or owner, or paid to others.

TRUCKERS DECLARATIONS (Continued)

ITEM FIVE
SCHEDULE FOR NON-OWNERSHIP LIABILITY

Rating Basis	Number	Premium
Number of Employees		$
Number of Partners		$
		$

ITEM SIX
TRAILER INTERCHANGE COVERAGE

COVERAGES	LIMIT OF INSURANCE	DAILY RATE	ESTIMATED PREMIUM
COMPREHENSIVE		$	$
SPECIFIED CAUSES OF LOSS	STATED IN ITEM TWO	$	$
COLLISION		$	$
			TOTAL PREMIUM

TRUCKERS DECLARATIONS (Continued)

ITEM SEVEN

SCHEDULE FOR GROSS RECEIPTS RATING BASIS - LIABILITY COVERAGE

Estimated Yearly Gross Receipts	RATES Per $100 of Gross Receipts		PREMIUMS	
	LIABILITY COVERAGE	AUTO MEDICAL PAYMENTS	LIABILITY COVERAGE	AUTO MEDICAL PAYMENTS
	TOTAL PREMIUMS			
	MINIMUM PREMIUMS			

When used as a premium basis:

Gross Receipts means the total amount to which you are entitled for shipping or transporting property during the policy period regardless of whether you or any other carrier originate the shipment or transportation. "Gross Receipts" includes the total amount received from renting equipment, with or without drivers, to anyone who is not a "trucker" and 15% of the total amount received from renting any equipment to any "trucker". Gross Receipts does not include:

A. Amounts you pay to railroads, steamship lines, airlines and other motor carriers operating under their own ICC or PUC permits.

B. Advertising Revenue.

C. Taxes which you collect as a separate item and remit directly to a governmental division.

D. C.O.D. collections for cost of mail or merchandise including collection fees.

E. Warehouse storage fees.

Copyright, Insurance Services Office, Inc., 1993 CA 00 14 12 93 ☐

MOTOR CARRIER COVERAGE FORM DECLARATIONS

ITEM ONE

NAMED INSURED _____ POLICY NO. _____

FORM OF BUSINESS:

☐ CORPORATION   ☐ INDIVIDUAL

☐ PARTNERSHIP   ☐ OTHER _____

ITEM TWO

SCHEDULE OF COVERAGES AND COVERED AUTOS

This policy provides only those coverages where a charge is shown in the premium column below. Each of these coverages will apply only to those "autos" shown as covered "autos". "Autos" are shown as covered "autos" for a particular coverage by the entry of one or more of the symbols from the COVERED AUTO Section of the Motor Carrier Coverage Form next to the name of the coverage.

COVERAGES	COVERED AUTOS (Entry of one or more of the symbols from the COVERED AUTOS Section of the Motor Carrier Coverage Form shows which autos are covered autos)	LIMIT THE MOST WE WILL PAY FOR ANY ONE ACCIDENT OR LOSS	PREMIUM
LIABILITY		$	
PERSONAL INJURY PROTECTION (or equivalent No-Fault Coverage)		SEPARATELY STATED IN EACH PIP ENDORSEMENT MINUS $ Ded.	
ADDED PERSONAL INJURY PROTECTION (or equivalent Added No-Fault Coverage)		SEPARATELY STATED IN EACH ADDED PIP ENDORSEMENT	
PROPERTY PROTECTION INSURANCE (Michigan only)		SEPARATELY STATED IN THE P.P.I. ENDORSEMENT MINUS $ Ded. FOR EACH ACCIDENT	
MEDICAL PAYMENTS		$	
UNINSURED MOTORISTS		$	
UNDERINSURED MOTORISTS (When Not included in Uninsured Motorists Coverage)		$	
TRAILER INTERCHANGE COMPREHENSIVE COVERAGE		ACTUAL CASH VALUE, COST OF REPAIR OR $ WHICHEVER IS LESS	
TRAILER INTERCHANGE SPECIFIED CAUSES OF LOSS COVERAGE		ACTUAL CASH VALUE, COST OF REPAIR OR $ WHICHEVER IS LESS, MINUS $25 Ded. FOR EACH COVERED AUTO FOR LOSS CAUSED BY MISCHIEF OR VANDALISM	

Table continues on next page.

CA 00 19 12 93   Copyright, Insurance Services Office, Inc., 1993   **Page 1 of 7**

MOTOR CARRIER COVERAGE FORM DECLARATIONS (Continued)

ITEM TWO (Continued)

COVERAGES	COVERED AUTOS (Entry of one or more of the symbols from the COVERED AUTOS Section of the Motor Carrier Coverage Form shows which autos are covered autos)	LIMIT THE MOST WE WILL PAY FOR ANY ONE ACCIDENT OR LOSS	PREMIUM
TRAILER INTERCHANGE COLLISION COVERAGE		ACTUAL CASH VALUE, COST OF REPAIR OR $ WHICHEVER IS LESS, MINUS $ Ded. FOR EACH COVERED AUTO	
PHYSICAL DAMAGE COMPREHENSIVE COVERAGE		ACTUAL CASH VALUE OR COST OF REPAIR, WHICHEVER IS LESS, MINUS $ Ded. FOR EACH COVERED AUTO. BUT NO DEDUCTIBLE APPLIES TO LOSS CAUSED BY FIRE OR LIGHTNING.	
PHYSICAL DAMAGE SPECIFIED CAUSES OF LOSS COVERAGE		ACTUAL CASH VALUE OR COST OF REPAIR, WHICHEVER IS LESS, MINUS $25 Ded. FOR EACH COVERED AUTO FOR LOSS CAUSED BY MISCHIEF OR VANDALISM	
PHYSICAL DAMAGE COLLISION COVERAGE		ACTUAL CASH VALUE OR COST OF REPAIR, WHICHEVER IS LESS MINUS $ Ded. FOR EACH COVERED AUTO	
PHYSICAL DAMAGE TOWING AND LABOR (Not Available in California)		$ for each disablement of a "private passenger auto"	
		PREMIUM FOR ENDORSEMENTS	
		ESTIMATED TOTAL PREMIUM	

 CA 00 19 12 93

MOTOR CARRIER COVERAGE FORM DECLARATIONS (Continued)

ENDORSEMENTS ATTACHED TO THIS COVERAGE FORM:
  IL 00 21 - Broad Form Nuclear Exclusion (Not Applicable in New York)

ITEM THREE

SCHEDULE OF COVERED AUTOS YOU OWN

Covered Auto No.	DESCRIPTION Year, Model, Trade Name, Body Type Serial Number (S) Vehicle Identification Number (VIN)		PURCHASED Original Cost New	Actual Cost & NEW (N) USED (U)	TERRITORY Town & State Where the Covered Auto will be principally garaged
1					
2					
3					
4					
5					

Covered Auto No.	Radius of Operation	CLASSIFICATION Business use s=service r=retail c=commercial	Size GVW, GCW or Vehicle Seating Capacity	Age Group	Primary Rating Factor Liab. Phy. Dam.	Secondary Rating Factor	Code	EXCEPT FOR Towing, all physical damage loss is payable to you and the loss payee named below as interests may appear at the time of the loss
1								
2								
3								
4								
5								

Table continues on next page.

MOTOR CARRIER COVERAGE FORM DECLARATIONS (Continued)

ITEM THREE (Continued)

Covered Auto No.	COVERAGES - PREMIUMS, LIMITS AND DEDUCTIBLES (Absence of a deductible or limit entry in any column below means that the limit or deductible entry in the corresponding ITEM TWO column applies instead)					
	LIABILITY		PERSONAL INJURY PROTECTION		ADDED P.I.P.	PROP. PROT. (Mich. only)	
	Limit	Premium	Limit stated in each P.I.P. End. minus deductible shown below	Premium	Limit stated in each Added P.I.P. End. Premium	Limit stated in P.P.I. End. minus deductible shown below	Premium
1							
2							
3							
4							
5							
Total Premium							

Covered Auto No.	COVERAGES - PREMIUMS, LIMITS AND DEDUCTIBLES (Absence of a deductible or limit entry in any column below means that the limit or deductible entry in the corresponding ITEM TWO column applies instead)	
	AUTO MED PAY	
	Limit	Premium
1		
2		
3		
4		
5		
Total Premium		

MOTOR CARRIER COVERAGE FORM DECLARATIONS (Continued)

ITEM THREE (Continued)

Covered Auto No.	COVERAGES - PREMIUMS, LIMITS and DEDUCTIBLES (Absence of a deductible or limit entry in any column below means that the limit or deductible entry in the corresponding ITEM TWO column applies instead.)						
	COMPREHENSIVE		SPECIFIED CAUSES OF LOSS	COLLISION		TOWING & LABOR	
	Limit stated in ITEM TWO minus deductible shown below	Premium	Limit stated in ITEM TWO Premium	Limit stated in ITEM TWO minus deductible shown below	Premium	Limit Per Disablement	Premium
1							
2							
3							
4							
5							
Total Premium							

ITEM FOUR

SCHEDULE OF HIRED OR BORROWED COVERED AUTO COVERAGE AND PREMIUMS.

LIABILITY COVERAGE - RATING BASIS, COST OF HIRE - AUTOS USED IN YOUR MOTOR CARRIER OPERATIONS

ESTIMATED COST OF HIRE	RATE PER EACH $100 COST OF HIRE	TOTAL ESTIMATED PREMIUM

LIABILITY COVERAGE - RATING BASIS, COST OF HIRE - AUTOS NOT USED IN YOUR MOTOR CARRIER OPERATIONS

STATE	ESTIMATED COST OF HIRE FOR EACH STATE	RATE PER EACH $100 COST OF HIRE	FACTOR (If liab. Cov. is primary)	PREMIUM
				TOTAL PREMIUM

MOTOR CARRIER COVERAGE FORM DECLARATIONS (Continued)

ITEM FOUR (continued)

PHYSICAL DAMAGE COVERAGE

COVERAGES	LIMIT OF INSURANCE THE MOST WE WILL PAY DEDUCTIBLE	ESTIMATED ANNUAL COST OF HIRE	RATE PER EACH $100 ANNUAL COST OF HIRE	PREMIUM
COMPREHENSIVE	ACTUAL CASH VALUE, COST OF REPAIRS OR $ WHICHEVER IS LESS, MINUS $ Ded. FOR EACH COVERED AUTO BUT NO DEDUCTIBLE APPLIES TO LOSS CAUSED BY FIRE OR LIGHTNING			
SPECIFIED CAUSES OF LOSS	ACTUAL CASH VALUE, COST OF REPAIRS OR $ WHICHEVER IS LESS, MINUS $25 Ded. FOR EACH COVERED AUTO FOR LOSS CAUSED BY MISCHIEF OR VANDALISM			
COLLISION	ACTUAL CASH VALUE, COST OF REPAIRS OR $ WHICHEVER IS LESS, MINUS $ Ded. FOR EACH COVERED AUTO			
			TOTAL PREMIUM	

Cost of Hire means:

(a) The total dollar amount of costs you incurred for the hire of automobiles (includes trailers and semi-trailers), and if not included therein,

(b) The total remunerations of all operators and drivers helpers, of hired automobiles whether hired with a driver by lessor or an employee of the lessee, or any other third party, and,

(c) The total dollar amount of any other costs (i.e. repair, maintenance, fuel, etc.) directly associated with operating the hired automobiles whether such costs are absorbed by the insured, paid to the lessor or owner, or paid to others.

ITEM FIVE

SCHEDULE FOR NON-OWNERSHIP LIABILITY

Rating Basis	Number	Premium
Number of Employees		$
Number of Partners		$
		$

MOTOR CARRIER COVERAGE FORM DECLARATIONS (Continued)

ITEM SIX

TRAILER INTERCHANGE COVERAGE

COVERAGES	LIMIT OF INSURANCE	DAILY RATE	ESTIMATED PREMIUM
COMPREHENSIVE		$	$
SPECIFIED CAUSES OF LOSS	STATED IN ITEM TWO	$	$
COLLISION		$	$

TOTAL PREMIUM

ITEM SEVEN

SCHEDULE FOR GROSS RECEIPTS RATING BASIS - LIABILITY COVERAGE

Estimated Yearly Gross Receipts	RATES Per $100 of Gross Receipts		PREMIUMS	
	LIABILITY COVERAGE	AUTO MEDICAL PAYMENTS	LIABILITY COVERAGE	AUTO MEDICAL PAYMENTS
	TOTAL PREMIUMS			
	MINIMUM PREMIUMS			

When used as a premium basis:

Gross Receipts means the total amount to which you are entitled for shipping or transporting property during the policy period regardless of whether you or any other carrier originate the shipment or transportation. "Gross Receipts" includes the total amount received from renting equipment, with or without drivers, to anyone who is not a "motor carrier" and 15% of the total amount received from renting any equipment to any "motor carrier". Gross Receipts does not include:

A. Amounts you pay to railroads, steamship lines, airlines and other motor carriers operating under their own ICC or PUC permits.

B. Advertising Revenue.

C. Taxes which you collect as a separate item and remit directly to a governmental division.

D. C.O.D. collections for cost of mail or merchandise including collection fees.

E. Warehouse storage fees.

IL 00 17 11 98

COMMON POLICY CONDITIONS

All Coverage Parts included in this policy are subject to the following conditions.

A. Cancellation

1. The first Named Insured shown in the Declarations may cancel this policy by mailing or delivering to us advance written notice of cancellation.

2. We may cancel this policy by mailing or delivering to the first Named Insured written notice of cancellation at least:

   a. 10 days before the effective date of cancellation if we cancel for nonpayment of premium; or

   b. 30 days before the effective date of cancellation if we cancel for any other reason.

3. We will mail or deliver our notice to the first Named Insured's last mailing address known to us.

4. Notice of cancellation will state the effective date of cancellation. The policy period will end on that date.

5. If this policy is cancelled, we will send the first Named Insured any premium refund due. If we cancel, the refund will be pro rata. If the first Named Insured cancels, the refund may be less than pro rata. The cancellation will be effective even if we have not made or offered a refund.

6. If notice is mailed, proof of mailing will be sufficient proof of notice.

B. Changes

This policy contains all the agreements between you and us concerning the insurance afforded. The first Named Insured shown in the Declarations is authorized to make changes in the terms of this policy with our consent. This policy's terms can be amended or waived only by endorsement issued by us and made a part of this policy.

C. Examination Of Your Books And Records

We may examine and audit your books and records as they relate to this policy at any time during the policy period and up to three years afterward.

D. Inspections And Surveys

1. We have the right to:

   a. Make inspections and surveys at any time;

   b. Give you reports on the conditions we find; and

   c. Recommend changes.

2. We are not obligated to make any inspections, surveys, reports or recommendations and any such actions we do undertake relate only to insurability and the premiums to be charged. We do not make safety inspections. We do not undertake to perform the duty of any person or organization to provide for the health or safety of workers or the public. And we do not warrant that conditions:

   a. Are safe or healthful; or

   b. Comply with laws, regulations, codes or standards.

3. Paragraphs 1. and 2. of this condition apply not only to us, but also to any rating, advisory, rate service or similar organization which makes insurance inspections, surveys, reports or recommendations.

4. Paragraph 2. of this condition does not apply to any inspections, surveys, reports or recommendations we may make relative to certification, under state or municipal statutes, ordinances or regulations, of boilers, pressure vessels or elevators.

E. Premiums

The first Named Insured shown in the Declarations:

1. Is responsible for the payment of all premiums; and

2. Will be the payee for any return premiums we pay.

F. Transfer Of Your Rights And Duties Under This Policy

Your rights and duties under this policy may not be transferred without our written consent except in the case of death of an individual named insured.

If you die, your rights and duties will be transferred to your legal representative but only while acting within the scope of duties as your legal representative. Until your legal representative is appointed, anyone having proper temporary custody of your property will have your rights and duties but only with respect to that property.

POLICY NUMBER:

IL DS 00 07 02

COMMON POLICY DECLARATIONS

COMPANY NAME AREA	PRODUCER NAME AREA

NAMED INSURED: _____

MAILING ADDRESS: _____

_____

POLICY PERIOD: FROM _____ TO _____ AT 12:01 A.M. STANDARD TIME AT YOUR MAILING ADDRESS SHOWN ABOVE.

BUSINESS DESCRIPTION	

IN RETURN FOR THE PAYMENT OF THE PREMIUM, AND SUBJECT TO ALL THE TERMS OF THIS POLICY, WE AGREE WITH YOU TO PROVIDE THE INSURANCE AS STATED IN THIS POLICY.

THIS POLICY CONSISTS OF THE FOLLOWING COVERAGE PARTS FOR WHICH A PREMIUM IS INDICATED. THIS PREMIUM MAY BE SUBJECT TO ADJUSTMENT.

	PREMIUM
BOILER AND MACHINERY COVERAGE PART	$ _____
CAPITAL ASSETS PROGRAM (OUTPUT POLICY) COVERAGE PART	$ _____
COMMERCIAL AUTOMOBILE COVERAGE PART	$ _____
COMMERCIAL GENERAL LIABILITY COVERAGE PART	$ _____
COMMERCIAL INLAND MARINE COVERAGE PART	$ _____
COMMERCIAL PROPERTY COVERAGE PART	$ _____
CRIME AND FIDELITY COVERAGE PART	$ _____
EMPLOYMENT-RELATED PRACTICES LIABILITY COVERAGE PART	$ _____
FARM COVERAGE PART	$ _____
LIQUOR LIABILITY COVERAGE PART	$ _____
POLLUTION LIABILITY COVERAGE PART	$ _____
PROFESSIONAL LIABILITY COVERAGE PART	$ _____
	$ _____
TOTAL:	$ _____

Premium shown is payable: $_____ at inception. $ _____

FORMS APPLICABLE TO ALL COVERAGE PARTS (SHOW NUMBERS):

Countersigned:	By:
(Date)	(Authorized Representative)

NOTE

OFFICERS' FACSIMILE SIGNATURES MAY BE INSERTED HERE, ON THE POLICY COVER OR ELSE-WHERE AT THE COMPANY'S OPTION.

COMMERCIAL AUTO
CA 00 38 12 02

THIS ENDORSEMENT CHANGES THE POLICY. PLEASE READ IT CAREFULLY.

WAR EXCLUSION

This endorsement modifies insurance provided under the following:

BUSINESS AUTO COVERAGE FORM
BUSINESS AUTO PHYSICAL DAMAGE COVERAGE FORM
MOTOR CARRIER COVERAGE FORM
SINGLE INTEREST AUTOMOBILE PHYSICAL DAMAGE INSURANCE POLICY
TRUCKERS COVERAGE FORM

With respect to coverage provided by this endorsement, the provisions of the Coverage Form apply unless modified by the endorsement.

A. Changes In Liability Coverage

The War exclusion under Paragraph **B. Exclusions** of **Section II – Liability Coverage** is replaced by the following:

WAR

"Bodily injury", "property damage" or "covered pollution cost or expense" arising directly or indirectly, out of:

a. War, including undeclared or civil war;

b. Warlike action by a military force, including action in hindering or defending against an actual or expected attack, by any government, sovereign or other authority using military personnel or other agents; or

c. Insurrection, rebellion, revolution, usurped power, or action taken by governmental authority in hindering or defending against any of these.

B. Changes In Garagekeepers Coverage

If the Garagekeepers Coverage endorsement or the Garagekeepers Coverage – Customers' Sound Receiving Equipment endorsement is attached, the following exclusion is added:

We will not pay for "loss" caused by or resulting from the following. Such "loss" is excluded regardless of any other cause or event that contributes concurrently or in any sequence to the "loss":

WAR

(1) War, including undeclared or civil war;

(2) Warlike action by a military force, including action in hindering or defending against an actual or expected attack, by any government, sovereign or other authority using military personnel or other agents; or

(3) Insurrection, rebellion, revolution, usurped power, or action taken by governmental authority in hindering or defending against any of these.

C. Changes In Auto Medical Payments

If the Auto Medical Payments Coverage endorsement is attached, then Exclusion **C.6.** is replaced by the following:

6. "Bodily injury", arising directly or indirectly, out of:

a. War, including undeclared or civil war;

b. Warlike action by a military force, including action in hindering or defending against an actual or expected attack, by any government, sovereign or other authority using military personnel or other agents; or

c. Insurrection, rebellion, revolution, usurped power, or action taken by governmental authority in hindering or defending against any of these.

D. Changes In Uninsured/Underinsured Motorists Coverage

If Uninsured and/or Underinsured Motorists Coverage is attached, then the following exclusion is added:

This insurance does not apply to:

WAR

1. "Bodily injury" or "property damage", if applicable, arising directly or indirectly, out of:

a. War, including undeclared or civil war;

b. Warlike action by a military force, including action in hindering or defending against an actual or expected attack, by any government, sovereign or other authority using military personnel or other agents; or

c. Insurrection, rebellion, revolution, usurped power, or action taken by governmental authority in hindering or defending against any of these.

E. Changes In Personal Injury Protection Coverage

1. If Personal Injury Protection, no-fault, or other similar coverage is attached, and:

   a. Contains, in whole or in part, a War exclusion, that exclusion is replaced by Paragraph **2.**

   b. Does not contain a war exclusion, Paragraph **2.** is added.

2. This insurance does not apply to:

   WAR

   "Bodily injury" or "property damage", if applicable, arising directly or indirectly, out of:

   a. War, including undeclared or civil war;

   b. Warlike action by a military force, including action in hindering or defending against an actual or expected attack, by any government, sovereign or other authority using military personnel or other agents; or

   c. Insurrection, rebellion, revolution, usurped power, or action taken by governmental authority in hindering or defending against any of these.

F. Changes In Single Interest Automobile Physical Damage Insurance Policy

The War exclusion is replaced by the following:

   a. War, including undeclared or civil war;

   b. Warlike action by a military force, including action in hindering or defending against an actual or expected attack, by any government, sovereign or other authority using military personnel or other agents; or

   c. Insurrection, rebellion, revolution, usurped power, or action taken by governmental authority in hindering or defending against any of these.

 CA 00 38 12 02 ☐

POLICY NUMBER:

COMMERCIAL AUTO
CA 99 10 09 02

THIS ENDORSEMENT CHANGES THE POLICY. PLEASE READ IT CAREFULLY.

DRIVE OTHER CAR COVERAGE – BROADENED COVERAGE FOR NAMED INDIVIDUALS

This endorsement modifies insurance provided under the following:

BUSINESS AUTO COVERAGE FORM
BUSINESS AUTO PHYSICAL DAMAGE COVERAGE FORM
GARAGE COVERAGE FORM
MOTOR CARRIER COVERAGE FORM
TRUCKERS COVERAGE FORM

With respect to coverage provided by this endorsement, the provisions of the Coverage Form apply unless modified by the endorsement.

This endorsement changes the policy effective on the inception date of the policy unless another date is indicated below.

Endorsement Effective:	Countersigned By:
Named Insured:	(Authorized Representative)

SCHEDULE

Name Of Individual	Liability		Auto Medical Payments	
	Limit	Premium	Limit	Premium

Name Of Individual	Uninsured Motorists		Underinsured Motorists		Physical Damage	
					Comp.	Coll.
	Limit	Premium	Limit	Premium		

Note – When uninsured motorists is provided at limits higher than the basic limits required by a financial responsibility law, underinsured motorists is included, unless otherwise noted. If Underinsured Motorists Coverage is provided as a separate coverage, make appropriate entry in the Schedule above.

(If no entry appears above, information required to complete this endorsement will be shown in the Declarations as applicable to this endorsement.)

CA 99 10 09 02 © ISO Properties, Inc., 2002 Page 1 of 2 ☐

A. This endorsement changes only those coverages where a premium is shown in the Schedule.

B. Changes In Liability Coverage

1. Any "auto" you don't own, hire or borrow is a covered "auto" for Liability Coverage while being used by any individual named in the Schedule or by his or her spouse while a resident of the same household except:

   a. Any "auto" owned by that individual or by any member of his or her household.

   b. Any "auto" used by that individual or his or her spouse while working in a business of selling, servicing, repairing or parking "autos".

2. The following is added to **Who Is An Insured:**

   Any individual named in the Schedule and his or her spouse, while a resident of the same household, are "insureds" while using any covered "auto" described in Paragraph **B.1.** of this endorsement.

C. Changes In Auto Medical Payments And Uninsured And Underinsured Motorists Coverages

The following is added to **Who Is An Insured:**

Any individual named in the Schedule and his or her "family members" are "insured" while "occupying" or while a pedestrian when being struck by any "auto" you don't own except:

Any "auto" owned by that individual or by any "family member".

D. Changes In Physical Damage Coverage

Any private passenger type "auto" you don't own, hire or borrow is a covered "auto" while in the care, custody or control of any individual named in the Schedule or his or her spouse while a resident of the same household except:

1. Any "auto" owned by that individual or by any member of his or her household.

2. Any "auto" used by that individual or his or her spouse while working in a business of selling, servicing, repairing or parking "autos".

E. Additional Definition

As used in this endorsement:

"Family member" means a person related to the individual named in the Schedule by blood, marriage or adoption who is a resident of the individual's household, including a ward or foster child.

COMMERCIAL AUTO
CA 99 33 02 99

THIS ENDORSEMENT CHANGES THE POLICY. PLEASE READ IT CAREFULLY.

EMPLOYEES AS INSUREDS

This endorsement modifies insurance provided under the following:

BUSINESS AUTO COVERAGE FORM
MOTOR CARRIER COVERAGE FORM
TRUCKERS COVERAGE FORM

With respect to coverage provided by this endorsement, the provisions of the Coverage Form apply unless modified by the endorsement.

The following is added to the **Section II – Liability Coverage,** Paragraph **A.1. Who Is An Insured** Provision:

Any "employee" of yours is an "insured" while using a covered "auto" you don't own, hire or borrow in your business or your personal affairs.

THIS ENDORSEMENT CHANGES THE POLICY. PLEASE READ IT CAREFULLY.

INDIVIDUAL NAMED INSURED

This endorsement modifies insurance provided under the following:

BUSINESS AUTO COVERAGE FORM
BUSINESS AUTO PHYSICAL DAMAGE COVERAGE FORM
GARAGE COVERAGE FORM
MOTOR CARRIER COVERAGE FORM
TRUCKERS COVERAGE FORM

With respect to coverage provided by this endorsement, the provisions of the Coverage Form apply unless modified by the endorsement.

If you are an individual, the policy is changed as follows:

A. Changes In Liability Coverage

1. The Fellow Employee Exclusion does not apply to "bodily injury" to your or any "family member's" fellow employees.

2. **Personal Auto Coverage**

   If any "auto" you own of the "private passenger type" is a covered "auto" under Liability Coverage:

   a. The following is added to **Who Is An Insured:**

      "Family members" are "insureds" for any covered "auto" you own of the "private passenger type" and any other "auto" described in Paragraph **2.b.** of this endorsement.

   b. Any "auto" you don't own is a covered "auto" while being used by you or by any "family member" except:

      (1) Any "auto" owned by any "family members".

      (2) Any "auto" furnished or available for your or any "family member's" regular use.

      (3) Any "auto" used by you or by any of your "family members" while working in a business of selling, servicing, repairing or parking "autos".

      (4) Any "auto" other than an "auto" of the "private passenger type" used by you or any of your "family members" while working in any other business or occupation.

   c. The Pollution Exclusion and, if forming a part of the policy, the Nuclear Energy Liability Exclusion (Broad Form), does not apply to any covered "auto" of the "private passenger type".

   d. The following exclusion is added and applies only to "private passenger type" covered "autos":

      This insurance does not apply to:

      "Bodily injury" or "property damage" for which an "insured" under the policy is also an "insured" under a nuclear energy liability policy or would be an "insured" but for its termination upon its exhaustion of its limit of liability. A nuclear energy liability policy is a policy issued by Nuclear Energy Liability Insurance Association, Mutual Atomic Energy Liability Underwriters or any of their successors. This exclusion does not apply to "autos" registered or principally garaged in New York.

B. Changes In Physical Damage

PERSONAL AUTO COVERAGE

If any "auto" you own of the "private passenger type" is a covered "auto" under Physical Damage Coverage, a "non-owned auto" will also be considered a covered "auto". However, the most we will pay for "loss" to a "non-owned auto" which is a "trailer" is $500.

C. Additional Definitions

As used in this endorsement:

1. "Family member" means a person related to you by blood, marriage or adoption who is a resident of your household, including a ward or foster child.

© ISO Properties, Inc., 2000

2. The words "you" and "your" include your spouse if a resident of the same household except for notice of cancellation.

3. When the phrase "private passenger type" appears in quotation marks it includes any covered "auto" you own of the pick-up or van type not used for business purposes, other than farming or ranching.

4. "Non-owned auto" means any "private passenger type" "auto", pick-up, van or "trailer" not owned by or furnished or available for the regular use of you or any "family member", while it is in the custody of or being operated by you or any "family member".

CA 99 17 10 01 □

POLICY NUMBER:

COMMERCIAL AUTO
CA 20 01 10 01

THIS ENDORSEMENT CHANGES THE POLICY. PLEASE READ IT CAREFULLY.

LESSOR – ADDITIONAL INSURED AND LOSS PAYEE

This endorsement modifies insurance provided under the following:

BUSINESS AUTO COVERAGE FORM
BUSINESS AUTO PHYSICAL DAMAGE COVERAGE FORM
GARAGE COVERAGE FORM
MOTOR CARRIER COVERAGE FORM
TRUCKERS COVERAGE FORM

With respect to coverage provided by this endorsement, the provisions of the Coverage Form apply unless modified by the endorsement.

This endorsement changes the policy effective on the inception date of the policy unless another date is indicated below.

Endorsement Effective:	Countersigned By:
Named Insured:	(Authorized Representative)

SCHEDULE

Insurance Company Policy Number Effective Date	
Expiration Date	
Named Insured Address	
Additional Insured (Lessor) Address	
Designation or Description of "Leased Autos"	

Coverages	Limit Of Insurance
Liability	$ Each "Accident"
Personal Injury Protection (or equivalent no-fault coverage)	$
Comprehensive	ACTUAL CASH VALUE OR COST OF REPAIR WHICHEVER IS LESS; MINUS: $ For Each Covered "Leased Auto"
Collision	ACTUAL CASH VALUE OR COST OF REPAIR WHICHEVER IS LESS; MINUS: $ For Each Covered "Leased Auto"
Specified Causes of Loss	ACTUAL CASH VALUE OR COST OF REPAIR WHICHEVER IS LESS; MINUS: $ For Each Covered "Leased Auto"

(If no entry appears above, information required to complete this endorsement will be shown in the Declarations as applicable to this endorsement.)

A. Coverage

1. Any "leased auto" designated or described in the Schedule will be considered a covered "auto" you own and not a covered "auto" you hire or borrow. For a covered "auto" that is a "leased auto" **Who Is An Insured** is changed to include as an "insured" the lessor named in the Schedule.

2. The coverages provided under this endorsement apply to any "leased auto" described in the Schedule until the expiration date shown in the Schedule, or when the lessor or his or her agent takes possession of the "leased auto", whichever occurs first.

B. Loss Payable Clause

1. We will pay, as interest may appear, you and the lessor named in this endorsement for "loss" to a "leased auto".

2. The insurance covers the interest of the lessor unless the "loss" results from fraudulent acts or omissions on your part.

3. If we make any payment to the lessor, we will obtain his or her rights against any other party.

C. Cancellation

1. If we cancel the policy, we will mail notice to the lessor in accordance with the Cancellation Common Policy Condition.

2. If you cancel the policy, we will mail notice to the lessor.

3. Cancellation ends this agreement.

D.
The lessor is not liable for payment of your premiums.

E. Additional Definition

As used in this endorsement:

"Leased auto" means an "auto" leased or rented to you, including any substitute, replacement or extra "auto" needed to meet seasonal or other needs, under a leasing or rental agreement that requires you to provide direct primary insurance for the lessor.

 CA 20 01 10 01

COMMERCIAL AUTO
CA 99 44 12 93

THIS ENDORSEMENT CHANGES THE POLICY. PLEASE READ IT CAREFULLY.

LOSS PAYABLE CLAUSE

This endorsement modifies insurance provided under the following:

BUSINESS AUTO COVERAGE FORM
GARAGE COVERAGE FORM
MOTOR CARRIER COVERAGE FORM
TRUCKERS COVERAGE FORM
BUSINESS AUTO PHYSICAL DAMAGE COVERAGE FORM

With respect to coverage provided by this endorsement, the provisions of the Coverage Form apply unless modified by the endorsement.

A. We will pay, as interest may appear, you and the loss payee named in the policy for "loss" to a covered "auto".

B. The insurance covers the interest of the loss payee unless the "loss" results from conversion, secretion or embezzlement on your part.

C. We may cancel the policy as allowed by the CANCELLATION Common Policy Condition.

Cancellation ends this agreement as to the loss payee's interest. If we cancel the policy we will mail you and the loss payee the same advance notice.

D. If we make any payments to the loss payee, we will obtain his or her rights against any other party.

CA 99 44 12 93   Copyright, Insurance Services Office, Inc., 1993   Page 1 of 1   □

POLICY NUMBER:

COMMERCIAL AUTO
CA 20 15 10 01

THIS ENDORSEMENT CHANGES THE POLICY. PLEASE READ IT CAREFULLY.

MOBILE EQUIPMENT

This endorsement modifies insurance provided under the following:

> BUSINESS AUTO COVERAGE FORM
> BUSINESS AUTO PHYSICAL DAMAGE COVERAGE FORM
> MOTOR CARRIER COVERAGE FORM
> TRUCKERS COVERAGE FORM

With respect to coverage provided by this endorsement, the provisions of the Coverage Form apply unless modified by the endorsement.

This endorsement changes the policy effective on the inception date of the policy unless another date is indicated below.

Endorsement Effective:	Countersigned By:
Named Insured:	(Authorized Representative)

SCHEDULE

Coverages	Covered "Auto" Vehicle Numbers	Limit Of Insurance	Premium
Liability		$ Each "Accident"	$
Auto Medical Payments		$ Each Person	$
Personal Injury Protection or Equivalent No-Fault Coverage		Separately Stated in Each P.I.P. Endorsement	$
Uninsured Motorists		$ Each "Accident"	$
Underinsured Motorists (Indicate Only When Coverage Is Not Included in Uninsured Motorists Coverage)		$ Each "Accident"	$
Comprehensive		ACTUAL CASH VALUE OR COST OF REPAIR, WHICHEVER IS LESS, MINUS $ DED. FOR EACH COVERED AUTO, BUT NO DEDUCTIBLE APPLIES TO LOSS CAUSED BY FIRE OR LIGHTNING	$
Collision		ACTUAL CASH VALUE OR COST OF REPAIR, WHICHEVER IS LESS, MINUS $ DED. FOR EACH COVERED AUTO	$

CA 20 15 10 01   Copyright, Insurance Services Office, Inc., 2000   Page 1 of 2   □

Specified Causes of Loss		ACTUAL CASH VALUE OR COST OF REPAIR, WHICHEVER IS LESS, MINUS $ DED. FOR EACH COVERED AUTO FOR LOSS CAUSED BY MISCHIEF OR VANDALISM	$

Vehicle No.	Description Of Vehicles That Are Covered "Autos"

(If no entry appears above, information required to complete this endorsement will be shown in the Declarations as applicable to this endorsement.)

A. This endorsement provides only those coverages where a premium is shown in the Schedule. Each of these coverages applies only to the vehicles shown as covered "autos".

B. The vehicles described in the Schedule will be considered covered "autos" and not "mobile equipment".

C. Liability Coverage does not apply to "bodily injury" or "property damage" resulting from the operation of any machinery that is on, attached to or part of any of these vehicles.

SAMPLE

Copyright, Insurance Services Office, Inc., 2000 CA 20 15 10 01 ☐

POLICY NUMBER:

COMMERCIAL AUTO
CA 99 23 12 93

THIS ENDORSEMENT CHANGES THE POLICY. PLEASE READ IT CAREFULLY.

RENTAL REIMBURSEMENT COVERAGE

This endorsement modifies insurance provided under the following:

BUSINESS AUTO COVERAGE FORM
GARAGE COVERAGE FORM
MOTOR CARRIER COVERAGE FORM
TRUCKERS COVERAGE FORM
BUSINESS AUTO PHYSICAL DAMAGE COVERAGE FORM

With respect to coverage provided by this endorsement, the provisions of the Coverage Form apply unless modified by the endorsement.

This endorsement changes the policy effective on the inception date of the policy unless another date is indicated below.

Endorsement Effective	
Named Insured	Countersigned By

(Authorized Representative)

SCHEDULE

Coverages	Auto No.	Designation or Description of Covered "Autos" to which this insurance applies	Maximum Payment Each Covered "Auto"			Premium
			Any One Day	No. of Days	Any One Period	
Comprehensive	1		$		$	$
	2		$		$	$
Collision	1		$		$	$
	2		$		$	$
Specified	1		$		$	$
Causes of Loss	2		$		$	$
			Total Premium			

(If no entry appears above, information required to complete this endorsement will be shown in the Declarations as applicable to this endorsement.)

A. This endorsement provides only those coverages where a premium is shown in the Schedule. It applies only to a covered "auto" described or designated in the Schedule.

B. We will pay for rental reimbursement expenses incurred by you for the rental of an "auto" because of "loss" to a covered "auto". Payment applies in addition to the otherwise applicable amount of each coverage you have on a covered "auto." No deductibles apply to this coverage.

C. We will pay only for those expenses incurred during the policy period beginning 24 hours after the "loss" and ending, regardless of the policy's expiration, with the lesser of the following number of days:

1. The number of days reasonably required to repair or replace the covered "auto". If "loss" is caused by theft, this number of days is added to the number of days it takes to locate the covered "auto" and return it to you.

2. The number of days shown in the Schedule.

D. Our payment is limited to the lesser of the following amounts:

1. Necessary and actual expenses incurred.

2. The maximum payment stated in the Schedule applicable to "any one day" or "any one period".

E. This coverage does not apply while there are spare or reserve "autos" available to you for your operations.

F. If "loss" results from the total theft of a covered "auto" of the private passenger type, we will pay under this coverage only that amount of your rental reimbursement expenses which is not already provided for under the PHYSICAL DAMAGE COVERAGE Coverage Extension.

       CA 99 23 12 93   ▢

POLICY NUMBER:

COMMERCIAL AUTO
CA 99 30 10 01

THIS ENDORSEMENT CHANGES THE POLICY. PLEASE READ IT CAREFULLY.

TAPES, RECORDS AND DISCS COVERAGE

This endorsement modifies insurance provided under the following:

BUSINESS AUTO COVERAGE FORM
BUSINESS AUTO PHYSICAL DAMAGE COVERAGE FORM
GARAGE COVERAGE FORM
MOTOR CARRIER COVERAGE FORM
TRUCKERS COVERAGE FORM

With respect to coverage provided by this endorsement, the provisions of the Coverage Form apply unless modified by the endorsement.

This endorsement changes the policy effective on the inception date of the policy unless another date is indicated below.

Endorsement Effective:	Countersigned By:
Named Insured:	(Authorized Representative)

SCHEDULE

Additional Premium
$

(If no entry appears above, information required to complete this endorsement will be shown in the Declarations as applicable to this endorsement.)

A. The **Physical Damage Coverage** Section is amended as follows:

   1. The exclusion referring to tapes, records, discs or other similar audio, visual or data electronic devices designed for use with audio, visual or data electronic equipment does not apply.

   2. The following is added to Paragraph **A. Coverage:**

   Under Comprehensive Coverage we will pay for "loss" to tapes, records, discs or other similar devices used with audio, visual or data electronic equipment. We will pay only if the tapes, records, discs or other similar audio, visual or data electronic devices:

   a. Are your property or that of a family member, and

   b. Are in a covered "auto" at the time of "loss".

   The most we will pay for "loss" is $200.

B. No Physical Damage Coverage deductible applies to this coverage.

CA 99 30 10 01   © ISO Properties, Inc., 2000   Page 1 of 1   □

COMMERCIAL AUTO
CA 99 03 07 97

THIS ENDORSEMENT CHANGES THE POLICY. PLEASE READ IT CAREFULLY.

AUTO MEDICAL PAYMENTS COVERAGE

This endorsement modifies insurance provided under the following:

BUSINESS AUTO COVERAGE FORM
GARAGE COVERAGE FORM
MOTOR CARRIER COVERAGE FORM
TRUCKERS COVERAGE FORM

With respect to coverage provided by this endorsement, the provisions of the Coverage Form apply unless modified by the endorsement.

A. Coverage

We will pay reasonable expenses incurred for necessary medical and funeral services to or for an "insured" who sustains "bodily injury" caused by "accident". We will pay only those expenses incurred, for services rendered within three years from the date of the "accident".

B. Who Is An Insured

1. You while "occupying" or, while a pedestrian, when struck by any "auto".

2. If you are an individual, any "family member" while "occupying" or, while a pedestrian, when struck by any "auto".

3. Anyone else "occupying" a covered "auto" or a temporary substitute for a covered "auto". The covered "auto" must be out of service because of its breakdown, repair, servicing, loss or destruction.

C. Exclusions

This insurance does not apply to any of the following:

1. "Bodily injury" sustained by an "insured" while "occupying" a vehicle located for use as a premises.

2. "Bodily injury" sustained by you or any "family member" while "occupying" or struck by any vehicle (other than a covered "auto") owned by you or furnished or available for your regular use.

3. "Bodily injury" sustained by any "family member" while "occupying" or struck by any vehicle (other than a covered "auto") owned by or furnished or available for the regular use of any "family member".

4. "Bodily injury" to your "employee" arising out of and in the course of employment by you. However, we will cover "bodily injury" to your domestic "employees" if not entitled to workers' compensation benefits. For the purposes of this endorsement, a domestic "employee" is a person engaged in household or domestic work performed principally in connection with a residence premises.

5. "Bodily injury" to an "insured" while working in a business of selling, servicing, repairing or parking "autos" unless that business is yours.

6. "Bodily injury" caused by declared or undeclared war or insurrection or any of their consequences.

7. "Bodily injury" to anyone using a vehicle without a reasonable belief that the person is entitled to do so.

8. "Bodily Injury" sustained by an "insured" while "occupying" any covered "auto" while used in any professional racing or demolition contest or stunting activity, or while practicing for such contest or activity. This insurance also does not apply to any "bodily injury" sustained by an "insured" while the "auto" is being prepared for such a contest or activity.

D. Limit Of Insurance

Regardless of the number of covered "autos", "insureds", premiums paid, claims made or vehicles involved in the "accident", the most we will pay for "bodily injury" for each "insured" injured in any one "accident" is the Limit Of Insurance for Auto Medical Payments Coverage shown in the Declarations.

No one will be entitled to receive duplicate payments for the same elements of "loss" under this coverage and any Liability Coverage Form, Uninsured Motorists Coverage Endorsement or Underinsured Motorists Coverage Endorsement attached to this Coverage Part.

CA 99 03 07 97   Copyright, Insurance Services Office, Inc., 1996   Page 1 of 2   □

E. Changes In Conditions

The Conditions are changed for Auto Medical Payments Coverage as follows:

1. The Transfer Of Rights Of Recovery Against Others To Us Condition does not apply.

2. The reference in Other Insurance in the Business Auto and Garage Coverage Forms and Other Insurance – Primary And Excess Insurance Provisions in the Truckers and Motor Carrier Coverage Forms to "other collectible insurance" applies only to other collectible auto medical payments insurance.

F. Additional Definitions

As used in this endorsement:

1. "Family member" means a person related to you by blood, marriage or adoption who is a resident of your household, including a ward or foster child.

2. "Occupying" means in, upon, getting in, on, out or off.

COMMERCIAL AUTO
CA 25 01 12 93

THIS ENDORSEMENT CHANGES THE POLICY. PLEASE READ IT CAREFULLY.

BROAD FORM PRODUCTS COVERAGE

This endorsement modifies insurance provided under the following:

GARAGE COVERAGE FORM

With respect to coverage provided by this endorsement, the provisions of the Coverage Form apply unless modified by the endorsement.

LIABILITY COVERAGE is changed as follows:

The DEFECTIVE PRODUCTS Exclusion does not apply. However, subject to the Each "Accident" Limit of Insurance – "Garage Operations" – Other Than Covered "Autos", the coverage only applies to that amount of "property damage" to your "products" that exceeds $250 for any one "accident".

COMMERCIAL AUTO
CA 25 14 10 01

THIS ENDORSEMENT CHANGES THE POLICY. PLEASE READ IT CAREFULLY.

BROADENED COVERAGE – GARAGES

This endorsement modifies insurance provided under the following:

GARAGE COVERAGE FORM

The coverages provided by this endorsement are applicable only to "garage operations" other than the ownership, maintenance or use of the covered "autos".

With respect to coverage provided by this endorsement, the provisions of the Coverage Form apply unless modified by the endorsement.

This endorsement changes the policy effective on the inception date of the policy unless another date is indicated below.

Endorsement Effective:	Countersigned By:
Named Insured:	
	(Authorized Representative)

SCHEDULE

Personal and Advertising Injury Limit of Insurance	$
The Fire Legal Liability Coverage Limit of Insurance is $50,000 for any one fire unless another limit is shown below:	
Fire Legal Liability Limit of Insurance	$
The premium for this endorsement is	$

(If no entry appears above, information required to complete this endorsement will be shown in the Declarations as applicable to this endorsement.)

SECTION I – PERSONAL AND ADVERTISING INJURY LIABILITY COVERAGE

A. Coverage

We will pay all sums the "insured" legally must pay as damages because of "personal and advertising injury" caused by an offense arising out of your business but only if the offense was committed in the Coverage Territory during the Policy Period.

We will have the right and duty to defend any "insured" against a "suit" asking for these damages. However, we have no duty to defend any "insured" against a "suit" seeking damages for "personal and advertising injury" to which this insurance does not apply. We may investigate and settle any claim or "suit" as we consider appropriate. Our duty to defend or settle ends when the Personal And Advertising Injury Limit of Insurance has been exhausted by payment of judgments or settlements.

1. Who Is An Insured

The following are "insureds":

a. You and your spouse.

b. Your partners (if you are a partnership) and their spouses or members (if you are a limited liability company) and their spouses. None of your partners (if you are a partnership) or their spouses nor your members (if you are a limited liability company) or their spouses is an "insured" for "personal and advertising injury" resulting from the conduct of any other partnership.

c. Your "employees", executive officers, directors and stockholders but only while acting within the scope of their duties.

2. Coverage Extensions

SUPPLEMENTARY PAYMENTS

In addition to the Personal And Advertising Injury Limit of Insurance, we will pay for the "insured":

a. All expenses we incur.

b. The cost of bonds to release attachments in any "suit" against an "insured" we defend, but only for bond amounts within the Personal And Advertising Injury Limit of Insurance.

c. All reasonable expenses incurred by the "insured" at our request, including actual loss of earnings up to $250 a day because of time off from work.

d. All costs taxed against the "insured" in any "suit" against an "insured" we defend.

e. All interest on the full amount of any judgment that accrues after entry of the judgment in any "suit" against an "insured" we defend; but our duty to pay interest ends when we have paid, offered to pay, or deposited in court the part of the judgment that is within the Personal And Advertising Injury Limit of Insurance.

B. Exclusions

1. This insurance does not apply to:

a. "Personal and advertising injury":

(1) For which the "insured" has assumed liability assumed under any contract or agreement. But this exclusion does not apply to liability for damages that the "insured" would have in the absence of the contract or agreement.

(2) Caused by or at the direction of the "insured" with the knowledge that the act would violate the rights of another and would inflict "personal and advertising injury".

(3) Arising out of oral or written publication of material, if done by or at the direction of the "insured" with knowledge of its falsity.

(4) Arising out of oral or written publication of material whose first publication took place before the effective date of this insurance.

(5) Arising out of a criminal act committed by or at the direction of any "insured".

(6) Arising out of breach of contract, except an implied contract to use another's advertising idea in your "advertisement".

(7) Arising out of the failure of goods, products or services to conform with any statement of quality or performance made in your "advertisement".

(8) Arising out of the wrong description of the price of goods, products or services stated in your "advertisement".

(9) Committed by an "insured" whose business is advertising, broadcasting, publishing or telecasting. However, this exclusion does not apply to Paragraphs **a.**, **b.** and **c.** of "personal and advertising injury" under the Additional Definitions Section.

(10) To:

(a) A person arising out of any:

(i) Refusal to employ that person;

(ii) Termination of that person's employment; or

(iii) Employment-related practices, policies, acts or omissions, such as coercion, demotion, evaluation, reassignment, discipline, defamation, harassment, humiliation or discrimination directed at that person; or

(b) The spouse, child, parent, brother or sister of that person as a consequence of "personal injury" to that person at whom any of the employment-related practices described in Paragraphs **(i)**, **(ii)** or **(iii)** above is directed.

This exclusion applies:

(a) Whether the "insured" may be liable as an employer or in any other capacity; and

(b) To any obligation to share damages with or repay someone else who must pay damages because of the injury.

© ISO Properties, Inc., 2000   □

(11) Arising out of the actual, alleged or threatened discharge, dispersal, seepage, migration, release or escape of "pollutants" at any time.

b. Any loss, cost or expense arising out of any:

(1) Request, demand, order or statutory or regulatory requirement that any "insured" or others test for, monitor, clean up, remove, contain, treat, detoxify or neutralize, or in any way respond to, or assess the effects of, "pollutants"; or

(2) Claim or "suit" by or on behalf of a governmental authority for damages because of testing for, monitoring, cleaning up, removing, containing, treating, detoxifying or neutralizing, or in any way responding to, or assessing the effects of, "pollutants".

2. The following is added to Paragraph **B. Exclusions** of **Section II – Liability Coverage:**

Personal And Advertising Injury

"Bodily injury" arising out of "personal and advertising injury".

C. Personal And Advertising Injury Limit Of Insurance

The following is added to the **Aggregate Limit Of Insurance – "Garage Operations" – Other Than Covered "Autos"** Provision in **Section II – Liability Coverage:**

Subject to the Aggregate Limit Of Insurance – "Garage Operations" – Other Than Covered "Autos" and regardless of the number of "insureds", claims-made or "suits" brought or persons or organizations making claim or bringing "suits", the most we will pay for the sum of all damages because of all "personal and advertising injury" sustained by any one person or organization is the Personal And Advertising Injury Limit of Insurance shown in the Schedule of the Broadened Coverage – Garages Endorsement.

The Each "Accident" Limit of Insurance – "Garage Operations" – Other Than Covered "Autos" for Liability Coverage does not apply to damages we pay because of "personal and advertising injury".

D. Additional Definitions

As used in this endorsement:

1. "Personal and advertising injury" means injury, including consequential "bodily injury, arising out of one or more of the following offenses:

a. False arrest, detention or imprisonment;

b. Malicious prosecution;

c. The wrongful eviction from, wrongful entry into, or invasion of the right of private occupancy of a room, dwelling or premises that a person occupies, committed by or on behalf of its owner, landlord or lessor;

d. Oral or written publication of material that slanders or libels a person or organization or disparages a person's or organization's goods, products or services;

e. Oral or written publication of material that violates a person's right of privacy;

f. The use of another's advertising idea in your "advertisement"; or

g. Infringing upon another's copyright, trade dress or slogan in your "advertisement".

2. "Advertisement" means a notice that is broadcast or published to the general public or specific market segments about your goods, products or services for the purpose of attracting customers or supporters.

SECTION II – HOST LIQUOR LIABILITY COVERAGE

Liability Coverage is changed by adding the following:

We will also pay all sums the "insured" legally must pay as damages because of "bodily injury" or "property damage" arising out of the giving or serving of alcoholic beverages at functions incidental to your garage business provided you are not engaged in the business of manufacturing, distributing, selling or serving of alcoholic beverages.

SECTION III – FIRE LEGAL LIABILITY COVERAGE

Liability Coverage for "garage operations" is changed as follows:

A. The insurance applies to "property damage" caused by fire to premises while rented to you or temporarily occupied by you with the permission of the owner.

B. Exclusions **3.** through **17.** do not apply to the insurance provided by this endorsement.

C. Subject to the Aggregate Limit Of Insurance – "Garage Operations" – Other Than "Auto", the most we will pay for all "property damage" resulting from any one fire is $50,000 unless another limit is shown in the Schedule of the Broadened Coverage – Garages Endorsement.

D. This insurance is excess over any collectible property insurance (including any deductible portion of that insurance) available to the "insured".

SECTION IV – INCIDENTAL MEDICAL MALPRACTICE LIABILITY COVERAGE

Liability Coverage is changed by adding the following exclusion:

This insurance does not apply to any "insured" in the business or occupation of providing any of the services listed under the following definition.

As used in this endorsement:

"Bodily injury" means bodily injury, sickness or disease sustained by a person including death resulting from any of these.

"Bodily injury" also includes injury resulting from:

1. Providing or failing to provide any medical or related professional health care services;
2. Furnishing food or drink connected with any medical or other professional health care services; or
3. Furnishing or dispensing drugs or medical, dental or surgical supplies or appliances.

SECTION V – NON-OWNED WATERCRAFT COVERAGE

Liability Coverage is changed as follows:

A. The **Watercraft Or Aircraft** Exclusion is replaced by the following:

This insurance does not apply to:

1. Any aircraft; or
2. Any watercraft except a watercraft under 26 feet that is not owned by you nor being used to carry persons or property for a charge.

But this exclusion does not apply to watercraft while ashore on premises where you conduct "garage operations".

B. If there is other applicable insurance covering damages payable under Non-Owned Watercraft Coverage, we will not make any payments under this coverage.

SECTION VI – ADDITIONAL PERSONS INSURED

Liability Coverage is changed by adding the following to **Who Is An Insured**:

If you are a partnership, the spouse of a partner is an "insured" with respect to the conduct of your garage business.

SECTION VII – AUTOMATIC LIABILITY COVERAGE – NEWLY ACQUIRED GARAGE BUSINESSES (90 DAYS)

As used in this endorsement:

"Insured" means any person or organization qualifying as an insured in the Who Is An Insured Provision of the applicable coverage. Except with respect to the Limit of Insurance, the coverage afforded applies separately to each insured who is seeking coverage or against whom a claim or "suit" is brought.

"Insured" also includes as named "insured" any garage business that is acquired or formed by you and over which you maintain ownership or majority interest.

However, "insured" does not include any garage business:

1. That is a joint venture;
2. That is an "insured" under any other similar liability or indemnity policy;
3. That has exhausted its Limit of Insurance under any other similar liability or indemnity policy; or
4. 90 days or more after its acquisition or formation by you.

SECTION VIII – LIMITED WORLDWIDE LIABILITY COVERAGE

A. The **Policy Period, Coverage Territory** Garage Condition is changed by adding the following:

We also cover "bodily injury", "property damage", or "personal and advertising injury" that:

1. Occurs during the policy period shown in the Declarations; and
2. Is caused by an "insured" who permanently lives within the coverage territory while the "insured" is temporarily outside of one of those places.

The original "suit" for damages resulting from such "bodily injury", "property damage", or "personal and advertising injury" must be brought within the coverage territory.

B. We will not provide **Limited Worldwide Liability Coverage** for any "work you performed".

 CA 25 14 10 01 □

COMMERCIAL AUTO
CA 25 02 12 93

THIS ENDORSEMENT CHANGES THE POLICY. PLEASE READ IT CAREFULLY.

DEALERS DRIVEAWAY COLLISION COVERAGE

This endorsement modifies insurance provided under the following:

GARAGE COVERAGE FORM

With respect to coverage provided by this endorsement, the provisions of the Coverage Form apply unless modified by the endorsement.

PHYSICAL DAMAGE COVERAGE is changed as follows:

The exclusion relating to collision "loss" to covered "autos" driven or transported more than fifty road miles from point of purchase or distribution to their destination does not apply, provided that:

1. You must include in your regular monthly or quarterly reports a statement of the points of origin, the destination and the factory price of each of these covered "autos".

2. If on the date of your last report the total value of these covered "autos", driven or transported during the period the report covers, exceeds what you reported we will pay only a percentage of what we would otherwise be obligated to pay. We will determine this percentage by dividing the total value reported by the total value you actually had on the date of your last report.

CA 25 02 12 93   Copyright, Insurance Services Office, Inc., 1993   **Page 1 of 1**

GARAGE COVERAGE FORM - AUTO DEALERS' SUPPLEMENTARY SCHEDULE

INSTRUCTIONS

1. This schedule must be attached to the **GARAGE COVERAGE FORM DECLARATIONS** when the **GARAGE COVERAGE FORM** is used to write an "auto" dealer garage risk, other than a trailer dealer.

2. This schedule is one way **BUT NOT THE ONLY** way that all of the material needed to write an "auto" dealer risk may be arranged.

3. Companies may amend the arrangement and format of the supplementary schedule to serve their own policy preparation needs and procedures.

4. **WARNING.** If the arrangement or format of the declarations is altered, the major **ITEMS** of this supplementary schedule must be kept in the same order because of specific references in the **GARAGE COVERAGE FORM,** the **GARAGE COVERAGE FORM DECLARATIONS** and in some of the endorsements that may be attached.

5. **ITEM NINE** which deals with covered "autos" insured on a specified car basis or covered "autos" furnished to someone other than a Class I or Class II operator may be omitted at the company's option.

CA 00 07 12 90　　　　　　Copyright, Insurance Services Office, Inc., 1990　　　　　　☐

GARAGE COVERAGE FORM—AUTO DEALERS' SUPPLEMENTARY SCHEDULE

ITEM THREE
LOCATIONS WHERE YOU CONDUCT GARAGE OPERATIONS

Location No.	Address state your main business location as Location No. 1
1	
2	
3	

ITEM FOUR
LIABILITY COVERAGE—PREMIUMS.

Location No.	Classes of Operators	Rating Factor	Number of Persons	Rating Units	Total Rating Units	Liability Premium	Personal Injury Protection Premium	Property Protection Premium
1	Class I—Employees Regular Operators							
	Class I—Employees All Others							
	Class II—Non-Employees Under age 25							
	Class II—Non-Employees Age 25 or over							
2	Class I—Employees Regular Operators							
	Class I—Employees All Others							
	Class II—Non-Employees Under age 25							
	Class II—Non-Employees Age 25 or over							
3	Class I—Employees Regular Operators							
	Class I—Employees All Others							
	Class II—Non-Employees Under age 25							
	Class II—Non-Employees Age 25 or over							
	TOTAL PREMIUMS							

Definitions:
Class I—Employees
Regular Operator — Proprietors, partners and officers active in the "garage operations," salespersons, general managers, service managers; any employee whose principal duty involves the operation of covered "autos" or who is furnished a covered "auto."

All Others — All other employees.

NOTE: 1. Part-time employees working an average of 20 hours or more a week for the number of weeks worked are to be counted as 1 rating unit each.
2. Part-time employees working an average of less than 20 hours a week for the number of weeks worked are to be counted as ½ rating unit each.

CLASS II—Non-Employees

Any of the following persons who are regularly furnished with a covered "auto": Inactive proprietors, partners or officers and their relatives and the relatives of any person described in Class I.

GARAGE COVERAGE FORM—AUTO DEALERS' SUPPLEMENTARY SCHEDULE—(Continued)

ITEM FIVE
LIABILITY COVERAGE FOR YOUR CUSTOMERS.

In accordance with paragraph a.(2)(d) of WHO IS AN INSURED under SECTION II—LIABILITY COVERAGE. Liability coverage for your customers is limited unless indicated below by "☒".

☐ If this box is checked, paragraph a.(2)(d) of WHO IS AN INSURED under SECTION II—LIABILITY COVERAGE does not apply.

ITEM SIX
GARAGEKEEPERS COVERAGES AND PREMIUMS.

Location No.	Coverages	Limit of Insurance For Each Location (Absence of a limit or deductible below means that the corresponding ITEM TWO limit or deductible applies)
1	Comprehensive	$ MINUS $ DEDUCTIBLE FOR EACH COVERED AUTO FOR LOSS CAUSED BY THEFT OR MISCHIEF OR VANDALISM SUBJECT TO
	Specified Causes of Loss	$ MAXIMUM DEDUCTIBLE FOR ALL SUCH LOSS IN ANY ONE EVENT.
	Collision	$ MINUS $ DEDUCTIBLE FOR EACH COVERED AUTO.
2	Comprehensive	$ MINUS $ DEDUCTIBLE FOR EACH COVERED AUTO FOR LOSS CAUSED BY THEFT OR MISCHIEF OR VANDALISM SUBJECT TO
	Specified Causes of Loss	$ MAXIMUM DEDUCTIBLE FOR ALL SUCH LOSS IN ANY ONE EVENT.
	Collision	$ MINUS $ DEDUCTIBLE FOR EACH COVERED AUTO.
3	Comprehensive	$ MINUS $ DEDUCTIBLE FOR EACH COVERED AUTO FOR LOSS CAUSED BY THEFT OR MISCHIEF OR VANDALISM SUBJECT TO
	Specified Causes of Loss	$ MAXIMUM DEDUCTIBLE FOR ALL SUCH LOSS IN ANY ONE EVENT.
	Collision	$ MINUS $ DEDUCTIBLE FOR EACH COVERED AUTO.

Comprehensive	$
Specified Causes of Loss	$
Collision	$

GARAGEKEEPERS COVERAGE applies on a legal liability basis unless one of the Direct Coverage Options is indicated below by "☒".

DIRECT COVERAGE OPTIONS

☐ EXCESS INSURANCE. If this box is checked, GARAGEKEEPERS COVERAGE is changed to apply without regard to your or any other "insured's" legal liability for "loss" to a covered "auto" and is excess over any other collectible insurance regardless of whether the other insurance covers your or any other "insured's" interest or the interest of the covered "auto's" owner.

☐ PRIMARY INSURANCE. If this box is checked, GARAGEKEEPERS COVERAGE is changed to apply without regard to your or any other "insured's" legal liability for "loss" to a covered "auto" and is primary insurance.

GARAGE COVERAGE FORM—AUTO DEALERS' SUPPLEMENTARY SCHEDULE—(Continued)

ITEM SEVEN
PHYSICAL DAMAGE COVERAGE—
TYPES OF COVERED AUTOS AND INTERESTS IN THESE AUTOS—
PREMIUMS—REPORTING OR NONREPORTING BASIS

Each of the following PHYSICAL DAMAGE coverages that is indicated in ITEM TWO applies only to the types of "autos" and interests indicated below by " X ").

Coverages	Types of "autos"		Interests covered			
	New "Autos"	Used "autos." Demonstrators and Service Vehicles	Your interest in covered "autos" you own	Your interest only in financed covered "autos"	Your interest and the interest of any creditor named as a loss payee	All interests in any "auto" not owned by you or any creditor while in your possession on consignment for sale.
Comprehensive	☐	☐	☐	☐	☐	☐
Specified Causes of Loss	☐	☐	☐	☐	☐	☐
Collision	☐	☐	☐	☐	☐	☐

Location No.	Coverages	Limit of Insurance For Each Location	Rates	Premium
1	Comprehensive / Specified Causes of Loss	$ MINUS $ DEDUCTIBLE FOR EACH COVERED AUTO FOR LOSS CAUSED BY THEFT OR MISCHIEF OR VANDALISM SUBJECT TO $ MAXIMUM DEDUCTIBLE FOR ALL SUCH LOSS IN ANY ONE EVENT.		
2	Comprehensive / Specified Causes of Loss	$ MINUS $ DEDUCTIBLE FOR EACH COVERED AUTO FOR LOSS CAUSED BY THEFT OR MISCHIEF OR VANDALISM SUBJECT TO $ MAXIMUM DEDUCTIBLE FOR ALL SUCH LOSS IN ANY ONE EVENT.		
3	Comprehensive / Specified Causes of Loss	$ MINUS $ DEDUCTIBLE FOR EACH COVERED AUTO FOR LOSS CAUSED BY THEFT OR MISCHIEF OR VANDALISM SUBJECT TO $ MAXIMUM DEDUCTIBLE FOR ALL SUCH LOSS IN ANY ONE EVENT.		

Location No.	Coverages	$ MINUS $ DEDUCTIBLE FOR EACH COVERED AUTO			Adjustment Factor	Premium
All	Collision	BLANKET ANNUAL COLLISION RATES				
		First $50,000	$50,001 to $100,000	Over $100,000		

	TOTAL PREMIUM	

Our limit of insurance for "loss" at locations other than those stated in ITEM THREE.
$ Additional locations where you store covered "autos"
$ In transit

PREMIUM BASIS—Reporting (Quarterly or Monthly) or Nonreporting (Indicate Basis Agreed Upon by " X ").

☐ **REPORTING BASIS (Quarterly or Monthly as indicated below by " X ").**

You must report to us on our form the location of your covered "autos" and their total value at each such location. For your main sales location identified as location no. 1, you must include the total value of all covered "autos" you have furnished or made available to yourself, your executives, your employees or family members and other Class II—Non-Employees, and covered "autos" that are temporarily displayed or stored at locations other than those stated in ITEM THREE above. For your main sales location you must include the total value of all service vehicles.

YOUR REPORTING BASIS IS:

☐ **QUARTERLY** You must give us your first report by the fifteenth of the fourth month after the policy begins. Your subsequent reports must be given to us by the fifteenth of every third month. Your reports must contain the value for the last business day of every third month coming within the policy period.

☐ **MONTHLY** You must give us your reports by the fifteenth of every month. Your reports will contain the total values you had on the last business day of the preceding month.

Premiums will be calculated pro rata of the annual premium for the exposures contained in each report. At the end of each policy year we will add the monthly premiums or the quarterly premiums to determine your final premium due for the entire policy year. The estimated total premiums shown above will be credited against the final premium due.

☐ **NONREPORTING BASIS.** Stated limit of insurance shown above applies.

Loss Payee—Any loss is payable as interest may appear to you and:

GARAGE COVERAGE FORM—AUTO DEALERS' SUPPLEMENTARY SCHEDULE—(Continued)

ITEM EIGHT

MEDICAL PAYMENTS COVERAGE. REFER TO ITEM TEN FOR COVERED AUTOS INSURED ON A SPECIFIED CAR BASIS.

Coverage	Premium Determination	Premium
Auto Medical Payments Only	Auto Medical Payments Premium equals _____ % of the Liability Premium	
Premises and Operations Medical Payments (Does not apply to bodily injury caused by any auto)	Premises and Operations Medical Payments Premium equals _____ % of the Liability Premium	
Premises and Operations and Auto Medical Payments	Premises and Operations and Auto Medical Payments Premium equals _____ % of the Liability Premium	

ITEM NINE

SCHEDULE OF COVERED AUTOS WHICH ARE FURNISHED TO SOMEONE OTHER THAN A CLASS I OR CLASS II OPERATORS OR WHICH ARE INSURED ON A SPECIFIED CAR BASIS.

Covered Auto No.	DESCRIPTION: Year Model, Trade Name, Body Type / Serial Number (S) Vehicle Identification Number (VIN)		PURCHASED: Original Cost New	Actual Cost & NEW (N) USED (U)	TERRITORY: Town & State Where the Covered Auto will be principally garaged

Covered Auto No.	CLASSIFICATION								Except for towing all physical damage loss is payable to you and the loss payee named below as interests may appear at the time of the loss
	Radius of Operation	Business use s = service r = retail c = commercial	Size GVW, GCW or Vehicle Seating Capacity	Age Group	Primary Rating Factor Liab.	Phy. Dam.	Secondary rating Factor	Code	
1									
2									
3									
4									
5									

CA 00 07 12 90   Copyright, Insurance Services Office, Inc., 1990   Page 4 of 5 □

GARAGE COVERAGE FORM—AUTO DEALERS' SUPPLEMENTARY SCHEDULE—(Continued)

Covered Auto No.	COVERAGES—PREMIUMS, LIMITS AND DEDUCTIBLES (Absence of a deductible or limit entry in any column below means that the limit or deductible entry in the corresponding ITEM TWO column applies instead)							
	LIABILITY		PERSONAL INJURY PROTECTION		ADDED P.I.P.	PROP. PROT. (Mich. only)		
	Limit	Premium	Limited stated in each P.I.P. End. minus deductible shown below	Premium	Limit stated in each Added P.I.P. End. Premium	Limit stated in P.P.I. end. minus deductible shown below	Premium	
1								
2								
3								
4								
5								
Total Premium								

Covered Auto No.	COVERAGES—PREMIUMS, LIMITS AND DEDUCTIBLES (Absence of a deductible or limit entry in any column below means that the limit or deductible entry in the corresponding ITEM TWO column applies instead)	
	AUTO. MED PAY	
	Limit	Premium
1		
2		
3		
4		
5		
Total Premium		

Covered Auto No.	COVERAGES—PREMIUMS, LIMITS AND DEDUCTIBLES (Absence of a deductible or limit entry in any column below means that the limit or deductible entry in the corresponding ITEM TWO column applies instead)							
	COMPREHENSIVE		SPECIFIED CAUSES OF LOSS		COLLISION		TOWING & LABOR	
	Limit stated in ITEM TWO minus deductible shown below	Premium	Limit stated in ITEM TWO Premium		Limit stated in ITEM TWO minus deductible shown below	Premium	Limit Per Disablement	Premium
1								
2								
3								
4								
5								
Total Premium								

Covered Auto	Person or organization to which the Covered "Auto" has been furnished (Do not include Covered "Autos" which have been furnished to Class I or Class II operators)
1	
2	
3	
4	
5	

ITEM TEN

LIABILITY PREMIUM FOR PICK UP AND DELIVERY OF AUTOS—NON-FRANCHISED DEALERS ONLY

	Number of Driver Trips	Rate	Premium
51-200 miles			$
Over 200 miles			$
			$

CA 00 07 12 90   Copyright, Insurance Services Office, Inc., 1990   Page 5 of 5 □

COMMERCIAL AUTO
CA 25 05 07 97

THIS ENDORSEMENT CHANGES THE POLICY. PLEASE READ IT CAREFULLY.

GARAGE LOCATIONS AND OPERATIONS
MEDICAL PAYMENTS COVERAGE

This endorsement modifies insurance provided under the following:

GARAGE COVERAGE FORM

With respect to coverage provided by this endorsement, the provisions of the Coverage Form apply unless modified by the endorsement.

A. Coverage

We will pay reasonable medical and funeral expenses to or for each person who sustains "bodily injury" to which this coverage applies, caused by an "accident" and resulting from:

1. The maintenance or use of the locations shown in the Declarations and that portion of the roads or other accesses that adjoin these locations for garage business.

2. All operations necessary or incidental to a garage business.

We will pay only those expenses incurred for services rendered within one year from the date of the "accident".

B. Exclusions

This insurance does not apply to:

1. "Bodily injury" resulting from the maintenance or use of any "auto".

2. "Bodily injury" to a person, whether or not an "employee" of any "insured", if benefits for the "bodily injury" are payable or must be provided under a workers' compensation or disability benefits law or a similar law.

3. "Bodily injury" caused by declared or undeclared war or insurrection or any of their consequences.

4. "Bodily injury" to any "insured".

C. Limit Of Insurance

Regardless of the number of persons who sustain "bodily injury" or claims made, the most we will pay for "bodily injury" for each person injured in any one "accident" is the Limit of Medical Payments Coverage shown in the Declarations.

D. Changes In Conditions

The **Transfer Of Rights Of Recovery Against Others To Us** Garage Condition does not apply.

POLICY NUMBER:

COMMERCIAL AUTO
CA 99 37 10 01

THIS ENDORSEMENT CHANGES THE POLICY. PLEASE READ IT CAREFULLY.

GARAGEKEEPERS COVERAGE

This endorsement modifies insurance provided under the following:

BUSINESS AUTO COVERAGE FORM
MOTOR CARRIER COVERAGE FORM
TRUCKERS COVERAGE FORM

With respect to coverage provided by this endorsement, the provisions of the Coverage Form apply unless modified by the endorsement.

This endorsement changes the policy effective on the inception date of the policy unless another date is indicated below.

Endorsement Effective:	Countersigned By:
Named Insured:	(Authorized Representative)

SCHEDULE

Location No.	Coverages	Limit Of Insurance For Each Location
1	Comprehensive	$ MINUS $ DEDUCTIBLE FOR EACH "CUSTOMER'S AUTO" FOR "LOSS" CAUSED BY THEFT OR MISCHIEF OR VANDALISM SUBJECT TO $ MAXIMUM DEDUCTIBLE FOR ALL SUCH "LOSS" IN ANY ONE EVENT; OR
	Specified Causes Of Loss	$ MINUS $ DEDUCTIBLE FOR ALL PERILS SUBJECT TO $ MAXIMUM DEDUCTIBLE FOR ALL SUCH "LOSS" IN ANY ONE EVENT.
	Collision	$ MINUS $ DEDUCTIBLE FOR EACH "CUSTOMER'S AUTO".
2	Comprehensive	$ MINUS $ DEDUCTIBLE FOR EACH "CUSTOMER'S AUTO" FOR "LOSS" CAUSED BY THEFT OR MISCHIEF OR VANDALISM SUBJECT TO $ MAXIMUM DEDUCTIBLE FOR ALL SUCH "LOSS" IN ANY ONE EVENT; OR
	Specified Causes Of Loss	$ MINUS $ DEDUCTIBLE FOR ALL PERILS SUBJECT TO $ MAXIMUM DEDUCTIBLE FOR ALL SUCH "LOSS" IN ANY ONE EVENT.
	Collision	$ MINUS $ DEDUCTIBLE FOR EACH "CUSTOMER'S AUTO".
3	Comprehensive	$ MINUS $ DEDUCTIBLE FOR EACH "CUSTOMER'S AUTO" FOR "LOSS" CAUSED BY THEFT OR MISCHIEF OR VANDALISM SUBJECT TO $ MAXIMUM DEDUCTIBLE FOR ALL SUCH "LOSS" IN ANY ONE EVENT; OR
	Specified Causes Of Loss	$ MINUS $ DEDUCTIBLE FOR ALL PERILS SUBJECT TO $ MAXIMUM DEDUCTIBLE FOR ALL SUCH "LOSS" IN ANY ONE EVENT.
	Collision	$ MINUS $ DEDUCTIBLE FOR EACH "CUSTOMER'S AUTO".

LOCATIONS WHERE YOU CONDUCT "GARAGE OPERATIONS"	
Location No.	Address State Your Main Business Location As Location No. 1.
1	
2	
3	

Premium For All Locations	
Comprehensive	$
Specified Causes Of Loss	$
Collision	$

DIRECT COVERAGE OPTIONS

Indicate below with an "X" which, if any, Direct Coverage Option is selected.

☐ **EXCESS INSURANCE**

If this box is checked, Garagekeepers Coverage remains applicable on a legal liability basis. However, coverage also applies without regard to your or any other "insured's" legal liability for "loss" to a "customer's auto" on an excess basis over any other collectible insurance regardless of whether the other insurance covers your or any other "insured's" interest or the interest of the "customer's auto's" owner.

☐ **PRIMARY INSURANCE**

If this box is checked, Garagekeepers Coverage is changed to apply without regard to your or any other "insured's" legal liability for "loss" to a "customer's auto" and is primary insurance.

(If no entry appears above, information required to complete this endorsement will be shown in the Declarations as applicable to this endorsement.)

A. This endorsement provides only those coverages:

1. Where a Limit of Insurance and a premium are shown for that coverage in the Schedule; and

2. For the location shown in the Schedule.

B. **Coverage**

1. We will pay all sums the "insured" legally must pay as damages for "loss" to a "customer's auto" or "customer's auto" equipment left in the "insured's" care while the "insured" is attending, servicing, repairing, parking or storing it in your "garage operations" under:

   a. **Comprehensive Coverage**

   From any cause except:

   (1) The "customer's auto's" collision with another object; or

   (2) The "customer's auto's" overturn.

   b. **Specified Causes Of Loss Coverage**

   Caused by:

   (1) Fire, lightning or explosion;

   (2) Theft; or

   (3) Mischief or vandalism.

   c. **Collision Coverage**

   Caused by:

   (1) The "customer's auto's" collision with another object; or

   (2) The "customer's auto's" overturn.

2. We will have the right and duty to defend any "insured" against a "suit" asking for these damages. However, we have no duty to defend any "insured" against a "suit" seeking damages for "loss" to which this insurance does not apply. We may investigate and settle any claim or "suit" as we consider appropriate. Our duty to defend or settle ends for a coverage when the Limit of Insurance for that coverage has been exhausted by payment of judgments or settlements.

3. **Who Is An Insured**

The following are "insureds" for "loss" to "customer's autos" and "customer's auto" equipment:

   a. You.

   b. Your partners (if you are a partnership), or members (if you are a limited liability company), "employees", directors or shareholders while acting within the scope of their duties as such.

4. Coverage Extensions

The following applies as Supplementary Payments. In addition to the Limit of Insurance, we will pay for the "insured":

a. All expenses we incur.

b. The costs of bonds to release attachments in any "suit" against an "insured" we defend, but only for bond amounts within our Limit of Insurance.

c. All reasonable expenses incurred by the "insured" at our request, including actual loss of earnings up to $250 a day because of time off from work.

d. All costs taxed against the "insured" in any "suit" against an "insured" we defend.

e. All interest on the full amount of any judgment that accrues after entry of the judgment in any "suit" against an "insured" we defend; but our duty to pay interest ends when we have paid, offered to pay, or deposited in court the part of the judgment that is within our Limit of Insurance.

C. Exclusions

1. This insurance does not apply to any of the following:

   a. **Contractual Obligations**

   Liability resulting from any agreement by which the "insured" accepts responsibility for "loss".

   b. **Theft**

   "Loss" due to theft or conversion caused in any way by you, your "employees" or by your shareholders.

   c. **Defective Parts**

   Defective parts or materials.

   d. **Faulty Work**

   Faulty "work you performed".

2. We will not pay for "loss" to any of the following:

   a. Tape decks or other sound reproducing equipment unless permanently installed in a "customer's auto".

   b. Tapes, records or other sound reproducing devices designed for use with sound reproducing equipment.

   c. Sound receiving equipment designed for use as a citizens' band radio, two-way mobile radio or telephone or scanning monitor receiver, including its antennas and other accessories, unless permanently installed in the dash or console opening normally used by the "customer's auto" manufacturer for the installation of a radio.

   d. Any device designed or used to detect speed measurement equipment such as radar or laser detectors and any jamming apparatus intended to elude or disrupt speed measurement equipment.

D. Limit Of Insurance And Deductible

1. Regardless of the number of "customer's autos", "insureds", premiums paid, claims made or "suits" brought, the most we will pay for each "loss" at each location is the Garagekeepers Coverage Limit of Insurance shown in the Schedule for that location minus the applicable deductibles for "loss" caused by collision; and

   a. Theft or mischief or vandalism; or

   b. All perils.

2. The maximum deductible stated in the Schedule for Garagekeepers Coverage Comprehensive or Specified Causes of Loss Coverage is the most that will be deducted for all "loss" in any one event caused by:

   a. Theft or mischief or vandalism; or

   b. All perils.

3. Sometimes to settle a claim or "suit", we may pay all or any part of the deductible. If this happens you must reimburse us for the deductible or that portion of the deductible that we paid.

E. Additional Definitions

As used in this endorsement:

1. "Customer's auto" means a customer's land motor vehicle or trailer or semitrailer. This definition also includes any customer's auto while left with you for service, repair, storage or safekeeping. Customers include your "employees", and members of their households who pay for services performed.

2. "Loss" means direct and accidental loss or damage and includes any resulting loss of use.

3. "Garage operations" means the ownership, maintenance or use of locations for the purpose of a business of selling, servicing, repairing, parking or storing "customer's autos" and that portion of the roads or other accesses that adjoin these locations. "Garage operations" also includes all operations necessary or incidental to the performance of garage operations.

4. "Work you performed" includes:

   a. Work that someone performed on your behalf; and

   b. The providing of or failure to provide warnings or instructions.

POLICY NUMBER:

COMMERCIAL AUTO
CA 25 08 10 01

THIS ENDORSEMENT CHANGES THE POLICY. PLEASE READ IT CAREFULLY.

PERSONAL INJURY LIABILITY COVERAGE – GARAGES

This endorsement modifies insurance provided under the following:

GARAGE COVERAGE FORM

With respect to coverage provided by this endorsement, the provisions of the Coverage Form apply unless modified by the endorsement.

This endorsement changes the policy effective on the inception date of the policy unless another date is indicated below.

Endorsement Effective:	Countersigned By:
Named Insured:	(Authorized Representative)

SCHEDULE

Personal Injury Limit Of Insurance	$
Premium	$

(If no entry appears above, information required to complete this endorsement will be shown in the Declarations as applicable to this endorsement.)

A. Coverage

We will pay all sums the "insured" legally must pay as damages because of "personal injury" caused by an offense committed:

   a. In the conduct of your business; and

   b. In the Coverage Territory during the Policy Period.

We will have the right and duty to defend any "insured" against a "suit" asking for these damages. However, we have no duty to defend any "insured" against a "suit" seeking damages for "personal injury" to which this insurance does not apply. We may investigate and settle any claim or "suit" as we consider appropriate. Our duty to defend or settle ends when the Personal Injury Limit of Insurance has been exhausted by payment of judgments or settlements.

1. Who Is An Insured

The following are "insureds":

   a. You and your spouse.

   b. Your partners (if you are a partnership) and their spouses, or members (if you are a limited liability company) and their spouses. None of your partners (if you are a partnership) or their spouses nor your members (if you are a limited liability company) or their spouses is an "insured" for "personal injury" resulting from the conduct of any other partnership.

   c. Your "employees", executive officers, directors and stockholders but only while acting within the scope of their duties.

2. Coverage Extensions

The following applies as Supplementary Payments. In addition to the Personal Injury Limit of Insurance, we will pay for the "insured":

   a. All expenses we incur.

   b. The cost of bonds to release attachments in any "suit" against the "insured" we defend, but only for bond amounts within the Personal Injury Limit of Insurance.

c. All reasonable expenses incurred by the "insured" at our request, including actual loss of earnings up to $250 a day because of time off from work.

d. All costs taxed against the "insured" in any "suit" against the "insured" we defend.

e. All interest on the full amount of any judgment that accrues after entry of the judgment in any "suit" we defend; but our duty to pay interest ends when we have paid, offered to pay, or deposited in court the part of the judgment that is within the Personal Injury Limit of Insurance.

B. Exclusions

1. This insurance does not apply to:

a. Liability assumed under any contract or agreement. But this exclusion does not apply to liability for damages that the "insured" would have in the absence of the contract or agreement.

b. "Personal injury" arising out of advertising, publishing, broadcasting or telecasting done by or for you.

c. "Personal injury" arising out of oral or written publication of material, if done by or at the direction of the "insured" with knowledge of its falsity.

d. "Personal injury" arising out of oral or written publication of material whose first publication took place before the effective date of this insurance.

e. Arising out of a criminal act committed by or at the direction of any "insured".

f. "Personal injury" to:

(1) A person arising out of any:

(a) Refusal to employ that person;

(b) Termination of that person's employment; or

(c) Employment-related practices, policies, acts or omissions, such as coercion, demotion, evaluation, reassignment, discipline, defamation, harassment, humiliation or discrimination directed at that person; or

(2) The spouse, child, parent, brother or sister of that person as a consequence of "personal injury" to that person at whom any of the employment-related practices described in Paragraphs **(a)**, **(b)** or **(c)** above is directed.

This exclusion applies:

(a) Whether the "insured" may be liable as an employer or in any other capacity; and

(b) To any obligation to share damages with or repay someone else who must pay damages because of the injury.

g. "Personal injury" arising out of the actual, alleged or threatened discharge, dispersal, seepage, migration, release or escape of "pollutants" at any time.

h. Any loss, cost or expense arising out of any:

(1) Request, demand, order or statutory or regulatory requirement that any "insured" or others test for, monitor, clean up, remove, contain, treat, detoxify or neutralize, or in any way respond to, or assess the effects of, "pollutants"; or

(2) Claim or "suit" by or on behalf of a governmental authority for damages because of testing for, monitoring, cleaning up, removing, containing, treating, detoxifying or neutralizing, or in any way responding to, or assessing the effects of, "pollutants".

2. The following is added to Paragraph **B. Exclusions** of **Section II – Liability**:

Personal Injury

"Bodily injury" arising out of "personal injury".

C. Limit Of Insurance

The following is added to the **Aggregate Limit Of Insurance – "Garage Operations" – Other Than Covered "Autos"** provision in **Section II – Liability Coverage**:

Subject to the Aggregate Limit Of Insurance – "Garage Operations" – Other Than Covered "Autos" and regardless of the number of "insureds", claims made or "suits" brought or persons or organizations making claims or bringing "suits", the most we will pay for all damages because of all "personal injury" sustained by any one person or organization is the Personal Injury Limit of Insurance shown in the Schedule of the Personal Injury Liability Coverage – Garages Endorsement.

The Each "Accident" Limit Of Insurance – "Garage Operations" – Other Than Covered "Autos" for Liability Coverage does not apply to damages we pay because of "personal injury".

 CA 25 08 10 01 □

D. Changes In Conditions

The **Policy Period, Coverage Territory** Garage Condition is changed by adding the following:

We also cover "personal injury" that:

1. Occurs during the policy period shown in the Declarations; and

2. Is caused by an "insured" who permanently lives within the coverage territory while the "insured" is temporarily outside of one of those places.

The original "suit" for damages resulting from such "personal injury" must be brought within the coverage territory.

E. Additional Definition

As used in this endorsement:

"Personal injury" means injury, including consequential "bodily injury", arising out of one or more of the following offenses:

1. False arrest, detention or imprisonment;

2. Malicious prosecution;

3. The wrongful eviction from, wrongful entry into, or invasion of the right of private occupancy of a room, dwelling or premises that a person occupies, committed by or on behalf of its owner, landlord or lessor;

4. Oral or written publication of material that slanders or libels a person or organization or disparages a person's or organization's goods, products or services; or

5. Oral or written publication of material that violates a person's right of privacy.

COMMERCIAL AUTO
CA 00 40 02 03

THIS ENDORSEMENT CHANGES THE POLICY. PLEASE READ IT CAREFULLY.

WAR EXCLUSION –
GARAGE COVERAGE FORM

This endorsement modifies insurance provided under the following:

GARAGE COVERAGE FORM

With respect to coverage provided by this endorsement, the provisions of the Coverage Form apply unless modified by the endorsement.

A. Changes In Liability Coverage

1. The **War** exclusion under Paragraph **B. Exclusions** of **Section II – Liability Coverage** is replaced by the following:

   WAR

   "Bodily injury", "property damage" or "covered pollution cost or expense" arising directly or indirectly, out of:

   a. War, including undeclared or civil war;

   b. Warlike action by a military force, including action in hindering or defending against an actual or expected attack, by any government, sovereign or other authority using military personnel or other agents; or

   c. Insurrection, rebellion, revolution, usurped power, or action taken by governmental authority in hindering or defending against any of these

B. Changes In Garagekeepers Coverage

If Garagekeepers Coverage in the Garage Coverage Form is selected or the Garagekeepers Coverage – Customers' Sound Receiving Equipment endorsement is attached, the following exclusion is added:

We will not pay for "loss" caused by or resulting from the following. Such "loss" is excluded regardless of any other cause or event that contributes concurrently or in any sequence to the "loss":

   a. **War**

   (1) War, including undeclared or civil war;

   (2) Warlike action by a military force, including action in hindering or defending against an actual or expected attack, by any government, sovereign or other authority using military personnel or other agents; or

   (3) Insurrection, rebellion, revolution, usurped power, or action taken by governmental authority in hindering or defending against any of these

C. Changes In Medical Payments

If the Auto Medical Payments Coverage endorsement or Garage Locations And Operations Medical Payments Coverage endorsement is attached, then the exclusion which refers to declared or undeclared war or insurrection is replaced by the following:

This insurance does not apply to:

"Bodily injury", arising directly or indirectly, out of:

   a. War, including undeclared or civil war;

   b. Warlike action by a military force, including action in hindering or defending against an actual or expected attack, by any government, sovereign or other authority using military personnel or other agents; or

   c. Insurrection, rebellion, revolution, usurped power, or action taken by governmental authority in hindering or defending against any of these.

D. If the Personal Injury Liability Coverage – Garages endorsement is attached, the following exclusions are added to Paragraph **B. Exclusions**:

This insurance does not apply to:

1. "Personal injury", arising directly or indirectly, out of:

   a. War, including undeclared or civil war;

   b. Warlike action by a military force, including action in hindering or defending against an actual or expected attack, by any government, sovereign or other authority using military personnel or other agents; or

c. Insurrection, rebellion, revolution, usurped power, or action taken by governmental authority in hindering or defending against any of these.

E. If the Broadened Coverage – Garages endorsement is attached, the following exclusion is added to Paragraph **B. Exclusions** of **Section I – Personal And Advertising Injury Liability Coverage:**

1. This insurance does not apply to:

   a. "Personal and advertising injury" arising, directly or indirectly, out of:

      (1) War, including undeclared or civil war;

      (2) Warlike action by a military force, including action in hindering or defending against an actual or expected attack, by any government, sovereign or other authority using military personnel or other agents; or

      (3) Insurrection, rebellion, revolution, usurped power, or action taken by governmental authority in hindering or defending against any of these.

F. **Changes In Uninsured/Underinsured Motorists Coverage**

If Uninsured and/or Underinsured Motorists Coverage is attached, then the following exclusions are added:

This insurance does not apply to:

WAR

1. "Bodily injury" or "property damage", if applicable, arising directly or indirectly, out of:

   a. War, including undeclared or civil war;

   b. Warlike action by a military force, including action in hindering or defending against an actual or expected attack, by any government, sovereign or other authority using military personnel or other agents; or

   c. Insurrection, rebellion, revolution, usurped power, or action taken by governmental authority in hindering or defending against any of these.

G. **Changes In Personal Injury Protection Coverage**

1. If Personal Injury Protection, no-fault, or other similar coverage is attached, and:

   a. Contains, in whole or in part, a War exclusion, that exclusion is replaced by Paragraph **2.**

   b. Does not contain a war exclusion, Paragraph **2.** is added.

2. This insurance does not apply to:

   WAR

   "Bodily injury" or "property damage", if applicable, arising directly or indirectly, out of:

   a. War, including undeclared or civil war;

   b. Warlike action by a military force, including action in hindering or defending against an actual or expected attack, by any government, sovereign or other authority using military personnel or other agents; or

   c. Insurrection, rebellion, revolution, usurped power, or action taken by governmental authority in hindering or defending against any of these.

H. **Changes In Single Interest Automobile Physical Damage Insurance Policy**

The War exclusion is replaced by the following:

   a. War, including undeclared or civil war;

   b. Warlike action by a military force, including action in hindering or defending against an actual or expected attack, by any government, sovereign or other authority using military personnel or other agents; or

   c. Insurrection, rebellion, revolution, usurped power, or action taken by governmental authority in hindering or defending against any of these.

 CA 00 40 02 03 □

POLICY NUMBER:

COMMERCIAL AUTO
CA 23 20 10 01

THIS ENDORSEMENT CHANGES THE POLICY. PLEASE READ IT CAREFULLY.

TRUCKERS ENDORSEMENT

This endorsement modifies insurance provided under the following:

BUSINESS AUTO COVERAGE FORM

With respect to coverage provided by this endorsement, the provisions of the Coverage Form apply unless modified by the endorsement.

This endorsement changes the policy effective on the inception date of the policy unless another date is indicated below.

Endorsement Effective:	Countersigned By:
Named Insured:	(Authorized Representative)

SCHEDULE

For those covered "autos" used in your operations as a "trucker" the liability "cost of hire" provisions in the Declarations are replaced by the following:

SCHEDULE OF HIRED OR BORROWED COVERED AUTO COVERAGE AND PREMIUMS – LIABILITY COVERAGE

LIABILITY COVERAGE – RATING BASIS, COST OF HIRE – AUTOS USED IN YOUR TRUCKING OPERATIONS

ESTIMATED COST OF HIRE	RATE PER EACH $100 COST OF HIRE	TOTAL ESTIMATED PREMIUM

"Cost of hire" means the total cost you incur for the hire of "autos" you don't own (not including "private passenger type autos" you borrow or rent from members of your household, your partners, "employees" or agents or members of their households).

The following provisions apply to those covered "autos" used in your operations as a "trucker" if gross receipts is used as a premium basis:

SCHEDULE FOR GROSS RECEIPTS RATING BASIS – LIABILITY COVERAGE

Estimated Yearly Gross Receipts	RATES		PREMIUMS	
	Per $100 Of Gross Receipts			
	LIABILITY COVERAGE	AUTO MEDICAL PAYMENTS	LIABILITY COVERAGE	AUTO MEDICAL PAYMENTS
TOTAL PREMIUMS				
MINIMUM PREMIUMS				

When used as a premium basis:

Gross Receipts means the total amount to which you are entitled for shipping or transporting property during the policy period regardless of whether you or any other carrier originate the shipment or transportation. Gross Receipts includes the total amount received from renting equipment, with or without drivers, to anyone who is not a "trucker" and 15% of the total amount received from renting any equipment to any "trucker". Gross Receipts does not include:

1. Amounts you pay to railroads, steamship lines, airlines and other motor carriers operating under their own ICC or PUC permits.
2. Advertising Revenue.
3. Taxes which you collect as a separate item and remit directly to a governmental division.
4. C.O.D. collections for cost of mail or merchandise including collection fees.
5. Warehouse storage fees.

SCHEDULE OF TRAILER INTERCHANGE COVERAGE

COVERAGES	LIMIT OF INSURANCE		DAILY RATE	ESTIMATED PREMIUM
COMPREHENSIVE	ACTUAL CASH VALUE, COST OF REPAIR OR $ WHICHEVER IS LESS		$	$
SPECIFIED CAUSES OF LOSS	ACTUAL CASH VALUE, COST OF REPAIR OR $ WHICHEVER IS LESS, MINUS $ Ded. FOR EACH TRAILER FOR LOSS CAUSED BY MISCHIEF OR VANDALISM		$	$
COLLISION	ACTUAL CASH VALUE, COST OF REPAIR OR $ WHICHEVER IS LESS, MINUS $ Ded. FOR EACH TRAILER		$	$
			TOTAL PREMIUM	

PHYSICAL DAMAGE COVERAGE

The **Physical Damage Coverage** exclusion in Paragraph **C.** of this endorsement is removed for each of the following coverages indicated by an "x" in the "☐".

☐ COMPREHENSIVE

☐ SPECIFIED CAUSES OF LOSS

☐ COLLISION

For any operations you engage in as a "trucker" the policy is changed as follows:

A. Who Is An Insured under Liability Coverage is replaced by the following:

  1. Who Is An Insured

    a. You for any covered "auto".

    b. Anyone else while using with your permission a covered "auto" you own, hire or borrow except:

      (1) The owner or anyone else from whom you hire or borrow a covered "private passenger type auto".

      (2) Your "employee" or agent if the covered "auto" is a "private passenger type auto" and is owned by that "employee" or agent or a member of his or her household.

      (3) Someone using a covered "auto" while they are working in a business of selling, servicing, repairing or parking "autos" unless that business is yours.

      (4) Anyone other than your "employees", partners (if you are a partnership), or members (if you are a limited liability company), or a lessee or borrower or any of their "employees", while moving property to or from a covered "auto".

© ISO Properties, Inc., 2000 CA 23 20 10 01 ☐

(5) A partner (if you are a partnership), or member (if you are a limited liability company) for a covered "private passenger type auto" owned by him or her or a member of his or her household.

c. The owner or anyone else from whom you hire or borrow a covered "auto" that is a "trailer" while the "trailer" is connected to another covered "auto" that is a power unit, or, if not connected:

(1) Is being used exclusively in your business as a "trucker"; and

(2) Is being used pursuant to operating rights granted to you by a public authority.

d. The owner or anyone else from whom you hire or borrow a covered "auto" that is not a "trailer" while the covered "auto":

(1) Is being used exclusively in your business as a "trucker"; and

(2) Is being used pursuant to operating rights granted to you by a public authority.

e. Anyone liable for the conduct of an "insured" described above but only to the extent of that liability.

However, none of the following is an "insured":

a. Any "trucker", or his or her agents or "employees", other than you and your "employees":

(1) If the "trucker" is subject to motor carrier insurance requirements and meets them by a means other than "auto" liability insurance.

(2) If the "trucker" is not insured for hired "autos" under an "auto" liability insurance form that insures on a primary basis the owners of the "autos" and their agents and "employees" while the "autos" are being used exclusively in the "truckers" business and pursuant to operating rights granted to the "trucker" by a public authority.

b. Any rail, water or air carrier or its "employees" or agents, other than you and your "employees", for a "trailer" if "bodily injury" or "property damage" occurs while the "trailer" is detached from a covered "auto" you are using and:

(1) Is being transported by the carrier; or

(2) Is being loaded on or unloaded from any unit of transportation by the carrier.

B. The following **Trailer Interchange Coverage** Provisions are added:

1. Coverage

a. We will pay all sums you legally must pay as damages because of "loss" to a "trailer" you don't own or its equipment. The "trailer" must be in your possession under a written "trailer" or equipment interchange agreement in which you assume liability for "loss" to the "trailer" while in your possession.

b. We will pay for "loss" to the "trailer" under:

(1) Comprehensive Coverage

From any cause except:

(a) The "trailer's" collision with another object; or

(b) The "trailer's" overturn.

(2) Specified Causes Of Loss Coverage

Caused by:

(a) Fire, lightning or explosion;

(b) Theft;

(c) Windstorm, hail or earthquake;

(d) Flood;

(e) Mischief or vandalism; or

(f) The sinking, burning, collision or derailment of any conveyance transporting the "trailer".

(3) Collision Coverage

Caused by:

(a) The "trailer's" collision with another object; or

(b) The "trailer's" overturn.

c. We have the right and duty to defend any "suit" asking for these damages. However, we have no duty to defend "suits" for "loss" not covered by this Coverage Form. We may investigate and settle any claim or "suit" as we consider appropriate. Our duty to defend or settle ends for a coverage when the Limit of Insurance for that coverage has been exhausted by payment of judgments or settlements.

d. **Coverage Extensions**

The following applies as Supplementary Payments. In addition to the Limit of Insurance, we will pay for you:

(1) All expenses we incur.

(2) The cost of bonds to release attachments, but only for bond amounts within our Limit of Insurance.

(3) All reasonable expenses incurred at our request, including actual loss of earnings up to $250 a day because of time off from work.

(4) All costs taxed against the "insured" in any "suit" against the "insured" we defend.

(5) All interest on the full amount of any judgment that accrues after entry of the judgment; but our duty to pay interest ends when we have paid, offered to pay, or deposited in court the part of the judgment that is within our Limit of Insurance.

2. **Exclusions**

a. We will not pay for "loss" caused by or resulting from any of the following. Such "loss" is excluded regardless of any other cause or event that contributes concurrently or in any sequence to the "loss".

(1) **Nuclear Hazard**

(a) The explosion of any weapon employing atomic fission or fusion; or

(b) Nuclear reaction or radiation, or radioactive contamination, however caused.

(2) **War Or Military Action**

(a) War, including undeclared or civil war;

(b) Warlike action by a military force, including action in hindering or defending against an actual or expected attack, by any government, sovereign or other authority using military personnel or other agents; or

(c) Insurrection, rebellion, revolution, usurped power or action taken by governmental authority in hindering or defending against any of these.

b. We will not pay for loss of use.

c. **Other Exclusions**

We will not pay for "loss" caused by or resulting from any of the following unless caused by other "loss" that is covered by this insurance.

(1) Wear and tear, freezing, mechanical or electrical breakdown.

(2) Blowouts, punctures or other road damage to tires.

3. **Limit Of Insurance And Deductible**

The most we will pay for "loss" to any one "trailer" is the least of the following amounts minus any applicable deductible shown in the Schedule:

a. The actual cash value of the damaged or stolen property at the time of the "loss".

b. The cost of repairing or replacing the damaged or stolen property with other property of like kind and quality.

c. The Limit of Insurance shown in the Schedule.

C. Physical Damage Coverage is changed by adding the following exclusion:

We will not pay for "loss" to:

Any covered "auto" while in anyone else's possession under a written trailer interchange agreement. But this exclusion does not apply to a loss payee; however, if we pay the loss payee, you must reimburse us for our payment.

D. The **Other Insurance** Condition is replaced by the following:

5. Other Insurance – Primary And Excess Insurance Provisions

a. This Coverage Form's Liability Coverage is primary for any covered "auto" while hired or borrowed by you and used exclusively in your business as a "trucker" and pursuant to operating rights granted to you by a public authority. This Coverage Form's Liability Coverage is excess over any other collectible insurance for any covered "auto" while hired or borrowed from you by another "trucker". However, while a covered "auto" which is a "trailer" is connected to a power unit, this Coverage Form's Liability Coverage is:

(1) On the same basis, primary or excess, as for the power unit if the power unit is a covered "auto".

(2) Excess if the power unit is not a covered "auto".

b. Any Trailer Interchange Coverage provided by this Coverage Form is primary for any covered "auto".

c. Except as provided in Paragraphs **a.** and **b.** above, this Coverage Form provides primary insurance for any covered "auto" you own and excess insurance for any covered "auto" you don't own.

d. For Hired Auto Physical Damage coverage, any covered "auto" you lease, hire, rent or borrow is deemed to be a covered "auto" you own. However, any "auto" that is leased, hired, rented or borrowed with a driver is not a covered "auto".

e. Regardless of the provisions of Paragraphs **a., b.** and **c.** above, this Coverage Form's Liability Coverage is primary for any liability assumed under an "insured contract".

f. When this Coverage Form and any other Coverage Form or policy covers on the same basis, either excess or primary, we will pay only our share. Our share is the proportion that the Limit of Insurance of our Coverage Form bears to the total of the limits of all the Coverage Forms and policies covering on the same basis.

E. Additional Definitions

As used in this endorsement:

1. "Trailer" includes a semitrailer or a dolly used to convert a semitrailer into a trailer. But for Trailer Interchange Coverage only, "trailer" also includes a container.

2. "Private passenger type" means a private passenger or station wagon type "auto" and includes an "auto" of the pick-up or van type if not used for business purposes.

3. "Trucker" means any person or organization engaged in the business of transporting property by "auto" for hire.

POLICY NUMBER:

COMMERCIAL AUTO
CA 23 09 02 99

THIS ENDORSEMENT CHANGES THE POLICY. PLEASE READ IT CAREFULLY.

TRUCKERS – INSURANCE FOR NON-TRUCKING USE

This endorsement modifies insurance provided under the following:

BUSINESS AUTO COVERAGE FORM

With respect to coverage provided by this endorsement, the provisions of the Coverage Form apply unless modified by the endorsement.

This endorsement changes the policy effective on the inception date of the policy unless another date is indicated below.

Endorsement Effective:	Countersigned By:
Named Insured:	
	(Authorized Representative)

SCHEDULE

Description of Covered "Auto":

(If no entry appears above, information required to complete this endorsement will be shown in the Declarations as applicable to this endorsement.)

Liability Coverage for a covered "auto" described in the Schedule is changed as follows:

1. The following exclusions are added:

   This insurance does not apply to:

   a. A covered "auto" while used to carry property in any business.

   b. A covered "auto" while used in the business of anyone to whom the "auto" is rented.

2. Who Is An Insured does not include anyone engaged in the business of transporting property by "auto" for hire who is liable for your conduct.

CA 23 09 02 99   Copyright, Insurance Services Office, Inc., 1998   Page 1 of 1   □

POLICY NUMBER:

THIS ENDORSEMENT CHANGES THE POLICY. PLEASE READ IT CAREFULLY.

TRUCKERS – UNIFORM INTERMODAL INTERCHANGE ENDORSEMENT FORM UIIE – 1

This endorsement modifies insurance provided under the following:

BUSINESS AUTO COVERAGE FORM
MOTOR CARRIER COVERAGE FORM
TRUCKERS COVERAGE FORM

With respect to coverage provided by this endorsement, the provisions of the Coverage Form apply unless modified by the endorsement.

This endorsement changes the policy effective on the inception date of the policy unless another date is indicated below.

Endorsement Effective:	Countersigned By:
Named Insured:	(Authorized Representative)

(If no entry appears above, information required to complete this endorsement will be shown in the Declarations as applicable to this endorsement.)

It is agreed that such insurance as is afforded by the policy for Auto Bodily Injury and Property Damage Liability applies to liability assumed by the named insured, as "Motor Carrier Participant", under Section **F.4.** of the Uniform Intermodal Interchange and Facilities Access Agreement, and any subsequent amendments thereto, reading as follows:

F. Liability, Indemnity, And Insurance

4. Indemnity

Motor Carrier agrees to defend, hold harmless, and fully indemnify the Indemnitees, against any and all claims, "suits", loss, damage or liability, for "bodily injury", death and/or "property damage" (including reasonable attorney fees and costs incurred in the enforcement of this Agreement) arising out of or related to the Motor Carrier's: Use or maintenance of the equipment during an interchange period; the performance of this Agreement; and/or presence on the Facility Operator's premises.

Subject to the following provisions:

1. The limit of the company's liability under this policy for damages because of "bodily injury" and "property damage" arising out of the use, operation, maintenance or possession of interchange equipment shall be the applicable amount stated below and designated by an "x" unless a greater amount is otherwise stated in the policy as applicable to such "bodily injury" or "property damage".

☐	Single Limit "Bodily Injury" and "Property Damage" (or the Equivalent)	$ Each "Accident"

2. The company shall:

   a. Upon issuance of this endorsement, furnish to the President, The Intermodal Association of North America, 7501 Greenway Center Drive, Suite 720, Greenbelt, Maryland 20770-6705, a properly executed Certificate of Insurance which carries the notation that the company has issued to the named insured Motor Carrier a policy of liability insurance; and

CA 23 17 09 00   © ISO Properties, Inc., 2000   Page 1 of 2   ☐

b. Upon cancellation or termination of the policy of which this endorsement forms a part, furnish a notice of such cancellation or termination NOT LESS THAN 30 DAYS prior to the effective date of such cancellation or termination, such notice to be mailed to said President at the above address.

© ISO Properties, Inc., 2000 **CA 23 17 09 00** □